Siva and Her Sisters

Studies in the Ethnographic Imagination

John Comaroff, Pierre Bourdieu, and Maurice Bloch, *Series Editors*

Siva and Her Sisters

Gender, Caste, and Class
in Rural South India

KARIN KAPADIA

WESTVIEW PRESS

Boulder • Oxford

In memory of
my father
Faridun H. Kapadia
Amicus aeternus

Studies in the Ethnographic Imagination

Copyright © 1995 by Westview Press, Inc. . A Member of the Perseus Books Group

Published in 1995 in the United States of America by Westview Press, Inc., 5500 Central Avenue, Boulder, Colorado 80301-2877, and in the United Kingdom by Westview Press, 12 Hid's Copse Road, Cumnor Hill, Oxford OX2 9JJ

Library of Congress Cataloging-in-Publication Data
Kapadia, Karin.
   Siva and her sisters : gender, caste, and class in rural South
India/Karin Kapadia
       p.   cm.—(Studies in ethnographic imagination)
   Includes bibliographical references and index.
   ISBN 0-8133-8158-4.—ISBN 0-8133-3491-8 (pbk.)
   1. Caste—India, South.   2. Women—India, South—Social
conditions.   3. Social classes—India, South.   I. Title.
II. Series
HT720.K2957   1995
305.4'0954—dc20

                                                                94-38588
                                                                CIP

Printed and bound in the United States of America

The paper used in this publication meets the requirements
of the American National Standard for Permanence of Paper
for Printed Library Materials Z39.48-1984.

10   9   8   7   6   5   4   3

PERSEUS
POD
ON DEMAND

Contents

Tables and Illustrations

Tables

Figures

Photographs

Following page 160

At the coming-of-age celebration of Uma's youngest sister
Kandan, pierced "through the chest" with Lord Murugan's spear, at the Aruloor festival
Siva and her baby boy, who survived a complicated birth

Preface and Acknowledgments

I AM INDEBTED TO MANY PEOPLE for their help and encouragement but can name only a few here. First and foremost, I thank Susila Raj and her husband, Professor Jeganath Raj. Professor Raj invited me, a complete stranger, to stay with them for two or three days until I found a house in the village; I stayed one and a half years instead! They and their sons, Provine and Deepoo, became my family, and Susila became my close friend and mentor. I also thank my other dear friend and mentor in Madras, Susila Rajagopal, who nurtured me with her excellent food and her knowledge. Without the inspiration of the two Susilas, this would be a much poorer book. In Madras, I thank K. Nagaraj, V. Athreya, and S. Guhan, all of the Madras Institute of Development Studies. I also thank D. K. Oza, who became a valued friend, for his substantial help. In London, I particularly thank my two doctoral supervisors, C. J. Fuller and J. P. Parry, for their inspiration and enormous support. I also thank Ramini Solomon of Lady Doak College, Madurai, for her hospitality, and Mrs. Jayalakshmi, retired head of the Department of Tamil Studies at Stella Maris College, Madras, for her invaluable help with transliteration. I gratefully remember the late K. Paramasivam of Madurai, a great Tamil teacher.

Much of this material has been discussed in various seminars and privately with colleagues whose comments have been invaluable. I especially thank Tone Bleie of Christian Michelsen Institute, Bergen, Norway; Sarah Skar, Marit Melhuus, and Ingrid Rudie of Oslo University; Julia Leslie, Chris Pinney, and Terry Byers of the School of Oriental and African Studies; Henrietta Moore, Jean Dreze, John Harriss, and Maurice Bloch of the London School of Economics; C. P. Chandrasekhar of Jawaharlal Nehru University; Meenakshi Thapan and Andrei Beteille of the Delhi School of Economics; Professor Thekkamalai of Tanjore University; Joan Mencher of City University, New York; and Gillian Hart of the University of California–Berkeley. In London, I thank John Knight and Francis Jayapathy and in Madras, Shanthakumari Sara Rajan, Ragini Raj, and Sister Mercy Parathazham. I also thank Shirley Ardener of Queen Elizabeth House, Oxford.

Aruloor, Nannikal, and Pettupatti are pseudonyms—as are the names of all informants in this book. This is because I hope to protect the identities of my informants, who so generously shared with me their time, their experiences, and their hospitality. In every caste-street, I met generous friends. I was particularly inspired by the cheerfulness and fortitude of the Pallar women, to whom my excellent Pallar research assistant, here called Siva, introduced me. I thank both my research assistants, "Siva" and "Mala," for their work and warm companionship.

The word "untouchable" is in quotation marks throughout because it is a label that denigrates and insults my friends. But I have not used a more anodyne term like "ex-untouchable" instead because caste discrimination still remains an ugly feature of daily life, even though it has been abolished by law. Siva's sisters are, in my understanding, not just the other Pallar women of Periyar Street but all the women in Aruloor. But this "sisterhood" did not exist in everyday life, where women (and men) remain sharply divided by caste and class. Their generous affection drew me to people of all castes in Aruloor, and I had hoped to reciprocate with a party to which *everyone* would be invited. But would everyone come? They were all my friends—but they remained sharply divided from each other. This is the sadness of social life in India. Things would have to change a great deal before I could have that party.

This book is formally dedicated to my father, my great friend and a passionate feminist. But inevitably it is also dedicated to the Pallar women of Aruloor. It must also be lovingly dedicated to my grandmother, Rodabe Kapadia; to my brother, Khushroo Kapadia; and to my mother, Anita Kapadia.

Karin Kapadia

Key to Kinship Notation

In this book, the following standard abbreviations are used to indicate kinship relationships:

M: Mother	S: Son
F: Father	W: Wife
Z: Sister	H: Husband
B: Brother	y: younger
D: Daughter	e: elder

These abbreviations are used to denote *both* genealogical relationships and classificatory relationships. That is, "MB" refers not only to the actual (genealogical) mother's brother of Ego but also to all such classificatory "uncles" (see the discussions in Chapters 2 and 3).

These abbreviations are combined to indicate other relationships. For example, MB: Mother's Brother, FZ: Father's Sister, MyB: Mother's Younger Brother, and so forth.

Part One

The Politics of Cultural Contestation

1

Introduction: The "Untouchable" Rejection of Hegemony and False Consciousness

Isn't our blood as red as theirs? In what way are they our superiors?
—Ambal (Pallar)

Forms of Resistance

IN HIS BOOK ON EVERYDAY forms of peasant resistance, James Scott argues that the notion of "false consciousness" "typically rests on the assumption that elites dominate not only the physical means of production but the symbolic means of production as well—and that this symbolic hegemony allows them to control the very standards by which their rule is evaluated" (1985: 39). Scott rejects this notion, arguing that such a view is blind to the "unwritten history of resistance" (1985: 28)—forms of resistance that are necessarily covert and underhand and that "typically avoid any direct symbolic confrontation with authority or with elite norms" (1985: 29). Apart from making the qualification that false consciousness does sometimes exist, I endorse this approach. Scott's conclusions resonate with those I came to in my own research, focused primarily on women in a village in rural Tamilnadu (Figure 1.1). I, too, found that subordinate groups—preeminently the so-called "untouchables" who are at the bottom of India's caste hierarchy—resisted and rejected upper-caste representations of themselves. I argue that "untouchable" Pallars in Aruloor village do not share the Brahminical values of elite groups. I therefore question the claims of Louis Dumont (1970) and Michael Moffatt (1979) that there is a pervasive "cultural consensus" between all groups in Hindu caste society. I contend, instead, that through distinc-

3

4

FIGURE 1.1   Tamilnadu

tive cultural representations, oppressed groups create for themselves a normative world in which they have dignity, self-respect, and power. I further argue that in indigenous perceptions, a sharp dichotomy exists between what are seen as "Brahmin" (upper-caste) values and "Tamil" (Non-Brahmin and lower-caste) values—and that this essentially political construction is of continuing importance to the ways in which women and men view their identities in Tamil South India today.

Gillian Hart, in her important paper "Engendering everyday resistance" (1991), has sharply critiqued the "androcentric" focus of Scott's account of peasant resistance in the Muda region of Malaysia. She points out that in Muda (where she, too, did fieldwork), there are "striking differences between women and men in both the organisation of labour arrangements and forms of resistance" (1991: 94). Her central question is: "Why were women more capable than men of asserting their identities and interests as workers" (1991: 94). She finds that Scott's analysis cannot answer this question because it is not a gendered analysis. She rightly notes that "to explain why class consciousness has differentiated along gender-specific lines, we *also* have to understand the operation of gender meanings in these interconnected sites of struggle" (1991: 94). Her insight is extremely relevant to my analysis because there are striking similarities between Aruloor and Muda: As we will see, Pallar women workers in Aruloor have a much greater ability than Pallar men to assert their rights as workers and to organize in defense of these rights.

One of the most difficult issues raised by the discussions of Hart and Scott is the question of the epistemological basis on which a critique of social practice and discourse can be undertaken. Hart rightly criticizes Scott for implying that subjects can have an entirely clear-sighted understanding of social oppression, and she states that "gender does indeed entail some degree of mystification and false consciousness" (1991: 117–118). This is an extremely important point, and it raises a crucial question: If I, as a social analyst, cannot "see" special reality "transparently," how can I then presume to critique South Indian discourse and practice? In short, on what epistemological basis can my (or any) social critique be conducted? The epistemology on which this study rests is offered by feminist critical theory, which has faced up to this difficult problem.

The Relevance of a Critical Feminist Theory

"Ideology" has been defined primarily in two ways. On the one hand, it is simply used descriptively to denote a system of thought or systems of belief. John Thompson characterizes this as "a *neutral conception* of ideology" (1984: 4, emphasis is added). On the other hand, "ideology" is also used negatively to criticize a system of ideas. This was the negative connotation used by Marx and Engels, and in this sense, the term continues to be associated with the critique of ideas. "Ideology," in this sense, is part of a process that sustains asymmetrical relations of power. Thompson calls this use of the term "a *critical conception* of ideology" and points out that, in sharp contrast to the neutral conception of the term, this critical conception "binds the analysis of ideology to the question of critique" (1984: 4, emphasis added). I use "ideology" solely in this critical sense in the following discussion; I use "discourse" to refer to a system of thought.

An intense discussion is currently going on among Western feminists regarding the very possibility of undertaking a critical analysis of ideology. If it is admitted that an empiricist view of the world is mistaken and that there are no facts "out there" but only facts that are "value-laden" and "theory-laden" (Hawkesworth 1989), then it becomes problematic to assume the possibility of an "objective" or "scientific" standpoint from which an observer can critique ideology. On what epistemological basis can this critique be conducted?

Mary Hawkesworth identifies three models for a feminist theory of knowledge that recur in this debate: feminist empiricism and feminist standpoint epistemologies claim to have a privileged perspective on the world but that both are refuted by "the insight generated by the long struggle of women of color within the feminist movement, that *there is no uniform 'women's reality' to be known,* no coherent perspective to be privileged" (1989: 537, emphasis added). This insight is very relevant to my own research. I found that there is no uniform women's perspective in Aruloor: Aruloor's Hindu women are positioned—and sharply divided—by caste and class, and their experience and understandings of the world vary greatly.

Hawkesworth states, "Critical reflection on and abandonment of certain theoretical presuppositions is possible within the hermeneutic circle; but *the goal of transparency, of the unmediated grasp of things as they are, is not,* for no investigation, no matter how critical, can escape the fundamental conditions of human cognition" (1989: 549, emphasis added). Above all, the analyst needs to be aware of *"the political implications of determinate modes of inquiry. The politics of knowledge must remain a principal concern of feminist analysis"* (Hawkesworth 1989: 552 emphasis added). This is why sociological analysts should be wary of claiming that a particular point of view is a consensual or encompassing view, shared by an entire society, as Dumont argues in *Homo Hierarchicus* (1970). Dumont presents a very Brahminical discourse as a central discourse that is "shared by all." Gerald Berreman (1971) and others have rightly challenged this; as Jonathan Parry puts it, "Dumont's emphasis on the values of purity and pollution derives from a rather brahmanical view of the world" (1974: 109). Richard Burghart (1978, 1983) points out that many equally important discourses are available in Hindu society. These writers are making an important political point: Social analysis that describes a dominant group's beliefs as consensually shared by all implicitly makes these beliefs appear both universal and legitimate.

Linda Alcoff emphasizes that "habits and practices are critical in the construction of meaning. ... Gender is not a point to start from in the sense of being a given thing but is, instead, a posit or construct, formalizable in a nonarbitrary way through a matrix of habits, practices, and discourses" (1988: 431). This formulation recalls Pierre Bourdieu's very influential work (1990) on the centrality of "habitus" and practices in the analysis of social inequality. Elaborating the concept of the subject as positionality, Alcoff says, "The concept of positionality shows how women use their positional perspective as a place from which values are interpreted and constructed rather than as a locus of an already determined set of values" (1988: 434–435).

Both Hawkesworth and Alcoff stress that subjects are capable of *interpreting and reconstructing* their identities within the cultural discursive contexts to which they have access. This epistemological perspective is central to this book, for I will argue, on the basis of both ritual and everyday discourses, that the "untouchable" Pallars have always interpreted their own identities differently from the way in which the upper castes have constructed them.

Thus, a critical feminist theory offers extremely suggestive insights for the analysis of the concepts of caste and class. Joan Scott emphasizes this when she calls for accounts "that focus on women's experiences and analyse the ways in which *politics construct gender and gender constructs politics.* Feminist history then becomes not the recounting of the great deeds performed by women but the exposure of the often silent and hidden operations of gender that are nonetheless present and defining forces in the organisation of most societies" (1988: 25, emphasis added).

As Hart has noted, the central insight of feminist theory has been the recognition of the need to extend the definition of politics: "Politics has increasingly come to be used in a broader sense to refer to the processes by which *struggles over resources and labour are simultaneously struggles over socially-constructed meanings, definitions, and identities.* By using an extended definition of politics, recent feminist analyses have shown how working class women's struggles in the workplace 'reverberate' or intersect with struggles in the household and the local community" (1991: 95, emphasis added). Hart adds, "reverberations among workplace, household, and community politics are just as important for men as they are for women" (1991: 95). My analysis is an attempt to understand such reverberations in Aruloor, as well as those between gender, caste, and class.

The Politics of Culture

I will examine the positional perspectives of both women and men in five castes in Aruloor. However, I will particularly focus on the experiences of "untouchable" Pallar women, for two reasons of differing importance.

The secondary reason is that the majority of anthropological accounts of Tamil South India have focused on so-called caste-Hindus (e.g., Dumont 1986; Beteille 1965; Barnett 1970; Beck 1972; Daniel 1984; Trawick 1990; Good 1991). The "untouchable" experience has largely been considered from the point of view of men (Berreman 1972; Mencher 1978; Moffatt 1979; Gough 1981, 1989; Deliege 1988). Virtually no accounts exist of the discourses and practices of "untouchable" women engaged in agricultural labor; even Maria Mies's useful study of poor women's work (1987) tells us little about the cultural construction of their identities.

But the primary reason why Pallar women stand at the center of this account is because their experiences provide a unique analytical focus that sharpens and clarifies the ways in which three axes of identity—gender, caste, and class—are represented and conceived in South India. Pallar women will, I hope, emerge from my account as women of great resourcefulness, independence, courage, and warmth. However, in their everyday lives, they are discriminated against as women, as "untouchables," and as landless agricultural workers.

I will make two central and interconnecting arguments. First, I will argue, as James Scott does, that elites who hold economic power and dominate the physical means of production do not necessarily dominate the symbolic means of production as well. I will focus this argument on the "untouchable" Pallars, and, using them as a test case, I will examine varied aspects of their concept, rituals, and everyday discourses to see whether Pillar cultural values and consciousness can be said to mirror the values and consciousness of the Brahminical elites. I will also comparatively examine caste and class dynamics in four other castes.

Second, I will argue, as Gillian Hart does, that it is not possible to study the dynamics of class—and, I would add, caste processes—without a *gendered* analysis. I will contend that in South India, both caste and class construct gender, and gender constructs both class and caste. So throughout this book, I will attempt "the exposure of the often silent and hidden operations of gender that are nonetheless present and defining forces in the organisation of most societies" (Joan Scott 1988: 25).

The Socioeconomic Background

Aruloor is a large village or agrarian town in Lalgudi Taluk (subdistrict), located in easternmost Tiruchi (Tiruchirappalli) District in Tamilnadu, South India. In Lalgudi Taluk, as elsewhere, caste has never correlated exactly with class, for there have always been poor Brahmins. However, in this rice-growing region, as in parts of neighboring Thanjavur District (which it closely resembles), caste very roughly correlates with class, for Brahmins and Vellan Chettiars (its highest castes) have been among the wealthiest landowners for centuries and the great majority of those in the "untouchable" castes are still landless laborers, constituting the regular agricultural workforce (See Beteille 1965, 1974, and Gough 1981, 1989, on Thanjavur). Brahmins and Chettiars never till the land themselves.

There are more than sixty endogamous castes and subcastes in Aruloor. Of them, the wealthy Vellan Chettiars and Telugu Brahmins form an upper class;

Vellalars and better-off Muthurajahs and Kallars form an upper middle class; and poorer Muthurajahs, Kallars, and better-off Pallars form a lower middle class. Landless Muthurajahs, Pallars, and Christian Paraiyars (CPs) largely form the indigent lower class, a sector that is becoming steadily more proletarianized and pauperized. All castes have members who are poorer and members who are richer than the caste average. Significantly, caste and class coincide less and less today.

Though a few Muthurajahs are very wealthy and landed individuals, the majority are small farmers. Many of them are landless, as is the case with the majority of Christian Paraiyars and Pallars. The Pallars, Christian Paraiyars, and Wottans (Hindu Paraiyars) in Aruloor all continue to be regarded as "untouchables," as they have been for centuries.

Aruloor village has been joined for administrative purposes with its three neighboring villages of Nannikal, Marukoil, and Pettupatti to constitute an administrative unit designated "Aruloor Town Panchaya," with a total population of 7,531 in 1987. With its sixty castes and a 1987 population of 6,176, Aruloor village had 82 percent of the population of this administrative unit. Nannikal village and Marukoil are almost entirely Muthurajah in population: With 1987 populations of 695 and 321, respectively, they constituted 9.2 percent and 4.3 percent of the Town Panchayat population. Pettupatti's 1987 population of 339 was, significantly, wholly Pallar: It formed the remaining 4.5 percent. With time, the villages of Aruloor and Nannikal expanded, so that by 1987, they were contiguous, their streets touching each other (see Figure 1.2).

The population of Aruloor and its neighboring villages in 1987 is given in Table 1.1, divided by caste and religion and ranked by percentage of population of Town Panchayat. The ranking in Aruloor village alone in that year was a little different: (1) Muthurajahs (25.8 percent), (2) Pathmasaliyars (13.8 percent), (3) Pallars and Paraiyars (both ranked at 12.6 percent), (4) Vellan Chettiars (8.2 percent), (5) Vellalar castes (4.4 percent), (6) Muslim castes (3.4 percent), (7) Brahmins (3.2 percent), and (8) Kallar castes (3.0 percent). Table 1.2 translates these population statistics into percentages.

This study is focused on five castes in Aruloor village: the "untouchable" Pallars; the "untouchable" Christian Paraiyars; the agriculturist Muthurajahs; the rich, landed, and mercantile Vellan Chettiars; and the wealthy Telugu Brahmins. These five castes together constituted 62.4 percent of Aruloor village in 1987. The 1,590 Muthurajahs were numerically the dominant caste in this large village, making up just over a quarter of its population (25.8 percent), but in terms of local power, they ceded primacy to the Vellan Chettiars. Today, the Vellan Chettiars not only control far more land and wealth than the Telugu Brahmins, they are also more respected by the general populace, who credit the Chettiars with having more "true" piety than the Brahmins.

This lower-caste attitude toward the Non-Brahmin Chettiars is influenced by the widespread anti-Brahmin bias found among Aruloor's Non-Brahmin castes.

10

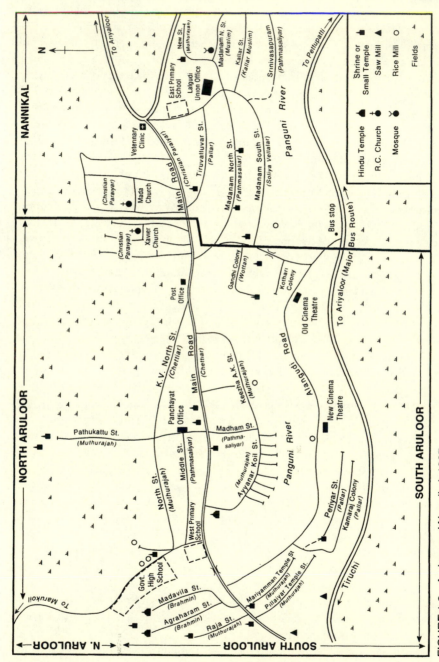

FIGURE 1.2 Aruloor and Nannikal, 1987

TABLE 1.1   Caste Populations in Aruloor Town Panchayat, 1987

	Aruloor	Nannikal	Marukoil	Pettupatti	Aruloor Town Panchayat
1. Muthurajah	1,590	512	266	—	2,368
2. Pallar	778	—	—	311	1,089
3. Pathmasaliyar	845	—	—	—	845
4. Christian Paraiyar	771	—	—	—	771
5. Chettiar	506	—	—	—	506
6. Brahmin	198	86	—	—	284
7. Vellalar	273	5	—	—	278
8. Kallar	188	45	—	—	233
9. Muslim	209	13	—	—	222
10. Other	818	34	55	28	935
Total	6,176	695	321	339	7,531

They see themselves as true Tamils, so-called sons of the soil, and largely endorse the political propaganda of the Dravidian political parties, which have depicted the "alien" Brahmins as "Aryan invaders from the North." Anti-Brahmin feeling has been a crucial factor in the consciousness of all Non-Brahmin castes in this area since the 1920s. Now, however, it is not deliberately whipped up by the Anna Dravida Munnetra Kazhagam (ADMK), which is led by the ex-film star Jayalalitha. Ironically, Jayalalitha, chief minister of Tamilnadu in 1994, is Brahmin.

It is worth noting that even though upper-caste Tamils, such as Aruloor's Vellan Chettiars, resent Brahmin social and political dominance, they have continued to imitate certain features of Brahmin lifestyle—for example, strict vegetarianism and the taboo on widow-remarriage. Their apparent "Brahminization" can perhaps be termed a qualified "Sanskritization," to use M. N. Srinivas's omnibus word, especially since Srinivas himself points out that there are many kinds of Sanskritization (1962b). However, the imitation of the Chettiar lifestyle by the upwardly mobile lower castes probably cannot, according to Srinivas's own criteria, be considered true Sanskritization. This is because, in a context of continued and strong anti-Brahmin feeling, this lower-caste adoption of upper-caste norms is, instead, an attempt to appropriate a prestigious cultural style that enhances their change in *class* status. They do not seek to make a claim to higher *caste* status. Thus, Brahminization now has more to do with class mobility than with the legitimation of a higher caste status.

The Chettiars control huge amounts of capital, mainly in land. Like Max Weber's Puritans (1985), the Chettiars, with characteristic acumen, have acquired religious legitimacy for their huge wealth through generous donations to the ancient Siva Temple. This has helped to secure their hegemonic position in Aruloor society, so that upwardly mobile Muthurajahs and Pallars attempt to emulate the Chettiar lifestyle, not that of the Brahmins. Consequently, Sanskritization in Aruloor is more a matter of imitating the Brahminized Chettiar, rather than the Brahmins.

TABLE 1.2   Population Profile in Aruloor Town Panchayat, 1987 (in percentages)

	Aruloor	Nannikal	Marukoil	Pettupatti	Aruloor Town Panchayat
Total population	100.00	100.00	100.00	100.00	100.00
1. Muthurajah	25.8	73.7	82.9	—	31.4
2. Pallar	12.6	—	—	91.7	14.5
3. Pathmasaliyar	13.8	—	—	—	11.2
4. Christian Paraiyar	12.6	—	—	—	10.2
5. Chettiar	8.2	—	—	—	6.7
6. Brahmin	3.2	12.4	—	—	3.8
7. Vellalar	4.4	0.7	—	—	3.7
8. Kallar	3.0	6.4	—	—	3.1
9. Muslim	3.4	1.9	—	—	3.0
10. Other	13.0	4.9	17.1	8.3	12.4

Classes Within Castes

Traditionally, the individual in Aruloor found support and security in her kin group and in the more extended classificatory kin of her caste in the village. Today, however, crucial aspects of these kin and caste ties are weakening. This is due to the very important phenomenon of increasing class stratification within castes. With a growing differentiation in terms of education and access to jobs, class divisions are now appearing within castes and kindreds. But due to the powerful hold of caste-based identity, these divisions do not result in a class consciousness that cuts across caste but, on the contrary, in an increasingly sharp class stratification within caste. There are at least two trajectories that this class-within-caste consciousness can take. In one, class interests are accentuated almost as much as caste. This has happened with some elite urban caste-groups who share common educational backgrounds and similar class interests and thus a degree of mutuality, despite their different castes. However, another trajectory is the deliberate strengthening of caste consciousness, regardless of the growing importance of economic differentiation. This trajectory is being intentionally encouraged at the political level, not just in Tamilnadu but throughout India. This is not a new trend; Srinivas discussed it in 1962 (1962a), and Andre Beteille took the discussion further (1969a, 1969b), pointing out that Kathleen Gough (1960) and Edmund Leach (1960) were quite wrong to argue that the politicization of caste would mean the end of caste. On the contrary, caste is now even more important in politics at both the state and national levels, and political parties now cater to caste interests.

2

"Kinship Burns!"
Kinship Discourses and Gender

You know how it is! Kinship burns! That's our life and that's what we have to put up with.

—Anuradha (Veerakodi Vellalar)

MUCH HAS BEEN WRITTEN on Tamil (or Dravidian) kinship (e.g., Dumont 1953, 1957, 1983; Traumann 1981), but few writers have related an analysis of the structure of Tamil kinship to women's views about their place in it. Structurally, kinship in Aruloor suggests that women have high status, because of the prominence of matrilateral affines. Yet from the female perspective, especially in the upper castes, kinship is regarded very ambiguously. It is portrayed in *male* discourse—the dominant discourse in Tamil kinship—as largely positive. This discourse suggests that there are always quarrels and tension between brothers within the *pankali* (patrilineage). But this notion is balanced against an idyllic view of marriage and affinal relations as a sphere of happiness and harmony. However, the female attitude toward marriage and affinity is highly ambivalent.

Kinship discourses and kinship systems vary considerably throughout Tamilnadu, and therefore, the following discussion does not claim that what exists in Aruloor represents Tamil kinship throughout Tamilnadu. On the contrary, the work of Dumont (1953, 1957, 1983), Steve Barnett (1970, 1976), Tony Good (1978, 1980, 1991), and others make it quite clear that there is enormous variation.

Cross-kin Tamil marriage is usually described as "isogamous." In anthropological discourse, this term means that the social statuses of the families that are linked through marriage are equal. However, those who hold this traditional view have not sufficiently considered the position of women within these families: They have tended to simply assume that there is no internal differentiation in status be-

13

tween men and women within these groups. But recent research has shown that there is very widespread subordination of women to men in many cultures. This is certainly true of Tamil culture. For this reason, I argue that the subordinate status of women relative to the status of men of their own family and social group must be recognized in an analysis of the structures of Tamil kinship. And if it is recognized, then we must also accept that the quality implicit in the term "isogamy" is the equality of affinal *males*.

Women are considered inferior to men in all the castes, though in differing degree. The social status of women is equal to that of the men in their caste only in dealings outside their caste. Within the caste, the social status of a woman is inferior to that of her brothers, her father, and her husband. This inferiority of women is constantly emphasized in family interaction; for instance, women never eat first, women have to perform demeaning household tasks, wives must always sit at a lower level than their husbands, and so on (see Sheryl Daniel 1980: 69, for a detailed list of "ranked interactions"). In these ways, the status of women as a "lower species" is emphasized in the upper castes. Not surprisingly, it is in these better-off castes that the dependence of women on men is most marked—and most insisted upon.

Because the status of women is, in most contexts, lower than that of men, marriage can create hierarchy even between close cross-kin who have been social equals. Consequently, when there are marital problems, it is usually the interests of the male that prevail. This is predominantly true even among the lowest castes, despite the fact that women in these castes have far more autonomy than those in the upper castes.

Another central argument in this chapter is that the Aruloor data suggest the importance of the matrilateral affinal kin in Tamil kinship has been greatly underestimated. These kin were the traditional focus of Non-Brahmin kinship in Aruloor, and it is probably the fact that affines were matrilateral that largely accounts for the comparatively high status of Non-Brahmin Tamil women. Hence, Dennis McGilvray, who studied matrilineal, Non-Brahmin Tamils in Batticaloa, Sri Lanka, is, in fact, mistaken to assume that Batticaloa Tamils were very different from other Tamils. He contrasts his Tamil area with "practically all of Tamil Nadu in south India ... [which] is patrilineal in emphasis, giving greater salience to Brahminical orthodoxy in ritual and belief" (1982b: 27). On the contrary, my Aruloor data are remarkably close to McGilvray's data in significant respects. Most importantly, they suggest that where patrilineal principles are weak, Brahminical beliefs are marginal or irrelevant. I contend that this correlation is evident in many aspects of Non-Brahmin culture in Aruloor.

However, the current move away from the matrilateral emphasis of traditional Non-Brahmin marriage in Aruloor, in the direction of less marriage with close kin and more dowry marriage with "strangers," is undermining women's traditional status. This, I will argue, is largely because these changes ignore or at least devalue the traditional affinal link with matrilateral kin. in traditional close-kin marriage, prestations (ritual gifts) followed a "bride-price" pattern, going from the groom's family to the bride's. In "dowry" marriage, these transfers are reversed—the bride's family must give gifts to the groom's family.

In this chapter, I will focus on the kinship ideas of four Non-Brahmin Tamil castes and two of the three Brahmin castes in Aruloor. The four Non-Brahmin Tamil castes are: the "untouchable" Pallars, the upwardly mobile agriculturist Muthurajahs, the "untouchable" Roman Catholic Paraiyars (the Christian Paraiyars, or CPs), and the wealthy Vellan Chettiars. The Pallars are impoverished, landless laborers. The Muthurajahs are becoming economically stratified—some families are moving into salaried urban jobs. The CPs are falling back economically, blaming this on the loss of church patronage. And the Chettiars remain the richest landowners in Aruloor; as noted, they also provide the role model for other Non-Brahmin Tamil castes in the village.

The two Brahmin castes examined are the Telugu Brahmins, who are the dominant Brahmin group in the Brahmin street, and the Tamil Brahmins, who number only a few households. I did not study the third Brahmin caste, the low-status, Telugu-speaking Pancangam (Almanac) Brahmins; they are the domestic priests of the caste-Hindus. None of these three Brahmin castes intermarry. The majority of Brahmins are well off, and most desire urban jobs and salaries and are keen to leave the village, though they have been major landlords there for generations. For many years, a massive migration of Brahmins from rural Tamilnadu to the big cities (Madras, Bombay, and Delhi) has been going on, and as a result, Aruloor's Telugu Brahmins now have kin in all these places. This migration is closely connected with the fundamental political changes that have occurred in Tamilnadu since the 1920s, creating a social climate that, until the 1980s, was distinctly hostile to Brahmins.

The traditional forms of Non-Brahmin Tamil kinship are, in the indigenous perception, being radically altered today. This apparent breakdown in traditional, close cross-kin marriage correlates with a fundamental devaluation of the status of the Non-Brahmin Tamil woman. I will discuss this breakdown and statistical evidence for it in the next chapter, when analyzing the implications of contemporary changes in marriage preference and practice. Here, I will limit myself to delineating the traditional ideas of Tamil kinship in Aruloor as these were represented in the discourses of my informants.

I will begin by examining the traditional kinship systems of Non-Brahmin Tamils and Brahmins. When these two rather different kinship discourses are contrasted, the changes occurring today emerge most sharply. In the area of kinship, Aruloor's Non-Brahmin Tamils feel they have very good grounds for clearly differentiating themselves from Brahmins.

The Categories of Tamil Kinship

Dravidian, or Tamil, kinship has a cross-kin marriage system. Traditionally, this was referred to in the literature as the "cross-cousin marriage system" (Dumont 1957, 1983, 1986; Yalman 1962), but as Good has pointed out (1978, 1991), this is an imprecise use of terms since the preferential system is really far wider than a cross-cousin system, given that all classificatory (or terminological) cross-kin consist of the children of the cross-sex siblings of Ego's parents and also of all those classificatory kin who are similarly related to Ego. Ego's MB's and FZ's children are Ego's genealogical cross-cousins: They are the most preferred spouses for Ego. (See the Key to Kinship Notation following the Preface.) The children of the parallel-sex siblings of Ego's parents—that is, Ego's MZ's and FB's children— are Ego's genealogical parallel-cousins. They are prohibited as spouses, and Ego is held to have a classificatory sibling relationship with them and with all classificatory kin who are like them. Thus, for a female Ego, MZ's son and FB's son are "brothers" whom she cannot marry but with whom she enjoys a warm "brother-sister" relationship. MB's son and FZ's son, on the other hand, are both highly eligible as husbands, though most Aruloor castes claim that they strongly prefer one or the other.

What Dumont and a host of other writers (detailed in Good 1980, 1991) fail to note is that marriage with MB himself is, in some areas, quite as important as cross-cousin marriage. Indeed, Brenda Beck's data (1972), Good's work (1978, 1980, 1981, 1991), and my own data from Aruloor make it clear that MyB/eZD marriage is often the preferred marriage. This is true with most of the Non-Brahmin Tamil castes in Aruloor, including the Roman Catholic Paraiyar caste (despite a church ban on cross-kin marriage) (see Kapadia 1990). Like Good (1980), I came across no caste that prohibited MyB marriage, though the Telugu Brahmins did state that they did not encourage it (unlike many Tamil Brahmin groups). This is another reason why "cross-cousin marriage" is an imprecise general term to describe the Dravidian marriage system, not only because classificatory cross-kin play such an important role as preferred spouses but because, in many areas, MyB (who is not a cousin at all) is a highly preferred spouse.

Another reason for dispensing with the term "cross-cousin" is that it forms no part of the indigenous vocabulary. Hence, the terms "marriageable kin" or "affines" are preferable, for they more closely translate the Tamil term *"kalyana murai."* There are two main Tamil terms (in Aruloor) for what anthropologists have translated as "cross-kin": the more formal term *"kalyana murai"* ("marriage tradition" or "marriageable kin"—*"murai"*: "rule, tradition") and the more commonly used *"maman-maccinan murai"* ("MB/WB-type" kin). Similarly, there are two main Tamil terms for "parallel-kin": the more formal *"pankali"* ("patrilineage"—*"pankali"*: "sharers") and the more common *"annan-tampi murai"* ("Eb-yB-type" kin). *"Pankali"* derives from *"panku"* ("share"); thus, the *pankali* are the sharers, namely, the male kin (normally brothers) who inherit and share property and other forms of wealth.

The *pankali* (male lineage), in the context of everyday discourse, is said to be of secondary importance in Non-Brahmin Tamil (but not Brahmin) kinship. The fact that it is represented in this manner relates to the primary importance of affinal matrilateral kin in the contexts of marriage and gift-giving. Dumont's influential characterization of the Tamil marriage system as a system of a "marriage alliance" (1957, 1983) goes some way toward abandoning earlier misconceptions that the descent group was primary in kinship everywhere. His analysis holds that "there is a principle which balances patrilineality. ... There is a balance of forces, but the forces are not of the same nature" (Dumont 1983: 93). These forces or complementary principles Dumont identifies as "descent" or "kin," on the one hand (1983: 103), and "alliance," on the other. Although this is generally acceptable for kinship in Aruloor, Dumont has assumed that the paradigmatic Tamil system was like that of the Pramalai Kallar (Dumont 1986), who had a strong preference for *bridges* from the mother's side (what anthropological terminology, habitually assuming a *male* Ego, has defined as "matrilateral marriage" [MBD/ FZS]). At the time of his study, Dumont did not know and could not take into account the fact that other ethnographies were to show that the opposite marriage preference was also popular with many Tamil groups. This is true of Good's data (1978, 1980, 1981, 1991) and also of mine (1990).

In the following analysis, instead of adhering to the convention of assuming a male Ego in the discussion of marriage preferences, I have adopted the point of view of a *female* Ego. I have done this not to make a feminist point but because this was the perspective of my informants. Indeed, the arguments that my informants made would be misrepresented if I tried to force them into the framework of anthropological convention. My informants (of both sexes) were primarily interested in whom a girl ought to marry. Their assumption in our frequent discussions of marriage, both actual and theoretical, was that marriage was far more important for a young woman than it was for a young man. This was because a Tamil girl did not become a "full woman" until she was married: Her social identity remained incomplete, and she was perceived as an incomplete human being until she married. This was not the case for young men, for whom marriage, though necessary, was not as urgent or as absolutely required as it was for women. In other words, marriage was not the foundation of a man's social identity as it was for a woman. As Sheryl Daniel points out, "A woman, traditionally, can have respect *only as a wife* ... marriage is not a necessary precondition for respectability for a man as it is for a woman" (1980 : 67, emphasis added). Getting married, my informants felt, was the central preoccupation for young women; young men did not worry so much about it. Thus, *the identity of the bridegroom* was the central question. Did this very significant male belong to the kin on the mother's side or the father's side?—this was the crucial question. To ask such a question was to adopt the perspective of a female Ego, and in doing this, my informants, far from showing feminist tendencies, were, on the contrary, being true to their culture in giving central importance to the identity of the significant male. In the following discussion, I therefore use the term "matrilateral" as they did, to denote a female Ego's marriage preference for a groom from the mother's side (MyB or MBS), and I use the term "patrilateral " to denote the marriage choice of a groom from the father's side (FZS).

For most informants, the choice of a groom from the girl's *mother's* side (the young woman's real or classificatory MyB or MBS) was a choice that valorized relations with the matrilateral kin and strengthened the position and status of the girl's mother. The choice of a groom from the young woman's *father's* side (her real or classificatory FZS) was, similarly, seen as a choice that strengthened her father's authority. This was explicitly stated by the Telugu Brahmins of Aruloor, who, like the Tamil Brahmins, favored such a patrilateral preference. These Telugu Brahmins expressed disapproval of the widespread Non-Brahmin Tamil preference for a woman's marriage with her MyB or her MBS because they saw this as weakening the authority of the patrilineage.

Because the four major Non-Brahmin Tamil castes of Aruloor all had a stated preference for grooms from the bride's mother's side, it was the matrilateral affinal kin who occupied center stage in kinship in Aruloor. Further, because they were the most preferred affines, they dominated all life-cycle rituals and gave the most important and expensive prestations (ritual gifts) at these events. Because they were gift-givers par excellence, they were very often described as the "most important" relatives. This flattering phrase was used repeatedly by informants from all Non-Brahmin Tamil castes to distinguish marriageable matrilateral kin from the patrilineage (the *pankali*). It is striking that even though inheritance rights and caste identity were transmitted in the male line (through the patrilineage), it was the affinal matrilateral kin who were spoken of more often. This view of the importance of affines derives both from the salience of marriage and life-cycle prestations and from the strong moral responsibility that rests with affines, especially Mother's Brother.

Dumont's perceptive paper *Hierarchy and Marriage Alliance in South Indian Kinship,* first published in 1957, provides some indication of why such importance should be given to affines. He says: "The most conspicuous feature of alliance ... consists in ceremonial gifts and functions ... ceremonial gifts are essentially affinal" (Dumont 1983: 79). Further, "this chain of gifts ... is the most important feature of marriage ceremonies" (Dumont 1983: 80). He emphasizes that "*the affinal nature of the giving relationship* is demonstrated by the fact that almost all givers are only in-laws" (Dumont 1983: 94, emphasis added). He concludes that alliance is "opposed to kin" ("kin" or descent groups being opposed to "alliance" or affinal relatives) but that, finally, it is "the principle of alliance" that is "the fundamental principle of South Indian kinship" (Dumont 1983: 103).

In short, it is the institution of marriage itself that is of greatest importance in South Indian kinship: Marriage is what Tamil kinship is about. Therefore, in Aruloor, it was said that "marriageable kin"—*"kalyana murai"*—were more important in everyday life than "lineage kin" (*"pankali"*). The simple fact was that one got more from them than from patrilineal kin, and for this reason, one was more involved with them. There was a strong economic reason for the greater affection felt for one's affinal kin.

However, there were also differences (though perhaps not fundamental ones) between the Kallar system that Dumont focuses on and Tamil kinship in Aruloor. Kallar kinship united through alliance clearly distinguished patrilineages, with lineage identity being an important part of the Kallar person. But among the Non-Brahmin Tamil castes in Aruloor, the ideological stress was, instead, on *the unity of the entire kindred* and on the importance of *"sondam"* ("relationship" or "kinship"). In both Kallar and Aruloor discourses, cross-kin marriage was seen as reproducing the existing links of *sondam*. But with Aruloor's Non-Brahmin Tamil castes, the principle of descent was very weak. This weak stress on the male patrilineage, who controlled most wealth, was balanced by a strong emphasis on the affinal (matrilateral) kin, who were characterized as the source of emotional and material support. So, as in Dumont's kinship paradigm, the Non-Brahmin Tamil kinship system in Aruloor is also essentially *bilateral* in emphasis—but with a stronger stress on the matrilateral kin than is found in Dumont's model.

Dumont uses the terms "affines"/"terminological affines" to designate *"maman-maccinan murai"* (MB/WB-type kin or marriageable kin) and "kin"/ "terminological kin"/"consanguines" to designate *"annan-tampi murai"* (eB/yB-type kin or unmarriageable kin) (1953, 1957). His dichotomy of "consanguines/affines" is confusing, however, and becomes misleading if applied to an area like Aruloor, where all castes assume that not only patrilineal "consanguines" but also *all* affines and potential affines are related "by blood" to Ego even before marriage. This assumption is not made everywhere in Tamilnadu, where, as Dumont notes, there is a remarkable variation in kinship systems (1983: 103). However, in Aruloor, given traditional cross-kin marriage, such consanguinity is considered a perfectly reasonable assumption because a genealogical MBS or FZS is related "by blood" to a female Ego even before marriage. Further, after marriage, it is said that both partners are related "by blood" to all their affinal kin, due to the creation of a "blood-bond" between them (which I will discuss later). Consequently, it is believed in Aruloor that there is a strong element of consanguinity in affinity and that affines are also "consanguineous." For this reason, I use the term "affines" (for "marriageable kin") but avoid the term "consanguines" (for "unmarriageable kin") because in this Non-Brahmin Tamil discourse, *all* relatives are regarded as consanguineous to some degree.

The Mother's Brother

The Non-Brahmin Tamil castes of Aruloor, in contrast to the Brahmins, give the *Tay Maman* (the Mother's Brothers) the preeminent role in their kinship system. The MB represents the natal family of his sister (especially her parents) at ritual events, but he also has great importance in his own right, for three reasons. The first is his right to claim in his marriage, either for himself or his sons, his ZDs (only his eZDs in his own case but any ZDs for his sons). This customary right (*urimai*) traditionally afforded great influence to MB (and MBS), for if he did not wish to claim these girls himself, he had a large say in deciding (jointly with the girls' parents) upon whom the girls would be bestowed in marriage. His opinion in this matter had traditionally been considered as important as that of the girls' parents, I was told, though it was waning in 1988. Thus, MB historically shared with a girl's parents control over her potential fertility through his joint say in the choice of her marriage partner. In this sense, he was described as "inheriting" women.

The second reason for MB's importance in Aruloor was derivative, stemming from the comparatively higher position of women in traditional Non-Brahmin Tamil culture as compared to traditional Brahmin culture. Women were—and, to a large extent, still are—highly valued in Non-Brahmin Tamil culture both as the producers of children and as active participants in agricultural labor (waged and unwaged). Therefore, through his marriage claims, MB shared in the control of not only his ZDs' fertility but also, in the Tamil lower castes, the allocation of their labor. It is true that, especially in the lower castes, women are generally independent earners who are, to some degree, economically independent of their husbands (see Mencher 1988). But even in these lower castes (such as the "untouchable" Pallars), both a woman's labor and her earnings are often seen as the "property" of her husband.

The third reason for MB's importance is the affective link between him and his sister and between him and his sister's children. As the following discussion will show, MB is believed to have immense affection (*pasam*) for his sister's children. But it is also widely accepted that the link between brothers and sisters is exceptionally close and that it endures throughout life, even after a sister's marriage. Margaret Trawick has discussed the remarkable intensity of brother-sister relationships more suggestively than anyone else. She says: "In most of Tamil Nadu … the brother-sister tie is neither clearly severed at marriage, nor is its emotional priority over other ties translated into social priority. The blood bond remains, and is affectively the strongest bond" (Trawick 1990: 1979).

The rights of the Mother's Brothers were carefully balanced with responsibilities. They were obliged to provide assistance to their sisters' husbands whenever needed and to provide important, expensive prestations at the life-cycle rites of their sisters' children, both female and male. They had to be present on these occasions and to give "gifts," particularly at the grand puberty rites of their ZDs. In this traditional context, MB's gifts were quintessential Tamil gifts, for they were viewed as *reciprocal* gifts: They were directly related to his assertion of his traditional "rights" in his ZDs. In a general sense, reciprocity was the dominant ideology of Tamil kinship. For everything given, there was an equal or greater return made—and all affines were equal. From this point of view, MB's gifts were investments, made with the intent of asserting and legitimizing his claim to his ZDs. Certainly, a MB who had not given ritual prestations and who had neglected his sister's children was not allowed to claim a ZD in marriage either for his son or for himself: His neglect of his obligation (to provide gifts) rendered his claims (and those of his sons) invalid. Thus, in Aruloor, a clear quid pro quo existed. MBs *earned* their right to "inherit" their ZDs.

A poor MB might actually be provided with "his" gifts by his sister and her husband. Rachel, a young woman of Christian Paraiyar caste, stated: "If the *maman* is very poor then the girl's parents might provide all the gifts necessary and only ask him to come to formally 'give' them." Malarkodi, a perceptive young woman of Muthurajah caste, gave an example from the ear-piercing of her FeB's daughter's child: "*Periappa's* [FeB's] family are very poor and so their married daughter—whose husband owns a 'hotel' [cafeteria] in Keyankondam—bought all the jewelry for the ear-piercing of her daughter [aged seven] and her son [aged five]. Her younger brother [their Mb] merely 'gave' it. This was known to everyone here—but in Jeyankondam they thought the younger brother had paid for it all!" This is what the children's parents would have wanted people to think because a poor *maman* brings discredit; conversely, a rich *maman* brings honor. However, poor *maman* were also being summarily left out of the most important kinship event—marriage—altogether. There was an increasing trend in Aruloor for wealthy parents to give their daughters in marriage to rich "strangers" (non-kin of the same endogamous group) instead of giving them to the MyBs who had the traditional right (*urimai*) to marry them. This had happened in Middle Street, where Devaki, a Lingayat woman from an upwardly mobile family, married her beautiful daughter to a wealthy bank officer rather than to her younger brother, an impoverished farmer. Everybody in her street had noted this, but nobody explicitly criticized it because the times were changing.

An important aspect of MB's gifts is the fact that they are widely seen as constituting his sister's share of parental property. These predators, known as *sir* (or *sir varisai*), are presented by MB at all the life-cycle rites of his sister's children. This aspect of MB's gifts is implied by the term used for these gifts: *Sir* (the Tamil corruption of the Sanskrit "stri") is an abbreviation of the Sanskrit *"stri dhanam,"* meaning "woman's wealth." In Tamil, this takes the form *"sidanam."* *"Sidanam"* (or *sir*) is generally understood to mean the premortem inheritance of a woman. This is also how the word "dowry" is understood in North India, Ursula Sharma states (1984), but she argues quite convincingly that this understanding is an ideological misrepresentation of reality because brides themselves do not gain control of the "dowry" that is supposedly theirs. However, Non-Brahmin Tamil women in Aruloor did seem to view *sir* as their share of parental property, and so they became very indignant when their brothers did not provide *sir,* as they saw it as their *right.* Thus, MB's gifts to his sister's children were, indeed, perceived as the rightful share of premortem inheritance of his sister. From this perspective, *sir* constituted an obligatory gift, and the MB who did not provide it was reneging on an unwritten contract. Dumont provides evidence for this view, noting: "If ceremonial gifts are essentially affinal and if they are important, it should follow that, in societies with male predominance, *property is transmitted from one generation to the next under two forms:* by inheritance in the male line, *and also by gifts* to in-laws. ... This is precisely what happens ... daughters have no formal share in their father's property, but they are entitled to maintenance and to the expenses necessary for their marriage and establishment. ... This double transmission of property confirms the opposition between kin and alliance" (1983: 79–80, emphases added).

I asked Paul, the influential Christian Paraiyar municipal council member from St. Xavier's Church Street, if the *sir* given by MB really added up to an equal share in the property the brothers had inherited, as men liked to claim. He replied:

> Yes, it does—the *maman* gives *sir* from the birth of the sister's children until the marriage of each child—and right until the death of the sister. So this *sir* usually adds up to more than the woman's share in property would have been. But men have become lax—reluctant to give *sir* to their sisters—so Indira Gandhi-amma brought in a law which stated that from now on women have an equal share in inheritance. No, nobody actually gives any property to the girls. That hasn't happened. But because of this new law, men have got a fright and now they give their prestations much more carefully. They're afraid that their sisters might take them to court. If they do give the *sir* properly then everyone is satisfied—and the sister, being happy that her brothers are giving her generous *sir,* does not wish to quarrel with them, by demanding a right in property.

Despite Paul's initial claim, his further words make it clear that women generally do *not* receive the equivalent of what their brothers inherit in landed property. If they did, brothers would have no reason to fear being taken to court.

Most women refrained from making any claims, but in the Muthurajah street, the case of Tilakambal was well known. Though in her fifties, she had sued her three brothers the previous year (1987). They had given no *sir* to her children for many years. Tilakambal and her husband, Ramasami (a retired railway clerk in his mid-sixties), were among the few wealthy Muthurajahs in the street and had a house in Tiruchi city. Urbanized and shrewd, they knew that the new legislation gave them a very strong case. So when Tilakambal demanded her share of the inheritance, she won her case (though she may have received less than she had hoped for) and was awarded half an acre of paddy land. She and her husband now got an income of twenty *kalam* (28.1 kilograms) of paddy per crop. It was said by neighbors that the reason Tilakambal's three brothers had not given any *sir* to her children was because of ill feelings between them and her husband from the very start. Ramasami had the reputation of being an aggressive man who was always fighting court cases.

However, Tilakambal's strategy was not typical among Muthurajah women and was regarded as quite exceptional by her neighbors. One of them said: "No sister would ever go to court if her brothers were giving *sir* to her children. She'd much prefer the goodwill of her brothers to *having* wealth but *not* having them to give it. Of what use is mere wealth? A woman's greatness lies in her having brothers who give *sir* to her children—'fame lies in *Maman* giving *sir* in front of ten others.'"

A CP man complained: "*Whenever* a woman comes to her natal home she has to be given gifts to take back to her husband's!" This was true for women whose mother's houses were in other villages. They visited their parental homes perhaps once a month on average, and as Malarkodi put it, "*Something* is always given: rice or [home-cooked] sweets or new clothes." But it was obviously not true for those women who were locally married and who consequently visited their mothers almost daily. Further, most people agreed that the *sir* that married daughters received amounted to only a tiny part of what their brothers inherited.

The obligatory nature of their gifts was as clear to the various MBs I spoke to as it was to the sisters who awaited their prestations. In the wealthy Chettiar caste, Devayanai Chettiar's younger brother, Annamalai, said: "*Maman's seyyum murai* [tradition of doing or giving] is a matter of duty [*kadamai*], not of mere desire [*ishtam*] or mere affection [*pasam*]. He *has* to do it—even if he has to take out loans to do it. And if he doesn't, he'll be told off by others. I have to give to the children of Devayanai and Janaki. So far, because our parents are alive, they pay for the events, but I perform the role." Many in Aruloor shared this unsentimental, hardheaded view of giving gifts as a man's bounden duty because of his inheritance of parental property and his responsibility to help his married sisters.

Women who had no brothers had a serious problem. "When looking for a bride for their son, people will generally *avoid* a girl who has no brothers. Because, with no brothers, who will give *sir* to her children? She'll have to always be chasing after *Cittappa's* son [FyBS] and *Periyappa's* son [FeBS] to act as *Maman* at 'necessary occasions' [life-cycle rites]. And the bridegroom too won't be happy about getting such a girl, because she has no brother to give him the traditional *maccinan*-ring [the ring from the WB]. On whose lap will the child sit at the ear-piercing? That's why girls who have no brothers aren't popular marriage choices." This was a Muthurajah opinion, but it was shared by all Non-Brahmin Tamils.

When I asked if only daughters were not *more* attractive because they inherited all their parents' wealth, I was told by a Muthurajah woman: "No one cares for wealth alone. Everyone considers honour [*madippu*] much more important than wealth. Everyone knows that there'll be problems with the *maman*-substitutes!" This had certainly been true in the case of Ambigai. She was a very beautiful, young, married woman, the only daughter of a rich Muthurajah family. Her father owned two acres of farm land and also lent money at interest. When her parents held the ear-piercing of Ambigai's little daughters, they asked Ambigai's two FyB's sons to act as *maman* and hold the two-year-old and one-year-old girls on their laps. But Ambigai's classificatory brothers had flatly refused to come, saying, "You didn't invite us for Ambigai's wedding, so why should we come now?" They had not been invited to her wedding due to an earlier quarrel between Ambigai's father and their own father over the division of their inheritance (the classic *pankali* quarrel between brothers). A delegation of several people went from the Muthurajah street to FyB's village to plead with them, and eventually the young men were persuaded to attend. Most persuasive of all was the promise that one of these young FyB's sons would certainly get half of Ambigai's inheritance one day. This was because she had no brother to light her father's funeral pyre. Her own son would not be allowed to light it because it had to be lit by a descendant in the direct *male* line; instead, her father's elder brother's son or his younger brother's son would light the pyre. And whoever did so would get half the wealth of the deceased man. This is one area in which the importance of the patrilineal kin is stressed, and consequently, the matrilateral kin have to give way before patrilineal prerogative. The result is a much smaller inheritance for widows and their daughters. It is remarkable that this system has persisted among the Muthurajahs, CPs, and Pallars despite the influence of the matrilateral kin. Not surprisingly, the system was sometimes (though rarely) challenged by a doughty lower-caste widow who had her *daughter* light her husband's pyre rather than give away half the family inheritance to a patrilineal kinsman. (At the time of my research, this had happened recently among Pallars in another village.)

Among the Chettiars, the same course was followed when substitute MBs were needed. Palani Chettiar, their ritual leader, had stated: "If there is no *maman*, then only the classificatory *maman* will be asked to give the gifts. *Pankali*-kin cannot give these gifts." But of course, given that it was often (among the Chettiars as well) a woman's FBS who was chosen to play the role of MB, this was a case of the classificatory *maman* also being a patrilineal kinsman. As Dumont rightly points out, this interesting choice of a patrilineal kinsman to "play" an affine was "an example of how an individual relationship is liable to a classificatory extension in agreement with the principle of descent" (1983: 90).

A classificatory MB was bound to provide *sir* if he had already been given a share of his classificatory sister's parental property, for instance, for lighting the funeral pyre of his "sister's" father. If this was not the case, he could not be expected to provide any gifts unless he was indemnified in some other way. For this reason, he was usually promised half the property that the only daughter was to inherit. In some cases, he was made the heir to her parental home.

This had happened in the Pallar street when Kannamma's husband died. Kannamma was elderly, with an only daughter. Her HyB's son had lit the pyre and had been duly promised half of Kannamma's property when she died, the other half going to her daughter. But the "half" promised to the young man was, in fact, far more than half, it was Kannamma's home. Some of her neighbors thought that she should leave the house to her daughter, but Kannamma refused. Her rationale was that in this way, her daughter (who was of marriageable age) would be provided with a "brother's home" (that is, the parental home normally inherited by the brother) to go to in case of marital difficulties. By accepting this arrangement, Kannamma's HyB's son (who was her daughter's classificatory brother) accepted both the obligation to provide *maman-sir* for the daughter's eventual children and the obligation to provide her with shelter in the event of a marital breakup.

Dumont notes that a MB must give presents to his sister's children and that these "are provided or compensated for by the fact that the sister had no formal share in the heritage, her share consisting precisely in such presents" (1983: 90). So the property a woman alienates to her classificatory brother (in order to persuade him to play the role of MB) is that property that her putative brothers would have inherited. Thus, the notion of a property share is central to the MB's obligation to give gifts to his sister's children.

However, though the prestations of their brothers are regarded as women's traditional share in parental property, these prestations add up to *far less* than the value of the inheritance received by the brothers (on this point, Sharma [1984] is quite right). This is because inherited immovable property has traditionally been seen as a male right. Most women in Aruloor accepted this, stating that they did not expect or even want an equal share in property with their brothers. What they wanted was *some* share: the small part that was theirs through *sir.* They added that they were anxious not to alienate their brothers because, above all, they wanted MB's goodwill and solicitous concern for their children in the future.

Despite the willingness of most women to allow their brothers to receive the traditional inheritance without sharing it with them, a few women openly expressed doubts about these brothers. They were very few, but their dissenting voices said that MBs were not to be trusted. One of them was Siva (Sivagami, known as Siva to her friends), my Pallar friend and research assistant who lived in Periyar Street. She was young, had completed high school, and was city-born and city-bred. She had come to Aruloor from Tiruchi at her marriage. As she said:

"Women usually try to have the ear-piercing of their children while their parents are alive because they don't trust their brothers. After marriage their brothers will listen to their wives, who may dissuade them from giving *sir.*" She spoke from bitter experience: Her only brother, who was older than she was, had never given her any *sir.* This was because he had had a serious quarrel with his parents when he married a Christian Pallar woman in Tiruchi. So in March 1988, when Siva was planning a grand ear-piercing celebration for her young son, she and Velayudham, her husband, were sure that her brother would refuse to participate and thus deeply embarrass them. In the event, a fine ear-piercing was held in May 1988. To the many guests, it looked perfectly normal, for Siva's smiling brother held her little boy as his ears were pierced and presented him with *maman-sir.* But Siva's close friends knew that this was a sham—her brother, though comparatively well off, had refused to spend a paise on the event. All the gifts and jewelry had been purchased by Siva's parents, and only by abjectly pleading with him had Siva and her husband persuaded her brother to come at all.

In all the four Non-Brahmin Tamil castes, a married woman was welcome to return to her natal home after marriage, and in the three poorer castes, she was expected to assist her natal kin with agricultural labor during her stay. In the poorest castes (Pallars and Christian Paraiyars), young couples lived separately in nuclear families after marriage, but young married women always went back to their natal homes to work on the family farms when labor demand peaked (primarily at harvesting time but also occasionally for transplanting). When a married woman of a laboring caste returned home, she was an economic asset to her natal family, immediately adding to the household income through her work. This was not the case with the Brahmins, for women in this caste were not free to return to their parental homes whenever they wished after marriage. Thus, the Non-Brahmin family's readiness to welcome a married daughter was closely connected to the fact that she, in her turn, provided them with free agricultural labor. This is consistent with the reciprocal ethos of Non-Brahmin Tamil kinship. So a central reason why lower-caste women continue to enjoy the strong support of their natal kin even today is because they render valuable economic assistance to their kin, through their agricultural work. Significantly, such support from natal kin has dwindled greatly for women in upwardly mobile groups, who are withdrawn from agricultural labor.

MB's *sir* emphasize the *continuity* of kinship links between a Non-Brahmin Tamil woman and her natal kin. These links do not weaken within a year or so of marriage as they do between a Brahmin woman and her parents. On the contrary, every prestation from the married woman's brothers reaffirms these links, exactly as every cross-kin marriage reaffirms existing kinship bonds. Non-Brahmin Tamil kinship seeks to reproduce existing kin links rather than establish new links with strangers. In this orientation, it is radically different from hypergamous North Indian kinship, which normally does not repeat alliances (Tambiah 1973a: 93, 1973b: 222; for exceptions to this pattern, see Parry 1979).

Affinal Kin and Patrilineal Kin

I will now turn to the second category of Non-Brahmin Tamil kinship, namely, the *pankali* (patrilineage or unmarriageable kin). In discussing the relative importance of *maman-maccinan* (marriageable kin) and *annan-tampi murai* (unmarriageable kin), a Chettiar man explained the difference with deceptive simplicity. The former were more important than the latter, he declared, "because we can marry with them!" This simple answer, however, carries important implications, for affines are important not only because they are married but also because they, rather than agnates, are perceived as providing the strongest moral and material support to their male affines. To quote Annamalai Chettiar in full: "*Maman* is so important becuase you can *marry* with his house—you can give and take spouses from his house. But you can't marry with your father's brothers' houses—therefore they aren't so important to you. *Maman* helps more and gives more to the family than *Cittappa* or *Periyappa*. This is what he *has* to do—it is his *kadamai* [duty]."

The significant fact that marriageable kin are constantly described as more important than patrilineal kin in Non-Brahmin Tamil kinship makes Aruloor a striking example of a society in which very little importance is given to descent lines. So when Dumont (1983) argues against the importance of descent lines (as propounded by Meyer Fortes and other Africanists) by insisting that Dravidian kinship illustrates a remarkable balance between patrilineal and affinal kin, he does not go far enough because, as far as Aruloor is concerned, Non-Brahmin Tamil kinship *tilts* the balance, giving preeminence to affines. However, this diminishment of the patrilineage is not carried as far as it is in Sri Lanka, where Nur Yalman has reported (1962, 1967) no descent groups exist at all. They do exist, though in attenuated form, in Aruloor, where inheritance, caste identity, and family-deity affiliation are transmitted in the male descent line (*pankali*). Thus, patrilineal descent is of considerable importance in certain contexts, but these contexts are not the ones that lower-caste Non-Brahmin Tamils emphasize in everyday life.

In his role as the wife's brother (*maccinan*), MB is seen as far more likely to aid his sister's husband than that husband's own brothers are. I was repeatedly told that a man turns for assistance not to his own brothers (his *pankali*) but to his WBs (his *maccinan*). In the accounts provided by informants, a certain pattern emerged: All were tales told *against* the *pankali*, who were characterized as greedy and unscrupulous; the matrilateral affinal kin, however, were elevated (in one account, to divine status, as I will discuss). I will provide three accounts, one of them mythical, of grasping *pankali*.

The first account came from Malarkodi (a Muthurajah): "Everyone says that the mother's-side relatives are *more* important. This must be because the *maman* gives *sir* and helps the family. The *cittappa-periyappa* are *supposed* to be 'substitute fathers' and to help the family, but in fact they never are: They're only out to grab as much wealth as they can from us. On the fifteenth day after my father's death, my *periyappa*, Ratnam—with whom my father had had *no* quarrel—suddenly came to our house in the night and told us we must get out of the house and leave the village [Aruloor]—that we had no business to stay on here." In the ensuing quarrel with her husband's *pankali* kin regarding her husband's house, Malarkodi's mother (a very strong-willed woman) was able to resist being thrown out of her own house with her children. The *pankali* kin remained obdurate, telling her to go back to Thannirpalli, her native village. From that time on, this woman (and her children) had no relations with her husband's *pankali*—even though these kin lived virtually next door.

The second account also came from the Muthurajah street and similarly concerned a widowed woman with children. Kannagi, whose children were quite young, was continually harassed by Ramasami (Tilakambal's spouse), who was her husband's eldest brother, and his two younger brothers. They wanted her to get out of her part of the house and go back to Kumbakonam (her "mother's place") because, they claimed, the official division of the house had not yet occurred. A very pleasant, forbearing woman, Kannagi had somehow managed to stay on in her house and to hang on to her share of land. She herself supervised agricultural labor on this land, eking out an income from farming.

Both these accounts focus on the death of a man and the vulnerability of his widowed wife and children, who are in danger of being cheated out of their patrimony by devious *pankali*. This is likely to have been a familiar tale of everyday life in Aruloor because in the third account, these elements come together in a mythic tale. It was told by Palani Chettiar, the wise and knowledgeable religious leader of the Chettiars. His story also vividly illustrated the importance of the MB, for in this tale, Sivan (Siva: God) takes the shape of a *maman* to settle a family quarrel:

> In a certain family, after the death of a man, his son didn't inherit his father's wealth because the boy's *cittappa-periyappa* grabbed it. So the boy's mother prayed to God, and Somasundaram [Siva] took the form of a *maman* [in that family]. He called each of these *pankali* relatives by their names, so they thought he really was that *maman*. And he said sternly to them: "Bring that boy's wealth here at once and present it to him with due respect—or else...!" And all of them obeyed. That's why the *maman* is so important. It is he alone who is important for all events. *Cittappa-periyappa* are not as important.

This story illustrates the moral authority of MB. He is represented as the arbiter of justice who protects the rights of his sister's children from their ever-grasping *pankali*. Indeed, in this account, *Maman's* importance could not be greater, for he is, through his moral qualities and his incarnation as protector of the oppressed, actually Siva himself. This potential "apotheosis" of MB is, in fact, regularly reenacted in the life-cycle rites in which he participates, where he is honored in what approaches a divine manner, especially among the Pallars.

Brahmins in Aruloor always invited their closest *pankali* kin to all their domestic celebrations and ceremonies. Significantly, Non-Brahmin Tamils do not; it is only affinal kin who are expected to be present and to give gifts, not patrilineal kin. This was put very clearly by a Muthurajah informant: "*Maman-maccinan* kin come for all our *nalladu-kettadu* [auspicious and inauspicious occasions] and we go for theirs. They must be present—if they don't come it's an insult. But *annan-tampi* don't have to come and usually aren't invited." Thus Non-Brahmin kinship has much to do with giving, and because Non-Brahmin *pankali* kin do not give, they are not invited. This confirms what Dumont means when he states that giving is central to affinal alliance (1983).

The Concept of the Blood-Bond

I will now explore the theory of blood-bond and its implications. I have already discussed why MB and the matrilateral affinal kin occupy a prominent position in Non-Brahmin Tamil kinship in Aruloor. This prominence is related to the importance of matrilateral kin as affines, but in Aruloor, this structural position is also legitimized by a fascinating cultural construct, the concept of the blood-bond (*iratta-sambandam*). This concept was central to the way in which many informants perceived relatedness. It was beguilingly simple and logical, and it was raised repeatedly when they discussed kinship. Their exegeses can be paraphrased as follows: "You grow for ten months in your mother's womb—it's her blood that nurtures you. So you *have more of your mother's blood than your father's blood in you*" (emphasis added). This had an unexpected corollary—unexpected in my view but self-evident in theirs—namely, that a man (or woman) was consequently "more related" to his MB than to his FB. This was readily explained: "This is because *Maman* shares Mother's blood—and a child has more blood from his mother's side in him than from his father's side: That's why the boy is more closely related to *Maman* than to *Cittappa* [FyB]. The *iratta-sambandam* [blood-bond] is stronger with *Maman*." These views are strikingly different from the views about blood relationship reported by Barnett (1976) for the Kontaikkatti Vellalars in Tamilnadu and by Kenneth David (1973) for Jaffna Tamils, as I will point out later. They are, however, remarkably similar to the views of many matrilineal Batticaloa Tamils, who told McGilvray that "the child's blood was definitely that of the mother" (1982a: 53).

I should add that when confronted with the claim that MB was more closely related to a child than FyB, I naturally enquired as to the status of Father: "Is *Maman* [MB] more closely related to a child than the child's father?" This question was treated with derision: "Of course not. Of course the child has more blood in common with his father than with his mother's brother. After all, he is his father's child too. But he has mainly his mother's blood. That's why he is less closely related to his *cittappa* [FyB] than to his *maman*."

One way to understand this extraordinary claim is to suggest that, of course, it was meant as a metaphor. But it was clear that some informants thought of MB's unique blood-bond with his sister's children as being a real, physical connection.

How did they reconcile this with their explicit (and repeated) statement that *pankali* kin were closer to them "in blood" than affines, including MB? By analyzing the following conversation about MB, *pankali*, and blood-bond, we may find clues to how some people understood these relationships.

The speakers were Devayanai Chettiar's younger brother, Annamalai (about fifty years old), and her younger sister, Janaki (in her mid-forties). Annamalai said: "*Maman* helps more and gives more to the family than do *Cittappa* or *Periyappa*. When the property is divided between brothers, in the formal document of division this phrase recurs: 'Having divided the wealth between us there is no other connection [*sambandam*] left between us other than the *iratta-sambandam* [blood-bond].' This is explicitly stated. But *Maman's* connection with us never ends."

His sister Janaki took over: "You *can* say that *Maman* has greater *iratta-sambandam* [with his sister's children] than *Cittappa-Periyappa*—firstly because *Maman* is connected with Mother who has greater *iratta-sambandam* with the child than does Father. Further, *Maman* has the *kalyana urami* [marriage right] with the children. Next, *Maman* has *pasam* [affection] for the child—which *Cittappa-Periyappa* don't necessarily have. And *Maman* has the *kadamai* [duty] to act on behalf of and to give to the children. For all these reasons his connection with them is much greater."

Thus, we are given a variety of reasons why MB is closer to his sister's child. Firstly, as Annamalai pointed out, although MB is constantly at hand to help, FBs take their share of the inheritance and then, despite their blood-connection, call it quits. One can expect little assistance or sympathy from them—there are "always" long-lasting quarrels between brothers after the division of the inheritance. But in contrast to the *pankali*, MB (in Janaki's argument) remains tied to his sister's children through his blood-connection (via their mother), through his genuine affection for them, through his duty and obligation to provide for them—and through his self-interest, embodied in his and his son's marriage rights. In this discourse, *Maman* is cast as the very opposite of the *pankali*: They represent grasping self-interest and a constant threat to the interests of their brother's children, but *Maman* emerges as the protector of these interests, just as he does in the mythic tale cited by Palani Chettiar. In a culture where "blood" is probably *the* dominant metaphor of "connectedness," it is, then, no surprise at all that MB is categorically stated to be "closer *in blood*" to a child than its FBs are. The cultural logic is flawless. Discussions of "difference in blood" and marriage partners belong to a quite separate sphere of logic.

Further, the sociological context of the argument is crucial to its logic; finally, it is context that validates the argument. To the Chettiars, it was entirely self-evident that MB had an extraordinarily close relationship with his sister's children—far closer than that of any FB—for the simple reason that MB lived in the same house with his sister's children, at least during the day. This family situation arose because among the Vellan Chettiars, married daughters spent more time daily in their natal home than they did in their marital home. Devayanai Chettiar explained why.

I had noticed that her two daughters' young children were very attached to her; they spent much more time at home with her than they did in their father's house. When I asked about this, she replied: "This is quite usual, actually—children are more with their mother's mothers, so they grow more attached to them." This was particularly true with the Vellan Chettiars, among whom a bride customarily continued to bathe daily at her mother's house for at least a year after marriage. In many cases, even after several years of marriage, young Chettiar wives continued to bathe at the mothers' homes and to spend most of the day there. They did the cooking at the marital home and ate with the marital family (and in-laws) and returned there to sleep at night, but apart from this, they—and their children—spent the entire day with their mothers.

In Aruloor, this custom was unique to the Chettiars, who explained it as the result of their extraordinarily localized marriage: Most girls were married to men living in the next street. As Devayani said, "This practice probably started because we all live in one place—Aruloor. Just a few of us live in Lalgudi."

But even in the other Non-Brahmin Tamil castes, the same sentiment was voiced. Malarkodi of the Muthurajah street commented: "Yes, children are generally more attached to their mothers' mothers." The fact that cross-kin marriage is very often local marriage is probably the main reason for the great closeness between a woman's parents, her brothers, and her children. In all four Non-Brahmin Tamil castes, there were many married women living only a few doors away from their mothers.

So the fact that *"amma vittu"* ("mother's house") has traditionally been very close by has had an important role in cementing the affection of MB for his sister's children. Significantly, only the Brahmins used the term "Father's house" when they spoke of a woman's parental home. *All* the Non-Brahmin Tamil castes used only one term to refer to this parental home—*"amma vittu."*

Mother's Brother, Astrology, and Divination at Childbirth

Dramatic evidence of the very special connection that exists between *Maman* and his sister's children is found in the astrological beliefs and practices of all four Non-Brahmin Tamil castes. *Maman's* central importance in these rites strongly contrasts with the marginality or absence of *"Cittappa-Periyappa"* ("Fyb-FeB) in these astrological discourses.

Most remarkable of all is the manner in which the horoscope of a child, either female or male, "says more about the house of *maman*" than it does about the fortunes of FyBs or FeBs. Marked differences existed between the castes: In the Chettiar caste, Devayanai Chettiar said, "The eldest son's horoscope speaks about this house and about his *maman's* house. It says *nothing* about the houses of his *cittappa-periyappa*." But later, her younger brother, Annamalai, amended this: "Yes, my *jadakam* [horoscope], as eldest son, 'speaks' a lot about my *maman's* house—but very little about my *cittappa-periyappa*. It does mention them though." Janaki, Devayanai Chettiar's younger sister, added: "More is said [in the horoscope] about *Maman* because he is the *Tay-Maman*, born with Mother—and so, very important."

Maman is central to another Non-Brahmin Tamil divinatory practice. When a child is born, the position of the umbilical cord augurs good or ill, especially for MB. As the Chettiars said: "If the child's umbilical cord is twisted round its neck this is 'bad' [dangerous, inauspicious] for *maman*. Such a birth is described as one in which the baby is "born circled by a garland" (*malai-sutti pirandal*). It is important to note that both at the puberty rite and at marriage, a ZD is garlanded (and thus "circled by a garland") by MB (just prior to her being wedded to the groom). This suggests that the divinatory practice has some connection with the fact that MB can marry his eZD. A male infant "garlanded" in this way also presages bad luck for his *maman*. Further, the Chettiars said, "If the cord is twisted around the waist of the newborn [like a belt] then this is 'bad' for the *cittappa-periyappa*." So the Chettiar practice does mention FBs, as well. The Muthurajah caste shared the belief that a "garlanded" newborn signaled bad luck for MB, but it had no such beliefs concerning FBs; they did not figure in birth-divination. To understand why, we must remember that the Chettiars were wealthier than any other Aruloor caste and also prided themselves on being more Brahminical in behavior. For these reasons, they took a greater interest in the patrilineage, even though they were strongly focused on the matrilateral affines. This greater interest in agnates is mirrored in their divinatory practices, which consequently do not exclude the FBs as those of the Muthurajahs do.

To dissolve the inauspiciousness of a "garlanded" birth so that MB's future is safe, Chettiars perform an additional rite at the *punniya danam* (purification) of the baby and its mother, which takes place soon after birth. The MB is not allowed to see the baby until then. At this purification rite, auspicious gingelli oil (*nallenney*) is poured into a broad-mouthed vessel or a tray. This is held in front of MB, who is seated. Bending down, MB should "see his face" (*"mokatte pakkanum"*) reflected in the oil. Then, the baby is brought and held above the head of MB (who is still looking down at his reflection) so that the baby's face, too, is reflected in the oil. In this way, the baby's face is first beheld by its MB in the auspicious oil. After this, the danger to MB is believed to have passed away. Exactly the same rite was performed by Chettiars to remove inauspiciousness for FBs. The rite was called "removing the [astrological] flaw" (*"dosham kalikkiradu"*) or "to do a pacification/purification rite" (*"parikaram seyyanum"*).

Malarkodi (my Muthurajah friend) described such a Muthurajah purification rite. She said: "You can see the reflections very clearly. My *periyappa's* daughter Banumathi had such a baby [Santhi]. At the *punniya danam* her face was shown to her *tay maman*, Arokiaraj. Arokiaraj was only three years old—it had been thought that he would marry his eZD [Santhi] but this idea was dropped when the cord was found around her neck. This is very 'bad' [inauspicious: *kettadu*]."

Palani Chettiar, on the other hand, said that among Chettiars, such a "garlanded" baby girl *could* marry her *maman*, after "seeing his face in oil." The fact that the Muthurajahs absolutely forbade this makes the Chettiar custom appear almost foolhardy. However, in allowing such a marriage despite the bad auguries, the Vellan Chettiars were bowing to necessity. They were a very small, endogamous community, with a notably high rate of actual MB-marriage. In such a context, with few alternative marriage partners available to them, it was unlikely that they would wish to further decrease their already limited pool of marriageable men.

The Blood-Bond and Non-Brahmin "Matrilateralism"

The central significance of the blood-bond concept is that it emphatically reiterates the secondary importance of patrilineal kin in Non-Brahmin Tamil kinship in Aruloor and shows that they are actually felt to be "less related" by "blood" to Ego (male or female) than certain matrilateral kin. Thus, rather surprisingly, though inheritance is solely in the male line and residence at marriage is virilocal (with the husband's kin), the kin relationship itself is seen as stronger in relation to the matrilateral kin. This discursive prominence in Non-Brahmin Tamil kinship of the *matrilateral* affinal kin suggests that we should view Non-Brahmin Tamil kinship as having a balanced bilaterality. This must not be confused with marriage preference: The Non-Brahmin Tamil castes in Aruloor (as noted) claim a unilateral marriage preference, preferring the matrilateral MB and MBS to the patrilateral FZs (but see Chapter 3 for the disjunction between stated preference and actual practice).

By "balance bilaterality," I mean the relative balance between the patrilineal kin and the matrilateral affinal kin in Aruloor. On the one hand, it is the matrilateral affinal kin (embodied in MB) who share control of the girl's fertility and labor with the girl's parents. On the other hand, it is the patrilineal kin who control all inheritable wealth and largely transmit caste identity. The bilateral elements in Non-Brahmin kinship in Aruloor are thus far more significant than the Dumontean model suggests (Dumont 1953, 1957, 1983). As I mentioned, these bilateral elements clearly make the kinship system of Aruloor similar in important respects to the Sinhalese and Sri Lankan Tamil systems (Yalman 1962, 1967; McGilvray 1982a, 1982b). However, the Sinhalese system's rule of prescriptive, bilateral, "cross-cousin" marriage makes its emphasis different from that of Aruloor's Non-Brahmin Tamils. This is because, according to Yalman's accounts, the Sinhalese emphasize the bilateral marriageability of "cross-cousins," but with Non-Brahmin Tamils, the normative stress—though little manifested in marriage practice—is on *either* marriage with MB and MBS (and, correspondingly, FZD) *or* marriage with FZS (and MBD). In other words, Yalman's Sinhalese are equally happy to marry with either matrilateral or patrilateral kin—but Aruloor's Non-Brahmins *claim* a marriage preference for one or the other, usually preferring their matrilateral kin.

The four Non-Brahmin castes thus prefer what they explicitly define as a "matrilateral" marriage preference (MyB/eZD or MBS/FZD); the Telugu Brahmins prefer what they view as a *"patrilateral"* marriage preference (FZS/MBD). The Telugu Brahmin preference is directly related by Brahmin informants to the cultural importance of the Brahmin patrilineage, though this is, in practice, a rather diluted descent system, as the occasional MB-marriage (rare though it is) testifies.

My informants explained why parallel-cousin marriage was "wrong" by recourse to the blood-bond theory. They stated that the children of Ego's MZ were prohibited as marriage partners "because your mother's sister is like your own mother." This was due to the fact that M and MZ were same-sex siblings who "had grown in the same womb"; consequently, their blood was virtually identical. Given that children inherit more of their mother's blood than their father's, the children of MZ had "too much" blood in common with Ego. Similarly, F and FB had grown in the same womb, and so FB's children were also prohibited as marriage partners for Ego. However, given that the blood-bond theory postulated a closer blood relationship between Ego (female or male) and MB than between Ego and FyB (or FeB), it should have logically followed that the children of FBs were *less* prohibited than the children of MZs. Some informants agreed that this should have been the case, but in practice, people never distinguished between the prohibitions on the two categories of parallel-kin. Instead, they saw the progeny of both MZ and FB as equally prohibited.

In discussing cross-kin marriage, my informants constantly stressed that the ideal marriage was one with the "closest" possible kin. This was why MB and cross-cousins were the ideal spouses. Yalman (1967) was the first to note this important point (for cross-cousins). Barnett, however, stated that his informants felt that "by marrying a cross-cousin you are marrying someone with whom you share the *least*" (1976: 148, his emphasis). My informants took the opposite view: They explained that Ego could not marry her own brothers because they had exactly the same blood, nor could she marry her male parallel-cousins because they were "like brothers" to her. But she could marry her male cross-cousins (MBS and FZS) because "though they were close to her in blood, yet they were of different blood."

As Sampoornam, a Chettiar friend, put it as she tried to explain things to me: "Your *maman-maccinan* are not so closely related to you as your *pankali*. That's why you can marry them—that's why they are your *kalyana murai* [marriageable kin]. Your father's side, the *pankali*, have blood that is, say, two-thirds identical with yours. But your *maman's* side have blood that is one-third related to you." I asked: "Does this mean that *all* your *sondarkarar* (relatives)—both *pankali* and affines—are related to you by blood to greater or lesser degree?" Sampoornam replied: "Yes, that is so—*all* your *sondam* are related to you by blood—your affines [*muraikkarargal*] a little—and your *pankali* a lot." I recalled that Palani Chettiar had said the same about the blood-bond: "One has *iratta-sambandam* with *both* one's mother's-side-relatives *and* one's father's-side-relatives—so you are related to *all* your relatives by blood-bond."

In this context, marrying MB was therefore even better than marrying a cross-cousin precisely because MB was even closer in blood to Ego than a cross-cousin and yet just sufficiently "different" in blood (through being cross-sex to Mother) to be marriageable. Informants explained that MB both did and did not have the "same blood" as Mother. He had the same blood because he came from the same womb, but he was significantly different from Mother in being male. His gender was crucial. It transformed his blood. Further, Ego did not have the same blood as her mother because Ego also carried her father's blood. Her father's blood differentiated Ego's blood sufficiently from MB's to allow her to marry him.

The Exchange of Blood

To conclude my examination of the blood-bond before moving on to consider its interesting implications, I will discuss another important blood-related theory. This is the notion, prevalent in all four Non-Brahmin Tamil castes, that married couples "*exchange* blood" in sexual intercourse. As Anjalai, a Muthurajah woman, put it: "When a husband and wife have sex, they exchange blood. Some blood from the husband enters the wife, in the form of his semen [*intiriyam*]; similarly, some of her blood in the form of [female] semen [also named *intiriyam*] enters him. So blood from each enters the other. From that time [their first sexual intercourse] on, each carries some blood of the other too." It is significant that both male and female sexual fluids have exactly the same name. This concept of sexual congress indicates an extraordinary equality between husband and wife because "blood from each enters the other." Sampoornam's explanation, from the Chettiar perspective, was very similar: "In sexual intercourse, the 'sperm-fluid' that is transferred from the man to the woman contains his blood as well. This blood joins the woman's blood to become the new blood of the baby that is formed when the woman conceives. So it's correct that through intercourse a little of the blood of each of them flows into the other. When people say this happens through 'marriage,' they actually mean through sexual intercourse. A blood-relationship [*iratta-sambandam*] is established between husband and wife. So, Palani Chettiar was right to say that after 'marriage' the husband was related by blood to his wife's brother—and to the rest of her family. Not very much, but certainly a little. That's why we say that *every one* of your relatives is related to you by blood—your *maman-maccinan* a little and your *pankali* a lot."

Thus, a prominent theme in these discourses of kinship is that "blood flows" during sexual intercourse, both from the man to the woman and from the woman to the man. This intimate exchange of blood is represented as entirely reciprocal and symmetrical, as are most exchanges in Non-Brahmin Tamil kinship. The representation of the sexual fluids of females and males as being "exchanged" during intercourse, so that female sexual fluid *enters the male* indicates that we are dealing here with a sexual universe that is very different from the patriarchal sexual universe described by H.N.C. Stevenson (1954).

Stevenson's views have gained wide currency: Yalman, among others, has considered him to be right (1963: 41). Seeking an explanation for "the fact that trans-status sexual congress affects males and females in different ways" (1954: 57), Stevenson unwisely rejects the possibility that this was primarily because eventual descendants would "become outcasts." Instead, he concludes: "A more consistent explanation is that, since in sexual intercourse it is the man who emits the polluting secretion and the woman who receives it internally, the man is exposed only to external pollution, which can be removed by a bath, whereas the woman is internally polluted to a greater degree than if she had eaten emission-polluted food such as domestic pork" (Stevenson 1954: 57). Whatever relevance Stevenson's distinction between "external pollution" and "internal pollution" may or may not have to North India, it clearly has little to do with these Non-Brahmin Tamil notions, which emphasize that both women and men "emit" sexual secretions and both men and women "receive" them internally.

Strong evidence that Aruloor's Non-Brahmins are not idiosyncratic in holding these egalitarian notions regarding sexual congress is afforded by the extremely detailed data on Non-Brahmin Tamil ideas provided by Valentine Daniel (1984: 163–181), which confirm and elaborate upon what I was told in Aruloor. Daniel states:

1. Excess intiriam is secreted from the systems of both partners into the yoni (vagina) of the female.
2. A physiologically healthy and controlled mixing of the two secretions takes place inside the yoni.
3. A portion of *this mixture,* which is *a new substance, is reabsorbed into the blood-stream of both partners,* and the blood thereby becomes enriched (1984: 165, emphases added).

This concept, Daniel points out, is elaborated in a number of contexts. Thus, if a "male has intercourse with a female much younger than himself, he will be unable to contain ... the female's intiriam. The result is that the female's intiriam contaminates his system" (Daniel 1983: 168). But even when "a young boy copulates with an older woman ... he cannot afford to lose all this (intiriam) without regaining something from his partner" (Daniel 1984: 169). Daniel also notes, "The consequence of intercourse during an impure period (such as menstruation) is *disease for the male*. ... It is contracted during intercourse *and transmitted to the bloodstream by the penis*" (Daniel 1984: 170, emphases added). This, I should point out, is remarkably different from the Tamil Brahmin notion of what happens if a couple have sex while the woman is menstruating. Tamil Brahmins know of no danger to the male; instead, they state that it is the female who will fall grievously sick with *"janni"* (fever with fits), and usually, she will die. This cautionary belief (strongly held by Tamil Brahmin women) suggests that Stevenson's theories are probably Brahmin-influenced, given that in Aruloor, only the Brahmins appear to have no theory of a reciprocal exchange of sexual fluids during intercourse. The emphatic stress on reciprocity in this sexual discourse is noted by Daniel as well, for he concludes: "To sum up, when a male and female are brought together in marriage ... the two are meant to give and receive from each other many bodily substances, chief among which are sexual fluids" (1984: 179). We are, indeed, a world away from the asymmetrical and unreciprocated sexual "givings" discussed by Stevenson.

McGilvray's account of Batticaloa Tamil discourses of conception indicates very similar ideas at work there. He states that "female semen ... was definitely seen as derived from blood and was assumed to resemble male semen" (McGilvray 1982b: 52). As he rightly notes, the important implication of this view of sexual intercourse "is that conception is seen by most people [as] fundamentally bilateral, involving substances from both parents" (McGilvray 1982b: 53).

This view, widely held by Aruloor's Non-Brahmins, is the diametrical opposite of the orthodox Brahmin view of pregnancy. Orthodox Brahmins in Aruloor believe that childbirth is due to *male conception* and *male pregnancy*. This remarkable view was shared by both Telugu Brahmins and Tamil Brahmins. It was put concisely by Gita, a close Brahmin friend of mine. She said: "A child is 'in the making' for twelve months—that is, a full year—because it first lives in the father for two months and thereafter in the mother for ten months. We believe that when a relative dies, the soul seeks to re-enter the world— and to re-enter the family that it left behind. So it's believed that if a woman conceives two months or so after a close relative has died, then that child, even if it is of another sex, is the dead person reborn. It comes to the father and then after living for two months in him the *jiva* [life] passes in the man's semen to the woman where it grows for ten months. So the *jiva* starts its life in the man and is transferred to the woman."

Another close Brahmin friend, Maitreyi, confirmed Gita's account. Her explanation indicates how profoundly influenced by Brahminical religious ideas the orthodox Brahmin view of conception is. Maitreyi said: "After death the spirit of a

dead person doesn't die. Depending on the meritorious deeds done by that person—that is, on the *karmam* he has gathered in this human life—he will be reborn
either as a human being—or as an animal or insect or plant. But this doesn't happen immediately. For the first eleven days after death the spirit of the person hov-
ers around. Finally, on the twelfth day the spirit enters a new body—human or
non-human. So it's on this twelfth day that we believe that the spirit enters the
sexual organ [the penis] of a man—and there it stays for two months. Then it is
transferred, in the semen of the man, to the woman and grows for ten months in
the woman's womb. Then it's born as a child, at the end." Maitreyi urbanely concluded, "This is what is *believed*—of course we don't know if it's true!"

Non-Brahmin friends were incredulous when they heard about these beliefs
from me—and then derisory. They joked that only Brahmins could have dreamed
up such an incredible theory of procreation: How absurd the idea of male pregnancy was! However, the rationale of this Brahmin discourse is, of course, not il-
logical when seen in terms of Brahmin priorities. It embodies the continuing
Brahmin preoccupation with "male" control of "female" power, here manifested
in the symbolic appropriation of conception and pregnancy. But these pregnancy
beliefs of orthodox Brahmins found no converts among the Non-Brahmins.

Implications of the Blood-Bond

I will now address some implications of the blood-bond concept. I noted earlier
that Non-Brahmin Tamil kinship in Aruloor shows a strong imperative toward
symmetry between affines: It balances patrilineal values with the importance of
matrilateral affines. Consequently, we can expect that among those Tamil groups
where such an equilibrium is not maintained but where the patrilineage is preeminent, ethnologists will find discourses that buttress this patrilineal dominance.
This is, indeed, the case with the distinctly Brahminicized Non-Brahmin Tamil
castes discussed by Barnett (1976) and David (1973).

Good records the "trans-sanguination" of women at marriage, noted by
Barnett and David, and adds that "trans-substantiation" (as in David's data, he
implies), if it does take place, presumably happens during the marriage rite (1978:
338). Good's informant "explained that wives were of the same blood as their
husbands, *and that this change took place during the wedding*" (1978: 435, emphasis added; also see Good 1991: 180). All this carries precisely the opposite cultural message from the *"iratta-sambandam"* (blood-bond) of Aruloor, for it
states that a woman's blood is transformed through marriage into blood that is
identical with the blood of her husband and his agnates. "Blood-bond," on the
contrary, announces that a woman's children have *more* of her blood and *less* of
their father's blood, which clearly implies that a woman's blood undergoes no
trans-sanguination and her body no trans-substantiation at marriage. It remains
the blood she was born with, derived from her parents—and it is this untrans-

formed blood that links her children more closely with their MB than their patri-lineal kin. Further, there is an emphatic discursive stress on the unity of kin and the "common blood" of the kin-group. Thus, the notion of a generalized blood-bond is also frequently expressed, as in the statement: "You are related by blood to your entire *sondam*." There is no ideological stress in this discourse on an op-position between the blood of the wife's kin and that of the husband's kin, as there is in Barnett's and David's data.

In this context, then, the distinction is not between "affines" and "consan-guines" but between those with whom one is either *"more"* or *"less"* related. My informants summed up the relationship between eligibility for marriage and the blood-bond in this way: "You're related by blood much more to some people and much less to others. You marry those to whom you are less related, with whom you share less blood. Obviously you can't marry your *annan-tampi* (eB-yB) be-cause you have the same blood, but you can marry your *maman-maccinan* (MB-WB) with whom you share less blood." The apparent contradiction in this logic is resolved when it is remembered that the ideal affine—the Mother's Brother—is the affine who is closest in blood of all affines to the bride. Dumont recognizes this as well in his southern Tamilnadu castes (even though they did not practice MyB/eZD marriage) when he notes that "'marrying a cross-cousin' is nothing but marrying an affine, i.e. the person who is *the closest affine* by virtue of the transmission of affinity ties from one generation to the next" (1983: 72, emphasis added).

Therefore, with Aruloor's Non-Brahmin Tamils, the unity of *sondam* is often so strongly emphasized that the categories of marriageable and unmarriageable kin are seen as different in degree rather than different in kind. The perspective chosen by informants depended on context or on the level considered. At one level, they spoke as if there were a structural opposition between the two catego-ries: This was when they described gift-giving and marriage. But on another level, they claimed to find only a difference of degree: This was the theoretical level at which they discussed the concept of *sondam*. However, at both levels, the idea of an opposition between the two categories remained, even if attenuated and un-stressed.

What Kinship Connotes

I will now consider more fully what the concept of *sondam* means to people in Aruloor. It has subtly varying meanings depending on context, ranging from "na-tal kin," "affinal kin," "kin," and "kinship" to "the entire kindred" ("relatives in general," as Good puts it [1991: 270]) and "marriage." The discourses of *sondam* are the key to Tamil kinship in Aruloor. "Sondam" most commonly de-notes all kin, both marriageable (*maman-maccinan*) and unmarriageable (*pankali*).

In informants' discussions, *"sondam"* suggested connectedness. The term had an extremely positive connotation in Tamil, which was significant for its ideological value. *"Sondakarar"* were all "relatives," both marriageable and unmarriageable. Only in certain contexts was stress laid on the division of *sondam* into two categories; instead, the crucial distinction in Tamil kinship in Aruloor was that between those who were kin (*sondakarar*) and those who were not kin (*sondakarar illai*).

Because the meaning of *"sondam"* subtly shifted with context, the word was often used in a restricted sense to mean "matrilateral affinal kin," especially when people spoke of the "joys" of "having *sondam.*" This was the case when married women who had "ungenerous" brothers were described as having "no *sondam*" or "inactive *sondam,*" even though they obviously possessed kin. Such use of the term made it quite clear that *"sondam"* had a strong economic content: It connoted power and wealth, particularly the honor, power, and wealth that women (and their husbands) derived through the stream of prestations flowing from their brothers to their children. Women who lacked the support and protection that were symbolized by the traditional prestations given by their brothers were considered pitiable because their affinal kin were likely to treat them disparagingly. This was particularly true of semisecluded, upper-caste women, who were financially dependent on their husbands and who relied on the continuing affection, moral support, and regular prestations of their brothers to maintain their standing. Such vulnerability did not characterize the self-reliant, wage-earning, lower-caste women, who did not seek economic security from their equally poor brothers. But for them, too, their brothers were just as important for a quite different reason, namely, their crucial role in lower-caste life-cycle rites.

In short, the profound emotive depth that the word *"sondam"* had for Non-Brahmin Tamils was closely connected with economics. When it was said that those who had *sondam* had little to fear in life, the meaning was clear. It was your kin—especially your affinal kin—who succored you, with material aid, honor, and affection. For this reason, it was said that you were *empowered* by *sondam,* but if you had no *sondam,* you had nothing. The central ideological point about *sondam* was precisely that it was represented in the discourse of all the castes as strongly positive: Family and kin were unquestionably the greatest good in life.

In this discourse, an opposition between affines and patrilineage was constructed so that, although the *pankali* tended to represent dissension and danger to one's interests, the *maman-maccinan* or affines represented emotional support and the protection of one's interests. This was clear in the three accounts presented earlier. However, a crucial elision occurs at this juncture in kinship discourses, for the identity of the individual whose interests are at stake remains opaque. Looking more closely, however, it emerges that the sphere of affinity and marriage that is represented as the sphere of all good, where divine *maman* step in to assist one against grasping *pankali,* is defined from a *male* perspective. It is the interests of *men* that are particularly protected by *maman* against *pankali*. More crucially, marriage and affinity can, indeed, be viewed as wholly positive by men because this is the domain where Tamil women have been trained since childhood to "sacrifice" themselves for the sake of the "family." In household discourse, it is *female* "selflessness" and "self-sacrifice" that are represented as great cultural ideals—these ideals are not viewed as relevant to male identity. In short, very different demands are made of women and of men.

Sheryl Daniel's depiction of this "double standard" does not quite apply to Aruloor's lowest castes, but it fits the upper castes well:

> From a young age, *girls are taught to make personal sacrifices for the good of the family,* first through assuming responsibility for household chores and child care and later, when they attain puberty, through the observance of the codes of modesty necessary to the preservation of family honor. Such restraints are accompanied by a didactic emphasis from kinsmen and others that women *think first of the welfare of their families and then only of their personal desires.* ... Similar training is not given to boys who ... are allowed to "sow their wild oats" and *expect to rely as husbands on the sacrifices of their wives* to preserve family prosperity and reputation. Part of the lenience in the upbringing of males is attributed to a *"double standard"* (1980: 72–73, emphases added).

In the impoverished lower castes, this double standard had rather different implications. In these poor castes, unlike the wealthy upper castes, very different sexual norms prevailed. In the upper castes, divorce and remarriage were prohibited for women, but men could take a second wife, and widowers were actively encouraged to remarry. In the lower castes, things were a bit more equal—separation, divorce, and remarriage were permitted for both women and men. However, things had changed within these castes, too. While other castes talked of how *marriage* had become much more expensive due to the current change from bridewealth to "dowry" marriage, the Pallars, for their part, talked of how much more expensive *divorce* had become. Ramaiyee, a Pallar woman in her fifties, said: "Previously people divorced very easily and quickly—but nowadays it is far more difficult, because today they try to get the couple to live together. They don't let them divorce—they mediate first." This is an important hint that lower-caste women are slowly losing the few privileges they had, a central one being the right to divorce. This became clear when college-educated Velayudham (Siva's husband) gave me a brief history of Pallar divorce.

> It's true that about thirty years ago divorce [*tirttuk-katturadu*] was easier, because life was much simpler. Fifty years ago people both cooked and ate out of mud pots, and used coconut-halves as spoons. And gold was cheap then ... and it wasn't in such demand. If there was a separation, there wasn't any wealth as such for the man to give the woman. But today it's different. Divorce has become much more expensive. If the persons concerned are very poor, it may still be only two or three hundred rupees [that the man gives his divorced wife]. Twenty-five years ago, at Kooloo's di-

vorce from Periavutai, he gave her only a hundred and fifty rupees. But if they're better off, today it's five hundred rupees, a thousand rupees or more!

So, even in Pallar society, the widespread change to "dowry" marriage in the upper castes was having repercussions. Pallar men were now less likely to formally divorce their wives and pay them the compensation demanded by customary law because in the new climate of opinion, a man could sometimes get away with simply moving in with another woman and deserting his wife and children. In short, the fundamental dynamics of gender relations among the Pallars were beginning to approximate those of the upper castes, in which men had more freedom to follow their inclinations and women had far fewer rights in customary law.

Traditionally, the sexuality of young Pallar women was not closely controlled, partly because there was little wealth to inherit. Consequently, premarital pregnancy was not seen as a catastrophe, as it was in the higher castes. This was because every child was viewed as a source of future income. Today, though so-called "modest" and "chaste" behavior is not imposed on young lower-caste women, they are still expected to be far more restrained than men in their sexual activities (as I will point out in Chapter 7).

However, in these poor castes, the crucial domain of male control is not the sexual but the economic, and here, the double standard flourishes vigorously. Although the ideology of "the male provider" prevails in the upper castes, the opposite norm exists in these lower castes. Both wife and husband have to do wagework to survive, but *the final responsibility for providing for the family lies with the woman*. So in these castes, it is socially acceptable for men to spend a large part of their incomes on themselves even though their families are in need. Women, on the contrary, are expected to spend their entire incomes on feeding their children and husbands, and they are socialized to see this inequity as required of them. Further, although many men contribute to the household budget very irregularly, all men expect to be fed by their wives every day. Frequent quarrels arise on this account, but the quarrels are always unequal, for men are allowed to beat their wives but women are not supposed to hit back. Male violence is a regular feature of lower-caste family life.

In these circumstances, it is clear that women's interest are *structurally* secondary to men's. Male prerogative is defined and protected through customary law and exalted in the upper-caste ideology of intrinsic male superiority (and intrinsic female inferiority). Even when this ideology is challenged by lower-caste women, it still survives because it resonates with the gender ideology of the dominant castes. For the sake of men, Tamil women have to be hardworking, self-sacrificing, and (in the upper castes) "chaste." And because this double standard of behavior permeates and influences the actions of both women and men, the discourses that describe "family" as the highest good are actually ideologies that serve the interests of men. It is clear that the ideological content of kinship discourses is not recognized as such by some women. Such women internalize the values that are commended to them and see their roles as wives as rightly founded upon their suffering and self-sacrifice. This is so with the Tamil women described by Margaret Egnor (1980), who exalt their suffering. But most of the women I came across recognized that they had an unfair deal under existing family norms. They are the ones who said privately that the demands made in the name of family in fact exploit women. In the words of their private discourse, "Kinship burns!"

"Kinship Burns!"

The interests of women are sacrificed more readily in the marriages of the Tamil middle and upper castes than in those of the lower castes. In a crisis in these castes, the woman is admonished to put the interests of the family (*sondam*) before her own—and these "family" interests are remarkably identical with those of men. This is why women regard the sphere of marriage and affinity ambiguously: They recognize that it can prove destructive to their interests. It is this hidden, muted discourse of women that is revealed in their saying, "Kinship burns!" (*Sondam sudum!*) This view is seldom spoken. Rather, it is a weak alternative discourse, voicing frustration and fear. Only at crises does it come into the open, and even then, it is spoken only between women. This explains why I came across it only very late in my fieldwork, when someone who had kept a brave face on her difficulties one day spoke out.

Anuradha belonged to the middle-ranking Veerakodi Vellalar caste, an upwardly mobile agriculturist caste that, like the Muthurajahs, was adopting Brahminical norms. She was in her late forties, with two grown but as yet unmarried children. Her beautiful face was worn and prematurely aged. She had been a most kind informant, though I had not visited her street much, for I had spent most of my time elsewhere in the village. I met with her shortly before leaving Aruloor. In that final talk, she suddenly gave me a very different life story from the impressionistic one I had pieced together over our year-and-a-half acquaintance. During the preceding period, I had understood that her husband, whom I had met only once or twice, was an accountant in the post office in Lalgudi, that they held land where Anuradha herself often supervised the work, and that Ravi, her likable twenty-year-old-son, was doing well at college in Tiruchi. On all counts, this had seemed a happy household with a harmonious family life.

Now, addressing herself to Nirmala, my close friend who had accompanied me, she was suddenly telling us things she had deliberately kept from me. She told Nirmala that, because I was unmarried, she had felt I should be protected from these harsh facts of married life. Now she was telling us that her husband had not lived with her for fifteen years, that he had deserted her, and that it was a constant struggle to make ends meet because he gave her and her children no financial support at all. They supported themselves solely through their meager agricultural in-

come. The one occasion when I had seen her husband in the house (and had assumed he lived there) had been a religious feast when he had merely been visiting.

Fifteen years earlier, he had begun an affair with a young woman who also
worked in the post office. This woman was of the same Veerakodi Vellalar caste
but almost ten years younger than Anurdha. When Anuradha heard about the affair, she went to her parents for help. Her husband was her genealogical MBS, her
mother was his own FZ. Anuradha demanded that they persuade him to end the
relationship: She had two small children by then, and, secluded at home, she depended entirely on her husband's income. She told us of her parents' reply, and
though she spoke clearly and dryly, her pain was evident. "They said I should do
nothing—that we should just let my husband do whatever he wanted. They said
that the most important thing was to preserve the family peace, to preserve
sondam. If they raised the issue there'd be a big quarrel. So they let him live with
her and marry her."

Anuradha's marriage had not been a marriage with non-kin; it had been the
most traditional marriage of all. Yet even here, her rights had been readily forgotten, and her husband's interests were given absolute preeminence. Her husband
now lived in the next street with his second wife and three children. And just a
couple of weeks earlier, he had refused to help Ravi, their son, find a job through
his Panchayat (municipal) contacts. During her marital crisis, nobody else had intervened to aid Anuradha, least of all her parents, who lived on the same street and
with whom she had remained on moderately good terms. She had retained the
house and an uncertain agricultural income—an income that was much less than
her husband's salary. Tuning to Nirmala—who was also of Non-Brahmin Tamil
caste, also a mother, and, most importantly, also married for more than fifteen
years—Anuradha said with quiet vehemence, "*You* know how it is! Kinship burns!
(*Sondam sudum!*) That's our life and that's what we have to put up with." And
Nirmala assented with heartfelt agreement.

Suddenly alerted that things were not quite what they had seemed and that
sondam was not the unalloyed good it had been portrayed as, I asked women of
other Non-Brahmin Tamil castes if they were familiar with the saying, "Kinship
burns!" They all recognized it and, without exception, stated, as Nirmala had
later done, that it exemplified women's negative experience of marriage. They
were surprised that I knew the saying, for it was part of a female discourse that was
seldom spoken. Their response suggested that they were well aware of their vulnerability to the damaging demands that were made of them in the name of family
and kin.

Thus, even in traditional Non-Brahmin kinship, where women have historically enjoyed high status and relative independence as compared with Brahmin
and North Indian women, women have found—as Anuradha did—that in a
crunch, it is their interests that are likely to be "sacrificed" to protect male interests. Earlier, perceptive informants had pointed out to me that even within

"equal" cross-kin marriage, a certain degree of hierarchy creeps in between both parties at marriage because, as they put it, "only one side can 'own' the male!" This subtle hierarchizing between affines is far more marked among upper-caste Non-Brahmins and far less evident among lower-caste Non-Brahmins. In 1993, it was minimal in marriages between close kin in Aruloor but was greatly increased in marriages with strangers or non-kin (*anniyam* or *pirattiyar*). Because the status of men is much higher than that of women in the upper castes, upper-caste marriage creates a subtle hierarchy between close cross-kin who have been social equals. This is why, in those upwardly mobile castes that are adopting Brahminic norms asserting male superiority, women's natal kin do not attempt to defend their interests but rather give way, as they did in Anuradha's case.

Today, there are unceasing complaints in Aruloor that affinal kin no longer behave like kin because they neglect their obligation to marry cross-kin and instead marry strangers. This perceived shift in Non-Brahmin marriage preferences is closely linked to the new *economic* differentiation that is occurring within endogamous caste groups. When this phenomenon is blamed for creating hierarchy between kin, the fact that deep inequality has always existed in Non-Brahmin marriage—the inequality between the genders—is entirely ignored. But this inequality has been well hidden in the public discourses of Tamil kinship that have represented marriage and affinity as life's greatest goods. It has not been hidden from women, however, which is why, though their frustration is seldom spoken, they continue to warn that "kinship burns!"

3

Marrying Money: Changing Preference and Practice in Tamil Marriage

> Today men no longer marry women, they marry money! They only ask one question:
> "How much gold will you put on her?"
>
> —Rachel (Christian Paraiyar)

A CENTRAL IRONY CHARACTERIZES changes in Non-Brahmin marriage today: Those upwardly mobile salaried groups (within larger caste-groups) that marry in a "modern" manner, for money and status rather than "for love of kin," are precisely the social groups in which Non-Brahmin women are losing their traditionally high status. In rural Tamilnadu today, consequently, "modernity" (*nagarikam*) and urbanization are not leading to the emancipation of women from patriarchal norms or to more options being made available to them but to precisely the opposite. It is this curious situation, arising out of economic differentiation within endogamous caste-groups and changes in marriage preference and practice, that I seek to explore here.

In this analysis of the changing context of Non-Brahmin marriage, I will focus primarily on upwardly mobile groups within the middle-ranking Muthurajah caste. Upward class mobility and changing caste status are resulting in a radical change in gender relations. This phenomenon is most clearly embodied in the Muthurajah community. Historically an impoverished agriculturist caste, the rising class position of its upwardly mobile families is now closely linked to their aspirations for higher social status.

In indigenous perceptions, the traditional forms of Non-Brahmin kinship are being irredeemably altered today. At the heart of this change is what people see as the breakdown of the traditional cross-kin marriage system and a simultaneous fall

46

in the status of the Non-Brahmin woman. Rural Non-Brahmins are now far more concerned with what they regard as becoming "urbanized" and "modernized" than with achieving higher caste ranking (what Srinivas described as "Sanskritization" [1962b]). Because Aruloor's Brahminized upper castes—especially the wealthy mercantile and landowning Vellan Chettiars—are also its upper *class*, upwardly mobile, rural Non-Brahmins "Brahminize some of their customs. They do this in order to appear upper-class themselves since class status is now becoming more important than caste status with urbanizing groups. In talking about a rise in class status (from lower class to middle class), I am also describing a change in the social status of a caste, in the specific sense of a low caste (such as the Muthurajahs) acquiring greater social respect without rising to a new position on the ladder of caste ranking. However, upwardly mobile groups hope to acquire the cultural capital that distinguishes the upper classes. And because upper-class behavior is perceived as being Brahminic in style, a "Brahminization" of behavior tends to occur in these groups. But, to repeat, this Brahminization is essentially concerned with legitimating a new class status and not with a rise in caste ranking, so it does not constitute "Sanskritization" in Srinivas's sense (1962b).

Non-Brahmin and Brahmin Marriage Preferences and Their Implications

An examination of traditional marriage preferences reveals important differences between Non-Brahmin and Brahmin kinship discourses. Many writers (e.g., Dumont 1983; Tambiah 1973a, 1973b) have rightly contrasted the hypergamous marriage system prevalent in North India with the cross-cousin marriage system generally found in South India, but they have implied that both Non-Brahmins and Brahmins share an isogamous marriage structure. This is not true. Different choices in cross-kin marriage lead to different marriage structures. The Non-Brahmin marriage system is, indeed, isogamous, but by consistently emphasizing a "patrilateral" preference (with FZS as the ideal spouse), the Brahmins have made the cross-kin system hypergamous.

Members of all four Non-Brahmin castes in Aruloor repeatedly stated that they had a strong preference for MB and MBS as the ideal spouses for their daughters. As already noted, my informants' discussions revolved around whom a girl ought to marry, implicitly assuming a *female* perspective and thus a *female* Ego in their discussions of marriage. They regarded a preference for marriage with MB and MBS as a "matrilateral" preference. Just as a choice of MB or MBS as groom favored the mother's natal kin, so, too, a preference for FZS was seen by Brahmins as signaling the ascendance of the father's natal kin and as a "patrilateral" choice. These definitions of marriage preference were shared by both Non-Brahmins and Brahmins. For both groups, it was the identity of the significant male—the groom—that was central. Consequently, I adopt the indigenous definition of "matrilateral preference" for describing a marriage preference for Mother's Brother and Mother's Brother's Son and "patrilateral preference" for describing a preference for Father's Sister's Son. The reader will need to remember that in my usage, therefore, these terms carry precisely *the opposite meaning* from what they conventionally do (given that conventional anthropology assumes that Ego is always male).

In choosing the indigenous orientation rather than the culturally irrelevant anthropological convention, I find support in the writings of one of the foremost analysts of South Indian kinship, Thomas Trautmann (1981). He, very relevantly, notes the arbitrariness of assuming a male Ego in his discussion of FZS/MBD marriage, which, as he observes, anthropological convention has termed a "matrilateral" marriage preference. He comments: "One other oddity of the foregoing formulation is trivial: that is, *its arbitrary male orientation*. It is from the male's point of view that the *matrilateral* cross cousin (MBD) acquires a name; but to that person the male in question is her *patrilateral* cross cousin (FZS), and vice versa. This, however, concerns only the anthropologist's choice of terms and says nothing of the indigenous way of looking at things" (1981: 201, emphasis added). Apart from noting that the male-biased convention is hardly trivial, I entirely endorse what Trautmann says.

In Aruloor, then, if we adopt the indigenous focus and concentrate on the identity of the preferred male, we find that all four Non-Brahmin castes have a strong matrilateral marriage preference. They strongly prefer MB or MBS as marriage partners; FZS rates a poor third. Most informants stated that MB himself was the first choice—as long as her younger brother remained unmarried, and elder sister needed to look no further in bestowing her daughter in marriage. Further, this brother had the *right* to claim his eZD in marriage. Good has pointed out, in his excellent discussion of eZD marriage, that the ages of the spouses in MB/eZD marriage do not show a disparity and that there is the same average age gap as in non-MB marriage (1980: 491). This is so in Aruloor, too. Further, Good points out that MB/eZD marriage (which was as strongly preferred in his study area as in Aruloor) is cross-generational and that therefore Dumont's four principles of classification) cannot stand, given eZD marriage (Good 1981: 115). Instead, Good suggests that we should speak of "terminological levels" (1981: 115) and rightly states that from this point of view (i.e., that of "terminologically-prescribed" categories), MB/eZD marriage emerges as no anomaly at all but as yet another of the cross-kin marriage rule. It becomes clear that *"a man has to marry a junior cross-relative of his own terminological level and a woman a senior cross-relative of her own level"* (Good 1981: 115, emphasis in original). Thus, there is no radical difference between MB/eZD marriage and MBS/FZD marriage. This point was repeatedly stressed by my own informants, who spoke of both types of marriage as very similar and of the same category.

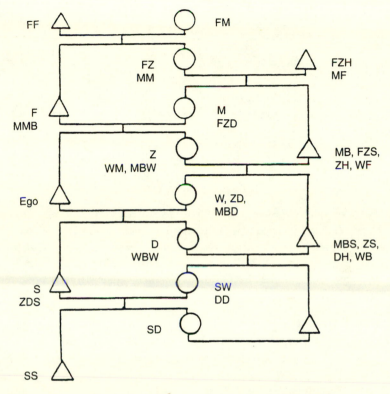

FIGURE 3.1   Repeated ZD/MB-Marriage.   *Source:* Good 1980: 486

This similarity emerges more clearly when we compare the implications of repeated MB/eZD marriage with the implications of MBS/FZD marriage ("matrilateral" preference). We find that the outcome of repeated MB marriage is exactly the same as that of repeated MBS marriage; namely, there is a reciprocal exchange of women across the generations. Figure 3.1 depicts repeated MB marriage; it is taken from Good (1980: 486). Figure 3.2 represents repeated MBS marriage; it comes from Trautmann (1981: 202). Figure 3.3 is also from Trautmann; it depicts repeated FZS marriage (1981: 202). What emerges from repeated FZS marriage is, clearly, a marriage structure that is markedly different from the previous two, for it is one in which there is no reciprocal exchange of women over the generations, but, on the contrary, a unilateral asymmetry. As Trautmann points out, repeated FZS marriage transforms the reciprocity of bilateral marriage (also termed "sister-exchange") into hierarchy. Trautmann says, ["FZS-marriage] introduces something new, the obligatory distinctions of affines as between wife-givers and wife-takers, and *the rule that wife-givers must not be*

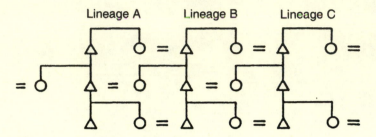

FIGURE 3.2   Repeated MBS/FZD-Marriage.   *Source:* Trautmann 1981: 202

wife-takers, and vice versa. This as we have seen is characteristic of Indo-Aryan [i.e., North Indian] systems and it is *a requirement of the kanyadana ideal"* (1981: 203, emphasis added). In short, it is a marriage system perfectly attuned to the hypergamy so desired by Brahmins (following their North Indian ideals), and it is consequently no surprise to find that FZS-marriage is strongly preferred by both Telugu Brahmins and Tamil Brahmins, despite the fact that the latter also allow MB-marriage. Of his figure illustrating MBS-marriage (Figure 3.2), Trautmann says: "Schematically, at least, wives flow in one direction only in any given generation; but from one generation to the next the direction reverses such that B gets wives from C and gives to A in one generation, but in the next gets from A and gives to C. A distinction of wife-giving and wife-taking affines could not easily be maintained under such a rule, and the corollary of the matrilateral rule [my informants' "patrilateral" preference: FZS-marriage] that givers cannot be takers, and vice versa, does not hold" (1981: 203–204).

Trautmann rightly points out that a FZS-marriage rule accords with "the Indian ideal of *kanyadan:* namely, the prohibition on sister-exchange, and the rule that wife-givers shall not be wife-takers, and wife-takers shall not be wife-givers" (1981: 204). He calls this "the matrilateral variant," but, as I said, in Aruloor, this is defined by all castes as a *patrilateral* choice. And this is precisely why the Telugu

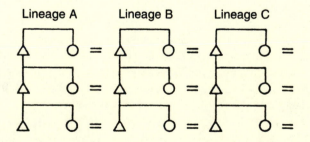

FIGURE 3.3   Repeated FZS/MBD-Marriage.   *Source:* Trautmann 1981: 202

Brahmins and Tamil Brahmins espouse it. This was made quite explicit when a Tamil Brahmin friend discussed the marriage preference of her caste with me. She stated that MBS/FZD-marriage was seen by Tamil Brahmins as a matrilateral type of marriage because the bride "returns to her mother's kin." She explained that a standard metaphor used to describe marriage among Tamil Brahmins was the botanical metaphor of a creeper (a climbing plant): When a girl was married to her MB or MBS, this was an "inward-turning creeper," which was formally disapproved of; the ideal marriage was to her FZS because here the creeper "turned outwards." She further explained this desire for marriage with FZ's kin rather than Mother's kin by reference to *gottiram*, the patrilineage groups that claim to have been founded by mythical sages. When a Brahmin woman married, her *gottiram* changed to that of her husband. If a Brahmin girl married her MB, this meant that her *gottiram* would revert to that of her mother's before marriage (that is, her MF's *gottiram*). This was disapproved of as "inward-turning." The ideal Tamil Brahmin marriage, my friend concluded, was with a distant kinsman who was a *classificatory* FZS.

My Telugu Brahmin informants agreed in every respect with this Tamil Brahmin account but claimed that, unlike Tamil Brahmins, they disapproved of MB-marriage. They admitted that it did sometimes occur among Telugu Brahmins but far more rarely than among Tamil Brahmins. They felt, somewhat more strongly than Tamil Brahmins, a strong dislike of giving brides to the matrilateral kin. Here, I have to reiterate (with Good 1981) that preference is not the same as practice. In practice, as we will find when examining a survey of marriage practice in Aruloor, Brahmins are not so very different from Non-Brahmin Tamils, but their *official* discourse of marriage preference is almost exactly the reverse of that of Non-Brahmins. Brahmins formally state a strong preference for patrilateral marriage (with FZS), in keeping with their patrilineal and male-centered ethos. Non-Brahmin Tamils formally and equally strongly prefer matrilateral marriage (with MB and MBS). However, the marriage practice statistics, discussed later, reveal a very different picture.

Bilateral marriage or sister-exchange (MBS/FZD- *and* FZS/MBD-marriage) occurs not infrequently among the four Non-Brahmin Tamil castes studied (see Figure 3.4). Trautmann rightly points out that "in ... the bilateral system every wife in the second and third generation is both MBD and FZD at one and the same time, and every husband is both FZS and MBS" (1981: 206). This is correct (see Figure 3.4, derived from Trautmann 1981: 202). A female Ego marries her MBS, but because MB has married FZ (in sister-exchange), MBS is *also* FZS. Similarly, a male Ego marries his FZD. But because FZ has married MB, FZD is identical with MBD. Though Brahmins occasionally practice MB- and MBS-marriage, they avoid sister-exchange and formally reject it entirely. Being the quintessence of reciprocal marriage, it is too blatantly opposed to hypergamous marriage, which is their ideal marriage.

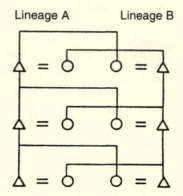

FIGURE 3.4   Repeated Bilateral Marriage.   *Source:* Trautmann 1981: 202

This leads Trautmann to conclude that a bilateral marriage structure is "the basic form of the Dravidian rule of cross marriage" and that the Dravidian kinship terminology is derived from it (1981: 206). This view has been implicitly challenged by Good, who has correctly rejected the assumption that the kinship terminology is based on "cross-cousin marriage" (1980: 494) and has advanced the thesis that it is actually based on cross-kin marriage that has "a jural preference for and behavioural incidence of eZDy marriage" (1980: 497). Good's argument is impressive: It distinguishes between terminological and genealogical identity and minutely examines the equivalences in each category. I shall not enter on an examination of his thesis here because it suffices for my own argument to point out that Good's discussion makes it quite clear that repeated MB/eZD-marriage has exactly the same reciprocal effect as bilateral marriage (see Figure 3.4). Thus, when Non-Brahmins in Aruloor speak of their strong attachment to MB- and MBS-marriage, they are indicating their commitment to the moral ideal of reciprocal and egalitarian relations between affines.

Good states that even anthropologists who encountered eZD-marriage conformed to the "majority view" that MB/ZD-marriage was an anomaly (1980: 496). Good cites Gough (1956: 849–853) as an example, but Trautmann falls into the same trap. He dismisses eZD-marriage as "a secondary derivative of the basic cross cousin rule" (Trautmann 1981: 206) and characterizes it as "a secondary derivative of patrilateral cross cousin marriage (FZD) in which that person (MB) anticipates, as it were, the claim of his son to the woman in question" (1981: 206). This is quite mistaken, with regard to Aruloor, for the claim of MB was always primary in my informants' minds: His right (*urimai*) to his ZD was apparently never seen as "anticipating" his son's claim. Their term *"urimaippen"* (*"pen"*: "girl" or "bride") was used in Aruloor, as in Good's area (1980: 486), and it was MB's *urimai* to his eZD that was pronounced strongest of all by Pallars,

Muthurajahs, Christian Paraiyars, and Vellan Chettiars. MB's *urimai* to his FZD came second in their opinion. Finally, Trautmann claims that eZD-marriage is of "restricted occurrence within the Dravidian region" and that "it is a derivative rule that, historically, represents a specialized development within a part of the South Dravidian area" (1981: 207). He appears to be mistaken here, for as Good shows (1978: 460, 1980: 497), eZD-marriage seems to have a very wide geographical spread. Indeed, Good claims that it has an "extremely wide distribution ... in South Asia" and that "the vast majority of the inhabitants of Sri Lanka and South India belong to castes having some degree of jural preference for and behavioural incidence of eZDy marriage" (1980: 497). Clearly, then, in discussing MB-marriage in Aruloor, we are dealing with an extremely important, though neglected, marriage preference and not merely a localized anomaly.

To conclude this part of my argument, I would add that Trautmann bemoans the lack of ethnographic data establishing correlations between marriage rules and caste in "the Dravidian kinship region" (1981: 204). By showing that hierarchizing, asymmetric FZS/MBD-marriage is the marriage preference of Telugu Brahmins and Tamil Brahmins and that MB/eZD-marriage and MBS/FZD-marriage are the preferences of the far more egalitarian Non-Brahmin castes, I hope to have established that there is a close correlation between the moral ideals espoused in both caste and kinship discourse. On the one hand, the values of equality and reciprocity of the Non-Brahmins manifest themselves in the symmetries of repeated MB- and MBS-marriage; on the other hand, the value of hierarchy avowed by the Brahmins is embodied in the hypergamy of repeated FZS-marriage. Further, it is no accident that a kinship discourse celebrating reciprocity exists in those castes where the subordination of women is relatively mild and that a kinship discourse valorizing hierarchy characterizes the Brahmin castes in which, traditionally, women have been most dramatically subordinated.

The Traditional Contexts of Non-Brahmin and Brahmin Marriage

The traditional marriage system of the Non-Brahmins, which still exists among the poorest groups in Aruloor, reflects the fact that women have been valued far more highly among Non-Brahmins than among Brahmins. In the Non-Brahmin traditional system, a young woman's parents do not seek a spouse for her, as Brahmin parents do. Instead, they wait for inquiries to be made about her by the parents of eligible men. Further, until very recently, it was the bridegroom's family who made the largest wedding prestations, thus making the Non-Brahmin system approximate a "bride-price" system. The groom's family traditionally bore the entire expense of the wedding feast, which was held, like the marriage rite itself, at the groom's home. This practice of holding the wedding virilocally continues largely unchanged today in all four Non-Brahmin castes.

Traditional Brahmin marriage, by contrast, has emphasized the subordination of the bride's family to the groom's in sharp contrast to Non-Brahmin marriage. It is the girl's parents who have to go in search of a groom, and it is they who give by far the largest wedding prestations. They also have to bear the entire cost of the wedding, which is held at their house.

The Advantages to Non-Brahmin Women in Close-Kin Marriage

Several Non-Brahmin women told me of the favorable position women enjoyed in close-kin marriage. They pointed out that in traditional close-kin marriage, a woman retained comparatively high status and a considerable degree of independence because of the equal relationship that existed between her family and the groom's family. Siva, who was in-married from Tiruchi city to an Aruloor husband who was non-kin (*anniyam*) to her, clearly envied the local Pallar women of her street, who were married to close kin (though she was very critical of them). She said:

> When a girl is married among her own close kin she is not among strangers—she is among the people she has grown up with. If she quarrels with her husband, she isn't worried at all—she goes straight to her parents, who come and tell off her in-laws and her husband. In fact, [she said,] they have too good a time. Look at Rajni—every time she quarrels with Sivarajan [her husband] she runs across the street to her mother's house, so she's in her parents' house half the time. I think girls should be married to non-kin—that'd teach them to behave and not be so quick to run home. Here they aren't scared at all because they know their parents will come and quarrel with their husbands if they scold them. This makes them bold and disobedient.

A similar criticism was voiced by my elderly Muthurajah friend, Anjalai: "You never have peace in marriages within close kin. The young couple are always quarrelling and the girl running off to her parents. And then her parents—your brother or sister—come and quarrel with you and a family feud breaks out. The irony is that these young people quickly make up, but their parents carry on quarrelling! That's why I'm all for marriage with non-kin now. You'd have more peace." Her wry comments reflect, once again, the unusually secure position of the young wife in traditional Non-Brahmin society. Significantly, both my friends belonged to upwardly mobile families. Their views therefore represent a fare more Brahminicized view than that of most Pallar women or most poorer Muthurajah women, which also accounts for their espousal of female obedience.

If maltreated, the Non-Brahmin woman could simply leave her husband's home and return to her parents' (or brother's) house, where she was readily accepted because she was seen as having the right to come home. This is an enormously important fact and indicates the very different social contexts in which

Non-Brahmin and Brahmin marriage take place. The Brahmin woman had no such right. Gowri, a Telugu Brahmin woman, had returned to Aruloor with her young son after being deserted by her husband. She lived alone, and to support herself, she worked as a professional astrologer. Both due to her marital situation and her occupation, she was regarded as a social anomaly, particularly by other Brahmins. However, due to her professional work with female Non-Brahmin clients from a wide range of castes, she had an extensive knowledge of both Brahmin and Non-Brahmin contexts. She gave me her explanation of why Brahmin women had no right to return to their natal homes.

At a Brahmin wedding the girl's family give the boy's side a huge dowry [*varadat-cinai*], often impoverishing themselves in the process. But with this dowry their responsibility ends: Their door closes on their daughter. She no longer has any rights in her father's house, and she is not supposed to return to it except for very brief ceremonial visits. So if she quarrels with her in-laws or her husband she has nowhere to go because it's very shameful for Brahmin parents to have a married daughter living with them. With the Tamil woman, it's completely different. At her wedding only a very small dowry is given, and she continues to have rights in her father's house. She can return to it whenever she wishes, and no one will criticise her. Just observe these Tamil women—they're always going off to their mother's house, but nobody says a thing. But the Brahmin girl has to stick it out in her husband's house, and if it becomes unbearable there, she has to fend for herself. I can't live in my father's house, so I live separately. I did live with my parents when I returned, but they felt so ashamed about this that they asked me to move out. My elder brother has supported me morally throughout, but he can't support me financially. That's why I had to take up this profession. Actually this is strictly forbidden to a Brahmin woman—she should stay quietly at home and never mix with other castes. But how could I do my work as an astrologer if I did that? My job demands mixing with them—so I've had to break many Brahmin prohibitions.

Gowri's account refers consistently to her Brahmin parents' house as her "father's house," but she used both this term and "mother's house" to refer to a Non-Brahmin woman's natal home. This is worth noting because, as already stated, Non-Brahmin women *never* speak of their natal home as their "father's house"; they only refer to it as their "*mother's* house." Conversely, all Brahmin women always refer to their natal home as their "father's house." This is another indication of the far greater emphasis on the mother and the matrilateral kin in Non-Brahmin kinship.

Gowri's analysis cited Brahmin "dowry" as a central reason why parents feel that they have fulfilled their duty to their daughter. But "dowry" is only part of the reason. Brahmins prohibit divorce and widow-remarriage (as do the Brahminized Vellan Chettiars): This is part of the reason for a daughter's vulnerability, as is their hypergamous marriage system, with its strong preference for FZS-marriage. Such a marriage system presupposes the higher status and greater authority of the bridegroom's family and goes together with the *kanyadanam* ethos that assumes that a married daughter "belongs" entirely to her husband's family.

Another central reason for the difference between Brahmin and middle- and lower-caste Non-Brahmin contexts is that Non-Brahmin women, like their husbands, have traditionally been engaged in agricultural labor and have been a highly valued source of labor power in both their marital and their natal homes. Brahmin women, on the other hand, have always been prohibited from participating in priestly work and traditionally been very strictly secluded in the home, engaged only in domestic work. The great value of the labor of married Non-Brahmin women to their natal families was clearly demonstrated during the harvest months (from January to March especially) when large numbers of women, in the weeks when work was slack in Aruloor, returned to their "mother's villages" to help their natal kin with harvest work.

The Bilaterality of Traditional Non-Brahmin Kinship

As already noted, the strong position of the matrilateral kin means that Non-Brahmin kinship in Aruloor has had a rather different structure of relations between affines than Brahmin kinship has. Brahmins have shared with Non-Brahmins a patrilineal system of inheritance. But though Brahmins have had a strongly patrilineal inheritance system, the Non-Brahmins have tended toward a bilateral system of inheritance. Matrilineal kin "inherit" women; that is, MBs and MBSs have had a customary claim on ZDs and FZDs. Patrilineal kin, on the other hand, have inherited land, immovable property, and other forms of wealth. Thus, the matrilateral kin have inherited the most important form of wealth—the women who provide both labor and children, who, in turn, provide future labor. In an agrarian economy with scarce land, control of labor has been the major source of wealth for those with little or no land—that is, the great majority of people.

Particularly among the poorer Non-Brahmin castes—the poorer Muthurajahs and the Pallars—children are more important as a source of labor than as heirs. Paddy agriculture in Aruloor today is primarily dependent on adult *female* labor (see Chapter 9). Further, it incorporates the labor of female children more than that of male children. Consequently, there is comparatively less stress on the supreme importance of male children and a greater valuation of female children in the laboring lower castes than in the Brahmin-influenced upper castes. Because women are more highly valued in the laboring castes, the status of the matrilateral kin who "inherit" them is enhanced. Thus, matrilateral kin, through their marriage right to ZDs, have traditionally controlled female sexuality, female fertility, *and* female labor.

A very important correlation that emerges here is that between affinal male reciprocity and female independence. Reciprocity between affinal males is greatest in those lower castes where women are most independent. Female involvement in waged and unwaged agricultural labor therefore correlates strongly with the importance of the matrilateral kin. This importance, in turn, establishes the equal relationship that exists between patrilineage (*pankali*) and matrilateral kin (*maman-maccinan*). As a result, the status of MB is very closely linked to female status in the caste concerned. MBs are most important in the lowest castes in Aruloor precisely because it is in these castes that females enjoy the highest status.

Changing Contexts:
From Close-Kin Marriage to Non-Kin Marriage

So far, I have dealt with Non-Brahmin marriage as it has historically functioned and have contrasted it with traditional Brahmin marriage. Today, however, with salaried jobs increasingly available to Aruloor's young men, the traditional marriage system is undergoing radical change. Previously, affines in Aruloor's Non-Brahmin castes—particularly the lower castes—were all engaged in agriculture and had comparatively equal agrarian incomes. But today, education has provided the means by which divisions arise between kin, for only some young men succeed in acquiring higher education and only a few of those who do eventually gain salaried jobs. A regular salary is much envied in Aruloor because it offers an escape from the increasingly uncertain returns of agriculture. Marginal farmers—and the majority of landholders here are small and marginal farmers—are keen to sell or lease out their land today and thereby get out of farming as an occupation. Parents send sons rather than daughters to college, partly because they wish to exercise strict control over the sexual behavior of their daughters and partly because sons are always given first preference where any outlay of money is concerned.

Consequently, the availability of higher education has meant its availability to *males.* Instead of increasing female opportunities, higher education and the salaried jobs it makes available have introduced a radical differentiation between young men and women in the middle and lower castes, which did not exist before. This differentiation is in occupation, and it is very recent. Previously, both women and men, whether from a middle caste (Lingayats, Veerakodi Vellalars, Muthurajahs) or lower caste (Pallars, Christian Paraiyars), were engaged in agricultural labor, either on their own farms or for wages or both. Today, quite suddenly, young middle-caste men are no longer entering agricultural labor. Instead, after high school, they are becoming government clerks, bus conductors, peons, and primary schoolteachers. Conscious of their vastly increased prestige, resulting from both their withdrawal from manual labor and their monthly salary, they have begun to demand wives with high school education who, also withdrawn from field labor, live in semiseclusion in the home, engaged primarily in household work. Whereas both wives and husbands had relatively equal occupations as agricultural workers, this relatively equal relationship has now given way to an extremely unequal one in which only the husband is—and is expected to be—the earner; the wife is transformed from a fellow earner into a financial dependent. This radically changed relationship between women and men lies at the heart of the changes that are occurring in marriage strategies.

The central change, my informants claim, is what they view as the collapse of close-kin marriage. In the past, few women with unmarried younger brothers would have given their daughters in marriage to someone else. Now, however, this is not unusual. The current situation is epitomized in the marriage of Devaki's daughter. Devaki, a Lingayat woman married to a high school teacher, had an unmarried younger brother who worked on the family farm. She herself claimed that a generation earlier, she would certainly have given her elder daughter to be her younger brother's wife. But today, she said, things were very different. Her eldest son had done exceptionally well at college and was a well-paid engineer at Neyveli. His status had risen, and he wished to see a corresponding rise in his family's status, so he had promised his parents that he would finance his sister's wedding if they found her a well-to-to, salaried bridegroom. His sister, Kamakshi, was beautiful and had a correspondence course degree, and so a bank officer groom from a rich Salem family soon materialized. Kamakshi's grand wedding in a Tiruchi marriage hall (*kalyana mandampam*) was readily financed by her brother, and for months thereafter, her happy parents basked in the reflected glory of their bank officer son-in-law.

Devaki's own unmarried brother was not even seriously considered as a match because he was too poor: He was only a small farmer living on an uncertain income and with only a little high school education. Devaki knew that he would have gladly received Kamakshi as his bride, but she doubted that he could have kept her in the style to which she was accustomed. In fact, Devaki's first break with the egalitarian small-peasant world had occurred a generation earlier, when she, a simple farmer's daughter, had been married to Natarajan, a salaried high school teacher. Natarajan's salaried status had raised Devaki to a new economic class, and she had been withdrawn from fieldwork immediately. Thus, Devaki had been of a higher social class than her younger brother for eighteen years, long before the question of a husband for Kamakshi arose. And when it arose, her impoverished brother was out of the running altogether. He did not quarrel about it or demand his right to marry his beautiful niece: He, too, recognized that they were now part of a new world in which considerations of wealth came first and kinship rights second. I met this MB in Devaki's house just before the marriage and noted a certain embarrassment in the air. But then Devaki showed me the gorgeous necklaces of synthetic diamonds they had made as part of Kamakshi's "dowry," and in the excitement of her forthcoming rise to glory in a fine house in distant Salem, all embarrassment faded. So Devaki's daughter was married to rich *"piratti"*—short for *"pirattiyar"* (strangers, non-kin)—even though there was an unmarried MyB. The fact was remarked on by Devaki's neighbors in Middle

Street, where she lived, but since they, too, were upwardly mobile, with educated sons seeking salaried jobs, their response was ambiguous.

For an unambiguous response to the new marriage market, we must move to a street where a few young men were college educated too but where their inflated "price" caused outrage among several young women. This was the case in Church of the Virgin Mother Street, where the young Christian Paraiyar men were—as in most other streets—demanding that more gold jewelry be "put on" their brides. This jewelry is formally the property of the bride, but everyone knows that a husband has the right to sell it if he chooses. The gold jewelry "put on" a bride is, in effect, the main "dowry" given to the groom's side.

It was this ever-escalating "bridegroom-price" that angered the young Christian Paraiyar women. Significantly, some of these young women were educated and had salaried jobs, too, but the "dowry" demanded from them was as high as that asked from uneducated brides. Angry and outraged, their unambiguous response was an impassioned condemnation of the new order of things. They saw how their parents were humiliated by the parents of the young men who asked for more and more gold. They also saw how, in the process, they themselves were devalued. Rachel, who had a high school education and who was the daughter of the most influential man in the street, worked as a clerk in the post office sorting center in Tiruchi city, and as her family was well off, she could expect to make a good marriage. But she had close female friends who had been rejected by their kin in favor of rich *anniyam* (stranger) girls, and it was of their plight that she spoke with vehemence: "Today men no longer marry women, they marry money! Previously they asked about the girl—'Is she well-behaved? Is she a good [sexually moral] girl? How well is she educated?' That's all they're interested in, because what they're really marrying is the gold. That's why I never want to get married. I'd rather have my job and stay with my parents."

Rachel's denunciation of the gold-digging parents of eligible males was echoed, but in more desolate tones, by the parents of marriageable young women of other castes. Families who were poor or who had many daughters were the hardest hit. But the problem was also related to caste and class. The impoverished Pallars were barely affected at all because their young men had little education and continued to do agricultural work, just as their young women did. Nor were the wealthy Chettiars much affected because they had Brahminized in this particular regard and had switched from huge bride prices to huge "dowries" some thirty years earlier. Of the four Non-Brahmin Tamil castes, the upwardly mobile Muthurajahs and Christian Paraiyars were most involved in the marriage game. These two castes had the largest numbers of college-educated young men, for the ultraconservative Chettiars still sent few young men to college and the Pallars were generally far too poor to do so. So it was particularly in the Muthurajah and Christian Paraiyar castes that parents with daughters were beginning to see them as financial liabilities. As Anjalai, my Muthurajah friend with an unmarried twenty-five-year-old daughter, lamented: "They're asking six *pavun* [A *"pavun,"* a Tamilized form of "pound," is one sovereign or eight grams of gold; one *pavun* of gold cost around Rs.2,500 in 1988.] Where are we to get six *pavun* from? We told them, 'We can put three *pavun* on her, but not more.' And he's my own *Maman paiyan venum* ([classificatory MBS]). How is one to get a girl married these days?"

Aruloor's mothers had varying opinions regarding the reason for the new marriage situation. Anjalai, whose eldest daughter had been married some eight years earlier, was an astute observer. Her analysis ran like this:

> It all started about twenty years ago, when they built BHEL [Bharat Heavy Electricals Limited, a mammoth government enterprise near Tiruchi city]. The young men who found employment there got good salaries—and so they thought they owned the world. They began asking for dowries and more marriage-gifts and more *pavun* on their brides. And they got it! Everyone wanted salaried husbands for their daughters, not impoverished farmers. We had a few men, of our caste, employed there from the early days. They only had low-paid jobs—watchman, peon—but if you worked at BHEL no one asked you what you actually did. Everyone was just hugely impressed. "Goodness!" they'd say, "He works at BHEL!" and they'd give him their daughter. Even if he was only the watchman and stood at the gate!

Anjalai's analysis was not the most popular one, however. More popular was a supply-and-demand analysis that was offered to me by women of all castes. They claimed: "It's because there are fewer men than women today—that's why it's become so difficult to get a bridegroom. And that's why they can ask whatever they like!" It is true that polygyny, which was more frequent in the past, has decreased; there has also been a huge increase in recent years in the migration of males from rural areas to the cities. Both these factors would lead to an apparent shortage of males. Further, population statistics for Tamilnadu indicate that considerable male out-migration from Tamilnadu has caused the southern districts, including Tiruchi District where Aruloor lies, to have a high female-to-male ratio (1,002 females to 933 males in 1981) (MIDS 1988: 38). So the most popular explanation for inflated "bridegroom prices" is objectively correct: There *are* fewer men than women in Tiruchi District today.

Another explanation, which connects with Anjalai's, held that the spiral in "bridegroom price" was due to the inflated cost of living and the great expense incurred in educating a son. Some of these female commentators, justifying their own behavior, claimed that parents were entirely correct in asking for a "reimbursement" for the expense incurred in educating their son: "After all, his wife is going to get the benefit of his salary, isn't she?" The unspoken assumption was always that the bride, having far less education than the groom, would be secluded at home and financially dependent on him.

Yalman recorded similar sentiments in 1967 in Sri Lanka, from families who preferred marriage with rich strangers to marriage with poor cross-kin. This suggests that the perceived breakdown of cross-kin marriage is a typical symptom of urbanization: It is a sign that new interests are supplanting the old obligations to kin.

It was with deep nostalgia that older Non-Brahmin women spoke of the "bride-price" gifts that had been showered on the bride, by the groom's side, in their day. Older Chettiar women spoke of how the families of some grooms had beggared themselves to gather the bride price, and they reported that some Chettiar men who were their contemporaries had never been married because their families had not been able to afford the bride price demanded. They were keenly aware of the irony that the situation is now exactly reversed, so that it is young Chettiar women who are left unmarried because their parents cannot afford the "dowries" demanded by the parents of eligible young kinsmen. Older women of the Muthurajah, Pallar, and Christian Paraiyar castes also spoke of how they had been sought in marriage, stressing that the groom's family had had to spend far more than the bride's on the marriage. At her engagement ceremony (*parisam podradu*), a young Non-Brahmin woman had been literally wooed into agreement through the bestowal of gifts on her. But now, this world was disappearing, slowly but irrevocably. What the Chettiar accounts indicate is that kinship obligations had always embodied a vulnerable moral code. This suggests that the contemporary situation in which kin ignore their marriage obligations to cross-kin if it does not suit them is not new at all, though most people speak as if it were. The central difference today is surely that a pragmatic self-interest can draw on powerful legitimation from the urban capitalist world and its ethos that class is more important than kinship, though not, as yet, more important than caste.

Class is becoming an increasingly important factor in Aruloor. And it is creating a new kind of division between "marriageable" and "unmarriageable" kin, a division that is based on the new educational and economic stratification *within* caste.

Marriage Strategies Today: Statistics on Marriage Practices in Aruloor and Their Implications

Statistical evidence suggests that marriage practices in Aruloor are changing and that they are very different from stated preferences. This evidence is provided in a survey of the actual marriage practices of the five castes studied (see Table 3.1), carried out in 1990. Informants from all the castes had constantly insisted that the ideal marriage for any girl was a cross-kin marriage to the closest possible male relative: MB and MBS in the four Non-Brahmin castes and FZS in the Telugu and Tamil Brahmin castes. However, when a survey of actual marriage practice

TABLE 3.1 Marriage in Aruloor: Statistics on 2,016 Marriages in Five Castes Through Three Generations

	Pallar				Muthurajah				Christian Paraiyar				Vellan Chettiar				Brahmin			
	MB	MBS	FZS	NK	MB	MBS	FZS	NK	MB	MBS	FZS	NK	MB	MBS	FZS	NK	MB	MBS	FZS	NK
WH	7	10	15	53	18	4	6	33	12	4	2	41	11	22	27		2	4	4	10
HP	5	18	9	53	15	8	2	36	9	6	2	42	7	46	8		2	4	4	10
WP	3	15	9	58	17	5	3	36	6	5	1	47	1	47	13		—	2	1	17
HMP	—	35	6	44	1	7	—	53	9	17	1	32	8	50	3		—	2	4	14
HFP	4	16	9	56	7	—	—	54	6	13	7	33	10	39	14		3	1	2	14
WMP	2	22	5	56	1	4	1	55	4	13	3	39	6	54	2		2	1	1	18
WFP	1	20	12	52	5	1	1	54	9	8	4	38	7	48	6		2	1	7	10
TOTAL	22	136	65	372	64	29	13	321	55	66	20	272	50	306	73		10	15	22	93
TOTAL%	3.7	22.9	10.9	62.5	15.0	6.8	3.0	75.2	13.3	16.0	4.8	65.9	11.3	69.4	16.6		7.1	10.7	15.8	66.4
PRF	2	16	7	60	4	7	9	41	12	6	8	33	13	37	11		—	—	1	19
PRF%	2.4	18.8	8.2	70.6	6.5	11.5	14.8	67.2	20.3	10.2	13.6	55.9	20.6	58.7	17.5		—	—	5.0	95.0

Castes Compared

	MB	MBS	FZS	NK	TOT
P	22	136	65	372	595
M	64	29	13	321	427
CP	55	66	20	272	413
VC	50	306	73	12	441
B	10	15	22	93	140
TOTAL	201	552	193	1070	2016
P%	3.7	22.9	10.9	62.5	100
M%	15.0	6.8	3.0	75.2	100
CP%	13.3	16.0	4.8	65.9	100
VC%	11.3	69.4	16.6	2.7	100
B%	7.1	10.7	15.8	66.4	100
TOT%	10.0	27.4	9.6	53.0	100

Key:

WH: Marriage of informant
HP: Marriage of Husband's Parents
WP: Marriage of Wife's Parents
HMP: Marriage of Husband's Mother's Parents
HFP: Marriage of Husband's Father's Parents
WMP: Marriage of Wife's Mother's Parents
WFP: Marriage of Wife's Father's Parents
PRF: Marriage preference expressed by informant
MB: Marriage with MB
MBS: Marriage with MBS

FZS: Marriage with FZS
NK: Marriage with Non-kin
P: Pallar
M: Muthurajah
B: Brahmin
MB: Mother's Brother
MBS: Mother's Brother's Son
FZS: Father's Sister's Son
(NB: Marriages both real and classificatory)

through three generations was carried out (by my friend and research assistant Susila Raja), a very different picture emerged.

The survey questionnaire had four categories of marriage: (1) marriage with MB, (2) marriage with FZS, and (4) marriage with non-kin. In the first three categories, both real *and classificatory* marriages have been included, in order to simplify the table. The survey thus gives information on the broad picture of Aruloor marriage in which the most significant questions, for my present purposes, are to what degree non-kin marriage is practiced and how far it is explicitly preferred. The survey asked what kind of marriage had been made (1) by the informant, (2) by the Husband's Parents, (3) by the Wife's Parents, (4) by the Husband's Mother's Parents, (5) by the Husband's Father's Parents, (6) by the Wife's Mother's Parents, and (7) by the Wife's Father's Parents. In this way, information on a total of 2,016 marriages in five castes through three generations was gathered (the Telugu and Tamil Brahmin castes are considered as one "Brahmin" caste). Out of 595 Pallar marriages, 372 (62.5 percent) were with non-kin, and 223 (37.5 percent) were with cross-kin. Out of 427 Muthurajah marriages, 321 (75.2 percent) were with non-kin, and 106 (24.8 percent) were with cross-kin. Out of 413 Christian Paraiyar marriages, 272 (65.9 percent) were with non-kin, and 141 (34.1 percent) were with cross-kin. Out of 441 Vellan Chettiar marriages, 12 (2.7 percent) were with non-kin, and 429 (97.3 percent) were with cross-kin. Out of 140 Brahmin marriages, 93 (66.4 percent) were with non-kin, and 47 (33.6 percent) were with cross-kin. As mentioned, in the category "marriages with cross-kin" used here, even marriages with distant classificatory cross-kin are included.

The survey concluded with a general question asking whether the informant thought cross-kin marriage or non-kin marriage more desirable. The answer—in direct contradiction to what had been reiterated to me in all discussions of marriage—was decidedly in favor of non-kin marriage in the Pallar caste, where 85 informants, 70.6 percent were in favor and 29.4 percent were against. Similarly, in the Muthurajah caste, of 61 informants, 67.2 percent were in favor of non-kin marriage and 32.8 percent were against it. Opinions were more uniformly divided in the Christian Paraiyar caste, where of 59 informants, 55.9 percent were for non-kin marriage and 44.1 percent were against. Of the four Non-Brahmin castes, only the Chettiar caste answered this question in exactly the same way as they had discussed it with me. They were overwhelmingly against non-kin marriage and strongly for cross-kin marriage: Only 3.2 percent were for non-kin marriage, and 96.8 percent were against it. It was far less surprising that the Brahmins (both Telugu and Tamil) were strongly in favor of non-kin marriage given that they had always said that they preferred marriage with *distant* kin. They had repeatedly stressed that their ideal preference, unlike that of Non-Brahmin castes, was not a genealogical FZS but a distantly related classificatory FZS. Out of 20 Brahmin informants, 95 percent were for non-kin marriage, with 5 percent against it.

The reasons for a choice in favor of non-kin marriage varied considerably, but many claimed that it was because kin were "too demanding": They expected and asked for too much *sir* (ritual prestations). This is rather surprising, for one would have expected the opposite, namely, that strangers would ask for far more in marriage prestations. Apart from this striking preference for non-kin marriage in the three Non-Brahmin lower castes, the rest of the data vary but indicate a high incidence of non-kin marriage through the three generations considered. This makes it clear that there has been a deep discrepancy between marriage preference and marriage practice in the Non-Brahmin lower castes for at least five decades. When Pallar and Muthurajah informants were asked why earlier generations had often married non-kin, their answer usually was that the parents or grandparents in question had had no suitable kin available to marry.

The survey indicates that a few Muthurajahs (3 percent) have married FZSs (genealogical and classificatory), even though they view this as a "patrilateral" preference, and that several Pallars (10.9 percent) have done so. A few Telugu and Tamil Brahmins have married their MBs (7.1 percent). It is the wealthy Chettiars who exhibit the most conservative pattern in their actual practice, for even today they primarily marry (classificatory and genealogical) MBs and MBSs (11.3 percent and 69.4 percent, respectively). Christian Paraiyars have married in all categories, indicating that the Catholic Church's ban on MB-marriage and on cross-cousin marriage has generally been ignored: 13.3 percent have married "MBs," and 16 percent have married "MBSs."

Thus, the actual practices of the four Non-Brahmin castes for the last three generations emerge as rather different from their clearly stated preference for "matrilateral" marriage. Significantly, the caste in which upwardly mobile groups are most evident today—the Muthurajah caste—also shows the highest incidence of non-kin marriage (75.2 percent) through an extended period of time (three generations). The increasingly Brahminized lifestyles of these Muthurajah groups make their adoption of a non-kin-type of marriage quite logical because, unlike the Non-Brahmin castes, the Brahmins have always had a stated preference for marriage with distant rather than close kin.

The total picture, though extremely complex, suggests that occupational change is not the sole reason for changes in marriage patterns but that rising educational attainment is equally important. This is not surprising when one remembers that occupational change is not easy: Aruloor's economy is still largely agricultural, and salaried jobs in the urban sector remain very elusive. In these circumstances, well-educated young men with landed fathers have to content themselves with remaining farmers.

Muthurajahs comprise 25.8 percent of the 6,176 people in Aruloor village. There are three main areas of Muthurajah residence: Ayyanar Koil Street, Pathukattu Street, and Three Streets (*Munu Teru*). In the Three Streets area, where the wealthiest Muthurajahs live, upward mobility is most striking. The area encompasses about 120 households. A random survey of half of them (60 households) was undertaken in 1990. It showed that the male "head" of household was engaged in a nonagricultural occupation in 30 of them—that is, in 50 percent of the sample. Of these 30 Muthurajah men, 22 were engaged in "new" occupations, requiring higher education or at least fluent literacy and numeracy. They included 11 Secondary School Leaving Certificate (SSLC) school-leavers (who may or may not have passed their final exams), 3 PUC (pre-university course) graduates, 1 university BA graduate, and 7 men whose educational qualifications ranged from the third standard in primary school to the ninth standard in secondary school. The group included 2 carpenters, 1 typesetter, 3 bank clerks, 4 teachers, 1 librarian, 3 policemen, 2 drivers, 1 papermill worker, 1 retired railway clerk, 1 low-ranking village official, 1 village Executive Officer, 1 tailor, and 1 government bill collector. In the ranks of the other 8 men, whose occupations arguably required less education, 4 were small shopkeepers (or kiosk-keepers), 1 flower garland vendor, 1 utensil polisher, 1 low-paid temple servant, and 1 craftsman who made synthetic diamonds (this is a widespread cottage industry around Tiruchi city). Of these 30 men, 18 had married non-kin, and 12 had married kin (8 claimed to have married real cross-kin, and 4 had married classificatory cross-kin).

Significantly, the other 30 Muthurajah men in Three Streets, who had remained in agricultural occupations, showed a similar marriage pattern and fairly similar educational attainment: 15 had married non-kin, and the other 15 had married kin (here, 14 claimed to have married real cross-kin, and 1 had married a classificatory cross-kin). Among these 30 Muthurajah farmers were 1 Bachelor of Commerce university graduate, 1 PUC graduate, and 3 SSLC school-leavers. Out of the total sample of 60 Three Streets men, only 3 were entirely uneducated.

The crucial reason for the similarity between the marriages of Three Streets men engaged in agriculture and those in "modern sector" employment appears to be the comparatively high educational attainment of both groups. In sharp contrast to the largely illiterate, impoverished Muthurajah men living in Ayyanar Koil Street who were engaged in casual agricultural labor, most Three Streets Muthurajah male farmers held land, were considerably wealthier, and were far better educated. In all the 60 Three Streets households, the women had withdrawn entirely from regular agricultural wage-labor, though they remained active in other unpaid roles on the family farm. This is in marked contrast to the agricultural wage-labor in which the Muthurajah women of Ayyanar Koil Street continued to engage. Marriage links had existed between the two areas in the past, but new marriages between residents of Ayyanar Koil Street and of Three Streets had virtually ceased by 1988.

The widespread trend toward non-kin marriage is clearly related to Aruloor's growing urbanization. In the Muthurajah community, this urbanization has manifested itself particularly in the growing differentiation between various sections of this previously endogamous community in male education, male occupation, and male earnings. Most of my poorer Muthurajah informants condemned the new trend as the maximizing strategy of avaricious, "dowry"-seeking parents. But my better-off Muthurajah informants stated that it was only reasonable to seek marriage with those of equal financial status and education rather than with uneducated, impoverished kin. Those whose marriage-age daughters had been rejected by wealthier kin were the most bitter.

Two strongly polarized attitudes emerge: On the one hand, non-kin marriage is seen as "immoral"; on the other, it is seen as "pragmatic" and even as "progressive," embodying "modern urban refinement" (*nagarikam*). The former attitude reveals a poignant nostalgia for a lost golden world in which life centered on the cooperation and solidarity between affines. Whether such an ideal world ever really existed is a moot question: The statistical data suggest that marriage obligations were often ignored even in the past. The crucial point is that cross-kin marriage is perceived as being tied to a moral order in which solidarity and reciprocity between affines are central. All kinship preferences have a strong moral content (Bloch 1971), and so the obvious preference for non-kin espoused so widely in the survey suggests that the new moral order has arrived in Aruloor. This new moral world is focused on the private interests of individual families, and since these private interests may no longer have any place for kin, the old kindred and caste-group loyalties take second place.

The survey of marriage practices in Aruloor also indicates that Dumont is mistaken when he claims that the marriage practices of Dravidians could be read off from their kinship terminology (1953). This is clearly not correct, for as the survey data clearly indicate, though the terminology has not changed, the marriage practices have. This is an important point, which Good has also noted (1978, 1981).

Conclusion

The changing context of rural Non-Brahmin marriage has resulted in a drastic fall in the status of women. This is intimately connected with the simultaneous fall in the status of the matrilateral kin. Thus, the dominance of MB (*Maman*) on the stage of Non-Brahmin kinship is revealed to have been wholly dependent on the high valorization of women in Non-Brahmin culture. This high value was largely due to women's participation in productive work outside the home. When higher education and salaried employment recently became available to young men, these options remained closed to young women. This has meant that at marriage, the traditional bride-price system has been reversed, with the parents of salaried sons now demanding "dowry" from the parents of prospective brides. After marriage, these young women are withdrawn from agricultural labor and thus transformed from agricultural earners into semisecluded housewives. Consequently, they are viewed as economic burdens by both their natal kin and their marital kin.

Their natal kin become far less interested in taking them back now that they cannot go out to work and can make no contribution to the household income. Thus, the married Non-Brahmin woman's easy access to her parental home (a right so envied by Brahmin women) is steadily being withdrawn today among the upwardly mobile groups.

These dramatic changes have, as yet, only marginally affected the poorest strata in the Muthurajah caste and the majority of Pallars, among whom both women and men continue to be involved in daily subsistence wage-labor. This is largely because these groups are too poor to keep their children in school: A good education and the path to salaried employment it offers is entirely outside their reach. Because the income opportunities of men in these poorest classes have not altered, their demands at marriage are not radically different: Traditional bride-price gifts are still given, and today, both sides share the cost of the marriage. But the values of the upper castes and classes constitute a very powerful social influence, so impoverished young men are increasingly emboldened to demand a small "dowry" because it is the "sophisticated" thing to do. So far, I have only heard my Pallar woman friends sneer at such men and pour scorn on their pretensions. But the dominant discourse supports these male demands, and it is possible that "dowry" will soon be paid to such men even by Pallar brides who labor in the fields all day to support their families.

Class has therefore become a crucial factor in rural Non-Brahmin kinship, creating, within each endogamous caste-group, new, primarily economic, divisions between "marriageable" and unmarriageable" kin. As noted in the statistical survey of marriage, marriage to "non-kin" instead of cross-kin is frequently the practice today, even if it is not the stated preference. Kinship obligations and their moral order are being increasingly viewed as obsolete. It is "urban" norms and the new non-kin marriage patterns that are viewed as *"nagarikam"* (sophisticated, civilized behavior). Urban sophistication is not to everyone's liking in Aruloor, though, and there is still widespread condemnation of these norms. Many people see them as merely legitimating greed and economic ambition. But those who protest tend to be those whose daughters have been rejected in favor of brides whose parents could give more "dowry," and the new perception of daughters as a financial liability is rapidly spreading. The final irony is that it is now only the poorest groups in the middle and lower castes who still share the expenses of marriage between affines and still value women in the traditional way. Everyone else is busily "marrying money."

4

Blood Across the Stars: Astrology and the Construction of Gender

What does happiness in marriage depend on? The fertility of the woman of course.
—Gowri (Brahmin astrologer)

I N THEIR IMPORTANT APPRAISAL of theories of menstrual symbolism, Thomas Buckley and Alma Gottlieb note that almost universally in ethnographic reporting, menstrual blood has been "seen always as symbolically dangerous or otherwise defiling" (1988: 4). Ethnographers have repeatedly focused on menstrual taboos and menstrual pollution, and the elaboration of pollution theory (especially in the work of Mary Douglas [1984]) has been the main analytical interest. Buckley and Gottlieb point out that the varying contexts of menstrual symbolism have often been ignored, as has the ambiguity and diversity of much of this symbolism. They rightly conclude that "above all, menstrual taboos are cultural constructions and must be approached as such—symbolic, arbitrary, contextualized, and potentially multivalent—whose meanings emerge only within the contexts of the fields of representations in which they exist" (Buckley and Gottlieb 1988: 24).

As Susan Wadley has correctly said, "The importance of puberty rites in south India can only be appreciated when we recognize their absence in north India. In the north, puberty is not only not celebrated, but is hidden. Yet puberty rites are common throughout south India and among Hindu, Buddhist, and Muslim groups in Sri Lanka" (1980: 163). Accounts that deal with North Indian women either have little or no discussion of menstruation (e.g., Jeffrey 1979; Parry 1979; Sharma 1980, 1986). It is an occasion that is not talked about and that is regarded as fundamentally polluting. I wish to argue here that in Tamilnadu, a very different perception of menstruation exists, particularly among the Non-Brahmin castes who form the vast majority of the population. Among them, menstruation is viewed in a manner that is radically different from that in North India. Further, this Non-Brahmin perception of menstruation is a crucial example of the considerable differences that exist between Brahmins and Non-Brahmins in their symbolic representations of kinship and gender.

As I have pointed out, a central discourse of kinship in Aruloor concerns the fact that children are primarily constituted of their mother's blood: They are said to have more of their mother's blood than their father's blood in them. Further, marriage preference in Aruloor is oriented toward bridegrooms from the matrilateral kin. It is felt that marriage with Mother's Brother or with Mother's Brother's son constitutes the ideal marriage. These discourses suggest that Non-Brahmin kinship in Aruloor is strongly oriented toward the matrilateral kin. This "matrilateralism" of Non-Brahmins in Aruloor is of great significance in explaining their representation of menstruation.

In Aruloor, in both the Hindu and Christian Non-Brahmin castes, the first menstruation of a girl is celebrated in a grand, public manner, with lavish feasting by the entire community and the ceremonial presentation of gifts to the newly pubescent girl. In the expense involved and in the elaborate ritual display, the sequence of puberty ceremonies—especially the final circling rite—rival wedding rites. Indeed, the rites of first menstruation initiate a ritual sequence that ends with marriage, even though marriage may only occur some years later. Good has argued that this is true over a wide area; in fact, many cultural groups across "Dravidian" South India appear to share this pattern of a sequence of elaborate female puberty rites ending in marriage rites (Good 1991). Further, very significantly, puberty rites in Aruloor take the form of a *symbolic marriage,* and this, too, is not unique but is widespread throughout South India (see Good 1991). The fact that puberty rites constitute a symbolic marriage is a crucial clue to their varied purposes.

Of all the castes in Aruloor, only the Brahmins have initiatory rites for boys. An ear-piercing rite is done for all children (Non-Brahmin and Brahmin); it does not constitute a distinctive male rite. Further, in many Non-Brahmin castes, though male children have a horoscope made for them at birth, it is only at first menstruation that a menstruation-horoscope is made for girls. At marriage, this female menstruation-horoscope is matched with a male birth-horoscope to pair eligible women and men. In short, because women have a menstruation-horoscope and not a birth-horoscope, it appears that menstruation is seen as a second birth for young females. At puberty, the mysterious power of creating children is "born" in women, and therefore, this moment is far more significant for a woman and her kin than her moment of birth, which is why women's horoscopes are made at this point and not at birth. Further, there is also the implicit suggestion that Non-Brahmin women are spiritually "reborn" through their puberty initiation rite.

Young Brahmin males are seen as spiritually reborn because they pass through an initiatory rite (the *upanayanam*), thus qualifying them to be viewed as "twice-born"—first physically and then (at the *upanayanam*) spiritually. In a parallel manner, young puberal Non-Brahmin girls are "twice-born," too; the important implication is that the puberty rites re-create them. This has further implications: In Brahminical discourse, women are re-created (in blood and flesh) in the image of their husbands at and through the marriage rites in the "trans-substantiation" (Good 1991: 180). In contrast, the Non-Brahmin puberty rites symbolically re-create women in the image of the divine, and there is no trans-substantiation of their flesh or blood at the time of marriage.

Puberty points to the tremendous importance of a Non-Brahmin woman's sexuality and fertility. Fertility (or the potential fertility marked by menstruation) is essential to the complete identity of a woman. Neither her sexuality nor her gender are complete until she starts menstruating. Thus, in the Non-Brahmin view, young females become gendered women only when they start menstrual bleeding.

Female blood is of great symbolic importance among all the Non-Brahmin castes. It is viewed as the living stream through which kinship and connectedness (*sambandam*) are transmitted. But what the rites of first menstruation reveal is that a "blood-bond" exists not only between the menarchal girl and her wider kin but with the stars as well. This powerful connection, set up between the girl and the destiny-giving planets at menarche, makes it crucial to guard the girl from harm—a harm that, through her, can affect both her natal family and her mother's natal kin.

Probably because the first menstruation of a Tamil girl is believed by Non-Brahmins to be a most momentous event "in which change involves numerous aspects of ... life" (Pugh 1983: 143), it is therefore considered to be influenced by the stars. This is what Judy Pugh's analysis (1983) of North Indian astrology suggests, and this interpretation fits Aruloor understandings well. She says: "The more auspicious or inauspicious the situation and the more numerous the aspects of life which it involves, the more directly and explicitly is the situation considered a manifestation of planetary influences and the workings of destiny" (Pugh 1983: 143). As noted, the astrological dimension of menstruation is made explicit by the Non-Brahmins' choice of menarche as the time to make a girl's horoscope and by the fact that the worship and propitiation of the divine Nine Planets is a central purpose of the grandest puberal rite of all, the Circling. Crucially, Non-Brahmins regard first menstruation as of enormous importance because, unlike the Brahmins, they believe that the girl's "stars" intimately affect her family as well. Conversely, Brahmins believe that the destiny found in a Brahmin girl's menstrual *natcattiram* (star chart) (Brahmins do not call it a "horoscope," for reasons I shall examine) affects her alone. So the Tamil Non-Brahmin family is represented as having great permeability to influences that affect the menarchal girl. In protecting her through the elaborate puberal rites, her family members are, in effect, protecting themselves.

In sharp contrast with Brahmins, Non-Brahmins view female fertility as the primary source of children: It is primarily through women that children are created. This is what gives menstruation its importance. It is the sign that the preeminent female powers of generation have "entered" a young woman.

Menarche, in this understanding, is a happy event and a sacred event. The divine Nine Planets direct it, making it a biospiritual event; that is, it is a biological event that confers positive mystical power on the girl. It is through her body, now linked to the celestial bodies in their orbits around the earth, and through her blood, blood that will nourish and create progeny, that the next generation is born. It is therefore through women's flesh and blood that society is reproduced. Men participate in this reproduction, but it is uterine blood—the blood of menstruation—that is the central symbol of community and the renewal of life. This symbolic understanding of the female body was shared by all four Non-Brahmin castes—Pallars, Chettiars, Christian Paraiyars, and Muthurajahs. Only the Brahmins castes did not share it.

It is, therefore, in the context of this symbolic universe that the Non-Brahmin menarchal rites of Aruloor must be understood and in the context of the profound symbolic significance of uterine blood that the meaning of menstrual "pollution" must be sought. First, menstruation practices cannot be understood independently of Tamil Non-Brahmin discourses of kinship, the female body, and astrology. Within this symbolic domain, pollution emerges as secondary to the main concerns of people, which are with female fertility and the reproduction of the community.

Why is first menstruation, which is regarded as extremely auspicious, also seen as an occasion of great ritual impurity? What exactly does "pollution" imply here? In seeking to answer these questions, we will find that deep differences exist between Non-Brahmin and Brahmin astrological representations of menstruation. In *all* castes, representations of menstrual astrology are complex and ambiguous, but nowhere are they more so than with the Non-Brahmins (Pallars, Muthurajahs, Christian Paraiyars, and Chettiars) for whom menarche is both an occasion of great auspiciousness and mystical power *and* a very "polluting" and potentially dangerous event.

The Chettiars, though typically Non-Brahmin in their marriage preferences and kinship discourses, liked to display Brahminical behavior in their religious rituals. Consequently, they formally claimed a Brahminical stance in matters astrological, but in practice, they were much closer to other Non-Brahmins. They occupied an intermediate position, halfway between the lower-caste Non-Brahmins and the Brahmins: Their intermediacy was nicely epitomized by the fact that "half" of them were said to use the menstrual-horoscope in arranging marriage while the other, more Brahminical "half" did not.

In the following discussion of astrological discourses, because of this division within the Chettiars, I will use the term "Brahminical castes" to mean both the Brahmin castes and the Brahminized section of the Chettiars. By "Non-Brahmin castes," I will mean the Muthurajahs, Pallars, Christian Paraiyars, and the remaining Chettiars who do use the menstruation-horoscope. Upper-class castes tend to appropriate Brahminic lifestyles because these give higher social status. Their vegetarianism is a clear sign that the Chettiars aspire to Brahmin-type behavior, so is their prohibition of divorce and of widow-remarriage. None of these norms are typical of the average Non-Brahmin caste in Aruloor: They are not shared by the Muthurajahs, Pallars, or Christian Paraiyars. For this reason, it is in the lower-class castes that we find more "typical" Non-Brahmin ideas and practices, and it is the practices of the lower castes that we find more "prototypical" Non-Brahmin norms, though there are no watertight normative compartments between groups.

In the Brahminical castes, a woman's *birth*-horoscope is used to arrange her marriage. In the Non-Brahminical castes, it is her *menstrual*-horoscope that is used. In both cases, the horoscope may show inauspicious signs with regard to her marriage. This inauspiciousness, which presages problems in her prospective marriage, is identified through *dosham* (astrological flaws or dangers) that are detected by the astrologer who makes the star-chart either at birth or at first menstruation. This star-chart was called *"natcattiram"* ("star," "constellation") by the upper castes and both *"natcattiram"* and *"caturam"* ("square") by the lower castes: Chris Fuller's informants call it *"cakkaram"* ("circle") (1980b: 56, 58). Importantly, in the Non-Brahmin castes, men are liable to have astrological dangers (*dosham*) in their horoscopes as often as women; thus, men are represented as transmitters of astral evil, too. But in Brahminical astrology, it is women's horoscopes that are afflicted by far more *dosham* than men's horoscopes. In short, in Brahminical representations, it is primarily women who transmit astrological danger. However, all the castes, though in differing degree, view menarchal women as both vulnerable to danger from "bad stars" (*ketta girakangal*) and as potential transmitters of such danger to others. In the Brahminical castes, those significant others who can be endangered are solely the young woman's future affines: her future husband and her future father-in-law (and, to lesser degree, her future mother-in-law). In the Non-Brahmin castes, however, the range of affected kin is much wider. It includes her parents, her siblings, her Mother's Brothers and their families, *and* her future husband and parents-in-law. Given local preferences in cross-kin marriage, it is a MB's family that is likely to provide the woman's future in-laws. Therefore, there is virtually an overdetermination of the fact that the fortunes of Mother's Brother show up prominently in his ZD's menstrual-horoscope.

All the castes depict menarchal women as being potentially dangerous to men, but this is particularly true of the Brahminical castes. Perhaps because astrology is primarily a Brahminic science in which Brahmins themselves have the greatest interest, Brahmins' normative tendency to represent women as subordinate to men is strongly emphasized in astrological discourse. This explicit gender hierarchization is most vividly apparent in the astrological rules (*poruttam*) for matching marriage-horoscopes.

Astrology and Cultural Contestation

Two very different views of menstruation interact in Aruloor, making astrological representations a prime example of cultural contestation between the Non-Brahmin and the Brahminical castes. On the one hand, there is the orthodox Brahminic scriptural view of menstruation as wholly polluting: In this paradigm, it is because of their menstruation that women constitute an inferior species (*jadi*: caste, species). Menstruation makes them polluted (men are clean), inferior to men, and more sinful than men. Every Brahmin woman hopes to perform the elaborate and expensive Rishi Pancami rituals when she is past her menopause—rituals that are very explicitly said to remove what is represented as the sin of menstruation from them. Further, from first menstruation onward, Brahmin women in Aruloor are strictly excluded from the house and treated remarkably like "untouchables" are for the ritually prescribed duration of their seclusion.

Non-Brahmin representations of menstruation are markedly different. Non-Brahmin menstruation is the most important event in a woman's life and is given elaborate rituals to *celebrate* it. Further, menstrual blood is seen as a form of the uterine blood that is central to the symbolic discourse of Non-Brahmin kinship. After first menstruation, Non-Brahmin women are not subject to menstrual exclusion, unlike Brahmin women (see Good 1991: 130). In Aruloor, only the Chettiars practice menstrual seclusion *within* the house, and they treat this in a far more relaxed manner than the Brahmins do.

For this reason, when menarchal practice and the discourse are defined by Non-Brahmins, it is the auspiciousness and mystical generative powers of the young woman that are stressed. In Brahmin representations, conversely, her impurity and dangerousness are stressed. It is important to recognize that there is no absolute cultural dichotomy here. Rather, there are clear differences in *emphasis* along a continuum.

The Non-Brahmin understanding of femaleness is far more positive than that of the Brahmins. Significantly, it is in these Non-Brahmin castes that in other contexts, too, discourses of impurity are very weak, particularly in relation of female gender and caste identity.

Astrology as a science is primarily an esoteric, upper-caste interest: Its complexities and subtleties mirror this. Consequently, in the lower castes, even what counts as "astrological" is very different. Upper-caste astrology is adapted and radically redefined so that the astrological domain is both widened and concretized to include supernatural and physical phenomena of various kinds. For example, central importance is given by the lower castes to what they call the "Cobra Flaw" (*Naga Dosham*) in a menstrual-horoscope. This important lower-caste astrological danger does not even exist in the astrology of either Brahmins or Chettiars. What is most significant about the lower-caste mode of detecting astrological dangers is that these dangers are viewed as being due to physical proximity or to bodily manifestation. In these ways, upper-caste astrology is transformed and literally *embodied* in lower-caste astrological discourses in order to make it fit with lower-caste values and priorities. Of these astrological reconstructions and embodiments, none is more striking than the way the Non-Brahmin lower castes have embodied destiny within the female body in the menstruation-horoscope. They have rejected the female birth-horoscope of the Brahminical castes in order to give pride of place to the event of menstruation.

The Menstruation-Horoscope

Fertility and Identity

When a Non-Brahmin girl reaches puberty, she is described as having "come of age" (*"vayasukku vandadu"*). She is now considered to be ready for marriage, even if she is only fourteen or fifteen. Informants stressed that it was the girl's availability as a bride that was advertised through the major puberty celebration, the Circling (*Suttaradu*), that followed her period of incarceration and her ritual purification (the *punniya danam*).

Female fertility is seen as the key to the greatest joy in life, the joy of having children. (In the upper castes, the wish is especially for male children who will be heirs.) In all castes, *male* fertility is taken for granted: It is almost never admitted that a man can be impotent. So, if a couple have no children, it is universally assumed that it is the woman's "fault." Moreover, all castes see childlessness as a perfectly legitimate reason for a man to take a second wife. However, even if her husband's impotence is known, a woman is never allowed a second husband. At best, in a lower caste, she may be able to divorce him and remarry. If a second wife is also childless, she, too, might be regarded as "at fault." Only if a third wife is childless do people admit that the husband might be impotent. So male impotence is not a concern. *Female* fertility, on the other hand, is regarded as dicey, unpredictable, and subject to dangerous astrological influences. This difference, I suggest, is not primarily due to a macho assumption that males are always sexually potent but rather to the far greater symbolic importance that is given to female fertility.

Pubescent female fertility is understood as being controlled by powerful astrological influences. This is predominantly because in the everyday cosmology of ordinary people, *all* of human life is believed to be controlled by the stars. Astrology occupies a position of paramount importance in the cosmology of all castes in Aruloor. Pugh's following observation therefore closely fits Aruloor thought: "Hindus believe that the heavenly bodies—the planets (*girakangal*), constellations (*rasi*), and asterisms (*natcattirangal*)—have a natural influence on the earth and on the person. ... Hindus consider the planets to be deities who influence earthly life and who may be worshipped and propitiated" (1983: 134).

Although the young woman's parents and Mother's Brothers decide which eligible young man is to benefit from her fertility through marriage, whether she has a successful reproductive capacity at all is determined by the stars. It is well known that horoscopes based on the time and date of birth are often used to match potential spouses in India. However, the existence of menstrual-horoscopes in India has apparently not been recorded in the anthropological literature so far. My research shows that many Tamil Non-Brahmin castes in Aruloor use horoscopes based on the time and date on which a girl starts menstruating as the only female horoscopes for marriage. Remarkably, this fact was not noted earlier for Tamil South India. For instance, there is no mention of menstrual-horoscopes in Gabriella Eichinger Ferro-Luzzi's 1974 study of Tamil women's menstrual cycles. The menstruation-horoscope has been reported only for Sri Lanka, in brief references by Yalman (1963), a fleeting reference to Yalman in Edmund Leach (1970), and a brief discussion in Deborah Winslow (1980).

Discussing the Kandyan Sinhalese female puberty-horoscope, Yalman points out that the menstrual-horoscope indicates "a new life" but describes it as superseding the birth-horoscope of the woman (1963: 29). This is not true of Aruloor, where no proper birth-horoscope is made for Non-Brahmin women (except for Brahminized Chettiar women). Further, when Yalman observes that the menstrual-horoscope is based on "the exact time" when the bleeding started (1963: 29), he fails to note the fact that this "exact time" can virtually never be established; it is actually only a guess that is simply assumed to be correct. Thus, this procedure is very different from that done at childbirth, when the exact moment of birth can be far more accurately established. Interestingly, Yalman makes no mention at all of astrological flaws in the menstrual-horoscope. This is remarkable because *dosham*, being a major cause of misfortune, are a central concern in Non-Brahmin menstrual-horoscopes. Their presence and their removal are potential worries, and many horoscopes appear to have *dosham*. Concern with horoscope-flaws is, as we will see, as much tied to the safety of the Non-Brahmin girl's *family* as it is to her protection. Yalman also states that the period of menstrual seclusion varies and depends on the horoscope (1963: 30). This is not true in Aruloor, where each caste has a fixed period of ritual seclusion. Winslow discounts Yalman's data on menstrual-horoscopes because her Sinhalese informants rejected the notion that the menstruation-horoscope could be primary for a woman: The female birth-horoscope remained more important among her informants and was used for marriage (1980: 622–623).

Menstrual-horoscopes are consulted to arrange marriage among all Muthurajahs, Pallars, Christian Paraiyars, and Non-Brahminical Chettiars, as well as several other castes in Aruloor. They appear to be widely used in surrounding villages as well (where Aruloor's castes have their kin), and wider inquiry in Tiruchi city showed that menstrual-horoscopes were used there, too. Menstruation is seen as preeminently important in a woman's life, and, as noted, a young woman who has not yet started menstruating is regarded as incompletely gendered. A Brahminical view was offered by Gowri, a local Brahmin woman astrologer with much experience with female Non-Brahmin clients: "What does happiness in marriage depend on? The fertility of the woman, of course. If there are no children, is there happiness? No, not for the woman, because her husband will take a second wife. Her life is destroyed. So—*everything* depends on her being fertile. That's why the menstruation horoscope [*vayasukku vanda jadakam*] is so important." This is a Brahminical view because a lower-caste Non-Brahmin woman can (at least in theory) divorce and remarry, thereby avoiding the misery of being an ignored co-wife.

The Non-Brahmin view is that the event of menstruation is the new birth or rebirth of a girl as an empowered, auspicious woman: In Leach's comment on the Sinhalese rites, "The girl is treated as 'reborn' from the moment of onset of her menstruation" (1970: 82). It is her newfound sexual maturity and fertility that, in Non-Brahmin eyes, make her a full person. Thus, menarche is, in a sense, a pseudo-birth, for it is represented as of greater importance to the girl's identity than her actual birth. This also connects with the great symbolic importance accorded to uterine blood—here, menstrual blood—in Non-Brahmin discourses.

However, though the symbolic identity a Non-Brahmin woman acquires at puberty is discursively represented as far more significant than male identity at puberty, this discourse remains ambivalent because male identity does not depend on evidence of sexual potency. An impotent man is still fully designated a man. Men are *automatically gendered*: Their gender is given, assumed. But women who have not menstruated are *less* than women: They remain incompletely gendered. Thus, female gender has to be achieved. Brahmins traditionally conferred wifely status on little Brahmin girls when they were married as children, several years before they reached puberty. But even with them, a child-wife who failed to menstruate was not sent to join her husband, and therefore, she failed to achieve full womanhood.

Without exception, all the five major caste-groups of Aruloor subscribe to the use of some form of the menstrual-horoscope. Future research in Tamilnadu will show how widespread the menstruation-horoscope is; my casual inquiries in Madras, Tiruchi, and Madurai established that menstrual-horoscopes were traditionally used in several castes in these far-flung cities.

The Process of Making the Menstrual-Horoscope

As soon as a girl's first bleeding is detected, the clotting of the blood is studied by older women to determine when the bleeding started. The computed time is only a rough guess, but it is assumed to be correct. The horoscope that the astrologer computes as a result is accepted as authoritative, unless it forebodes an evil future. In that case, some "adjustment" in the horoscope is usually sought, but there is a limit to such adjustments because the twenty-seven *natcattirangal* (lunar asterisms) of the astrological calendar correspond to the lunar month of thirty days (see Fuller 1980b). Thus, there are one and one-ninth days to each asterism (or lunar constellation). This rough correspondence of one day to one asterism means that if the day on which the first menstruation started is publicly known, the lunar constellation that corresponds to it cannot be easily changed if it is unpropitious. However, if the girl started bleeding during the night, then a choice between two asterisms may be available.

The astrologer (*josiar*) computes the horoscope by first determining these asterisms. "*Natcattiram*" literally means "star" or "lunar constellation," but, in practice, it refers to the entire astrological conjunction that influences a horoscope at a particular time. There are one and one-ninth days or twenty-six hours and twenty minutes during which asterism prevails. It is this prevailing lunar constellation that is believed to have a determining influence on a person's future. Menstrual-horoscopes and birth-horoscopes are computed in exactly the same way. So, to know the lunar constellation that was ascendant when a person was born or when she began to menstruate is to know the crucial factor in her horoscope.

It is important to remember that birth asterisms and birth menstrual asterisms are computed in the same way. The central difference between the castes are the *uses* to which they are put. In Aruloor, when a birth asterism is used *to arrange marriage,* it is termed a "*jadakam*" (horoscope). When it is not used for marriage but is only briefly consulted (at birth) and thereafter disregarded, it is merely termed "*natcattiram*" (lunar asterism).

Brahmins and Chettiars do ask the astrologer to compute a menstrual asterism for their daughters at puberty, but because they do not use it to determine marriage compatibility, they do not call it a menstrual-horoscope. They therefore stated to me that they did not use menstrual-horoscopes but readily admitted that they did check a girl's menstrual asterism for inauspicious influences. Similarly, the wealthier lower castes often check the birth asterism of a female infant, but since they do not use it for marriage, they state that they do not use female birth-horoscopes. Thus, among *all* the Hindu castes studied in Aruloor, all those who could *afford* it checked for astrological influences both at birth and at menstruation and acted upon these star-charts. But only the Non-Brahmin Tamil castes used the menstrual star-charts as horoscopes to determine marriage. The terminological difference between the Brahmins and the Non-Brahmin Tamils is an important pointer to significantly different astrological ideas. The fact that Telugu and Tamil

Brahmins never used menstrual star-charts for the purpose of determining marriage may derive from the historical fact that these Brahmin castes traditionally married off their daughters in child-marriage long before they reached puberty, unlike the Non-Brahmin Tamil castes who traditionally did so only after puberty.

The primary use of the menstrual-horoscope within the lower castes is at marriage. It is of utmost importance then, when it is matched to a male birth-horoscope to find a suitable husband. However, the menstrual-horoscope is of crucial importance to the girl's entire family and her mother's natal kin from the moment she starts bleeding because her stars are believed to have a powerful effect on their fortunes. This is a fundamental difference between Brahmin and Non-Brahmin astrology: With Brahmins, a girl's menstrual asterism affects *her alone,* but with Non-Brahmins, her menstrual-horoscope affects *all her family* as well. To understand why this is so, we must understand what the birth of a child signifies in Non-Brahmin culture.

The Portents of a Horoscope

Class is very relevant here. Better-off families of *any* caste generally have a child's birth-horoscope made. Proper horoscopes are seen as particularly important in the wealthy upper castes, and thus, they confer social status. The very poor (this includes most Pallars and many Muthurajahs) never have elaborate horoscopes of any kind made. They go to cheaper astrologers, often belonging to the low Valluvar caste, and use a much cheaper astrological system called "matching of names" (*peru poruttam*) to arrange marriage. The following discussion therefore concerns only the socially aspiring and slightly better-off members of the lower castes who do have horoscopes made.

Because these upwardly mobile groups seek to appropriate Brahminical norms, the tenor of their astrological discourses is distinctly Brahminical. As we will see, these discourses reveal a far more negative view of women than the discourses of the puberty rites. This is because astrology, even when reframed in lower-caste contexts, remains strongly influenced by its Brahminic origins. The opposite is true of the menarchal ceremonies: They are quintessentially Non-Brahminical, and they are most elaborated in the practices of the lower Tamil castes. Only there, in the discourses of these rites, does a strongly positive tenor emerge, celebrating the Non-Brahmin view of women as the source of that greatest wealth, children.

Here, I will focus on aspiring and upwardly mobile classes of Non-Brahmins and examine what the birth of a child means to them. Above all, the birth of a child *portends.* The child spells the future destiny of the family it is born into because the moment of its birth is meaningful, imbued with good or evil portents. This applies to both female and male children, but there was a marked tendency for informants of all castes to take the reigning stars at the birth of a male child more seriously than those of a female child. Opinions differed, but the majority seemed to agree that since a girl was only "a temporary thing" in her parent's house, the portents of her birth would not weigh so seriously on the family's future; "after all," they said, "she will move away to her husband's house and the good or bad luck that she brings will go with her to his house."

The fact that this upper-caste orientation is also implicitly upper-class becomes quite explicit in discussions of male horoscopes. The portents at a male birth, many felt, had to be taken more seriously "because the sons will always remain with their parents—and the parents will have to depend on these sons in their old age. So their fortunes are inextricably knit—they will always be in the same house." This is a very upper-class view, for only wealthy families can afford to live together in joint families. Most Chettiars and Brahmins did, but very few Muthurajahs could afford to do so. Impoverished Muthurajahs and most Pallars lived in nuclear households, and elderly parents had to fend for themselves. The stars thus take due note of household residential patterns: Better-off parents treat their sons' horoscopes as more significant because they will continue to live with and eventually depend on these sons. Yet with all these castes, the stars of the daughter were also regarded with anxiety, for "bad stars" (*ketta girakangal*) in her star-chart could cause misfortune to her family. Such bad outcomes were avoided through appropriate prayers and ritual offerings made to pacify the Nine Planets.

The Non-Brahmin castes stated that the menstrual-horoscope of a girl gave information about the health and job prospects of *all* her family, but the Brahminical castes rejected this view, stating that it gave information solely regarding the future of the girl (particularly relating to her marriage). All castes agreed, however, that the birth-horoscope of a son gave more information about the family than did a daughter's menstrual-horoscope.

Horoscopes and the Patterns of Male Control

The fact that horoscopes are essentially an upper-caste creation is revealed in the manner in which various horoscopes become successively important in a woman's life, reflecting the chronological pattern of male control of upper-caste women. The following account would be generally agreed upon by both upwardly mobile Non-Brahmins and the well-off Brahminical castes, though the individual caste may well differ in certain specific details from the system described.

When a child is born, better-off families usually check with an astrologer to confirm that it was born at a "good time" (*nalla neram*), even if a full-fledged horoscope (a birth-horoscope) is not completed for the child. The Chettiars and Brahmins had birth-horoscopes made for both male and female children. The poorer Pallars, Muthurajahs, and Christian Paraiyars, however, often never bothered to get the horoscopes of even male babies cast. Instead, they simply gave the time and date of birth of the child, female or male, to an astrologer and merely inquired if it was *"nalla neram"* (good or auspicious time). This was done to save expense. But even the quick check of "good time," at a cheap rate of maybe a rupee or less (depending on the standing of the astrologer), was not always done. As one Pallar man put it, "If you're not having any trouble, why go to the expense and bother? Only people who are suffering from *ketta neram* [bad, inauspicious time, implying continual bad luck] consult the astrologer about a birth! We didn't." An upwardly mobile Muthurajah man, however, rejected this view, saying, "How do you know whether the child will bring you bad luck or not? It's better to know beforehand. Most people check it out, as a matter of course."

That is, even the large majority of Non-Brahmin castes who consult only the menstrual-horoscope of the girl at marriage, do check that her birth is auspicious if they can afford it. Several people spoke of the good fortune brought by a daughter. In a Muthurajah account, the father, unemployed for some ten years, was immediately given a long-sought job as a government high school teacher on the birth of his baby girl; his family claimed that they had prospered ever since her birth. Interestingly, despite the Brahmin claim that a daughter's horoscope never affected her family, a Tamil Brahmin woman whom I knew well described how her mother had brought great good luck to *her* parents (my friend's grandparents) and how this luck had "transferred" to my friend's family when her mother had married her father. Moreover, her mother's natal family's fortunes had declined very sharply as soon as she left her parents' house. This suggests that despite their claims to the contrary, Tamil Brahmins are not unsympathetic to the Tamil Non-Brahmin belief that a woman's family members, both natal and marital, are permeable to influences in her horoscope.

When a female child reaches sexual maturity and begins menstruating, her "menses-*jadakam*" (to use the part-English term that educated Non-Brahmins used) is quickly computed by the astrologer because her parents desire to marry her off as soon as possible. Pallar and Muthurajah women who were between thirty and forty in 1988 had usually been married within one or two years of reaching puberty. Today, however, this time period, within the same castes, is a bit longer: Girls now typically marry three to four years after puberty. The reasons for this significant delay are primarily the greater demands made by the parents of eligible men and the decline in cross-kin marriage. In any case, today, as earlier, this means that the "menses-*jadakam*" must be ready within a couple of months of first menstruation because inquiries start coming in from the parents of prospective grooms. This, as noted, is significantly different from Brahmin practice. In traditional Brahmin marriage, the parents of a woman have to go in search of a husband for her. Traditional Non-Brahmin marriage is arranged in exactly the opposite way: The parents of the man have to find a bride for him.

In the upper castes and the socially aspiring castes, a startling change with regard to a woman's "astrological" life occurs at marriage. After marriage, a woman effectively ceases to possess a horoscope (either birth or menstrual) at all, because thereafter, her future is "read" by consulting the birth-horoscope of her husband. This is vital, for it implies, among other things, that she thereafter has no separate destiny. This suggests that the woman's identity is inseparable from that of her husband, with the further implication that she has no access to divorce. And this is, indeed, the case, for in these castes, which are largely sympathetic to Brahmini-cal mores, one of the first acts of upward mobility is to withdraw from women the right to divorce and remarriage. Thus, there is, in all the castes, a close correlation between their social practices and their astrological discourses, though contradictions between their own theory and practice may also exist.

With the birth of a first child, even the horoscope of a woman's husband falls into abeyance. It is no longer consulted if the child is male because this son's horoscope is thereafter consulted for all the affairs of the family. If the child is female, the father's horoscope usually does continue to be consulted, but, very significantly, several Pallar women claimed that a daughter's horoscope could replace the father's and serve as the family horoscope if the daughter was a first child. This remained a minority opinion even among the Pallar, but it offers striking evidence of the importance of women among the poor lower castes. It also reflects the strategic importance of Pallar women, who, unlike women in the wealthier castes, are often major breadwinners for their families.

The Non-Brahmin castes agreed that it was either the horoscope of the eldest or the youngest son that was most important. But striking caste- and class-based differences emerged here. The Muthurajahs and Pallars claimed that it was the horoscope of the *youngest* son that was most important, but the Chettiars gave greatest importance to the *eldest* son's horoscope. This connects with economic class. The former castes tend to be very poor, so there is little for sons to inherit. Therefore, at marriage, among the Pallars and Muthurajahs, sons move out to set up separate households. Consequently, parents in these castes usually end up living with and depending on the youngest son, who inherits the parental home. The wealthy Chettiars, however, own large estates. A wealthy Chettiar household, unlike the impoverished, nuclear lower-caste household, usually remains a joint-family household until the father's death. At this point, the eldest son, who has normally already taken over as effective family head, divides the family property and traditionally inherits more than his younger brothers, even though, in theory, the division of property is equal. The eldest son's responsibility toward his parents is seen as greatest.

Among Non-Brahmins, a child's horoscope affects his Mother's Brothers and their families as well. So the fortunes of the Mother's Brother are very prominent in his sister's son's horoscope. Pallar and Muthurajah informants claimed that a male child's horoscope would say even more about his *Maman*'s (Mother's Brother's) family than about his own. This recalls the Non-Brahmin view that a child is "closer in blood" to Mother's Brother than Father's Brother. Informants explained MB's prominence in the horoscope as deriving from his gift-giving: "The *Maman* plays a very important part in the life of his sister's children—indeed, sometimes it is almost as important as their father's role, because on all important occasions it is he who bears the expenses and gives the gifts. Further, if the child's family is in financial trouble, they turn to *Maman*. That's why a son's horoscope says a lot about *Maman*—because in many areas, including marriage, his future depends on his *maman*'s goodwill." Palani Chettiar himself confirmed that this was true for the Chettiar caste, telling us sadly and shamefacedly that his horoscope, as eldest son, had been very inauspicious for his eldest *maman*. It had caused great misfortune to his eldest MB's family, which had suffered several deaths. Daniel, too, notes the importance of a boy's horoscope for the fortunes of his *maman* (1984).

Whether it is the horoscope of the eldest or youngest son that replaces that of a father, what is striking is that in the better-off Non-Brahmin castes, a woman's destiny after marriage, writ in the stars, is first read from her husband's horoscope and thereafter from her son's. This reflects the pattern in which control of a woman's life, in these wealthier classes, passes first from her father (whose horoscope ruled her youth) to her husband and finally, after the death of her husband, to her son, whose horoscope "rules" her life from the day he is born. In all this, the woman's own menstrual-horoscope is of only temporary importance, despite its great significance to a large number of her kin.

Astrological Problems in a Horoscope

Flaws and Faults (*Dosham*)

An examination of the "problems" that might arise in a menstrual-horoscope suggests that astrological discourses have a decidedly negative tenor, for there is great concern that there might be astrological *"dosham"* (faults or flaws) in a girl's horoscope. These *dosham* bode an inauspicious future. Though many menstrual-horoscopes do appear to have *dosham* in them, most of these flaws are simple enough to be easily removed through rituals conducted on the advice of the astrologer. Some, however, pose major obstacles to the marriage of the girl.

"Problems" in a horoscope are also called *"dosham."* This multivalent word (meaning fault, flaw, danger, sin) is generally understood, in the Tamil astrological context, to connote dangers in a horoscope. If not removed through specific rituals prescribed by an astrologer, "flaws" in a person's horoscope cause that person grave misfortune. In a girl's menstrual-horoscope, *dosham* are astrological factors that affect her marriage prospects and her fertility, directly or indirectly, and that cause misfortune to others "through" her. The central concern here is with the *vulnerability of the girl,* who has to be protected from bad or inauspicious influences. But there is also great concern with protecting the family of the girl, who (except among the Brahmins) are viewed as also being very vulnerable to dangers from her *dosham*. Apart from *dosham,* there is also concern that a puberal girl might be at risk from the evil eye (*dirushti*) and from evil ghosts (*pey-pisasu*). But these dangers are dealt with particularly at the circling rite (the *sutti*), which is the most important puberty rite and occurs some time after her purification rite. These rites are discussed in the next chapter.

Some *dosham* are deducible from the menstrual-horoscope; others manifest themselves in other ways. Those "in the horoscope" are diagnosed by the astrologer; it is he who tells the girl's parents if she has *Mula Natcattiram* or *Sevvay Dosham* in her horoscope.

Mula Natcattiram and *Sevvay Dosham*

These are two of the most feared "flaws" that can be found in a horoscope. The various castes had very different understandings about their significance in a menstrual-horoscope. Interpretations varied widely, making it clear that in its astrology, each caste constructed itself differently.

Mula Natcattiram (*Mula* **Constellation**). Muthurajah and Pallar understandings were quite close. Both castes claimed that if a bride had *Mula Natcattiram* in her horoscope, either her father-in-law or her mother-in-law or both would die within thirty days of her marriage, given the malign power of this lunar constellation. The only way to avoid this was for the bride to be married to a groom with only one living parent. This nullified the dangerous influence of the asterism.

Muthurajah and Pallar informants claimed that men, too, could have *Mula Natcattiram* in their birth-horoscopes, with the same dire results on their affines' lives. But Chettiars and Brahmins scoffed at this suggestion (when they heard of it through me), stating emphatically that this particular *dosham* could be found only in female horoscopes—it did not exist in male horoscopes. This significant difference between lower and upper castes appears to connect with the fact that lower-caste women enjoy a more equal status with men. And as always, in practice, the Chettiar woman friend described to me how both her parents had suddenly died after the marriage of her younger sister: "Her husband must certainly have had *Mula Natcattiram*!" she concluded.

Sevvay Dosham (**Mars Flaw**). Sevvay (meaning "Red") is Mars, the red planet; it is a deity, one of the sacred Nine Planets. *Sevvay Dosham* is, in lower-caste usage, also referred to as *Sevvay Natcattiram*. This is apparently on the analogy of most other *dosham* being due a particular *natcattiram* (constellation), though Mars has nothing to do with the twenty-seven asterisms (see Pugh 1983 and Fuller 1980b for detailed discussions of the planets and asterisms).

This *dosham* is dreaded because if it appears in a girl's menstrual-horoscope, it means that the bridegroom will die immediately after the marriage. Here, Chettiars agree with Muthurajahs and Pallars on both the effect and the cure for the *dosham*. It can be averted only if both bride and groom have *Sevvay Dosham* in their horoscopes. Similarly, if the bridegroom has *Sevvay Dosham* and the bride does not, she will die immediately after the marriage. So the parents of a child with *Sevvay Dosham* have to hunt high and low for a potential spouse with the same *dosham*. Krishnan Chettiar (of the low-ranking Pathmasaliyar weaver caste) had a son whose horoscope was "afflicted" with it. He had to go to far-away Kullithalai to find his son a bride who also had *Sevvay Dosham*.

Ayilya Natcattiram. Chettiars and the Brahmins added a third *dosham*— *Ayilya Natcattiram*. This *dosham* was entirely unknown to the Pallars, who said they had never even heard of it. *Ayilya Natcattiram* was similar to *Mula Natcattiram,* endangering the lives of parents-in-law. The difference was that this upper-caste asterism particularly threatened the father-in-law and that it had a malign effect solely when it appeared in female horoscopes. Even more remarkably, if a male horoscope had *Ayilya Natcattiram,* it had a benign influence. In this way, the Brahminical astrology of the upper castes represented affinal women as a source of danger from which harm could come to the husband and the father-in-law.

A central difference therefore emerges between Brahminical and Non-Brahmin discourses. In the former, it is primarily women's horoscopes that can transmit misfortune, but with the Non-Brahmins, the horoscopes of both men and women are equally liable to be afflicted with *dosham*.

Bad Planets

Dosham are specific dangers arising from "bad planets" (*ketta girakangal*), which cause an inauspicious future. Apart from recommending specific rituals to remove specific *dosham,* the astrologer is likely to advise the precaution of worship of the Nine Planets to ensure that "flaws" that have slipped his notice are guarded against. Otherwise, a delay in the marriage of the girl is possible. This would be considered a great misfortune by both the girl and her parents, for it is generally agreed that a girl should be married very soon after puberty.

Propitiatory worship of the Nine Planets consists in making ritual offerings at their shrine in Aruloor's ancient Siva Temple. These offerings are made by the girl to "pacify" the "angry" *girakangal* (planets). (The reason for their anger may or may not be known.) Such a pacificatory offering is called a *santi parikaram* (*santi*: peace; *parikaram*: circling). A typical ritual of *santi parikaram* consists of the pubescent girl offering sesame oil and lighting a small oil-lamp at the shrine of the Nine Planets for forty consecutive days. Forty days is the duration of major periods of purification, including that following childbirth. Another ritual is for the girl to offer "lime-lights." She squeezes a half lime, turns it inside out, and uses it as a lamp, filled with sesame oil. She cuts and lights one for the goddess Durga (Kali) every Tuesday, and she must do this during a period of "inauspicious time" (*iragu kalam*) on seven or nine successive Tuesdays. Durga is the Sanskritic great goddess Parvathi (Siva's wife) in her incarnation as "terrible" goddess. In this aspect or embodiment, she is associated with "uncontrolled" and malign powers. For this reason, an "inauspicious" time is proper for her. Both these rituals are Brahminic in inspiration.

Brahmins and the Menstrual *Natcattiram*

All the Brahmins I talked to said that they did not use menstrual-horoscopes. They would say: "No, we don't use coming-of-age horoscopes [*vayasukku vanda jadakam*] at all—only the *Sudra* do!" *Sudra,* meaning "servant caste," was their derogatory term for the Non-Brahmin castes. As a result of this unambiguous reply, I did not pursue the issue. But then, one day, describing her own puberty, Revathipati, my friend Uma's grandmother (MM), mentioned that the time and date of the onset of menstruation were always noted by Brahmins and that the star-chart based on them was always computed by the astrologer. This menstrual *natcattiram,* giving the lunar constellation in dominance at the time, was, in essence, a horoscope. Since it was used to determine whether menstruation had caused bad astrological influences to affect the girl, it was clear that Brahmins, too, used a menstrual star-chart. This surprised me because of their earlier claims, but now I learned that they did not use the term *"jadakam"* (horoscope) for this star-chart but only the term *"natcattiram"* (constellation) because in all the castes, *"jadakam"* was used solely to denote a star-chart used to arrange marriage.

Revathipati was in her seventies. She said that she had not been sent to her husband's house on reaching puberty because the astrologer had found bad planets (*ketta girakangal*) in her menstrual-*natcattiram*. These inauspicious stars had been so powerful that even after the *santi parikaram* (propitiatory worship) of the Nine Planets had been done, their influence would have caused her young husband's death. The astrologer therefore advised her parents not to send her to her husband but to keep her away from him for three more years. In the context of child-marriage, then universal among the Brahmins, this had been very embarrassing. She had been married to her child-husband when she was only nine years old and then, as usual, kept at her parental home for several more years to await the onset of puberty. At this time, she would normally have been immediately sent to start living with her husband.

Two sisters in a Brahmin family I knew well reached menarche during the one and a half years I spent in Aruloor. Rituals celebrating their "coming of age" were performed very privately at home (see Chapter 5). A Brahmin astrologer residing near the major Saivite temple of Tiruvanaikovil in Srirangam was asked to make their star-charts. The menstruation-*natcattiram* of both girls were found to be "good," that is, auspicious. Neither of them had any *dosham* that needed to be removed.

Naga Dosham

Nagappa and Nagamma: The Cobra Deities

Naga Dosham is the most common major *dosham* reported by Pallars and Muthurajahs. Both Brahmins and Chettiars said, "We don't have *Naga Dosham*— we don't know about such things. Only the lower castes have them!" *Nagam* means "snake." In this context, it primarily refers to the Cobra-God Nagappa, who is the king of snakes. But it can also include the Cobra-Goddess Nagamma. The central iconic representation of Nagappa is actually a representation of both Nagappa and Nagamma engaged in serpentine copulation. A carved pillar shows two cobras intertwined in a long, sinuous embrace. Normally represented as a composite icon depicting sexual union, the symbolic significance of the Cobra deity is better understood as normally constituted by both Nagappa and Nagamma—that is, both male and female and as possessing a joint identity.

It is extremely interesting that in Tamil South India, this *jointly gendered* icon is one of the most important symbols of human procreation and fertility. It is important to not that the *two* genders, equally represented (the serpents are identical), are both necessary to this important symbol of sexual fruition. This is noteworthy because in certain contexts, the solitary male cobra, standing erect with its hood swollen, is understood as a phallic fertility symbol. It is particularly associated with the Sanskritic great god Siva, who is himself represented in temples by the preeminently male *lingam* (his phallus). This *lingam* is depicted by a small stone pillar standing within an oval line that represents the *yoni* (a symbolic vagina). This symbolic vagina (representing Parvathi, the female principle) is merely etched or ridged on the ground and is therefore far less prominent than the *lingam*. It is thus explicitly represented as secondary: It is Siva's *lingam* that is the focus of worship.

However, with the *doubly gendered* icon of Nagappa-Nagamma, the Cobra deities who symbolize fertility, we move away from the male-dominated world of Brahminic religion to the world of Non-Brahmin popular religion, in which the chief deities are either *female* or of dual gender. Here, male deities are demoted to the position of the goddess's watchmen or guards. The sole male deity to win popular favor is Murugan (Skandha), whose childlike and "female" qualities are a large part of his charm.

Nagappa-Nagamma are seen as bestowers of fertility. Tamil women who believe themselves to be infertile pray to them in their sexual embrace, hoping to conceive. A small shrine to this composite Cobra deity stands under a sacred *arasumaram* (*ficus religiosa* tree) in every village. Next to it, there is always a small shrine to Pillaiyar (Ganesa/Vinayak), the divine Remover of Obstacles. "Infertile" women circle the sacred tree and its sacred images and pray before both shrines, especially to that of the Cobra deity. In popular belief, the copulation of the male and female cobra is believed to be not only very fertile but also a very auspicious sight, if one is lucky enough to see it. Pallar informants claimed that copulating cobras left a yellow stain that, if caught on a cloth, brought great good fortune to the house where the cloth was later hung up.

Naga Dosham (Cobra Dosham)

Naga Dosham, unlike most lower-caste *dosham,* occurs only in female horoscopes. It primarily affects the girl alone, in its most common manifestations, so it is not a Brahminic representation of women as a source of danger to affines. What it does reflect is the overpowering concern about female fertility evinced in the Non-Brahmin castes and linked to their view of women as the source of children.

The Cobra *Dosham* is also a very striking example of the way in which the lower castes have adapted and refashioned upper-caste astrology, for unlike other *dosham,* this astrological flaw usually manifests itself in physical, tangible ways. It occurs in three forms.

First, it occurs astrally, in the conjunction of stars in a girl's menstruation-horoscope. The astrologer who discovers it will advise her how to get rid of the *dosham.* Its inauspiciousness results in the girl's marriage being repeatedly delayed.

Second, it occurs physically as a large cobra-shaped mark on the upper part of a girl's thigh, near her groin. This birthmark is said to resemble a cobra with its hood open. None of my informants knew of anyone in Aruloor who had the mark, or if they knew, they did not say so. Such a mark on a girl's body is greatly feared because this kind of *Naga Dosham* is said to result in the death of the girl's bridegroom. It is significant that this birthmark is believe to usually occur on the front of the upper thigh, near the woman's genitalia. This implies that an invisible cobra lurks there, "in" the young woman's sexual organs, ready to kill the first man who has sex with her. The idea that the sexuality of a puberal virgin is extremely dangerous and that sex with her can cause her partner's death is an ancient Tamil idea that, in varying forms, is retold in many temple myths of Tamil goddesses (Shulman 1980). This concept is of some importance in explaining the structure of the puberty rites, and so I will reserve discussion of it until the next chapter. Because the cobra birthmark is so greatly feared, it is kept a secret by parents because no one will marry their daughter if she has it. Therefore, when a group of Muthurajah kinswomen go to inspect a young man's prospective bride, they take her aside and, on some pretext, push up her sari to check that the mark is not there. One of them said, "Why else do you suppose that it's so important to see the girl yourself? You have to make sure she has no mark on her thigh! We pretend to have seen a lizard run up her leg. But she knows what we are looking for!" Men never have this birthmark: It exists only on women.

The third manifestation of *Naga Dosham* is again quite different. It occurs when a cobra (which is, of course, Nagappa or Nagamma incarnated) crawls across the menstrual-cloths that the young woman has washed and spread on the ground to dry. The Cobra-God (or -Goddess) is polluted by these "unclean" cloths and is angered that they lay in his or her path. Consequently, due to the deity's anger, *Naga Dosham* arises and affects the girl. "That is why women have to be very careful where they spread their menstrual-cloths to dry," said a Pallar woman.

There is a fourth manifestation, called *Garuda Dosham*, but this is merely a variation of the third category of *Naga Dosham*. It occurs when a kite (or eagle) flies over menstrual-cloths that are drying. The *garuda* (kite or eagle) is considered a deity, for the Eagle-God is the vehicle (*vakanam*) of Vishnu (one of the Hindu trinity of great gods). Just like Nagappasami (*sami*: god), Garuda is angered to find "unclean objects" in the "path" where his shadow falls. Because his shadow touches the cloths, the Eagle-God is polluted and angered. *Garuda Dosham* has the same results as the third kind of *Naga Dosham*.

Getting Rid of *Naga Dosham*

Removal of *Naga Dosham* in the Menstruation-Horoscope. *Naga Dosham* in the menstrual-horoscope is only a mild form of the *dosham*. It can be "removed" (removing: *kalikkiradu*) entirely; the astrologer will advise how this is to be done. Usually, the girl has to go to the shrine of Nagappasami, the Cobra-God, in the local temple and offer an egg and a glass of milk there for a certain number of days. The shrine of the Cobra-God is typically in the open air and sited to enclose a termite mound (*pambu-puttu*: snake mound), which is a common home for snakes. The unbroken raw egg and the cup of milk are placed near one of the mouths of the mound. Quite often, the mound is actually inhabited by a cobra, but in any case, people offer eggs and milk in the firm belief that they will be consumed by a real cobra. When the offering has been made for the stipulated number of days, the *dosham* is believed to have disappeared. This horoscope *Naga Dosham*, if unremedied, delays the marriage of the girl.

Marriage can be delayed indefinitely if no action is taken to remove the *dosham*. Lalitha, a young Muthurajah woman, had reached puberty more than ten years earlier; she was in her late twenties and "still" unmarried. Prospective bridegrooms and their parents came to see her from time to time, but, "inexplicably," they never returned. "The Cobra bit them," explained Lalitha's mother. "We didn't know that she had *Naga Dosham*—but when this happened again and again, we felt something must be wrong and showed her horoscope to another astrologer. And this man found at once that she had *Naga Dosham*. What we need to do now is for Lalitha to offer eggs and milk at the temple—and to have a major *pujai* [rite of worship] at the astrologer's house. But he is demanding a hundred and fifty rupees for the *pujai* and we don't have enough money just now, so it's got to wait." When Lalitha's mother said that "the Cobra had bitten" the prospective bridegrooms, she meant that Nagappasami had caused them to suddenly withdraw. Lalitha's mother assured me that the long-delayed *pujai* would be performed. But when the family did get some money, they decided to spend it on a bribe-fee to secure a job for Lalitha's twenty-year-old brother, Ramu. Lalitha and her marriage had to wait.

Naga Dosham **as Birthmark.** Nothing can be done about this kind of *dosham*: If the girl marries, her bridegroom will certainly die. In this connection, my friend Siva told a cautionary tale. It was a true story, she claimed, involving the classificatory brother of her husband. This young man fell in love with his young cross-cousin and wanted to marry her even though his parents knew that the girl had the dangerous mark on her thigh. The girl's parents, too, being his close-kin, opposed the match. However, the young couple secretly eloped in the company of the young man's friend. Having married the girl by tying a *tali* round her neck, the young man went to a nearby temple to arrange for a thanksgiving *pujai* (worship). Just as they approached the temple, a cobra flashed out of the bush, bit the bridegroom, and disappeared. The groom was hauled home by his friend but died in the hospital shortly thereafter. "So, you see," concluded my friend, "there's nothing you can do. If you marry such a woman, you'll die. He knew the danger, yet he went ahead. What a fool!"

However, if the couple had just lived together without marrying, the young man might have survived. This was the view of a Muthurajah woman who described how a young woman with the mark had eloped with her suitor but had not married "because of the danger. They can never marry. However, they have three children and are quite happy so there is no problem." The Muthurajahs, like the Pallars, tolerate open cohabitation, something that would be impossible in the upper castes.

Removal of *Naga Dosham* and *Garuda Dosham* Caused by Offending a Deity. The third category of *Naga Dosham,* the result of offending the Snake-God or the Eagle-God by leaving washed menstrual cloths lying about, causes a girl's marriage to be indefinitely delayed. Propitiatory offerings of milk and eggs at the snake mound and any further *pujai* prescribed by the astrologer will remove the *dosham.* Interestingly, for *Garuda Dosham,* it is Nagappa, the Cobra-God, who is propitiated on the Eagle-God's behalf, even though they are enemies in the natural world.

Dosham and *Karmam*

Brahmins and Chettiars share the view that the word *"dosham"* can also mean "sin." That is, it implies that the former sins of a person in earlier births manifest themselves as the *karmam* of her present life, as "given" by the stars. *Karmam* is generally explained as "the fruits of deeds in previous lives reaped in one's present life." This abstract and moralized understanding of *dosham,* which links it to sin (*pavam*) and *karmam,* exemplifies the far greater interest in causal origins shown in the discourses of these Brahminical castes. Such metaphysical concerns are markedly absent from the lower-caste understanding of *dosham,* which is far more earthbound. The most common lower-caste *dosham* (*Naga Dosham*), as we have just seen, is manifested in physical signs rather than in astrological phenomena. But the fundamental difference between the Brahminical castes and the Non-Brahmins is that the Non-Brahmin orientation in astrology is not toward seeking the causes of afflictions but rather toward predicting future dangers. This pragmatic Non-Brahmin view can therefore be termed a *prognostic* orientation, and the upper-caste obsession with causation can be termed an *etiological* orientation. There is a far greater inclination in Brahminical discourse of *dosham* to view it as the "karmic" fruit of the previous misdeeds of the woman concerned. However, these two orientations are not mutually exclusive. Both can be simultaneously present when people seek to understand the implications of a particular menstrual-horoscope. Helen Lambert, from whom I borrow these contrasting terms, has shown that both perspectives often coexist in popular medicine in Rajasthan (1992). Just as in Aruloor astrology, Lambert found that a prognostic orientation is characteristic of the popular mode of medical treatment and that the etiological orientation is typical of the medical traditions derived from "bramanical Hinduism and its textual sources" (1992: 1070).

In upper-caste astrology, a negative view of femaleness is clearly apparent. Given that *dosham* also means "fault" and given that it is primarily in female horoscopes (here, the birth-horoscopes of upper-caste women) that these faults are diagnosed, it is seen as self-evident that women themselves are to blame for the bad luck that may befall them. This blame implicitly attaches to them because a belief in reincarnation and *karmam* exists at the back of every Brahminical mind. Aruloor's Brahminical castes therefore believe that people *are* their stars: Their deeds in previous lives have created the *karmam* (results) that are embodied by their stars in this life. So, in upper-caste discourse, the stars are *moral*. Their impact on human life may *seem* like chance, but it is actually the working out of the divine law of cause and effect. In this view, good deeds earn a happy life in the next birth; that is, they earn "good stars!"

But all this is very remote from the Non-Brahmin view, which is best typified by the lower castes. Not only is no connection made between good deeds in previous lives and one's chances in this, but there is also a general assumption that the stars are *amoral*. They are not subject to any divine rule but move in their orbits according to their own natural laws. In other words, the stars are mystical entities with enormous power over human life, but they are not moral because they are not concerned about human deservings.

The stars follow their own physical laws in their orbits, and not even the intercession of deities can alter their course. As Pugh puts it, "There is ... something autonomous and irrevocable about the power and movements of the heavenly bodies, and many Hindus feel that God cannot completely control the planets" (1983: 136). She adds, "Hindus feel that there are kinds of planetary afflictions which God has little or no power to alter" (Pugh 1983: 138). These observations are particularly applicable to the lower-caste (and lower-class) view of astrology in Aruloor. Unfortunately, Pugh does not tell us which class or caste holds these views in North India. Thus, her otherwise fine account of astrological conception suffers from the fact that informants are not positioned by caste and class—they are only referred to as "Hindus" or "Muslims." Possibly for this reason, Pugh gives the impression that her informants simultaneously believe in a karmic theory of astrology (i.e., that they get the stars they deserve) and that the stars are amoral. Of course, it is perfectly true that people everywhere are often self-contradictory and may therefore hold conflicting views at the same time. This may be the case with Pugh's informants. However, although I run the risk of overemphasizing differences between Non-Brahmins and Brahmins, it is very important to point out salient differences in discourse, especially when these differences correlate with differences in caste and class.

Major differences emerge between the astrological discourses of the Brahminical and the Non-Brahmin castes, both in their orientations and in their representations of gender. The astrology of the wealthy upper castes takes a distinctly negative view of femaleness, representing women as transmitters of bad luck This view is somewhat modified in lower-caste astrology, where the sexes are represented as more equal in the astrological effects they have on others. Further, the Brahminical fascination with the etiology of temporal events, reflected in a preoccupation with the notion of *karmam,* is replaced in pragmatic lower-caste astrology by a prognostic orientation.

Conclusion: Astrology and the Construction of Gender

This analysis of astrological discourses has focused largely on upper-caste Brahminical perspectives because astrology remains colored by its upper-caste origins even when used by Non-Brahmins.

In the Brahminical castes, the primary agents of *dosham* are women, and the prime "victims" are men, especially the newly wed husband and the father-in-law. This sexual asymmetry raises the question of whether it is that the horoscopes of husbands do not afflict their wives or whether it is merely that wives are actually not important and so nobody takes any notice of what may cause potential harm to them. Given the sexual asymmetry that pervades gender relations in the upper castes, where males are remarkably free from malign astrological influences (compared to females), it seems likely that it is not so much in the theory of astrology that the main asymmetry lies but rather in the fact that in these castes, people care much more about men than about women. The fact that in lower-caste astrology, the horoscopes of men *can* transmit inauspiciousness, just as those of women do, suggests that it is perceptions of gender that determine perceptions of the stars.

5

The Vulnerability of Power: Puberty Rituals

The brothers of a woman think, "The daughter born of our mother's house must not feel her stomach burn." So they will give *all* the gifts that they ought to give.
—Pechiyai (Pallar)

THE RECENT POLITICAL HISTORY of Tamilnadu has had a profound effect on the relationships between Non-Brahmins and Brahmins. The Non-Brahmin political goal of affirming a strong and positive "Tamil" identity has influenced all other areas of life, not least the sphere of ritual. Thus, due to the influence of the atheist doctrines of "Periyar" (E. V. Ramaswami Naicker) and his Dravida Kazhagam party, the "untouchable" castes in this part of Tiruchi District gave up sacralized marriage rites performed by Pallar priests in favor of very simple "Self-Respect" marriages, in which a political leader or local elder merely witnessed a marriage contract. The "Self-Respect" movement rejected all Brahmin/priestly authority. The readiness of the Pallars to adopt this virtually ritual-less wedding was due to their enthusiastic support of "Periyar," who became the hero of Tamil "untouchables" in 1924 when he led the Vykom satyagraha that successfully protested the banning of "untouchables" from the use of certain roads (Irschick 1969).

Because "Dravidian" or "Tamil" identity has remained a cornerstone of the political propaganda of the various "Dravidian" (Non-Brahmin) parties in Tamilnadu since the 1920s, there is a sharp opposition between Brahmins and Non-Brahmins in local perceptions today. This may have affected the female puberty rites as well, for though Brahmins (both Telugu and Tamil) celebrated female puberty publicly in quite a grand manner until the 1930s and 1940s, their celebrations became more and more private thereafter so that in Aruloor today, they are very low-key, private, all-female rituals. This is true elsewhere as well (e.g., in Tiruchi city). It is very probable that this decline in the importance of the Brahmin puberty rites is connected with Brahmin embarrassment at the fact that their daughters are married *after* puberty today, whereas they were always married several years *before* puberty prior to the 1940s. This has made the Brahmin puberty celebration an almost shamefaced event, for it has lost its traditional significance. Historically, it celebrated the happy moment when a child-wife, who was still living with her parents, reached menarche and could therefore be sent to her parents-in-law's house to join her young husband at last. Both Non-Brahmins and Brahmins feel that a girl who does not menstruate does not reach "full" womanhood: She continues to be perceived as "unfinished" and ungendered, no matter what her age. Male sexual potency is not put in question, for it is always assumed that a male *is* sexually potent. The gendering of men is automatic.

Both Non-Brahmins and Brahmins regard menstruation as a very auspicious (*nalla*) event, and both groups also believe it is affected by impurity (*tittu*). Yet, though Brahmins regard the event as happy and auspicious, they simultaneously ritually construct the menarchal girl as an inauspicious female, until she is purified. This is quite different from the ritual construction of the Non-Brahmin pubescent girl. These remarkably varying representations of the menarchal girl have much to do with very different attitudes to monthly menstrual impurity. When menstruating, the Non-Brahmin woman continues with her daily life; the sole prohibition is that she should not enter a temple while menstruating. But the Brahmin woman, at every monthly period, is viewed as very polluted and is physically excluded from the home: She may not cook for her family, she may not sleep with them, she eats separately, and she must stay "far away" (*duram*) from them.

In the following discussion, I will first focus on Pallar puberty rites. This is because, being least touched by Brahminization, they appear to provide a typical example of this Non-Brahmin ritual. I will then briefly compare them with the rites of the Muthurajahs, Christian Paraiyars, Chettiars, and Brahmins.

I will argue that the puberty rites are quintessentially Non-Brahmin for three reasons. First, the rites are an attempt to safeguard what Non-Brahmins perceive as the precious, distinctively female ability to create children. Second, they enact a symbolic marriage that emerges as a necessary corollary of the symbolic construction of fertility as sacred female power. Third, the rites resonate with central aspects of the roles of both women and men in Non-Brahmin kinship.

Pallar Puberty Rituals

The Pallar rituals consist of three separate events:

1. the "first day" rituals, celebrating the day on which the girl starts bleeding;

2. her purification ritual on the seventeenth day (known as the *punniya danam* among caste-Hindus), and
3. the grand circling ceremony *suttaradu* that takes place a few months later. This is also called the *Puppuppunita Nirattu Vila* (Blossoming Sacred Bath Festival) (cf. Good 1991: 97).

Today, the days on which these rituals are performed have changed. The first day rites have remained on the first day, but the second ritual—the purification—is today often done as early as the ninth or eleventh day after the onset of bleeding instead of on the traditional seventeenth day. The third ritual—the *suttaradu* (or *sadangu*)—is often delayed for some years until the day before the girl's wedding. However, though their dates have changed over the last twenty years, the rituals themselves have not changed substantially. I will now examine what happens on the first day, when it is discovered that a young girl has started menstrual bleeding.

Coming of Age: "Seeing the Blood"

"To come of age" (*vayasukku vandadu*) is the most common term used in all castes for a girl's attaining puberty. When a Pallar girl "comes of age," she is seated quietly outside the house, either on the front porch if it is secluded or in the backyard. Older women, not necessarily kin, are called to come and witness the happy "evidence" that she has "attained age." They examine the patch of blood on her clothing. All castes, including the Telugu Brahmins, believe that it is inauspicious if the mother of the girl discovers the bleeding first. The reason for this may be that the girl's "powerful" uterine blood is inimical to that of her mother. Indeed, the mother of the girl is prohibited from participating in the purificatory bathing of her daughter (but see Winslow 1980 on Sinhalese mothers who do bathe their daughters). In one Brahmin family, the mother, seeing the blood first, quietly waited until an elderly aunt discovered it. All castes also felt that it was extremely dangerous if a widow saw the blood first. A Pallar woman, Thanjayee, told of how a young widow (*kammanatti*) had first seen the blood on her skirt when she had started menstruating, concluding, "That is why I became like her, a (widow) too." She had lost her husband after just four years of marriage. This emphasizes the extreme vulnerability of the girl to dangerous influences, such as the "evil eye" (*dirushti*).

The official discoverer of the bleeding is always a woman; even if a man noticed it, he would be expected to remain silent. This may be because the girl's uterine blood is considered very dangerous to men until her symbolic marriage has been performed during the puberty rites. This danger to men is also implied in the ban on the girl talking to—or even seeing—a man, not excepting her own father, while she is ritually secluded. The newfound sexuality of the girl is emphasized. The Pallar and other castes agreed that the father of the girl must maintain extreme reserve in dealing with his daughter once she came of age. But fathers were not prohibited from passing on the happy news of this important event to other relatives. I heard men, including Brahmin men, telling their neighbors the joyful news or expressing their pleasure at hearing of the first menstruation of a niece. The universal reaction, in all castes, was of pleasure at receiving good news: A happy and auspicious event had occurred and should be celebrated.

Central to the Non-Brahmin celebration is the girl's *Maman* or, more precisely, *Tay Maman* (Mother's Brother), and a messenger is dispatched to summon him as soon as the bleeding is discovered. The *Tay Maman* is of crucial importance to the Non-Brahmin puberty rituals but is comparatively unimportant to the Telugu Brahmin rites, indicating how much less important the MB is to Telugu Brahmin kinship as a whole. Pallar women stated that if an elder *Maman* (MeB) was married but a younger one (MyB) was not, then it would be MeB and his wife who came on this first day, not the unmarried MyB who was a potential groom for the girl. This choice of an unmarriageable MB (unmarriageable because he is *already* married) as officiant at the rites is particularly important in the context of the symbolic marriage in which he participates. The *Maman's* wife is also a central protagonist in these rituals.

Coming of Age: Impurity and Kinship

To the Non-Brahmin castes of Aruloor, the occasion of a girl's puberty is a very auspicious moment, but it is also fraught with ritual impurity. This first menstrual bleeding is called *"talaittittu,"* that is, "first impurity" (*talai:* first or foremost). It was also called *"kannittittu"* or "menarchal girl-impurity." For all Non-Brahmins, the ritual impurity (*tittu*) of the pubescent girl affects her immediate family and her home as well. This impurity exceeds both that incurred at childbirth by a mother and child and at death by a bereaved household. At death, the food of a bereaved household was not eaten by nonpatrilineal kin for two days, but after two days, the ban was not strictly observed. However, nonpatrilineal kin could not eat the food of a household with "menarchal girl impurity" for a full sixteen days. Only at the seventeenth day feast, after the girl had been purified, could affines eat food cooked by that household. But during the seclusion period, the affines bring fine food to the house and cook small feasts there for the girl (who eats in seclusion) and her family. Such food is shared by both lineage kin (*pankali*) and affines.

Though, in practice, such shared celebration continues between affines and lineage kin for the duration of the girl's seclusion, the ritual impurity that affects the girl is, in theory, dangerous to others. This is primarily because it is regarded as repugnant to the purity of the deities: It is, some said, "detested by all the deities." This is the basis of the sole prohibition that continues for the entire period of a Non-Brahmin woman's fertile years: She must not enter a temple when bleeding. This is also explained as the main reason why the prohibition on accepting hospitality from the girl's household is so strictly observed. Pallar women warned that if you ate the food of her house and then prayed at your domestic shrine, you would incur the anger of the deity, who would "punish you by sending scorpions and *puran* (a poisonous, large centipede) to bite you."

So, to pray at a shrine after having casually touched the girl (even by accident) or after entering her house or eating food prepared in it or touching those who had touched the girl (including little children of her family) is to incur the deity's anger. Like most Hindus, most Pallar's had simple domestic shrines in their homes at which family members worshipped daily. The deity formally worshipped at this shrine was the family lineage deity (*kulateyvam*). These family deities were very offended by menarchal impurity from *another* house, but significantly, the deity was not perturbed by the menarchal impurity of a girl belonging to the household. Therefore, the girl's family members could continue to worship at their domestic shrine throughout her seclusion, even though they, too, were "polluted" by her menarche. Only affines and strangers had to be careful not to touch either the girl or her family members. This is particularly striking because it indicates how differently (potential) inauspiciousness and impurity are regarded by Non-Brahmins. Both affect the girl's family, too, but though her impurity does not endanger them, her inauspiciousness (if she has bad stars) does. It is this possible inauspiciousness that is the central concern, not the girl's ritual impurity.

Day One: The First Bathing

After the menarchal blood on the girl's skirt has been witnessed by elder women called to the scene, all the Mother's Brothers are sent for, particularly the eldest Mother's Brother. He and his wife are the chief protagonists in the ensuing rituals. The girl, who is seated in a secluded spot close to but outside the house, is not supposed to eat or drink anything except water until *Maman* (MB) and his wife show up and she has been ritually bathed. Fasting is associated with ritual purity in all the castes. By fasting, the girl does not add to her impurity; she only eats after she has been purified by a ritual bath. But this can be hard on the girl, who may go without food a whole day if *Maman* lives far away. Normally, she is allowed "uncooked" food because *Maman* is always late, as he has to first rush out to buy the gifts that he must bring to his Sister's Daughter.

An example from the street of my friend Siva is illustrative. When young Manimeghalai was waiting for her Elder Sister's Husband (her classificatory *Maman*) to show up, she was allowed a couple of cups of coffee and a bread roll before the feast that was eventually prepared that evening by her *Attai* (MBW). Because Manimeghalai's impurity was offensive to Siva's family deity, Siva (who knew the girl must be hungry and bought her the snacks) placed the roll and a cup of coffee on the ground for Manimeghalai to pick up. If Siva had handed them to her, she would have incurred impurity.

Maman and his wife arrive, bringing *sir* (ritual gifts,—short for *sir varisai*). The ritual gifts that *Maman* bears are those that must always be offered at an auspicious occasion; they are primarily food items, including the foremost ritual food item, betel leaf and nut, which confers honor. Specifically, they are (1) roasted chickpeas (*pottukkadalai*), usually one kilogram, (2) sugar, half a kilogram, (3) betel leaves (*vetle*), one *kelli* (100) (4) areca nut (*pakku*), 100 grams, (5) two coconuts, (6) bananas, two *sippu* (cluster, about a dozen) (7) a piece of auspicious turmeric-root (*manjal*), and (8) for the girl's hair, some jasmine, threaded together. The total cost of these items is only twenty to thirty rupees. Women carry these gifts into the house, but *Maman* himself carefully remains standing outside the house. To enter would be to incur ritual impurity, for he is marriageable-kin, not *pankali*.

It is significant that the central gift on this first day is food because, from this day on, Mother's Brother symbolically *feeds* the girl, and in this way, he makes her more "like" himself. Food is a multivalent symbol: The sharing of food expresses the sharing of their own bodily substance between people (cf. Marriott 1976), and only those of equal or nearly equal social and ritual status share ritual food. But there is also sexual symbolism here, for the sharing of food between a marriageable couple implies shared sexual activity. This is important because, as we will see, Mother's Eldest Brother, who is normally already married, is represented throughout these puberty rites as the symbolic bridegroom of the menarchal girl.

As soon as *Maman* arrives, the girl can be bathed (it is usually late afternoon by then, if the messenger went early that morning), and so seven or nine women (always an auspicious odd number) who are close relations of the girl go to the river to bring water back in brass water pots (*kodam*). These female relatives are both affines and *pankali*. They normally include *Maman's* wife (addressed as *attai*), Father's Sister (FZ), who is also called *attai*, and the girl's Elder Sister (*akka*). The girl is taken to the backyard and there, in an all-female ritual, each of the seven women, starting with *Maman's* wife, slowly pours her pot of water over the head of the girl, who is standing dressed in a half-petticoat which has been pulled up to cover her breasts. Each woman also gives the girl a piece of *manjal* (turmeric) to rub over her face, arms, and legs. (Turmeric-root is very auspicious and is also a beautifier.) Thus, from the moment of her purificatory bath on the very first day, the beautification and adornment of the Non-Brahmin girl begins.

Significantly, the turmeric passes from hand to hand here, even between affines like MBW and FZ and the girl. Because the family-deities of MBW and FZ are different from the girl's, they theoretically incur severe ritual impurity, but this is totally disregarded in practice. Women are eager to have the honor of bathing the girl; to be asked to do so is a privilege. The sole qualifications are that a woman must be a *kattukkalutti* (which is glossed as "a married woman with a living husband") *and* have many children. The hope is that the auspiciousness of these women, derived from marriage and many children, will rub off on the girl. The implication is that a multitude of children counts for more than marriage, given that divorce and remarriage are practiced by the Pallar. This emphasis on fertility, rather than marriage—a very *un*-Brahminical emphasis—is quite explicit in the ritual that follows.

During this rite, the Pallar women officiants said to me: "We hope that she will be married very soon and have many children!" The hope for "uncountable" children is symbolized by the seeds of the *tandu* spinach (*tandu kirai vedai*) that the girl drinks in a glass of milk immediately on completing her bath. There are more than a hundred tiny black seeds in the bottom of the glass. "We hope that she will have as many children as the seeds she's swallowed!" I was cheerfully told. It is extremely significant that the wish here is for children of unspecified sex. In the equivalent Brahmin blessing (at marriage), the specific hope is for *sons*; daughters are not required. There is also explicit sexual symbolism here, with the spinach seeds signifying the semen of the male who will father the girl's children; milk symbolizes semen, too. The girl stands facing the east, the auspicious direction, as she swallows the half-handful of seeds. The fact that the symbolic pregnancy of the girl is enacted *before* her symbolic marriage (on the seventeenth day) reflects Non-Brahmin priorities here: It is fertility that is crucial; marriage is secondary. (This symbolic emphasis is echoed in the Muthurajah first day rites.) This multivalent event is also a rite celebrating the autonomous procreative female power, for though no man was present, the girl "becomes pregnant" with the hundred seeds that are in her belly. The implication is that the fertile mothers around her have given the girl their own auspicious and fertile powers. This mystical gift or transference to the girl from the *kattukkalutti* is implied by the reciprocal gifts that are made to each of them on their departure: Each receives auspicious ritual gifts when she leaves—betel leaf and nut, sugar, bananas, and flowers. The seven *kattukkalutti* are also offered auspicious vermilion (*kunkumam*), which they smear in large blood-red dots on their foreheads. The other women and female children who cluster around are given small gifts of sugar or bananas. The girl's family provides these token gifts to the all-female gathering that has watched the event.

Then the girl is given "Washerman's clothes" to wear, brought by the Washerman (*Vannan*). They are clean, old clothes that once belonged to other menarchal girls. Whatever clothes a Non-Brahmin girl is wearing when she first starts bleeding must be given as a gift to the Washerman, who cleans them and lends them out to other pubescent girls. No matter how expensive the girl's blood-stained clothes may happen to be, they cannot be retained in the girl's house because of their extreme impurity. But, cleaned by the Washerman, the clothes find their way into new homes as the "loan-clothes" for other menarchal girls. In both the Pallar and the Muthurajah castes, the Washerman provides these clothes on loan, everyday during the period of seclusion. He is paid twenty to thirty rupees for this work. Today, however, with less importance being given to menstrual prohibitions, many families (both Pallar and Muthurajah) have stopped taking loan-clothes from the Washerman. The girl's blood-stained clothes *are* given to him, but thereafter, she just wears her own old clothes. This weakens the symbolic meaning of the traditional loan-clothes, which implied two new aspects of the menarchal girl's identity. First, because she suddenly had to live in the clothes of other girls, her identity was made ambiguous, and her earlier identity was lost. Second, because she now wore *purified* "blood-clothes," she was identified with the newfound mystic and fertile powers of those earlier menarchal girls. Here, the role of the Washerman as ritual specialist is already evident: He becomes even more prominent at the grand circling rite (*sutti*) some months later.

While the girl is bathed, her Mother's Brother engages in another important ritual, the setting up of a screen made of braided coconut leaves (*kittu*). In earlier days, he set up an actual menstrual hut, constructed outside the girl's home; today, it is a symbolic hut consisting of a single braided thatch screen. One massive coconut branch (*tenna-mattai*), with its long green fronds entwined, forms the screen. One or two such branches are braided by a specialist paid to do this job by the family and are kept in readiness for the arrival of *Maman*. When the specialist comes, Father or some other man assists him as he constructs the shelter in which the girl will stay secluded. Usually, the girl is kept on the front porch (*tinnai*), so *Maman* has to tie the thatch so that it screens a section of the porch from the street. Sometimes, if the porch is already well screened, the coconut screen is leaned against the porch wall. Its function is symbolic: The girl sits within the space created in this lean-to. The green, fresh thatch is called "green thatch" (*paccaikkittu*)—it dries within a few days, and its ritual burning forms yet another rite.

A sacred oil-lamp (*kuttuvilakku*) symbolizing the deities is placed within the shelter, and the girl kneels to the light when she first enters the space. This act is called "to worship [*kumbidu*] the good light [*nallavilakku*]." It is typically the girl's mother who puts the sacred lamp in the "room." Here, female fertility is symbolically linked to sacredness, for the seclusion area is now a sacred space. This implies that the menarchal girl is separated from her family and home as much for her own protection as for theirs. She is in flux. Her continuing blood-flow symbolizes a body and an identity in transformation. From being only partially gendered, she is now well on her way to "becoming female." But though the secluded girl is being slowly gendered and empowered, she remains extraordinarily vulnerable. She is at risk not only from her menstrual stars but also from evil ghosts (*pey-pisasu*) and the evil eye. Through her, her family members are vulnerable, too.

It is her affines—primarily the matrilateral kin—who protect and "engender" the new woman. In building her hut, Mother's Brother constructs a symbolic womb for the "newborn" girl-woman. This womb from which she emerges is that of her matrilateral kin. Mother's Brother himself is also a symbolic, parturient *"mother,"* who protects, enwombs, and creates the girl-as-woman. This interpretation is supported by the fact that the girl is actually fed by Mother's Brother and other affinal kin throughout her period in the "womb-hut."

Simultaneously, the girl's mother feeds her to prepare her for childbirth. Every morning right up to the beginning of the seventeenth day, she drinks one or two raw eggs and half a cup of sesame oil (*nallenney*) on awakening. These foods are believed to strengthen the womb and back and help guarantee safe childbirth. And on every odd-numbered day until the seventeenth day, *Maman* and his wife and other affinal kin take turns cooking small feasts to "strengthen" the girl. She is fed fine meals, including mutton, though this is a luxury for the poor.

The Seventh Day: The Burning of the Screen

The dried thatch screens the girl particularly from male view. It is burned very early on the morning of the seventh day. The girl and her mother carry the thatch to a spot where three roads meet. Such a place, called a *muccandi,* has great supernatural power. It is important in the funeral rites of the Pallars and Muthurajahs and also in causing and removing bewitchment and *dirushti*. The ideal *muccandi* is very near a river, as is the one used by both Pallars and Muthurajahs in Aruloor.

This burning suggests that a significant transformation in personhood is occurring. Interestingly, at Brahmin temple festivals, the burning of a broom of thatch is an important rite (Chris Fuller, personal communication, 1988). The officiant walks around the temple that is being purified, carrying the burning thatch. This is done at the beginning of major festivals, and it sets up a boundary of auspiciousness, protecting the temple. The analogy suggests that here, it is the girl's body that is being protected, while she is, through the passage of time, being purified and made auspicious. The girl's body has so far been enwombed in Mother's Brother's hut: MB protects her for the sake of himself and his own kin, too, for they, like her own family, are all dynamically connected with her. In this discourse, identities and bodies are dynamically interconnected, and very significantly, affinal kin participate in each other's identities and can succumb to each other's dangers. This is an important clue to why the puberty rites must be performed: They are essential because of the Dravidian system of marriage with very close kin. The identities and the bodies of affines are linked before marriage, too, which is why the menarchal girl's affines must protect themselves by protecting her while she is vulnerable to dangerous influences. There is constant concern about the vulnerability of her kin to *dosham* (astrological danger) through her. It is as though all their bodies were joined as one. And of course, this is how their relationship is represented symbolically, as *one blood* that flows through both natal kin and affines (see Chapter 2). It is, literally, this blood that is being protected now, while it flows out of the girl.

The girl bathes in the river after the thatch is burned and returns home "without looking back." This proviso is crucial because "*pey* [evil spirits] will possess her if she does look back," it was said. *Pey* are very attracted by menstrual blood and by nubile young women. Not looking back is synonymous with preserving one's courage: *Pey* cannot "catch" or possess someone who has courage. On this journey home, the girl walks "invisibly," cloaked in a blanket, in the dark before sunrise.

For the remaining nine days, she continues to sit on the porch but is now screened by saris that are hung up around her. She has a separate plate and cup and is served separately; she eats alone. But she is visited, throughout her seclusion, by her prepuberal female friends, who pass the time playing games with her.

Purification and Prohibitions

She bathes daily. When she goes to the latrine area, which is always outside the home, she covers her head (*mukkadu pottirukka*) with the end of her half-sari "because if a bird shits on her head it will cause *dosham*." She can incur *dosham* easily because, in her transformative state, she is particularly open to negative influences.

Why is the menarchal girl so vulnerable? Astrological discourses explain this very clearly, emphasizing that people are particularly vulnerable at times of radical transition or transformation. Here, the paradox is that the girl is vulnerable because she is being empowered. Pugh put this clearly: "The *more auspicious* or inauspicious the situation and the more numerous the aspects of life which it involves, the more directly and explicitly is the situation considered a manifestation of planetary influences and the workings of destiny" (1983: 143, emphasis added). The situation is dangerous because (as noted in the last chapter) the planets are unpredictable and potentially dangerous.

The prohibitions that surround the girl reveal the dangerous power of her menstrual (uterine) blood. She must not, for example, give her menstrual-cloths to be washed by anyone else but must wash them herself. This is a powerful prohibition among the Pallars and Muthurajahs, who were outraged to learn (from me) that wealthy Chettiar women merely rinsed their menstrual-cloths and then gave them to their Washerman's Wife (*Vannatti*) for washing and bleaching. "This is a great sin on their part," said a Pallar woman. Similarly, food remains must be discarded without endangering anyone else. The girl's food remains are dangerous "even to dogs and cats," and so "she should dig the earth and bury her leavings there." This indicates that it is dangerous power, not pollution, that is at stake, for animals cannot be polluted.

The girl's newly gendered "femaleness" is particularly dangerous to males. Throughout her seclusion, she is kept totally segregated from men and is warned that if she speaks to or even looks at a man, her face will be covered with pimples (*mukapparu*).

The Seventeenth Day Purification: "The Bathing by Mother's Brother"

The Pallars call this "the day of inviting [her back] into the home" (*uttukku alaikkira nalu*) or simply "the inviting home" (*uttukku alaikkiradu*). They also call it "the day when *Maman* bathes the head of the girl" (*Maman talaikku tannir uttara nalu*). The caste-Hindus use the term *punniya danam* for the purification rite. This may be a corruption of *punniyavatanam* (Hiltébeitel 1991: 64) or of *punniyavacanam* (from *punniyakavacanam*), which is the term for the purification rite that is part of the preparatory ceremony before a major temple ritual (Chris Fuller, personal communication, 1988).

Significantly, for all caste-Hindus (except Brahmins), the ritual is performed by a Pancangam Brahmin priest, but for the "untouchable" Pallars (whom the Brahmin priests refuse to serve), it is Mother's Brother who takes the priestly role and performs the symbolic purification. Because of the purification, the day retains a sacral dimension, but with the Pallars, the event celebrates *Maman's* munificence as much as it celebrates puberty. It also enacts a symbolic marriage between Mother's Brother and his sister's daughter, so on this occasion, he is, symbolically, first a priest and then a bridegroom.

The Purification of the House. Very early that morning, the girl's house is whitewashed and thoroughly cleaned; all the floors, including the porch, are rubbed with wet cow dung by the women. This not only smoothes the clay floor but also "purifies" the house of bacteria, it is said. The whitewashing is part of this purification. The building stands for its inhabitants—from this day on, they are clean, too.

Early that morning, the girl rubs sesame oil in her hair and then washes it out with soap-nut (*siyakkay*). This bathing-by-washing-the-head symbolizes a significant break with the past. This rite is performed by those who have attended a funeral: It marks the leaving behind of all impurity and inauspiciousness; impurity is particularly associated with the hair of the head.

The girl purifies herself by this ritual bath. She is then sprinkled with the purifying urine of a cow (*komiyam* is the Pallar term), and then all the corners of the house are sprinkled with it. No great formality is attached to this act, which is usually done by an older affinal woman. Interestingly, this is a recent custom, borrowed from the repertoire of the Brahmin priest who purifies the caste-Hindu girl. But the Brahmin priest's sprinkling of the girl and her house marks the *final* step in the caste-Hindu purification rite. This suggests that for the Pallars, purification is secondary to the main purposes of the event, which lie in *Maman's* gift-giving and his symbolic marriage to the girl.

***Maman's* Prestations.** It is the "home relatives" (*vittu sondham*) or affines, not the "outside relatives" (*velile sondam*) or patrilineal kin who are primarily invited for this event. They come either as part of *Maman's* large party or in their own little contingents. This indicates the greater importance of affines as opposed to lineage kin. "Only those who are *moraikarar*—that is, who can marry with the family—come for the Seventeenth Day," it was said. Some lineage kin do come, but their presence is not essential.

The fact that there are no comparative ceremonies for Non-Brahmin males at puberty indicates that very special powers are believed to invest the menarchal female. The structuring of the puberty rites as a symbolic marriage has much to do with the nature of these extraordinary female powers. It is *Maman's* gifts that identify both the Seventeenth-Day Purification *and* the grand Circling as symbolic marriages.

For this Seventeenth Day Purification, *Maman* brings:

1. a *davani* ("half-sari") or sari; this will be the first half-sari or sari the girl has ever worn, and it signifies her entrance to womanhood,
2. a garland (*malai*) of pink roses; a rose-garland is a marriage-garland,
3. sugar (*sakkarai*),
4. roasted chickpeas (*pottukkadalai*),
5. betel leaf and nut (*vetlepakku*),
6. threaded jasmine flowers for her hair (*mallipu*),
7. sweets (such as *bundi* and *laddu*).

He also brings cosmetics and toiletries, which acknowledge and celebrate the girl's new sexual attractiveness. They include:

1. a soap in a soapbox,
2. a comb,
3. a mirror,
4. a ribbon,
5. vermilion (*bottu* or *kunkumam*),
6. hairpins,
7. bangles, and
8. mascara (*mai*).

These cosmetics are considered extremely auspicious, as are the new clothes, flowers, and food items. The sugar and the chickpeas are mixed together and served as a snack as was done at the first day celebration. *Maman's* gifts symbolize beauty, honor, sexual attractiveness—and marriage.

His most important gifts are the rose-garland, which is explicitly described as "like a marriage-garland" and the sari (or half-sari), which is "like a wedding-sari." This sari also signifies the girl's new identity: From this day, she no longer wears the long skirt and blouse of an immature girl but the apparel of a sexually mature woman, the sari. As *Maman's* wife and other married women wrap the sari around the girl, they invest her with new identity.

Yalman (1967) noted that with the Sinhalese, a gift of clothes from a man to a woman signified an offer of marriage. By wearing the clothes, the woman accepted the offer. *Maman's* gift carries the same conjugal connotation: It is a symbolic offer of marriage, and the girl's acceptance restates the traditional promise implicitly made by her mother to her younger brothers, by which they have first marriage rights to her daughters.

In his excellent book on female puberty rites (1991), Anthony Good has argued (1) that they are an intrinsic part of a cycle of rites that ends with marriage, (2) that puberty rites in his research area and in many other parts of South India take the form of a symbolic marriage, and (3) that the main reason for the puberty rite being represented as a marriage is because the central concern of the group is with its caste purity and its group status.

In Good's words, his paradigm of puberty practices "starts from the assumption that what is at stake in all these rites is the protection of the group against the *status ambiguity* and *impurity* which would result from uncontrolled sexual activity on the part of, especially, its female members" (1991: 8; emphases added). This assumption may be *partially* true for the Non-Brahmin upper castes, but it does not explain why female puberty rites are most elaborate and important in the lowest Non-Brahmin castes. Among the "untouchable" Pallar, the "untouchable" Christian Paraiyar, and the poor Muthurajahs, there is comparatively little concern about "status ambiguity." A paradigm that takes account of the puberty practices of *all* castes must take account of these low castes as well. Further, it is in these castes that the puberty rites are given greater importance than in the upper Non-Brahmin castes. So, Good's paradigm, with its emphasis on purity and on caste status, does not satisfy me because it does not answer the question of *why* it is in the poorest, lowest Non-Brahmin castes that female puberty rites are most important.

There is, indeed, more at stake. To answer the question, we have to recall that the central symbol of Non-Brahmin kinship in Aruloor is uterine blood. It is through "Mother's blood" that kinship is created and it is "primarily her blood" that constitutes a child. In this symbolic discourse, female generative power is the source of children. But this female power, *sakti,* is both sacred and dangerous. It is sacred in its mystical ability to bring forth new human beings, but it is also dangerous. Its dangerousness is deeply ambiguous: To understand it, we must explore the meaning of *sakti* in the South Indian context.

Sakti is sacred female power; depending on context, it means "power," "strength," "energy," "the life force," and "the creative principle of the universe." Here, I draw on the researches of Shulman, Fuller, and Sheryl Daniel. Chris Fuller's research (1980a) in the Madurai Meenakshi temple shows that in Tamil religious discourse, the goddess Meenakshi, who embodies divine creative power, can only be controlled by being married to the great god Siva. This is because divine female power becomes uncontrolled and therefore dangerous in an unmarried goddess. Through marriage, Meenakshi's female *sakti* is harnessed by Siva's male wisdom (1980a).

But here, "marriage" also stands for "sexual intercourse," for, as Sheryl Daniel (1983) has shown, even the *sakti* of ordinary women—like that of the goddess—needs regular sexual intercourse to "lessen" it and keep it from becoming "dangerously powerful" and "uncontrolled." But this does not fully answer the question of why the puberty rites are represented as a symbolic marriage. Why does a sexually mature woman have to be married symbolically *before* she can be married "for real"? Shulman's fascinating research on Tamil temple myths (1980) provides the clue. A central theme that runs through these myths is that the *sakti* of the goddess is so powerful that it kills the god who marries or has sex with her. The goddess's *sakti* is too powerful for *any* male, however divine, to control. Being divine, the god who dies is triumphantly reborn. But mortal men cannot achieve this fate. Instead, to safeguard themselves from this too-powerful *sakti*, they arrange a symbolic marriage of the powerful, *sakti*-filled menarchal girl. In this symbolic marriage—during the circling rite of the Pallars and Muthurajahs—the girl's sacred powers are tempered, and inauspicious *dosham* and *dirushti* (other forms of danger) are also removed from her. By these means, she is made safe enough to marry. This interpretation is supported by the fact that the main puberty rite, the Circling, need not be done soon after puberty but *must* be done before the marriage of the girl. This is absolutely crucial, and it always is conducted prior to marriage, even if only hours before the actual wedding rite.

To return to Mother's Brother's prestations at the Purification, I would note that these are identical with the gifts that he later provides both at the girl's betrothal ceremony (*parisam podradu*) and at her marriage. The only exception is the new clothes; he only gives this gift again at *parisam* if his son is the groom.

The Ritual of Purification. Having processed grandly around the Pallar streets to the beating of drums, the *Tay Maman* arrives at the girl's house. In addition to the gifts he has brought her, Mother's Brother also has to provide the "Mother's Brother's cooked rice" (*Maman-soru*), the feast that is eaten on this seventeenth day. He has to bring all the items necessary to cook it (a considerable expenditure) because now everyone in the street is willing to come and eat—there is no longer any fear of menstrual pollution.

When *Maman's* procession reaches the girl's house, her sister offers *aratti* to him. To offer *aratti* normally consists of circling a tray of auspicious objects in front of the person being honored or protected. The rite shows great respect and solicitude, but its central purpose is to remove *dirushti* (the evil eye). Having been waved in front of *Maman* as he stands on the doorstep, the red *aratti* liquid is poured on the street outside the house. To tread on this area is dangerous because such contact might transfer the evil eye to passersby. Mother's Brother incurs great *dirushti* in his public display of generosity. It was said that "he needs this protection because many people enviously think, 'have you brought so much, then!'" *Maman* has his *sir* (gifts) installed in the house, but this is done by women; he himself does not enter because the house is not yet entirely pure, for the girl has yet to be purified by him.

Food is of central symbolic importance: Mother's Brother has fed the girl (and her family) throughout her seclusion, and now he feeds the entire local community. The women plunge into cooking the feast, which takes several hours to prepare; *Maman-pondatti* (Mother's Brother's Wife) takes charge. She is assisted by the girl's mother and all the female neighbors. Unlike caste-Hindus, the Pallars often eat mutton (a luxury) on this day. Caste-Hindus eat no meat on this day, "only *vadai-payasam*," a vegetarian festal meal. *Payasam* is a sweet milk-and-grain porridge (*"payas"* is Sanskrit for "milk"). It is possibly related to *"payasdan,"* a sweet milk-and-rice porridge that symbolizes semen (Parry 1985: 620, 629; O'Flaherty 1980: 18, 43). If so, then the caste-Hindu feast fills the bride-to-be with symbolic semen, once again implying its procreative meanings.

When the food is ready, the girl is dressed by affinal women in her first sari. These *kattukkalutti* (auspicious married women) adorn her with *Maman's* gifts: new bangles, flowers, vermilion (for the auspicious red dot on her forehead), and mascara. They also borrow gold jewelry to ornament her. When the girl is ready, *Maman* stands her, facing east, on the porch and garlands her with the marriage-garland of pink roses. This act of garlanding between man and woman symbolizes marriage; in Non-Brahmin marriage, the bride and groom exchange garlands. It is important that the girl does not garland *Maman* in return. If she did, the symbolic marriage would turn into a real one. Similarly, at the symbolic marriages that Good (1991) witnessed at puberty rites, the symbolic bridegroom was either a young female cross-cousin or a very small boy. In these ways, the "marriages" were kept merely symbolic.

The garlanded girl is led out by *Maman* to the *vasal,* the street immediately in front of the doorstep, and he places a small tray on her head. The tray is held in place by a *kattukkalutti.* Then *Maman,* using a metal beaker, pours a little water onto the tray. The tray (a modern intervention) is used "as otherwise the water will spoil the girl's new clothes." This minimalist ritual constitutes the symbolic "bathing" of her head and purifies the girl. What is washed away is her dangerous menstrual impurity; the "priest" is *Maman.* The participation of the chief affine (in this case, *Maman*) is a traditional marker of the end of impurity in ritual. If there is no genealogical *Maman,* the ritual is performed by a classificatory *Maman* (MFBS or EZH or even FZH)—no agnates can perform it because they share in the girl's menstrual impurity.

A piece of camphor (*sudam*) is lit and placed on the porch step (*vasal-padi*). The purified girl reenters her home by crossing the camphor flame on its threshold. This may symbolize both her auspicious power, for "crossing fire" recalls the rite of fire-walking, when, possessed by the great goddess Mariyamman, people walk on burning coals unscathed. At this point, the purification rite is over. *Maman* and other affines now enter the house freely, and the feast can begin.

The Circling Rite (*Suttaradu*)

The Advantages of Performing the *Sutti*. The third and final rite of puberty in all the Non-Brahmin castes is the *"sadangu," "sutti,"* or *"suttaradu,"* that is, the "circling" rite. *"Suttanam"* means "to circle." The Circling is a very public statement and celebration of the procreative powers and sexual maturity of the girl. Or, as informants put it: "It is an advertisement [*vilambaram*] that announces: 'Here is a girl ripe for marriage! Come and ask for her!'" But Circling is also done to remove the evil eye from the girl. The connection between the two was explained by a Pallar woman: "The girl looks exceptionally beautiful in a lovely sari, flowers, jewels—so envious hearts burn. This creates *dirushti*, which will harm the girl if it isn't removed. So the Circling must be done." But, as we will see, the circling rite also has more esoteric aims, for it also protects the girl from astrological dangers and inauspiciousness.

Chettiar circling rites have up to seven hundred guests; rich Muthurajahs have five hundred. In the Pallar street, guests number two to three hundred. The girl's father foots the bill. *Maman's* major gifts at his sister's daughter's Circling are (1) a very fine sari (as expensive as possible), (2) a rose-garland, (3) cosmetics, and (4) a gorgeous new item—ornate "cloth" of fresh flowers stitched together (a *tanda*) to cover her long braid of hair. *Tanda* are worn by sexually mature women almost only at their puberty and marriage rites. The girl is explicitly described as looking "like a bride," and she is dressed like one, with much borrowed gold jewelry.

The Circling, like a wedding, is an occasion for conspicuous giving. Younger Mother's Brothers bring kitchen vessels (*patram*) for her trousseau. The girl's parents hope to get a good return on their outlay because every family of guests brings a gift of some sort or at least a small gift of cash (*moy*). They also hope to gain a son-in-law more quickly, for a girl whose *sutti* is performed is believed to get married much more quickly.

Because it removes astrological *dosham* and inauspiciousness of all kinds, the Circling *must* be done before marriage. And to have a daughter married very soon after puberty reflects credit on her parents in all castes. This is partly because parents thereby avoid the problem (and social disgrace, in the upper castes) of a premarital pregnancy and also because early marriage implies that the girl's father is wealthy. It is essentially his financial standing that attracts or discourages suitors.

The Context of the Circling. Traditionally, the Circling followed the Purification and was held on the same day (in all Non-Brahmin castes): The Purification occurred in the morning, and the Circling and feast held that evening. Nowadays, however, the Circling is held separately by all the Non-Brahmin castes, usually some months later. The Brahmins, on the other hand, have no public Circling at all. It is interesting that in Good's research area (in Tirunelveli District, far to the south of Aruloor), the Purification and the equivalent of the Circling are celebrated on the same day in *one* event. There appears to be no celebration of first day rites. Thus, instead of three distinct ritual events, there is only one event

(Good 1991: 97–110). Good states: "The rite discussed here is practised by all local groups except the Nadars, who are of course Catholics" (1991: 97). But Catholic faith does *not* preclude sharing in "Hindu" rites. As we will see, in Aruloor, the Catholic Paraiyars have elaborate puberty rites as well.

There are many *sutti* in the Tamil months of *Tai* (mid-January to mid-February) and *Masi* (mid-February to mid-March) after the main harvest, when both money and rice are more plentiful. The Pallar *sutti* was usually fairly small in scale and held two months after the Seventeenth Day Purification ceremony. But today, some Pallar avoid even this expense and, like the upwardly mobile Muthurajahs, postpone the *sutti* to the day before the girl's wedding. Both events are combined, and money is saved. Only wealthy Chettiars can afford to hold grand *sutti* at which many hundreds sit down to a fine feast.

The act of circling auspicious objects in front of a person is a standard rite to remove inauspiciousness of all kinds and is usually referred to as *aratti*. This clue takes us to the heart of the circling rite—it is not concerned with purification but with the removal of inauspiciousness from the girl. This is why caste-Hindus do not use a Brahmin priest for this rite but have their own *kattukkalutti* (auspicious married women) officiate instead. Significantly, the Pallars did not use *kattukkalutti*. Instead, they used a ritual specialist, the Washerman. This may be because the discourse of the "auspiciousness" of the married woman is of secondary importance in the Pallar caste. Marriage is of far less importance to the identity of Pallar women than it is to the identity of upper-caste women. The Pallar Washerman is a professional "remover of inauspiciousness," who performs the same function at Pallar funerals.

The Ritual of the Circling Rite. Probably because the Circling used to occur on the same day as the Purification, it starts in exactly the same manner. *Maman* and his party arrive bearing their gifts, progressing around the Pallar streets and ending at the girl's house.

At young Sasikala's Circling, two Mother's Brothers came. The *Tay Maman*, the Eldest Mother's Brother, took the lead. Having delivered the gifts, he entered Sasikala's one-room home and offered worship to the deities. Both the *Maman*s exited, and Sasikala was called to come into the crowded room and dress. She undressed with the usual skill shown by women in Aruloor, modestly covering herself as she exchanged her simple half-sari for a bright pink, synthetic silk sari and pink blouse. This was her very first sari, and she looked gauche but pretty in the shiny material.

In the street, the Washerman had dressed up a thatch awning (*pandal*) to fine effect. He had skillfully pinned white cloths to the underside of the thatch to create a fine white awning, and he even had a decorative frill, in red cloth, traversing the middle of the awning. Decorating the awning for the Circling is one of his traditional duties.

When Sasikala was ready, her gold jewelry shining and the beautiful flowers of the *tanda* crowning her hair, the elder Mother's Brother was called. Standing on the porch, he garlanded her with a huge ring of pink roses. She then descended to the *vasal* (the area in front of the doorstep), which was now covered by the awning.

The Washerman, very sprucely dressed in a shining white shirt and *veshti* (waistcloth), stood ready. He had spread a white *veshti* on the ground and placed two small trays on it. One contained two small brass measuring cans (*padi*), the first filled with paddy and the other with rice, a coconut, a small cluster of bananas, and betel leaf and nuts. The other tray contained *manjal-neer* (auspicious turmeric-water), and in it was lit a *Lakshmi-vilakku*, an ornate small oil-lamp depicting Lakshmi, the goddess of wealth.

Sasikala, garlanded, came and stood on the white cloth in front of the Washerman and respectfully folded her arms. The Washerman at once bent down, lifted up a plate with seven small biscuits (*adai*) on it, and placed one on Sasikala's head, one on each shoulder, one on each elbow, and one on each foot. The seven *adai* are made by the girl's family from raw rice (*paccarisi*) that is ground, mixed with water and salt, shaped into small biscuits, and finally steamed. They are inedible, but even if they were edible, no one would dare to eat them because they are believed to draw out inauspiciousness from the girl.

While Sasikala stood with the seven biscuits perched upon her, the Washerman lifted up the tray with the two cans of grain to a point just above her head, then lowered it until it almost touched the ground. He did this thrice, then passed the tray to Podum, a young girl, who, in turn, passed it to Amudha, a young kinswoman, who passed it back to the Washerman, circling Sasikala entirely. This, too, was done thrice, for three is a very auspicious number. At all times, the circling was clockwise, in the auspicious direction. Podum and Amudha stood just off the white cloth, which marked the "consecrated" area of the ritual. Both of them should have been *kattukkalutti*; that is, eleven-year-old Podum should have been a mature married woman. On the final circling, when the rice-tray reached the Washerman, he placed it on the ground.

Then he picked up the smaller tray containing turmeric-water and the burning Lakshmi-lamp. He performed exactly the same ritual, first raising and lowering it three times in front of Sasikala, then passing it round her. The entire rite was done three times, so the total number of times each tray was raised and lowered in front of Sasikala was nine (again, an auspicious number, recalling the *Navagirakam,* or Nine Planets). The Washerman poured out the turmeric-water at the end of the rite, exactly as *aratti*-water is poured out. Both liquids remove *dirushti*. But before the Washerman poured out the turmeric-water, *Maman* had to drop money (*panam*)—usually one or two rupees in cash—in the liquid as a "gift" for him. This was because *Maman*'s son had traditionally married the girl whose Circling the Washerman was performing, it was said.

The raising and lowering during the Circling is referred to as *"ettaradu-erakkaradu"* ("raising-lowering"). It is performed at all Non-Brahmin circling rites. Gowri, the Brahmin astrologer, said: "This is a ritual of worship done to the *Navagirakam*. They are made happy and they leave, blessing the girl. Their blessing means that all malign astrological influences fade away." The Pallar Washerman confirmed this explanation.

After this, he lifted the biscuits off Sasikala, replacing them on the tray, starting with her head and ending with her feet. The circling rite was almost over. Sasikala started to step off the white cloth as Amudha rushed up and performed an *aratti* rite for her by circling a tray containing a camphor flame three times in front of her. This removed *dirushti* from her. Sasikala then reentered the house. As the Washerman pointed out later, she should have crossed a piece of burning camphor in doing so (as she had after her Purification). But this time, the camphor had been forgotten, so she merely walked inside. Her Circling was over.

Meanwhile, the Washerman deftly tied the paddy and the rice that had been in the first tray in two separate corners of the cloth on which Sasikala had stood, then rolled up the cloth exactly as a Brahmin priest does at the end of a ritual. He placed the coconut, bananas, and betel nut in a small bag. This was his traditional payment for the Circling; he was usually given one *padi* (measuring can) of paddy and one *padi* of rice.

People had stood around in clusters, watching the ritual: When it was over, they were invited to partake of the feast (*sappadu*). The first sitting had already been laid out on banana leaves on a neighbor's terrace. But all was not over, for now the *moy*-giving (cash gift) began, and as each donor gave her or his sum, the amount and the donor's name were announced to the gathering on the loudspeaker. In between, a male voice loudly exhorted people to contribute their *moy* without delay. Pallars, though very poor, give far more in *moy* than better-off castes, such as the Muthurajahs. A careful account of *moy*-gifts was made because here, as with the *sir*, every gift had to be reciprocated in the future. Not to do so was an unforgivable trespass that caused lasting quarrels between relatives.

Muthurajah Puberty Rituals

The Muthurajah puberty rituals are very similar to those of the Pallar. The main differences are that instead of Mother's Brother, it is a Pancangam Brahmin priest who performs the Muthurajah purification ceremony (*punniya danam*) and that it is conducted on the sixteenth day (not the seventeenth, as for the Pallar). Further, it is not the Washerman but a *kattukkalutti* (auspicious married woman) who performs the circling ceremony. She is usually Mother's Brother's Wife but not invariably so if a related *kattukkalutti* who is older and with even more children is available.

Christian Paraiyar Puberty Rituals

The Christian Paraiyar of Aruloor are Roman Catholic by religion, and so it might be assumed that they do not celebrate puberty rituals. Good appears to make this assumption when he notes of the *"sadangu"* (the joint equivalent of Aruloor's Purification and Circling) that "the rite discussed here is practised by all local groups except the Nadars, who are of course Catholics" (1991: 97). However, Tamil Christians do share in Tamil rituals, due to the enormous impact of Hindu culture on *all* religious groups. Living in an environment permeated by Hindu ideas, it is not surprising that the Christian Paraiyars celebrate puberty rituals, for they are deeply influenced by Hindu practices. They observe menstrual impurity prohibitions in the manner of the lower castes, and their puberty rituals are very similar to those of the Pallars and Muthurajahs.

First Day Rituals

Like the other Non-Brahmin castes, the Christian Paraiyars (or CPs, as they are politely referred to since they consider "Paraiyar" an offensive term) put the newly menstruating girl outside the house, on the porch or behind the house. The girl's *Maman* is called, and when he and his wife have arrived, Mother's Brother's Wife and *kattukkalutti* give the girl a ritual bath, handing her auspicious turmeric-powder to rub upon herself. Like the other Non-Brahmin castes, the CPs emphasize the girl's auspiciousness.

The Sixteenth Day *Punniya Danam* (Purification Rite)

Very early on the morning of the sixteenth day, unseen by anyone, the girl and her mother carry the thatch to the river to be burned. The house is whitewashed. The Purification consists of an actual ritual bath, given to the girl by her Elder Brother's Wife (*Anni*). The nomenclature of this female relative is significant because the truly important fact about her identity is that she is usually Father's Sister's Daughter or Mother's Brother's Daughter. The CPs practice cross-kin marriage and Mother's Brother's marriage; as with Non-Brahmin Hindus, these are their traditional marriage preferences. But because the Roman Catholic Church prohibits cross-kin marriage and MB-marriage, they use a term that disguises EBW's true identity. Every time the church notices an "irregular" cross-cousin or MB-marriage, the CPs have to pay a fine and get a dispensation from the bishop. So they have good reason for choosing an innocuous term like *Anni* (EBW), rather than a more genealogically explicit term. Mother's Brother Wife does not give the ritual bath; Elder Brother's Wife bathes the girl and rubs turmeric on her.

The final purification is curious because it has no ritual officiant and no explicit purificatory rite. All it consists of is a visit to the local Roman Catholic Church in the next street, where, significantly, there is no priest to give purification in the

Hindu style. *Maman* escorts the girl to the church, usually in the late evening. The Church of St. Francis Xavier is reached, with all the kin of the girl (practically the whole of Xavier Church Street) following *Maman* and the girl in a procession. At the church, the Church Warden (*Koyil-Pillai*), an old man, reads from the Bible. He also leads prayers during which all the women, in Roman Catholic fashion, cover their heads with their saris. Incense and candles are lit, and a garland of jasmine is placed at the bottom of the crucifix. With this, the simple church rite ends, and everyone returns to the girl's home where they sit in rows and eat a celebratory feast of banana leaves. This feast, like that of high-caste Hindus, is *vadai-payasam*—a purely vegetarian feast. This is noteworthy because the Paraiyar (at least by reputation) are not only meat-eaters but beef-eaters, whence their very low status in the caste hierarchy. All the CPs I knew were anxious to lose this reputation: They *never* ate beef.

Several women expressed resentment at the absence of the Roman Catholic priest, whose presence, they felt, would have lent dignity and importance to the occasion: "The *samiyar* (Roman Catholic priest) never comes for the *punniya danam* (Purification) or the *suttaradu* (Circling ceremony)." At this, other women tried to explain the priest's absence: "It's not because he disapproves that he doesn't come—it's just because it isn't important." But this was plainly untrue. The event was enormously important to the CPs, just as it was to their Hindu neighbors in other streets.

The Circling

As in the CP *punniya danam* (Sixteenth Day Purification), it is the Mother's Brother who brings the *sir* (ritual gifts) to the Circling, and the girl's father provides the feast. The *sutti* feast is larger, grander, and more expensive than the sixteenth day feast, and the change in its date has followed the same pattern as that of the Hindu lower castes, (the upwardly mobile Muthurajah, in particular). So today, for many CPs, a separate Circling has become too expensive, and it is, instead, held the day before the wedding. The traditional CP name for this rite was the *terandu suttaradu* (*terandu*: together), that is, the "circling together."

As with the Hindus, worship occurs first. The girl is dressed in the fine new sari brought by *Maman,* then she is garlanded by him. *Maman* escorts her in a long procession of kin to the church, where (as at the Purification), the Church Warden reads from the Bible and there is prayer. After this, the girl is brought home.

The Circling has two stages. In the first stage, Elder Brother's Wife is the officiant. *Udiripputtu,* a finely powdered mixture of raw rice and brown sugar (*vellam*), is put in a cloth that is tied in a bag. Holding this bag, Elder Brother's Wife gently beats (*kuttaradu*) the girl with it on the back three times. A lot of (*udiripputtu*) is made, which is later distributed by the girl's womenfolk to every home on the street.

In the second stage of the rite, Mother's Brother's Wife takes over. The girl sits in front of an array of auspicious objects: (1) a plate with sweets (*palakaram*) containing, especially, *adirasam, jilebi,* and *laddu*; (2) a stone grinding mortar (*ammi*); (3) an *olakkai*—the long, thick wooden beam that was used as a pestle for milling paddy when this was done manually at home; and (4) a standing oil-lamp (*kuttuvilakku*) that is lit and placed in front of the *sami-padam* (deities' pictures: here, pictures of Jesus, Mary, Joseph, and the Christian saints). The *kuttuvilakku* is significant because of its strong Hindu connections; the *ammi* and the *olakkai* represent the female duties that the girl will now shoulder. The pestle also has strong sexual connotations: It is universally regarded as a phallic symbol.

Now the Mother's Brother's Wife starts the Circling. If she is not present, the rite is done by Elder Brother's Wife. The girl kneels in front of her, and *Maman's* wife lifts up the plate of sweets. She then places a sweet—usually either an *adirasam* or a *jilebi* (both are flat)—on the head, shoulders, and palms of the girl. Then she circles the plate of sweets three times in front of the girl. This is the first *sutti* (circling). The sweets are removed, the girls sits crosslegged, and the flat sweets are placed on her again, this time with one sweet on each knee as well. The sweets in the plate are circled in front of her. Finally, while the girl remains crosslegged, the sweets are removed, and all of them are placed in the plate, which is circled three times above her head and handed directly to the Paraiyar Washerman who will carry both plate and sweets home. He had already been given the clothes that were stained with menstrual blood on the first day, and these sweets are another part of his "payment." When the *sutti* is over, he is also given rice, vegetables, and up to twenty-five rupees in cash. If wealthy, the girl's family may also give him a *veshti* and *tundu* (towel). The sweets are now held to be "polluted" and inauspicious, having absorbed *dirushti* from the girl. No CP would eat them. So here the pollution and dangers of inauspiciousness are removed by transferring them to a ritual specialist of lower caste who normally rids the caste of more mundane impurities, namely, the Washerman. This is the end of the Circling.

Vellan Chettiar Puberty Rituals

The Vellan Chettiars have interesting variations on the Non-Brahmin pattern that the Muthurajah and the Pallar customs define. I will consider very briefly how they differ from this pattern and what the significance of such differences might be.

The First Day Rituals

These rites are similar to those of the Pallar, in that MB and his wife are called. What is significant is that *Attai* (FZ) suddenly springs into prominence, for not only do Chettiar respondents speak of *Tay Maman* (eMB), his wife, and *Attai* (FZ) in the same breath but also it is not MBW but FZ who is most important in the ritual bath on the first day.

The Fifteenth Day Purification Ritual (*Vittukku Alekkaradu*)

Interestingly, the Chettiars use the simple Tamil phrase "invitation back to the home" (*"Vittukku alekkaradu"*) for this event (exactly as the Pallar do), not the Sanskrit *"Punniya danam,"* used by the Muthurajah. As with the Muthurajah, a Brahmin Pancangam priest (*Aiyar*) comes to purify the girl. For the Chettiars, there was, traditionally, no separate circling-ceremony after this until the marriage of the girl. Consequently, this fifteenth day ceremony became a very grand occasion for wealthy Chettiars. "That evening when the girl is invited into the house, *Attai* (FZ) and *Maman* (MB) bring *sir* (ritual gifts)—they bring silk saris, polyester saris and *patram* (vessels). When there are many *Attai-venum* (classificatory FZ) and *Maman-venum* (classificatory MB), this means the girl receives a lot, so it is like *kalyana-sir* [marriage gifts]. In the old days, they gave *nagai* [gold jewelry] too—and the *patram* were of silver. All the kitchen utensils I was given were of silver," concluded Devayanai Chettiar, a woman in her mid-fifties who is married to the second richest man in Aruloor.

On the afternoon of the *Vittukku alekkaradu*, a *madyanam sappadu* (lunchfeast) was traditionally held "for the village [ur]," which Devayanai Chettiar further glossed as "for the entire caste," and a *ratri-sappadu* (night-feast) was held for relatives only. This was not the girl's marriage day, however. Like the Pallars and Muthurajahs, the Chettiars normally waited at least a few months before they married off a daughter.

A major difference used to exist between the Chettiars and the other (lowercaste) Non-Brahmins: The Chettiars had held the Circling on the day before the girl's marriage. Today, however, a fascinating inversion of custom is occurring. Influenced by the wider Non-Brahmin pattern, the Chettiars have recently started celebrating a Muthurajah-Pallar type of Circling a few weeks after the Purification. Meanwhile, the Muthurajahs and Pallars, for their part, are abandoning this separate Circling because they can no longer afford it and, instead, are resorting to the older Chettiar custom of doing it the day before the girl's marriage. Chettiar women were quite aware of the exchange of customs, and when I asked why it was happening, they explained their newly instituted Circling event in this way: "It's purely due to the influence of the other castes. Because our people see the other castes having grand circling celebrations they feel we should have them too." What is so remarkable is that the "other castes" referred to here are the other Non-Brahmin castes, not the Brahmins, who were previously the exemplar for upper Non-Brahmin castes such as the Chettiars. But the Brahmins have suffered a radical downgrading in social esteem in Tamilnadu, due to several decades of anti-Brahmin propaganda by the ruling parties. The Chettiars' adoption of a *lowercaste* Non-Brahmin practice is a sign of both the decline in Brahmin status and a stronger Chettiar identification with a so-called "Tamil" (Non-Brahmin) identity.

Telugu Brahmin Puberty Rituals

Their Diminished Importance

The Brahmin castes are strikingly different from the Non-Brahmins in the way in which they represent human procreation. They state that it is the Brahmin *male* who primarily creates a child; the Brahmin female merely provides a "vessel." Further, the ideal pattern of Telugu Brahmin marriage in Aruloor is not marriage with very close genealogical kin but marriage with distant classificatory kin. Consequently, the Brahmins make rather less of female puberty. Today, their puberty rituals are minor and low-key, private not public in nature, and with no men present at any point. This may be tied to their embarrassment at having *unmarried* puberal daughters, in sharp contrast with Brahmin tradition. Sixty years ago, Brahmins still practiced child-marriage: In Aruloor, for example, the grandmothers of the young girls who were reaching puberty in 1987–1988 had all been married as child-brides, before puberty.

Brahmins now do not commemorate the first day in any way, and they have no separate Circling: They have only one very private, all-female Purification rite and celebration. But fifty years ago their female puberty celebrations were both quite elaborate and public, though never as important as those of Non-Brahmins.

On the first day of menstruation, no rites are performed for the Brahmin girl. She is given no ritual bath, and for three days, she is not allowed to bathe at all or to change her clothes or comb her hair. This was noted with some disgust by the Non-Brahmins who knew about it, being very different from their own tradition in which the girl bathes daily.

The Fourth Day Purification

In sharp contrast, the first bath that the menarchal Brahmin girl is allowed is the ritual purificatory bath that is administered to her by a *sumangali* (married woman) on the morning of the fourth day. Remarkably, no Brahmin priest is involved (unlike the Chettiar and Muthurajah rituals). The entire rite is performed by auspicious married women, for whom Brahmins use the Sanskritic term *"sumangali"* rather than *"kattukkalutti,"* the Tamil term used by the Non-Brahmin castes.

The Fourth Day Purification ritual is very simple. First, the *sumangali* are visited in their homes and formally invited to go to the girl's home by sexually mature young women of the girl's family who offer them *kunkumam* (vermilion) with which to dab an auspicious *bottu* (dot) on their foreheads. A *manakkolam* (auspicious chalk design) is drawn on the back porch of the house, that is, *outside* the house, because the girl (who has spent the last three days either on this porch or in an outside shed) is still impure. On this auspicious chalk pattern, a wooden *palakai* (low stool) is set. The items necessary for the purification are all very auspicious items: (1) betel leaf and nut, (2) threaded jasmine, (3) turmeric-powder, (4) *kunkumam,* (5) a brass container with sesame oil (*nallenney*), and (6) a small brass tray with red *aratti* liquid in which a few grains of *paccarisi* are placed.

At the end of *iragu-kalam* (inauspicious time), the girl is called. As *nalla neram* (good time) begins, she sits on the low stool. The *sumangali* who have gathered (only two kinswomen in the rite I witnessed), along with the womenfolk of the girl, sing that most auspicious of Telugu Brahmin songs, *"Gauri Kalyanam"* ("The Marriage of Goddess Gowri [Parvathi]"). As they sing, the chief *sumangali* is supposed to put a turmeric dot on the girl's forehead. At the ceremony I observed, it was, in fact, not a *sumangali* at all but Sita, a twenty-year-old, unmarried cousin of Bhuvana, the menarchal girl, who did so. This happened because the two *sumangali* present frankly said that they did not want to officiate: They "did not want to have the bother" of taking the purificatory bath that participation in the rite would entail. They therefore deputized Sita to be "acting-*sumangali*" on their behalf, though, being unmarried, she was entirely inappropriate for this role. This casual arrangement suggests the relative unimportance of the event to all concerned.

Sita mixed turmeric-powder and sesame oil and rubbed this paste first on the girl's cheeks (which turned bright yellow), on her hands, and on her feet. Then she rubbed sesame oil into Bhuvana's hair, and finally, she and another young, unmarried cousin (who would now also have to take a purifying "head-bath" later) did *aratti* for the girl, circling the *aratti* tray three times in front of her. The other cousin carefully carried the *aratti* tray right through the house to the area of the *vasal* (the street in front of the doorstep), where she poured it out into the very center of the *kolam* (auspicious chalk design). This, the Brahmins believe, destroys *dirushti.* Non-Brahmins merely pour the liquid out anywhere in the street.

Thereafter, Bhuvana was given a bath by Sita. With this bath, impurity ended, and Bhuvana was given new clothes (a half-sari) and flowers for her hair. Significantly, the new clothes were bought by her father—no Mother's Brother was involved at all in this particular ritual. This suggests how far the Brahmins are from the Non-Brahmins who, in the absence of a genealogical *Maman,* would have ensured that a classificatory *Maman* was present and giving fine gifts.

But the most remarkable aspect of this particular rite was that Sita was the menarchal girl's genealogical Father's Elder Brother's Daughter and therefore her classificatory sister and close patrilineal kin. This relationship would have entirely disqualified Sita from performing any purificatory role in a Non-Brahmin caste because, as *pankali* kin, she shared the girl's impurity and so could not purify her. For this reason, it is always *affines* who are the purifiers and celebrants at purificatory rites—Mother's Brother for the Pallars and affinal *kattukkalutti* for the Chettiars, CPs, and Muthurajahs. Though in Sita's case this unorthodox situation was due to the carelessness of the *sumangali* who had delegated their job to her, it suggests that Brahmins do not share the Non-Brahmin belief that the impurity of the pubescent girl pollutes her agnatic kin. This, as we shall see, is a fact of some importance.

The Effect of Menstrual-Horoscopes on Family and Kin

Menstrual impurity is removed through the purification rite, so it does not need to be removed at Circling. The Circling is focused primarily on removing inauspiciousness. But there are various kinds of inauspiciousness. Though young Pallar and Muthurajah women seemed ignorant of it, older women of these castes and upper-cast women as well stated that the removal of *dirushti* was only part of the reason for the Circling; another crucial reason was the removal of malign astrological influences.

Astrological dangers are taken very seriously by Non-Brahmins because inauspicious stars harm not only the menarchal girl herself but also her entire family. This fact is of major importance, and it points to a crucial difference between Brahminical and Non-Brahmin views. Brahmins and Brahminized Chettiars do not believe that menstrual stars have the power to influence the fortunes of the girl's entire family. But Pallars and Muthurajahs *do* believe this: They state that "bad menstrual stars" can cause the immediate death of the girl's father if the influence of these stars is not removed through appropriate rituals. Indeed, her entire family can meet sudden ruin because of her stars. (Conversely, her family can also prosper if she has a good menstruation-horoscope.) Thus, a crucial difference between Non-Brahmin and Brahminical astrological discourses is that the former represent a menarchal girl's family as being significantly permeable to astral influences that affect her, for good or ill.

Conclusion: Inauspiciousness, Gender, and Kinship

Cultural Constructions of Menarche

Quite unlike the Non-Brahmin girl, the young Brahmin female is deliberately kept unwashed, uncombed, and unkempt until the fourth day. Her menstrual impurity ends with her bath on this fourth day; in the Non-Brahmin castes, it ends only on the fifteenth (Chettiar), sixteenth (Muthurajah), or seventeenth (Pallar) day. It is striking that the lower the caste, the longer the period of menstrual seclusion. There are at least two ways of interpreting this correlation. One interpretation, taking the Dumontean, impurity-focused perspective, has related this to the Brahminic doctrine that a "purer" caste is able to rid itself of impurity more easily. Such an interpretation also assumes that because "pollution" periods for childbirth and death are similarly correlated with caste status, everything boils down to "purity beliefs."

However, those who support the second mode of interpretation, put forward in this book, ask "*Whose* purity beliefs?" and suggest that a close examination of lower-caste ritual practice reveals that lower-caste understandings of ritual purity and its salience for everyday life are very different from those of Brahmins. Further, such an interpretation also implies that when we take lower-caste perspectives and practices into account, an alternative interpretation suggests itself, namely, that it is not the pollution but the generative powers of the menarchal girl that are central.

What actually happens during the menarchal seclusion of Non-Brahmin girls is so different that to focus merely on the different durations of their seclusion is entirely inadequate. From the first day of seclusion, the Non-Brahmin girl is celebrated and feted: A long party begins. On every odd-numbered day, Mother's Brother, Father's sister, or some other affinal kin brings provisions and cooks a small feast for the girl and her family. The puberal girl takes pains to look beautiful and well groomed and is regarded as being very auspicious in herself. Even though she is formally supposed to be "hidden" in seclusion, she is on view from time to time on the porch and is considered very attractive, with flower-bedecked hair and "golden" (turmeric-beautified) skin. Both flowers and turmeric are symbols of auspiciousness and sexuality. So though there may be some anxiety about the astrological influences affecting her, every Non-Brahmin girl is regarded as the embodiment of auspiciousness. Sacred generative powers now invest her, transforming her into a creator of children. In this seclusion period, she is treasured. She is both fed and strengthened for childbirth and beautified for marriage.

The Brahmin view is rather different. True, there is happiness that the girl has reached puberty. But for the entire period of her brief seclusion, the menarchal girl is deliberately kept dirty, unbathed, and uncombed—with no flowers in her hair and no turmeric on her body. She is thus ritually constructed as unclean, and the lack of auspicious symbols indicates that for the duration of her seclusion, she is also represented as inauspicious. This interpretation is strengthened by the fact that at every menstrual period thereafter, the Brahmin woman does not bathe, wear flowers (though she normally does), rub turmeric on her face and body (though she normally uses it) for three days. Upper-caste widows are prohibited from using flowers and turmeric—for the upper castes, the widow is the epitome of the inauspicious woman. Further, a menstruating woman is also excluded from the home, having to spend three days in a shed outside the house: She may not cook for her family or touch them. She temporarily becomes an "untouchable." In short, in Brahmin ritual representation, menstruation is an inauspicious and very impure event.

The lower-caste Non-Brahmin woman, on the contrary, continues to wear flowers, to beautify herself with turmeric, and to bathe daily during her menstrual periods. She continues with her daily life in the normal way, cooking and caring for—and touching—her family. The only prohibition is on her entering a temple or shrine while she is menstruating.

These differences in the representation of menarche could not be more striking. In these symbolic representations, we have two very different paradigms. On the one hand, the Brahmin puberal girl is represented as very impure, inauspicious, and dirty even though there is actually delight that she has come of age. The girl's ritual impurity is foremost in this cultural construction, and because Brahmins regard impurity as linked to sin and inauspiciousness, the symbolic representation is very somber. On the other hand, the Non-Brahmin girl is represented as extremely auspicious, even though ritually impure, and as very beautiful and imbued with sacred generative powers. Her impurity is of entirely secondary importance; it is her auspiciousness that is central.

These very different constructions of female puberty suggest that the very understanding of what inauspiciousness and impurity are differs considerably between the Brahminical castes and the Non-Brahmins. It also suggests that these data can throw some light on the current debate on the meanings of inauspiciousness and impurity and the relation between these concepts in social discourse.

Local Exegeses

When I asked the Pallar Washerman, "What is the Circling for?" he replied, "To remove *sandi* [*sandi kalikkiradu*]." I inquired: "What is *sandi?*" He said, "*Sandi* is impurity [*tittu*]." I asked, "What is this impurity?" He explained: "At the time that the girl comes of age, there are certain *keravam* prevailing." ("Keravam" was his dialectal word for "*girakam*" or "*girakangal*," the nine "planets" of the Hindu zodiac.) He continued: "It is in order to remove the girl's planets that she is circled" (*"Ponnukku keravam kalikkiradukkaka suttaranga"*). He repeated that this was the main reason. But at another point, he added, "The Circling is done because the impurity of the pubescent girl must be dissolved" (*"Suttaradu edukkunna kannipponnukku tittu povanum"*). The Washerman was an intelligent and knowledgeable ritual specialist. I have quoted him in detail because his comments suggest the complexity and ambiguity of the terms involved and also the problems that surround their usage.

Most Pallar and Muthurajah informants felt that the planets were, without exception, unmitigatedly "bad." "The planets *are* inauspiciousness," they would say (*"Keravam tan kettadu"*). Significantly, Chettiars and Brahmins had a more nuanced view of the planets: "Only *some* planets are bad," said Palani Chettiar. Thus, the higher castes had a more sophisticated view of the planets, but for the lower castes, no good could come from the astrological bodies; they were inauspiciousness itself.

In all local analyses, removal was a central concept (*kalikkiradu*: to remove). The Washerman said that the Circling was done to remove *"sandi."* In Tamil, the letters d and t are interchangeable: *"Sandi"* is the same word as *"santi,"* which means "peace." But the Washerman was using it to mean *"tittu,"* or "impurity" and "bad planets" (*"keravam"*). This may be because, in ritual contexts, the lower castes hear of *"santi"* primarily in connection with the *"santi parikaram"* rite, which is, precisely as in the Washerman's gloss, a rite to remove inauspicious influences, especially bad planets. Muthurajah women explained that the Circling was done to remove *dosham* (astrological dangers). Both the Washerman and my Pallar and Muthurajah informants seemed to perceive a fundamental similarity between "impurity" (*"tittu"*), "astrological danger" (*dosham*), and (bad) "planets" (*"keravam"*). All three terms were spoken of as more or less synonymous with "inauspiciousness" (*"kettadu"*). But why did they discuss "impurity as if it was the same thing as "inauspiciousness"? And what does the apparent synonymity between "inauspiciousness" and "impurity" in this context signify?

The Washerman's exegesis, which pointed out that "removal" (*"kalik-kiradu"*) was a central concern of the Circling, equated the removal of bad planets with removing impurity. But what is this impurity? It is not menstrual impurity, for that was removed at the Pallar Purification (by Mother's Brother). It is, apparently, the impurity of bad planets. But this is generally understood as the dangers or astrological flaws from the Nine Planets. Can danger be described as impurity? In this ritual capacity, the Washerman is primarily a remover—or, to put it differently, a professional recipient—of inauspiciousness. Both he and the Barber-to-the-Pallar serve at the Pallar funeral and are paid for their services. At the Circling, he receives, as part of his payment, the paddy and rice that have been circled around the girl and that are, implicitly, tainted with the planetary inauspiciousness and the *dirushti* that he has removed from the girl. The only objects that the Washerman does not accept for consumption (and that he throws away) are the seven *adai* (biscuits) that are inedible. But at the Circling of the Christian Paraiyar girl, the Washerman-to-the-Paraiyar accepts (and, it is believed, eats) the various sweets that have been circled around the girl. Here, the ritual specialist is literally consuming the inauspiciousness that Parry's Mahabrahmans metaphorically found so difficult to "digest" (1980).

I contend that the Washerman very clearly means that what he is engaged in removing through the Circling rite is inauspiciousness. However, he interchangeably uses the word "impurity (*"tittu"*) to describe it because in other contexts (e.g., the Pallar funeral), he, as ritual specialist, removes both impurity and inauspiciousness. Thus, in discussing puberty, several informants used the terms "inauspiciousness" and "impurity" synonymously when speaking of their removal (*kalikkiradu*). These informants spoke of the "removal" of ritual impurity, the "removal" of astrological inauspiciousness, and the "removal" of the evil eye as being much the same thing. Aruloor usage therefore appears to be very different from that described for Pahansu (in Uttar Pradesh, North India) by Gloria Raheja, for she states that her informants distinguished very sharply between *"im-*

purity" and *"inauspiciousness"* in all contexts (1988: 46). T. N. Madan, too, argues for an absolute separation of auspiciousness and purity (1987: 48–71), and so does Frederique Marglin (1977, 1985). By contrast, lower-caste discourse in Aruloor provides strong support for Parry's recent argument that "auspiciousness and purity ... cannot ... be properly understood as entirely independent variables. ... It is surely rather more likely that 'purity' and 'auspiciousness' are 'fuzzy concepts' which have blurred overlapping boundaries" (1991: 268–269).

Raheja's arguments (1988: 46) require attention. She says, "First, impurity cannot be 'removed' through any sort of transferral to a recipient, as inauspiciousness is removed through the giving of *dan*." She continues, "Second, forms of impurity have little if any relevance for more generalized well-being or auspiciousness." And she adds that "Pahansu villagers also make explicit statements that auspiciousness and inauspiciousness entail a 'different reckoning' (*dusra hissab*) from that involved in concerns with purity and impurity." Let us consider these points.

The claim that impurity cannot be removed "through any sort of transferral" to a recipient takes us to the heart of the issue. At the Muthurajah Purification, I spoke to some of the menarchal girl's kin to ask specifically if they thought any transferral of impurity (such as Parry [1980] has described) was occurring. Two men stated that this was happening, but most of those I talked to were not aware of any such transferral. In their view, menstrual impurity had been removed through performing the Purification rite on the sixteenth day: Impurity had ended. But old Subbu Aiyar (the Pancangam Brahmin priest) had a very different perspective. He cut in to say to the "ignorant" Muthurajahs that of course this was precisely what had happened—the impurity of the girl had "transferred" to him "in the *gift*" he had received. Further, he would have to perform various religious rites, particularly recital of the Gayatri Mantra, to dissipate this impurity and rid himself of this burden. He was pleased that I "knew" that a transferral had been occurring. So the views of informants here depended on their position; the Brahmin priest's explanation of what was going on was entirely different from the understanding of the majority of his Muthurajah clients. They knew of no transferral, and they stated that the priest had received no gift: He had simply been paid for services rendered.

Notions of the transferral of impurity are not strong among the Non-Brahmin castes. Significantly, Mother's Brother purifies the Pallar menarchal girl without incurring any impurity himself. Yet such notions are not completely nonexistent. Though they are apparently absent when a very important affine (*Maman*) acts as purifier, they do emerge when a lower-caste ritual specialist is purifier. This happens at Pallar childbirth, where the Barber's Wife performs the purificatory rite: Childbirth *"tittu"* ("impurity") is said by the Pallars to transfer to her in the "gift" she receives. Interestingly, the Pallars also say that the Barber's Wife "is not bothered by" the impurity, the implication being that she, unlike them, is able to deal with it. She herself told me that it was no problem; she took a bath, and it disappeared. At the Muthurajah childbirth purification (*punniya danam*), it is the Brahmin priest who attends. The rite is very similar to that performed at a puberty *punniya danam*. Once again, I found that more "knowledgeable" informants agreed with the Brahmin notion of a transferral of impurity, although the majority were entirely unaware of this.

But Raheja claims that inauspiciousness is removed through the giving of *"dan."* In Aruloor, evidence for this varies with context. In the Chettiar, Muthurajah, and Christian Paraiyar Circlings, the ritual officiants are auspicious *kattukkalutti* (married women). In no case was it stated that inauspiciousness transferred to these women; on the contrary, in all three castes, it was asserted that the hope was that the good luck of the *kattukkalutti* would transfer to the girl, causing her to bear many children after marriage. Only in the Pallar caste, where the ritual officiant was not an affine but the Washerman, was it implied that a transferral of inauspiciousness had occurred. It was transferred to the Washerman in the "gifts" given to him.

A pattern emerges from these varying contexts: Whenever the ritual officiants are close affines, the notion of a negative transfer—either of impurity or of inauspiciousness—is entirely absent. But when the ritual officiant is a specialist of *another* caste (either the lower-caste Washerman or Barber or the higher-caste Brahmin priest), then suddenly, notions of a transfer (of impurity or inauspiciousness) *are* salient and present, either explicitly or implicitly. So the crucial factor appears to be not the nature of the transfer (inauspiciousness or impurity) but the identity of the officiant. And the implication seems to be that in Tamil culture, "bad" transfers do not occur between close affines.

This is remarkably different from the North Indian context that Raheja describes. There, she says, close kin—such as "married sisters, daughters and father's sisters (the women they call *dhiyani*)"—are traditionally designated as the appropriate "vessels" to receive the inauspiciousness that is transferred to them in gifts (Raheja 1988: 25). But this is an idea utterly foreign to the Non-Brahmin kinship ethos. This kinship world was, I noted, distinguished by an emphasis on the value of marriage with the closest possible cross kin and on a continuing stress on the unbroken link between a married daughter and her natal household: They continued to be of "one blood." Further, children were symbolically represented as having a "closer" blood link with their Mother's Brothers than with their Father's Brothers. This stress on the *matrilateral* kin is also evinced in the choice of such individuals as chief affines: The ideal bridegrooms are Mother's Brother and Mother's Brother's son. In short, Non-Brahmin marriage is symbolically represented as reciprocated marriage. Brothers and sisters grow up expecting to give their children in marriage to each other, and it is, in large part, these marriage preferences that account for the intense interest taken by brothers in their sisters' children. This ethos of an egalitarian and reciprocal relationship between affines explains why inauspiciousness cannot be transferred in such a context because all exchanges are reciprocated. In Raheja's own words: "Inauspiciousness can never be transferred in a reciprocated exchange" (1988: 120). Discussing the aversion felt by her Pahansu informants toward "exchange" marriages, she aptly notes, "They say they avoid exchange because such marriages suggest the 'taking for a price' ... of a bride, a transaction that contravenes the fundamental purposes of *dan,* inasmuch as inauspiciousness can never be transferred in a reciprocated exchange. The well-being and auspiciousness of the givers of a bride are only assured when the marriage is a *kanya dan,* an unreciprocated gifting away of a daughter" (Raheja 1988: 120). Nothing could be more foreign to the Non-Brahmin tradition of close cross-kin marriage.

Consequently, the fact that inauspiciousness does not transfer to kin at Non-Brahmin puberty rites is closely tied to the fundamental structure of traditional Non-Brahmin marriage, which, in turn, is based on a very distinctive cultural representation of femaleness. Female uterine blood emerges as the central symbol of Non-Brahmin identity; "female blood" creates children, and the most significant prestations flow along uterine blood lines, from Mother's Brothers to their sisters' children. It is this uterine blood that manifests itself at puberty and that is purified and made auspicious in the most elaborate ritual sequence known in Non-Brahmin culture. Through these rites, the Non-Brahmin castes have continued to recreate themselves and their identities, while simultaneously protecting and perfecting the life-giving "powers" of the women who will create new generations.

However, in reality, female uterine blood has always been appropriated and controlled by males. The centrality of "female generative power" in Non-Brahmin representations of procreation does not mean that women have had substantive power or even a secure social position. This has become very clear today. The changes in Non-Brahmin marriage among upwardly mobile groups are, in fact,. resulting in a steady devaluation of women. Thus, the proclamation of female power in the puberty rites jars sharply with the reality of women's new insecurity. A painful disjunction is emerging between Tamil ritual discourses and everyday practices.

6

Dancing the Goddess: Possession, Caste, and Gender

Yes, isn't it strange how the *Sami* comes only to those two women, the wives of the **muppan**s? We must be made of lesser stuff, that's why she never possesses any of us!

—Pandaiyee (Pallar)

UNLIKE BELIEF IN THE EVIL eye (*dirushti*) which is pervasive in all the castes, the phenomenon of possession (*pudiccikkiradu*) exhibits a distinct caste and gender differential. My argument here will focus primarily on the implications of this caste and gender differential. However, an intriguing class differential also emerges, especially in relation to the identity of those who become possessed by the Supreme Goddess.

I will first argue that the phenomenon of possession, in its various manifestations, provides further evidence for my claim that the lower castes do not share upper-caste assumptions regarding ritual purity. Although the upper-caste religious ethos, embodied in the practices of the Brahmins and Chettiars, emphasizes ritual purity and the necessity for the correct performance of ritual, the emphasis of the religious ethos of the Muthurajahs and Pallars is not on ritualism but on devotion. This lower-caste ethos claims that a supreme deity like Mariyamman or Murugan will only possess a person if that person—who is usually male—has "purity of heart" and true devotional love for the deity. Ritual purity is of secondary importance: It is merely necessary so that the person can be a fit vehicle for the deity. Consequently, certain simple measures (involving vegetarianism, chastity, and extreme cleanliness) are taken by the person seeking to be possessed. But it is devotion—*bakti*—that counts above all.

124

However, though the lower castes do not share conventional upper-caste assumptions regarding the primacy of ritual purity, such purity is a means to an end, not an ultimate principle, in both groups. The lower castes also believe that one must be pure to be possessed by the deity, but though their notion of purity includes Brahmin-style ritual purity, this is not what it *stresses*. Instead, the stress is on *bakti*-style purity of heart. The influence of *bakti*, or devotional Hinduism, is so pervasive in Tamilnadu that even many Brahmins would probably agree with the lower castes that devotion counts above all else. However, Brahmins generally express their devotion in a controlled, ritualistic manner. This allows the lower castes to argue—as they do in Aruloor—that Brahmins lack the humility and self-abandonment required for "true" religious devotion. Thus, what is essentially a difference of emphasis between lower- and upper-caste religious ethos is sharply stressed and rephrased in lower-caste discourse so that it is perceived as a dichotomy between the "true devotion" of the lower castes and the "mere ritualism" of the upper castes.

The religious discourse of the lower castes rejects the claims of the higher castes. It claims—and regularly demonstrates—that Deity descends to possess those of the most humble caste because Deity is concerned not with any temporal purity hierarchy but rather with devotion, love, and purity of heart—values that the ideology of caste hierarchy entirely discounts. My first argument therefore concerns the religious discourse of the lower castes.

My second argument is that possession provides clear evidence that a strong bias exists against women in the religious sphere, in all castes, including the Pallar caste. Consequently, all important benign possession, especially institutionalized possession, is experienced solely by men, even when the deity concerned is female. Thus we have the paradoxical situation that "dancing" or "being possessed by" the Great Goddess Mariyamman is solely a male activity. ("Dancing" is a synonym for "being possessed"—the deity causes the person to dance.) Further, most malign possession is experienced by women, for far more women than men are possessed by *pey* (evil ghosts). This recalls a related phenomenon—that far more women than men have *dosham* in their horoscopes.

Most remarkable of all is the fact that in their possession events, both lower-caste men and Brahmin men have to "become female" in order to be possessed by the deity (whether female or male). I argue that through this symbolic appropriation of "femaleness," women are marginalized in religious discourse in all castes because men are allowed to be both female and male. No such freedom is available to women; in these possession events, they remain comparatively passive "objects" who are allowed virtually no active role. They merely watch and applaud feminized men enacting the incarnations of Deity. The idea that a devotee is a "female" in relation to God is pan-Hindu, being especially stressed in the *bakti* tradition, so my argument is, I suggest, widely applicable.

Types of Possession

The state of possession (*"pudiccikkiradu"*: "being caught") is well known in Aruloor and occurs fairly frequently in a multitude of forms. It is, however, not a commonplace state, and whenever it occurs, it evokes great interest and often (in a benign possession) deep respect. Possession is, very broadly, of two sorts—either possession by a benign deity (*sami*) or possession by a demon or evil spirit (*pey*). The first evokes respect; the second, fear.

Linguistically, the two categories are clearly distinguished by the upper castes (Brahmins and Chettiars). They use the term *"pudiccikkiradu"* ("catches") for possession by an evil spirit but the term *"vandudu"* ("comes") for possession by a benign deity. So a benign deity "comes" to a person, but a demon "catches" a person. However, the lower castes (Pallars, CPs, and Muthurajahs) distinguish far less sharply between the two terms, for they speak of *both* benign and malign spirits "catching" a person. They also use the term *"adradu"* ("dances") and speak of *both* evil ghosts and benign deities "dancing" when they are in possession of someone. Finally, like the upper castes, they also use the term "comes" (*"vandudu"*) for benign possession. This means that the lower castes use all three terms for benign possession, but the upper castes use only one, namely, "comes." As we will see, this difference is directly related to the religious styles adopted by the upper and lower castes.

Although benign and malign possession constitute the two principal categories of possession, each has further subdivisions. I will primarily focus on the various forms of benign possession. First, I will briefly note what the various categories are; they are quite clearly delineated and differentiated in Non-Brahmin discourse but sometimes blur from one category into another in practice. Following the local descriptions, they are as follows:

1. the state of temporary possession or spontaneous possession by either a benign deity or an evil spirit;
2. institutionalized possession or hierarchized, inherited possession by benign deities, which has considerable political importance;
3. possession by a benign deity while "putting *alaku*" (*"alaku podradu"*), that is, "wearing" various metal objects pierced through one's body.

Temporary or Spontaneous Possession

This could be of two kinds—possession by a *sami* ("benign deity," female or male) or by a *pey* ("evil spirit"). Sudden and short-lived possession by an evil spirit was far rarer than such a possession by a benign deity; when a person became suddenly possessed, it was usually by a beneficent power. Yet the term *pudiccikkiradu* ("being caught") does not necessarily have a positive connotation. When people speak of someone as "being possessed," they do not necessarily mean by a deity. The term is ambivalent and is also used for long-term possessions by *pey*. It is worth noting that in all castes, sudden, minor misfortunes are not attributed to *pey* but to *dirushti*, the malignant power of the evil eye exercised by human beings. Thus, sudden occurrences of evil, especially disease, are blamed on human beings rather than on supernatural beings.

Temporary Possession by a Deity

A person who is suddenly and spontaneously possessed by a deity is usually someone known to have a marked inclination "that way." Typically, the person becomes possessed (by the same deity) from time to time—such possession is normally not a one-time occurrence. This was the case with Kannagi's sister-in-law, who had come for the *punniya danam* (puberty purification ritual) of Kannagi's daughter in the Muthurajah street. In the middle of the ritual, while we were all clustered around Subbu Aiyar and Manjula, there were suddenly cries from the street: "She has fallen! Come quickly!" Alarmed, everyone dashed out to find that the sister-in-law (who was in her early forties) had fallen in the street. At first, it was not clear what had happened, but it was soon established, by witnesses and the woman herself, that on smelling the *sambrani* (incense) lit for the ritual, she had suddenly been "overpowered by the *sami*," in this case, the goddess Mariyamman herself.

The woman and her husband (Kannagi's brother) lived in Kumbakonam. There, her tendency to become possessed was known, and, as a Muthurajah woman neighbor explained to me, there she would not have fallen. The neighbor said, "When someone becomes possessed they lose control of their bodies. They begin to twitch and vibrate, this becomes so violent that they end by throwing themselves around wildly, without caring that they might injure themselves. This is because they are no longer in control—they no longer even know what is happening: It is the *sami* who is in control. That's why, when you see this happening, you must rush up and grab them under the arms to prevent them falling. But here it happened so quickly that there was no time for passers-by to catch her." We learned that Kannagi's brothers had built a small Mariyamman shrine near their house to commemorate their deceased mother. Her sister-in-law was a great devotee of the goddess and worshipped daily at the shrine. "Consequently," explained Kannagi, "she has grown very close to the *sami*. She loves the *sami* deeply—and Mariyai returns this love, for God is always drawn by true devotion. That's why she becomes possessed—because the *sami*, recognising her love, comes to her readily, to satisfy her longing. That's when she becomes possessed [*pudiccikkiradu*] and falls down." The possession by Mariyai was taken as a very auspicious sign: The Great Goddess had "visited" the puberty ceremony, it was felt. The woman herself was drawn and pale but quite composed after the event.

She said that she remembered nothing, only the smell of the incense that had brought on the possession.

"This is quite common," said Anjalai, my Muthurajah friend. "There are actually many people who become possessed when they smell incense, but they are usually people who are devoted to a particular deity. Their particular deity [female or male] 'comes' to them, when they smell incense. They remember nothing about what happened, later." This was apparently true of the sister-in-law. Thus, those who become possessed may legitimately behave in a manner that would be considered improper or even obscene in normal circumstances. The round-bellied *sami-adi* (god-dancer) Selvam was famed for the occasion when his *veshti* (waistcloth) fell off entirely while he "danced," possessed by his god, in Mariamman Koil Street.

After the brief possession of Kannagi's sister-in-law, everyone filed back to watch the *punniya danam,* which continued as smoothly as if no interruption had occurred. Interestingly, the event also indicated that the expectation that someone was likely to be possessed influenced events. When someone shouted to Manjula, the pubescent girl being purified, "Your mum's fallen down in the street! Your mum's become possessed!" fourteen-year-old Manjula calmly replied, "Impossible! My mother doesn't become possessed!" And she was right, of course, for it was her *attai* (MBW) who had fallen down.

Much credit redounds to the possessed person, for she (or he) is seen to be pure (*suttama*) enough for the deity to "enter." This state of "purity" (*suttam*) is synonymous with "purity of heart" or spiritual virtue, and it carries status. This is not ritual purity in a Dumontean (caste hierarchy) sense. People who are often possessed by a deity are generally regarded with special respect: They have been hallowed and made the embodiment of the Supreme Deity whether female or male. The term *"Sami"*, though a male term usually meaning "God," was used by both lower- and upper-caste informants for *both* goddesses and gods. Kannagi's sister-in-law had keeled over before anyone could reach her; if she had been held and remained standing, several people (mainly women) would have fallen at her feet to worship her. This happened on every other such occasion that I witnessed, though the caste of the possessed person determined who worshipped him or her and who did not.

Temporary Possession by Evil Spirits

I now turn to sudden, spontaneous possession by an evil spirit. This is more problematic, given that nobody wishes to claim that they have suddenly been possessed by a *pey*. Consequently, on the only occasion when I witnessed possible *pey* possession, there was considerable doubt as to whether benign or malign spirits were acting. The occasion was the possession rituals of the Pallar village of Mallarchipuram at their Mariyamman festival. The *pusari* (priest) was beating his *udukkai* (a small hand drum that produces an eerie moaning sound) to induce possession in the men and women who were going to carry *pal-kodam* (milk-pots) when the intrusion by evil spirits—or deities—occurred.

Suddenly, several young female bystanders started jumping up and down, their eyes shut, throwing themselves about, and crying out. They were grabbed by others and held upright, so that they did not fall, and the *pusari* himself seemed annoyed by their possession because the people in whom he was trying to induce possession had not yet reacted. The immediate assumption of those present was that these supernatural agents were *pey,* not deities, so nobody worshipped the young women. On the contrary, bystanders sternly asked the spirits, "Who are you? What is your name? Reveal yourself!" But the young women merely moaned and shrieked louder as they struggled to tear free from the women who were holding them.

Siva, my Pallar friend, declared at once: "This shows that they are *pey* and not deities, because they can't identify themselves. *Pey* have no names—and know of no names—*pey* are stupid. But a *deyvam* [deity] will always identify itself. *Pey* come to these occasions because they're attracted by the sweet smells [of incense, joss-sticks, flowers] and the food-offerings. They come pretending to be the *sami,* hoping they'll get the offerings instead." Sacred ash (*tunnuru*) was thrown by the *pusari* on the possessed women, who were screaming and flailing about, as if in hysteria. The ash, which fell on their heads, seemed to calm them a little, but they were still quite agitated as they were dragged away. Siva explained: "The *tunnuru* causes the possession to end—it causes the *pey* to release the person, because it is sacred and *pey* are afraid of the sacred. Also, ash signifies fire and, of all things, *pey* are most terrified of fire. They never go near fire." This explanation is interesting because sacred ash is normally used to "cool" and calm a person. It is also used to halt possession by a deity. When Arulooor's young Brahmin priest became possessed, his father, the elder priest, threw ash on him when it was time to end the possession.

Women and Temporary Possession

Significantly, temporary possession is considered unimportant, particularly in comparison with institutionalized possession. This is because it is of short duration, because it is not hereditary, and possibly because it affects women, too. It appears that the fact that women can have it automatically devalues this category of possession. Further, it is usually women, not men, who are believed to be spontaneously possessed by evil spirits, as in the event just noted. It was felt that women were more liable to possession by *pey* "because," as a Pallar informant explained, "they are weaker and can't resist the *pey,* as men can. That's why it's usually women who are possessed by *pey* at festivals, not men." She added, "A person is always possessed by a *pey* of the *opposite sex*—for male *pey* desire to possess women while female *pey* desire to possess men." For this reason, *pey* are regarded as the sexual partners of those whom they possess. Both Muthurajah and Pallar informants agreed on this. However, among upwardly mobile lower castes, the Brahminical view that women are more vulnerable to possession by *pey* because they are "less pure" than men also existed. In this upper-caste perspective, women are less frequently possessed by benign deities because they are impure beings, being polluted by menstruation.

Institutionalized Possession

Because this kind of possession is hierarchized and inherited from father to son, I have called it "institutionalized possession" (as Dumont also did; see Dumont 1986). By "hierarchized," I mean that both deities and possessed are ranked: The higher deities are incarnated in the wealthiest men, and the lower deities are incarnated in less wealthy men.

The Muthurajah caste are, by far, the biggest caste-group in Aruloor. At a major festival in the Muthurajah Three Streets, I saw the clearest manifestations of institutionalized possession. Several important and wealthy men of this caste were hereditary *sami-adi* (god-dancers). In contrast, in the Pallar street in 1987, there was only one hereditary *sami-adi* left. *"Sami-adi"* is the term used for a man who has inherited the ability to be possessed by a deity. These possessions normally occur at the annual festivals of the deities concerned, when, by possessing the *sami-adis*, the deities manifest themselves. The ability to be possessed confers great prestige because it indicates the superior moral virtue and purity of the person who is possessed. Consequently, to be a *sami-adi* is to have considerable status in one's community. Further, as we shall see, the institutionalized possession embodied in the tradition of the *sami-adi* provides a focus for local rivalries and power politics. This became apparent in an ongoing quarrel in the Three Streets.

The Muthurajah Three Streets Feud Concerning Sami-Adi

In the small open shrine at the head of Mariamman Temple Street, there is only a rather rough painting of the goddess on the wall. An oil lamp is lit in this little three-walled room every evening. However, as the inhabitants of the street were very proud to tell me, two silver effigies of Mariyai (Mariyamman) and Kaliyai (Kali) were kept in a *koyil petti* (temple chest) in the house of an important family. The Muthurajahs of the Three Streets were inordinately proud of their silver goddesses (though they hardly ever saw them) because, they claimed, "No other community anywhere else, has a silver figure of Mariyai—all others only represent her by a *karagam* [sacred pot with a tall, conical flower decoration]." In 1987, there was to be a ceremony for the purification of the Mariyamman shrine, where there would be *sami-adi* representing not just Mariyai, but possibly also Kaliyai and the secondary gods Madurai-veeran (the Warrior of Madurai), Nagappasami (the Cobra-God), and Tevangudi-Karuppan (the Black God of Tevangudi). The feud centered on who Kaliyai's *sami-adi* was going to be.

The three male deities were described by Muthurajahs as the guardian deities (*kaval-deyvam*) of the two main deities: "They are the watchmen [*kaval*], the guards of Mariyai and Kaliyai. When you go to see a great man you have to flatter his subordinate officers, otherwise you'll get nowhere. Similarly here: You can't just march into the main shrine of a temple. You must first worship at the shrines of the watchman-deities and only thereafter proceed, with their blessings, to the inner shrine." Tevangudi-Karuppan or Karuppu, the Black God of Tevangudi, is a warrior-god: He was the family-deity (*kula-deyvam*) of "half" the Muthurajahs in the Three Streets *ur*, it was said. Nagappasami was the *kula-deyvam* of the other half. The *ur*, or community, consisted primarily of two large lineages (*pankali*).

The *sami-adi* were of greatest importance at the *Karagam-tiruvila* (Sacred Pot festival) of Mariyamman, which was usually held in the month of Masi (ca. February 15 to March 15) or in Cittirai (April 15 to May 15) every year. On this occasion, the *karagam*, or flower-ornamented pots—which embodied the two goddesses—were carried on the heads of the *sami-adi* who became possessed by Mariyai and Kaliyai. The silver effigies were tied to the fronts of the sacred pots. Meanwhile, *tirtta kodam* (pure-water pots) were carried on the heads of the *sami-adi* of the three male guardian-deities. As with the *karagam*, the male deities were said to enter into the water in the pots and simultaneously possess the pot-bearers. However, in 1987, the *karagam*-festival had not been held for more than five years. A bitter intrastreet feud lay behind this. Feelings were so strong that no one was willing to talk openly about it. But in private, it emerged that a local power struggle was going on. The struggle throws into sharp relief the political uses of being a *sami-adi*.

As noted, the feud centered on who was to be *sami-adi* for the goddess Kaliyai. A man called Maruday had been the last *sami-adi*, and one faction argued that the deceased Maruday's son should automatically become *sami-adi*. However, there were two problems, one major and one minor.

The minor problem was that the young man was as yet not married, and a *sami-adi* must be married. This has to do with "having power": Power is *sakti* and is personified by the goddess Sakti, Siva's consort. A *sami-adi* must be "in contact with his Sakti, just as Siva derives strength [*sakti*] from his wife, Sakti [or Parvati]," I was told. The implication is that men derive "power" from sexual intercourse with women, who embody this power. Fuller notes the same of the Madurai Temple priests, who "must have a living wife to perform the daily worship and other important rituals. It is believed that, in order to worship both the god and the goddess, they must have access to feminine power, only legitimately obtained through sexual relations with their wives" (1980a: 326, emphasis added). Fuller had noted earlier that "this explanation parallels the Tantric doctrine that in ritual intercourse the female is the incarnation of the goddess's power" (1979:

463). Beck mentions that the same marriage rule applies to the three main officiants at the Kannapuram Mariyamman festival (1981: 110). And Daniel points out
that even in an everyday, nonreligious context, semen or vaginal fluid (*intiriyam*)
is referred to as *"sakti"* (1984: 167). This has important implications, which will
be discussed later.

Maruday's son could easily marry, so nobody was too worried by the requirement of a wife: This was a minor dilemma. The major problem was that when a
test was carried out to decide who the successor should be, neither the "legal"
heir (Maruday's son) nor the contestant, Sibi, a young man from the rival faction,
had been able to pass it. The rival faction had a strong case because the hereditary
position of *sami-adi* for Kaliyai had run in Sibi's forefather's line. That is, before
Maruday, it had not been his father but Sibi's grandfather (from another lineage)
who, following his own father, had become *sami-adi*. However, when Sibi's
grandfather died, his son did not want to become *sami-adi* because he was a fanat-
ical Dravida Kazhagam party member and therefore a confirmed atheist. So he declared that the whole *sami-adi* business was a load of rubbish and would have
nothing to do with it. That was when Maruday claimed that the goddess (Kaliyai)
had come to him and told him that he was her new *sami-adi*, and he duly became
possessed by her. Sibi's father did not challenge Maruday, and therefore the right
to be *sami-adi* passed to Maruday's family. So went the story. The feud had
started on Maruday's death, when young Sibi declared that he had been possessed
by Kaliyai and claimed his hereditary right. He demanded that the role of *sami-
adi* be given back to him, arguing that Maruday's role had been a temporary intrusion. Consequently, in 1984, the street had tried to settle the quarrel by a test.

With many witnesses at hand, the test to determine the true *sami-adi* had been
held directly in front of the Mariyamman shrine. The test was one that was often
used. A tiny packet of *kunkumam* (vermilion powder) signifying the goddess
Kaliyai was hidden amid many tiny packets of *tunnuru* (sacred ash) (cf. Daniel's
1993 account of similar tests). The two young men were told to call upon Kaliyai
to help them, and each was given a turn at picking out the right packet. When neither was able to do so, they were given yet another try, but again both failed. As a
result, the feud had continued unabated. Those in the street who wished to hold
the *karagam*-festival with the goddess Kaliyai left out were threatened by Sibi's
supporters, who saw this as a trick by which Maruday's son's claims would be exalted. "They threatened that they would push Ganesan [Mariyamman's *sami-adi*]
so that Mariyai's *karagam* fell down. If it fell it would smash—this would bring
destruction on everyone in the street. They're such mad, drunken men that
they'd really do it. That's why we haven't dared to have the *karagam* festival for
several years now," said Ponnarsan, a wealthy young man who was on Maruday's
son's side. Many feared that if the Great Goddess was thus affronted, her anger
would know no bounds. She would probably kill them all as punishment for the
sacrilege. Older women recalled the terrible time, some forty years earlier, "when

Mariyai had been angry" and many had died in the smallpox (*ammai*) epidemic that had swept Tiruchi District.

A feud's ability to put a halt to a community's most important festival is quite common. Here, it indicated the absence of a dominant leadership among the Muthurajahs of the Three Streets. This contrasted sharply with the situation in the Pallar street where two hereditary leaders had long been the unquestioned street-bosses (*talaivar*). This suggests that traditional, inherited authority, such as that in the Pallar Street, is weakened and challenged in a context where salaried employment—and the power and status it gives—becomes widespread. This had happened in the upwardly mobile Muthurajah Three Streets. Ironically, although Lakshmanan, the man in whose house the *koyil-petti* (temple chest) with the two silver statuettes was kept, was among the most outspoken atheists, he supported Sibi's claim politically. This factionalism testifies to the resurgence of religion as a political strategy, due to the steady decline in the militant atheism of both the Dravida Kazhagam party and the DMK party.

Sibi himself had a critical need of higher social status, for he had recently acquired the newly created salaried post of *Vettiyan*. The *Vettiyan* was traditionally the "untouchable" Paraiyar funeral attendant, and his had been a most despised occupation. But as soon as this "untouchable" hereditary job was made a salaried Panchayat (Local Council) post, it was promptly grabbed by the dominant Muthurajah caste, and the unemployed Sibi, through his contacts, got the job. He clearly needed all the status he could get.

Spontaneous *Sami-Adi* Possession

Because of this quarrel, the great *karagam*-festival was not held at all in the Muthurajah street. Consequently, the occasion when I saw hereditary *sami-adi* possessed was not at the *karagam*-festival, which is clearly when they come into their own, but at a much smaller event, the "purification" of the Mariyamman shrine. The *sami-adi* were not required to be possessed for this, so the possessions of Ganesan (Mariyamman's *sami-adi*) and Selvam (Tevangudi-Karuppan's *sami-adi*) were actually "spontaneous" events. Neither man had any official role in the purification rite, which was carried out by the most senior Brahmin priest and his son, from Aruloor's Siva Temple. Therefore, neither man was ritually dressed, nor were they carrying either *karagam* (flower-ornamented pot) or *kodam* (water pot), as they would have been for the *karagam*-festival. Instead, they were, until the moments of their possessions, ordinary members of the audience. The young Brahmin priest became possessed too.

As the young Brahmin priest carried the *tirtta kodam* (pure-water pot) on his head around the shrine, his possession began. This happened so gradually that I was not aware of it until I noticed that he was swaying and in danger of smashing the pot. I had not noticed because a very much more spectacular possession was occurring. Ganesan, *sami-adi* of Mariyamman, had been standing on Main Road, which runs behind the shrine. As the Brahmin carrying the sacred pot, which embodied the goddess, came around the corner of the shrine and up the Main Road (which slopes down to the shrine), he was clearly possessed, for he walked unsteadily, as in a trance, with his eyes half closed. Both he and the pot were supported by two men (Ponnarsan and another rich and influential man, Srinivas). The Brahmin's unexpected possession—by the Great Goddess herself, as was readily understood by all who watched—triggered Ganesan's possession by her, too. He suddenly went rigid, his eyes becoming huge and staring, almost popping out of his head. He started jerking his hands, legs, and head, sticking out his tongue from time to time (reminiscent of "angry" representations of Mariyamman, whose fury is indicated by her bared teeth and outstretched tongue). His possession was not very violent, nor did he "dance" as such; instead, he seemed to find it difficult to move at all. He was grabbed at once and supported as he moved around the shrine to its front, where he was held up, his body still jerking slightly and his eyes, most dramatic of all, still huge and distended.

The most violent possession, however, was that of Selvam. It began while we were up on the Main Road, but we heard cries from the crowd below, by the shrine: "He's possessed! Watch out! Hold him!" But Selvam was leaping about so wildly that no one could hold him as we, the crowd accompanying the possessed Ganesan and the Brahmin, came around the corner of the shrine and returned to the front of it. A woman reported: "Selvam suddenly started quivering—first his legs began to tremble, then his whole body, then, suddenly, with a great yell, he sprang forward and danced from side to side. It was a very powerful possession—and a very good sign." It was universally agreed that the possessions were a most auspicious occurrence. Mariyamman herself had manifested in the Brahmin priest and in Ganesan, and Tevangudi-Karuppan had done so in Selvam, thus signifying their pleasure in and acceptance of the worship done.

Remarkably, although possession of a *sami-adi* is generally taken as evidence of the grace (*arul*) and happiness of the deity concerned, it is manifested as extreme pain and sorrow in its human vehicle (cf. Dumont 1986 for a similar observation). The Brahmin priest in trance wore no smile; on the contrary, it was clear that he was suffering physically. He told me later: "The pot became immensely heavy, for the *amman* [goddess] had entered it—and then she entered me and I remember nothing after that." Ganesan, too, had looked tortured, though he made not a sound: His eyes had shown a startled pain. But the divine agony had been most visible in Selvam. Even as we came around the shrine, this large, fat man was giving shouts and screams as he hurled himself around, his whole body and his whole face were beaded with sweat. He was the embodiment of a human being in extreme suffering, his face twisted in agony, his eyes wide open but unseeing. Many in the crowd (particularly women) raised their joined palms above their heads in worship to him—or, more precisely, to Tevangudi-Karuppan, now embodied in Selvam. So, too, others bowed before the Brahmin priest and before Ganesan. At the same time, the wobbling of the pot on the Brahmin's head caused great concern. If it fell, Mariyai would be dishonored and would devastate those gathered, so it was with genuine anxiety that the Muthurajah men held on to the pot—and the tottering Brahmin beneath it. "Mahamai! Mahamai! Great Mother! Have pity on us! Forgive us! Don't be angry with us!"—the cries and prayers of the women to the Great Goddess resounded: It was a moment of tremendous emotional intensity, a moment of extraordinary divine longing—and this groundswell of feeling created a sense of presence, of embodiment, of something, whether the Great Goddess herself or of human longing for her. In that moment, it was possible, even for an alien like me, to believe in the power and grace of Mariyamman—how much easier for those who lived in the shadow of her shrines and temples all their lives. The cries, the intense crescendo of feeling, were brought under control by the old Brahmin priest, who, ritually, threw ash on the head of his son to end his possession and then, in turn, on Ganesan and on Selvam. The two *sami-adi* remained standing where they were: The expressions of pain and suffering remained on their faces. It was, in fact, the young Brahmin who, after a few minutes of looking dazed, wiped his face and then set to work assisting in the ritual, thus returning from possession to normalcy fairly quickly.

The printed invitations to the purification ceremony had stated that worship would be offered to Mariyai, Kaliyai, and their three guardian deities, Nagappasami, Madurai-veeran, and Tevangudi-Karuppan. Mariyai and Tevangudi-Karuppan manifested themselves: Kaliyai could not since no *sami-adi* existed for her. The *sami-adi* of Madurai-veeran had moved away with his family to another village some years earlier: He never showed up at this rite but always came for the *karagam*-festival, it was claimed. Thus, moving away from the village did not mean that one lost one's hereditary *sami-adi* right. The fifth *sami-adi*, of the Cobra-God, Nagappasami, was actually present, but this man did not become possessed. Many people were disappointed by this and vigorously blamed him for not getting possessed: "He's a weak, drunken fellow, and very seldom sober these days. What god would come to such an impure [*asuttama*] fellow?"

Divine Grace and Wealth

The most significant aspect of *sami adradu* (god-dancing) or institutionalized possession is the striking fact that there is a close correspondence between economic wealth and divine possession. In short, social status and divine grace appear to go together. Ganesan, the *sami-adi* of Mariyamman, the supreme deity, God Herself, was the richest man in the Three Streets, possessing more land than anyone else (about twenty acres). The hereditary position of *sami-adi* had been in Ganesan's family for several generations; so, too, had their dominant economic power. Ganesan was a quiet, reserved man, but he could afford to maintain a low profile because everyone in the *ur* knew he was a man not only of great wealth but also blessed with the special grace of Mariyamman; he was her chosen vehicle, her *sami-adi.* The other three god-dancers of the "watchman" gods were also landed and comparatively wealthy. Several Muthurajahs in the upwardly mobile Three Streets were still very poor. None of them was a *sami-adi.*

In the Pallar *ur,* too, the very significant fact of this correspondence between earthly power and divine grace was equally apparent, but there, it was publicly commented on and sneered at, the Pallars being more brutally frank than the Muthurajahs.

Possession in the Pallar Street

In the Pallar street, the only *sami-adi* left was Ramaiah, the elderly *sami-adi* of Mariyamman. At the head of the street stood the goddess's temple, and ten years earlier, this street had been called Mariamman Koil (Temple) Street. Here, too, the *sami-adi*-ship had passed from generation to generation, and the family of Mariyamman's *sami-adi* was one of the two or three wealthiest in the community. Ramaiah was a well built, grey haired man in his sixties. He showed little interest in the legends of Mariyamman and did not seem to know much about them. His lack of interest cannot be faulted, perhaps, for all the other *sami-adi*-ships in the Pallar street had become defunct.

No *sami-adradu* (god-dancing) had occurred in Periyar Street for more than fifteen years, it was said. This may have been due to the ascendance, in the previous ten years or so, of Pechimuthu, a man of considerable wealth and great influence. As a very active member of the atheistic DMK party, he not only got himself elected as Ward Member for the street but was also Vice-President of the Aruloor Town Panchayat. But Pechimuthu had always shared power with another street-boss, Mani. Apparently not so atheistic, Mani took an interest in organizing the major Pallar religious festivals. Mani, Pechimuthu, and Ramaiah (the *sami-adi*) were, in fact, the hereditary *muppan* (three leaders) of the street. Traditionally, Pallar communities had had three village headmen, who, in turn, had two assistants. So these three were the modern triumvirate, though Ramaiah was much less important than the other two. Obviously, neither Pechimuthu nor his wife could be possessed by a deity, given his affiliation and prominence in a political party dedicated to atheism. Nor did Mani ever become possessed. But, most strikingly, the wives of both Mani and Ramaiah became regularly possessed, both of them by the Great Goddess herself. For instance, Valliammal, Ramaiah's wife, had very recently become possessed when she learned of the "uncleanliness" of a woman recovering from chicken pox: An infuriated "Mariyamman" had warned the woman's husband that they would be punished if they did not perform the necessary purification rituals following recovery from the disease. Valliammal may have been worried about the spread of infection to her neighboring house. Meanwhile, sharp-voiced Sellaiyee, the wife of Mani, ensured that she was "possessed" by Mariyamman at every festival. I use quote marks here because my Pallar women friends effectively did so when they sneered about Sellaiyee's divine shenanigans.

Faith in the divine possession of the wives of the two *muppan* was virtually nonexistent; scepticism abounded. A discussion on the issue with Marudambal on her open porch became an open, satiric attack on the two self-proclaimed vehicles of the goddess. Marudambal, who was in her fifties, was generally on her porch when not at work in the fields. She was both a noted satirist and an acute commentator on the social scene in the Pallar street. She had just heard about Valliammal's outburst "as Mariyamman" and promptly reenacted it for us. "Hooo!" Marudambal-as-Valliammal cried: "Haaa! You filthy man! You unclean thing! You refuse to give me the offerings that are my due, do you? You refuse to purify your wife? Repent, wretch, or I'll punish you both: go to Samayapuram without delay, or else! Hooo! Haaa!" Ending her performance to applause, Marudambal described how the frightened young man had fallen to his knees in front of Valliammal and promised to take his wife to Samayapuram at once. Her appreciative female audience laughed, and at this open display of contempt for the "false" Mariyammans, Pandaiyee, a quiet woman, gathered her courage and called out from in front of her house across the street, "Yes, isn't it strange how the *Sami* comes only to those two women, the wives of the *muppans?* We must be made of lesser stuff, that's why she never possesses any of us!" Marudambal gave a delighted cackle and shouted back: "Oh yes! Of course the *Sami* only possesses the *muppans'* families! What'd the *Sami* want with us?" Her irony was not lost on the members of her audience, who chuckled and grinned knowingly. They had had to put up with—and show respect to—Valliammal (now in her late sixties) and Sellaiyee (now in her fifties) for many years. It was a pleasure to get a dig at their "divine" cavortings.

I was told that when Sellaiyee became "possessed by Mariyai" at the *Somavaram* festival and threw out her hands and swayed from side to side, the other Pallar women were so exasperated by her "performances" that not one moved to catch her. "And she'd have fallen in the mud—it had been raining—if her own daughters hadn't rushed to catch her. No one else could be bothered!" Pallar skepticism with regard to possession is wide ranging, for several Pallar women were also contemptuous of the possessed Pallar men who took part in the festival for the goddess Periakka on Panguni Uttiram day in 1987, as we shall see.

Possession During the Process of "Wearing *Alaku*"

Preconditions and Preparations

"Alaku" are the various metal hooks, spikes, spears, skewers, and needles that the human body—always solely the *male* body in Aruloor—is pierced and wounded with in order to express submission, obedience, repentance, and devotion to a deity. Men "put *alaku*" (*"alaku podradu"*) either in order to fulfill a vow made in the past or to win divine favor for a boon that the devotee hopes will be granted in

the future. To "put *alaku*"—to wear hooks in his flesh or a spear through his cheeks—a man must be in a state of special ritual purity. This requires a period of preparation, often seven days, when a narrow strip of yellow cloth (dyed in auspicious turmeric) is worn wound around the left wrist. This wristband, called a *"kappu,"* protects the wearer from evil forces—such as *pey*—during this period of ritual purification. Just like the (all-male) Sabarimalai pilgrims, the man should have no sexual intercourse for this period, eat no meat, sleep and eat separately from others and refrain from noisy company, bathe twice daily, drink no alcohol and smoke no tobacco, and not go near any *tittu* (impure) object, "such as a menstruating woman." These are the restrictions observed by ascetics; thus, temporary asceticism is as important for those who are to be possessed as it is for pilgrims.

These observances leading to a state of purity are absolutely essential, because if he is not pure (*suttama*), a man will not win the grace of the deity and will consequently not be possessed. This results in public obloquy, publicizing his reprehensible character. When, after several hours of *udukkai*-beating, a young Pathmasaliar man was still not possessed during the Cittirai Paurnami festival in 1987, he had to go sadly home. All Aruloor speculated on what *tittu* (impurity) existed in his family to cause this fall from grace, for he had been a prominent *alaku*-wearer the previous year and was felt to be of very good character himself. Someone in his family had clearly sinned "in a big way," the village surmised. This indicates that the purity or impurity of an *alaku*-wearer's family affects him as well.

Thus, a state of purity is the precondition for possession, and being possessed is, in turn, the precondition for "putting" or "wearing" (*podradu*)—that is, being pierced by—*alaku*. The possession is believed to be essential to the successful "wearing of *alaku*" (*"alaku podradu"*) because then the body of the possessed man, when pierced, sheds "not a drop of blood. This is proof of the power of God!" as I was told, "God" being the deity to whom the *alaku*-wearer has dedicated his suffering and ritual wounding. The *kappu*-wearers or devotees gather at a riverbank, for the inducement of the possession. There should be flowing (and therefore "pure") water at this riverbank because all participants must first have a ritual bath in order to be purified. Sometimes their facial hair is also shaved; those whose cheeks are to be pierced by a spear often shave their heads entirely.

A crowd, large or small, gathers on the riverbank to watch, and if a shrine or temple is available in the immediate vicinity, then the possession ceremony occurs there. If there is no shrine, it occurs in the open, on the riverbank, as it did at Aruloor for the two major festivals I witnessed there. These were the Pallar festival in honor of the goddess Periakka (Elder Sister) on Panguni Uttiram day in April 1987 and the middle-caste, mainly Muthurajah, festival in honor of Murugan at Cittirai Paurnami on May 1, 1988. At the third major festival I observed, that of the Pallars of Mallarchipuram village, on the outskirts of Tiruchi city, they had an

Ayyalamman temple at hand on their riverbank, so they were able to hold their possession-ritual in this riverbank temple.

Political Implications

Possession, in the Non-Brahmin context, is essentially an exhibition, or display. It is a manifestation of a deity's power and grace. It is also a demonstration of the possessed person's claim to moral status in a society where moral status carries an enormous value. Further, possession, in this context, is generally a demonstration of the social prestige of a caste-group and is testimony to the ability of the group to cooperate and to organize. In other words, *alaku*-possession, which is "large-scale" possession because it normally consists of at least four or five men becoming possessed by a prominent deity, is a very major public event. The audience forms the largest part of the *alaku* procession as it winds its way around the village. Demonstrating the religiosity and the organizational strength of the caste concerned, the event embodies a public political claim to both ritual status and social status. Thus, the *alaku*-procession is implicitly a *political* demonstration; in the subtle cultural contestation that continues between castes in Aruloor, it issues a caveat to other castes while it simultaneously provides a powerful rallying point for its own members.

The Crowd

The crowd that collects at the riverbank is usually made up of men only, except for a few older postmenopausal women who do not run the risk of *tittu* (menstruation/impurity). It is important to note that this crowd is absolutely essential to the possession-process: If the crowd was not present, possession would probably not occur. This is because the crowd—always well disciplined, enthusiastic, and eager to see and, indeed, to induce possession—is "conducted" by the *pusari* (priest), much as an orchestra is conducted. He whips it into an emotional frenzy in order to cause the devotees to enter a state of trance and become possessed. The crowd shouts into the very ears of the man who is to be possessed; it deafens him, very deliberately, in a carefully orchestrated uproar, seeking to excite him so that his limbs start trembling. Once his legs are quivering, his whole frame is soon shuddering, and in a moment, the man is possessed—that is, he is in a trance-state in which he no longer feels or cares about the spear that is being pierced through his cheeks or through two points on the epidermis of his chest. This is suggested by the fact that he apparently feels no pain and does not bleed.

The Inducement of Possession

Many items must be assembled before the possession-ritual can start, including a food offering to the deity or deities involved, laid out on banana leaves. Coconuts are broken (the coconut is both a surrogate "life"-sacrifice and food offering), and incense and joss-sticks are lit. Then the priest performs a brief ritual-worship (*arccanai*), waving incense and, finally, a camphor flame in front of the portrait of Murugan or (depending on the deity being celebrated) the pot representing Mariyamman or Periakka. Thereafter, his attention—and that of the entire crowd—focuses on the man who is to be possessed first.

The man's male friends and male kin gather round him. Pressing upon him from all sides, they shout rhythmically, "Hao! Hao! Hao!" They shout in a deliberate effort to deafen and disorientate him: He stands erect, often rigid, his legs apart, eyes open. His eyes are focused on the priest until they lose focus as the trance begins. The priest is usually an *uddukai*-drum beater (*udduke-adikkiravar*), that is, a medium who communicates with spirits through his drum. He now stands directly in front of the devotee, beating the moaning *udukkai* and singing. His songs are an exhortation to the devotee to remember the grandeur and love of the deity, to remember the wonderful exploits of the god or the divine beauty of the goddess. All this is designed to help the devotee "lose" himself—to allow him to forget his fear and his personal desires and to submit himself, open himself, to the "entrance" of the deity. The sexual symbolism is implicit, though muted.

A Penetration of "Female" Men

This sexual symbolism, explicitly acknowledged in much *bakti*-literature, is implicit in the correspondence between the attitude of the devotee who desires to be possessed by the deity and pierced with "weapons" and that of a woman who desires to be sexually possessed by her lover. The correspondence was not spelled out but was clear in the way informants spoke of the "penetration" by the deity and the "painful joy" this caused. Though this may well be how the devotee feels himself, ideologically it distorts everyday reality, because it represents man, not woman, as the epitome of submissive self-sacrifice. It is men, not women, who silently bear "wounds" (in "wearing" *alaku*) for God: It is men who give themselves up, losing themselves in God. Women are not allowed to participate in this pageant of suffering; consequently, they have no role whatsoever in this supreme icon which, finally, on the Aruloor stage, represents not suffering, self-sacrificing humanity but suffering, submissive *men*.

Women are left out of the icon altogether. The *alaku*-procession has a tremendous impact on those who see it, and virtually everyone in the village does. Consequently, the ideological power of this masque of "female" men cannot be overestimated. It extracts all that Tamils consider most admirable in women, particularly the qualities of submission and self-sacrifice, and attaches these "female" characteristics to men. By celebrating these attitudes in men and not women, a subtle exclusion is made possible: Women are made ideologically irrelevant and thus utterly insignificant. If submissiveness and self-sacrifice can be seen to be epitomized—

and publicly honored—in men alone, there is clearly no need to invoke women, for men are, in this symbolic representation, both male and female. Hence, Tamil women are divested of the very features (submissiveness and self-sacrifice) in which, for this culture, their "greatness" lies. I suggest that this process of the ideological appropriation of "femaleness" occurs very widely in men's possession events throughout India.

The Piercing

I will return now to the *pusari*, who is drumming in front of the "female" devotee and crying out to him to remember the might and power of his deity. There is excitement and concentration in the crowd that huddles round the devotee, as well as a keen awareness that its participation is necessary to create the mood in which the devotee becomes exalted, literally "high." Normally, photography of a possession-event is disliked and prohibited, for two reasons: because the devotee is becoming a *sami* (deity)—and one should never photograph a deity—and because this may disturb the inducement of possession. At the village of Mela Valadi, I was not allowed to photograph the *alaku*-wearers in procession "because they were deities!"

In Aruloor, my friends allowed me to take pictures during the preparations for the Cittirai Paurnami procession on May 1, 1988, but suddenly, a young Muthurajah devotee, who was not becoming possessed, decided that I and my camera were to blame: We had angered the god (Murugan). So I was startled to see him snap out of his half-trance and, fixing me with a furious glare, point an accusing finger at me. He said nothing, but his meaning was clear, and bystanders urged me, in a friendly way, to put the camera out of sight, temporarily.

When the devotee's body has started trembling and shuddering and when his rigid stance suddenly relaxes into an open one—his hands either hanging loosely at his sides or held out, gracefully, welcoming what is to be done to him—the priest decides that he is possessed, in a state of trance, and signals to the professional *alaku*-piercer to get to work.

At the Muthurajah Cittirai Paurnami festival for Murugan, I talked with the professional piercer from Lalgudi. He was a well-built man of Muthurajah caste in his mid-thirties who said he had been doing this work for the last eight years. It had started when he himself "put *alaku*" to fulfill a vow: He had had a spear put through his cheeks. Thereafter, he had learned from another professional how to pierce the implements on or through a man's body and had bought his own set of spears, spikes, and hooks, which he rented out. He owned all the metal implements and weapons present, and they gleamed and were finely filed with very sharp points, particularly the spears. He said that he was paid fifty rupees for his services and for the rental of three spears, two spike-cages (worn over the chest, so that the devotee turns into a human porcupine), and innumerable hooks with little packets or fruits attached to them as weights. There were also two very large hooks that were to go into the back of the devotee, who would draw "Murugan's chariot" (a humble little cart, glorified with decorations of colored paper) after him. When the priest gave the word, the *alaku*-piercer and his assistant, a man of the same age, got to work. They were going to get the toughest jobs done first, starting with the spear-piercings.

This was also an implicit status move because those who were going to have spears driven through their cheeks were obviously going to suffer far more than the others, so they deserved to come first. The piercer and his man each grabbed an arm of the possessed devotee, standing him up; then the piercer grabbed the devotee's two cheeks and pulled at them, causing his mouth to open and close. Warning the crowd to keep back for a minute, he held the point of the spear to the devotee's cheek and carefully, swiftly, pierced it. He pulled the spiked cheek further out on the spear and pierced the next cheek, swiftly pulling the spear through so that the tiny hole grew to the three-quarter-inch diameter of the spear.

Not a drop of blood appeared, leaving me utterly amazed. My companions in the crowd were, however, entirely unsurprised: "It shows the power of God! Yes, of course you or I would bleed profusely if our cheeks were pierced with a spear!" The spears were very long, measuring some seven feet. The professional piercer stepped back, surveyed the equal lengths of the spear on each side of the devotee's face, pulled the two cheeks out a little so that the devotee's mouth opened, then released them. The devotee had his eyes open throughout and seemed to hardly feel the pain. When I asked the professional piercer about this later, he replied: "He feels it just as a pin-prick, because he is possessed." It was extraordinary to watch, at very close quarters, a man being willingly skewered with a spear; my feelings were confused, between fear, at the actual wounding, astonishment, and admiration. My companions, however, were most content. All was going well— "God is with us!" they said—for now the possessed devotees were not merely emblematic of Murugan, they *were* Murugan himself incarnate.

Murugan Incarnate

Murugan or Kandan is the younger son of Siva and Parvati and is enormously popular. He was the most popular *ishta-deyvam* (personal deity) in Aruloor and was equally popular with all the castes. This remarkable cross-caste appeal, very widespread throughout Tamilnadu, is due to his interesting intermediate position, for he is both a Sanskritic and a non-Sanskritic deity (Clothey 1978). Murugan is a hunter and is therefore often portrayed as holding a spear; he has two beautiful wives, Valli and Devayanai and is considered approachable, sympathetic, loving, and tender. These last qualities are particularly evoked by the numerous, very popular representations of him as a child holding a spear. Having the fresh beauty, vulnerability, and openness of a child, Murugan as a child-god also appeals (like the child Krishna) to the maternal instincts of women. Being *the* most popular of all deities, his shrine at Palani is the wealthiest and most visited shrine in

Tamilnadu. At Palani, Murugan is portrayed as the ascetic, Dandayudapani, holding a staff. Elsewhere, in his incarnation as Arumugam, he is the six-headed slayer of demons, and wielding a spear (*vel*). This spear is an important icon and is a central symbol of Murugan, whose other names include "Thangavelu" ("Golden Spear") and "Velayudham" ("Spear-Weapon"). Consequently, by causing themselves to be pierced by Murugan's *vel,* devotees offer themselves to be "destroyed" by him: They are annihilated as themselves and pierced through, transformed by his grace. Being publicly pierced by the phallic *vel* therefore signifies a spiritual transformation wrought by Murugan's grace, for possession by Murugan means that the god himself now masters the "female" devotee's body.

Though the religious devotion of devotees varies greatly, I was told that "genuine devotion shines through." This was what my companions believed, and I understood what they meant when I saw how irresistibly, in every street, the crowds were especially drawn to offer worship to one devotee in particular. This man's name, like that of the god who possessed him, was Kandan.

Kandan was of average height and of slightly stocky build, but he had a remarkably serene, well-chiselled face. In his early forties, he was a minor rice merchant of Muthurajah caste. He had taken great interest in organizing the festival. At the riverbank he was the one in whose shoulders the great hooks to pull the cart should have been pierced, but, to my surprise, he had refused this, having only the numerous small hooks (with little colored packets hanging from them) put all over his chest and back. I had thought that he had refused the hooks because he was not sufficiently possessed to bear the pain, but when we reached the front of the Ayyanar Temple, I realized that I was wrong. There was a teeming multitude there, far more people than down on the riverbank: Kandan had deliberately chosen to wait so that the piercing could be done at this site, watched by many and thus giving greater glory to his god. The hooks were put into his back, by the piercer, but only through the thin folds of the epidermis, I noted. Thus, he could hardly have pulled a cart—his skin would have torn off. In fact, he did not have to pull the cart (though to a casual observer, it appeared that he did so occasionally); instead, the cart was pushed along from behind by his friends and kin, and the ropes from the hooks in Kandan's back merely hung down slackly.

But the climax was yet to come, and it was so unusual and impressive that it made a profound impression on the crowd. This was because, unusually, Kandan was going to have a spear pierced "through his chest." Once again, the professional piercer expertly pinched up a fold of epidermis at two points, above and below the chest, and passed the spear through them. The piercing through the cheeks was possibly a more serious wounding of the body than Kandan's spear. However—and this was generally acknowledged—Kandan's aspect was so noble, with his eyes shut in rapture and a spear "through his chest," that he was indubitably the most touching and majestic of all the possessed devotees. The spear through his chest had an instantaneous effect: Women cried out and raised joined

palms above their heads in salutation to Murugan incarnate. Unlike the other devotees, Kandan had a slight smile on his face, and he would close his eyes from time
to time as he walked. This suggestion of deep serenity, of an inward contentment
and joy, gave him a most attractive appearance, and the public of Aruloor re-
sponded to it. Consummate actor or true devotee—or perhaps both, for a devotee
might well feel that he has to project the personality of the god who has entered
him—Kandan became the chief manifestation of Murugan that day.

Hierarchies of Submission

In all the streets that the procession went through, women came out to pour water on the feet of the five men who "wore" *alaku* and the three men who carried
pal-kodam (pots of milk) or *kavadi* (small palanquin-like frames made of bamboo
and ornamented with peacock feathers). In most of the streets, the women would
first pour their pots of water on the feet of as many of the *sami* (deities, for that
was how the possessed men were referred to) as possible, then they would kneel
down in the oozing mud and touch their heads to the slimy ground in front of the
sami. It was most striking that this ritual worship of the possessed men was performed almost solely by women: Many men stood watching too, but only a hand-
ful (all of them very young men) prostrated themselves. Thus, through the formal
obeisance done almost exclusively by women, there was a public enactment of the
submission of female to male. A hierarchy of submission was thus implied in this
Cittirai Full Moon pageant—the submission of women to men and of men to deities. This public subordination of women to men makes it quite explicit that by
appropriating "female" qualities, the possessed men do not become "women." If
they did, then, in symbolic terms, women would be their equals. On the contrary,
the possessed men become *more than men* in appropriating "femaleness," and
their superior position in the gender hierarchy is preserved by the repeated public
obeisance of women to them.

Ritual worship (*arccanai*) was offered to the *alaku*-wearers by many households, exactly as it would be to a deity passing in procession in his or her chariot
(*ter*). The procession therefore made frequent halts, stopping whenever anyone
wanted to perform worship of these men in whom Murugan had manifested himself. The male head of the household would give the Muthurajah *pusari* a tray
containing betel leaves and areca nut, two bananas, a few burning joss-sticks stuck
in a banana, burning camphor, and a coconut. The *pusari* would neatly cleave the
coconut in two, giving both halves back to the family, then wave the tray with the
burning camphor three times in front of the chosen devotee and return it to the
householder. The edibles were now *pirasadam,* food imbued with divine grace.

Most people chose to perform worship of Kandan. Several also stepped close to
him and murmured anxious questions about the future, to which they believed
the possessed man could give prophetic answers. Kandan (his eyes often closed)
replied readily, calmly, and fluently to all; and the questioners would step back,

looking more cheerful. I heard him tell several: "Do not worry: All will be well!" Convinced that they had heard Murugan himself, they were consoled. Kandan and the other *alaku*-wearers distributed sacred ash (*tunnuru/vibuti*) to all who asked for it, and a great many did. Every woman who poured water and prostrated herself requested ash, too. The *"sami"* would drop it in the recipient's cupped hands, and the latter would immediately rub some on her forehead with her right hand. To have sacred ash on one's forehead is considered purifying, and in this case, the ash was doubly holy because it was given by a man who was temporarily God himself in human form. Several parents brought babies or little children to be blessed, which the *"sami"* readily did by personally rubbing ash on their foreheads. However, the attitude of the Aruloor public was not purely devotional. This was also a grand spectacle to be enjoyed.

Spikes and Vows

At this Murugan festival, the devotees who had spears pierced through their cheeks also had star-shaped metal frames around their faces to help support and steady the spears. Their chests and backs were pierced with a multitude of little hooks, from which small packets or limes hung as weights. All the *sami* were profusely garlanded, some with four or five garlands each. They were all barechested and dressed very simply in clean white *veshti*. The two devotees, who, porcupine-like, wore cages of spikes, were also impressive.

The most demanding *alaku* of all, called the "airplane-*alaku*," was not done at the Murugan festival. This was an *alaku*-penance in which a man, suspended in midair from a beam, hung by hooks pierced through his back, his buttocks, and his calves, with his arms outspread, like an airplane. I had only seen this amazing *alaku* at Angarai village. But it had been done in Aruloor the previous year by a young Pathmasaliar man who was admired greatly for his extraordinary endurance and religious zeal. This Aruloor airplane-*alaku* had used a small mobile crane that was towed by a tractor to suspend the devotee—a striking instance of modern technology assisting ancient religious tradition.

The upper castes claimed that there was a large measure of exhibitionism in the "wearing" of *alaku*. This was the criticism made by Palani Chettiar, who echoed what several upper-caste informants had told me. However, exhibitionism apart, the main reason why anyone wounded his body with *alaku* was universally agreed to be a religious vow. No man did it merely to show his courage or strength; he did it because he had vowed to do it, either as thanksgiving for a boon fulfilled or in anticipation, having asked a favor of the deity. The ability to be pierced by the spear, hooks, or "porcupine"-cage without being harmed is visible proof of dedication to the deity concerned. A problem therefore arises if the devotee's wish is thereafter not fulfilled, for this implies that the devotee's behavior was wanting in some way. This may be why I was told, "You shouldn't tell others why you put *alaku*—it should remain your secret"—and, indeed, it was impossible to find out

why the five Aruloor men had taken their vows. At Mallarchipuram, the friendly
Pallar hamlet on the outskirts of Tiruchi, people were more forthcoming. One
young man had vowed to "wear" the spear-*alaku* in the hope that his devotion
would win a son for him: He and his wife had been married for two years but had
no child. The other young man (also with a spear through his cheeks) had done
this as his promised thanksgiving for a desired job that he had obtained. Others,
we learned, did it in the hope that they would be cured of some long-term ail-
ment. Several men "wore" *alaku* year after year, having vowed to do so for three,
five, or seven years, depending on the "greatness" of the boon desired from the
deity.

The Ending of Possession

In a possession-event, the most intense times are the beginning and the ending,
when the *alaku* are first pierced through the devotee's body and then taken out.
Immense excitement had attended the "putting-on" period, as I have noted. The
crowd had shouted, the *pusari* had sung and wept, and everyone had been most
concerned that the possession should occur. At the end, another kind of anxiety
grips the public, namely, that the *alaku* be taken out with no flow of blood, because this extraordinary fact indicates the continued power of the deity's possession. Just as the possession started in a "pure" area, on a riverbank near running
water, so too, it ends in a sacred space—in a temple directly in front of the deity
who has been incarnated. At the start of a possession-event, therefore, it is the deity who comes to the devotee, far away, on a riverbank; at the end, the devotee,
who now incarnates the deity, "returns" to the shrine of that deity. This movement is found in many festivals for deities who possess people. Fuller has suggested that it is a progress from an "impure" exterior to "pure" interior, where
the highest form of the deity is present (1988).

The devotee is held to have been in a state of possession since it was first induced, yet, in this final stage, the possession is *intensified* by the same means used
when it was first inspired—the crowd shouts and the *pusari* sings. Once again, a
peak of excitement is reached, while the *udukkai* is beaten. This time, the possessed devotee is standing directly facing the stone statue of the deity: God-made-
man views god-represented-in-stone. At the appropriate moment, when possession—or the trance state—is most intense, the priest gives the signal, and the professional piercer sets to work at great speed, removing the spear from the mouth
of the devotee. As he extracts it, he stuffs sacred ash into the holes (the ash is made
from cow dung, which is considered to be a very efficient antibacterial agent) both
to stave off any bleeding and to prevent an infection. At Mallarchipuram and in
Aruloor, the holes bled a little, but the bleeding was quickly stopped by pressing
more sacred ash on them.

After the spear had been removed, in Aruloor, the devotee closed his eyes and
collapsed and was then carried bodily to a corner in the cool temple corridor

where he was revived and given water. Yet the collapse may have had a touch of the histrionic about it, because no collapses occurred at Mallarchipuram, where, if anything, the Pallar men with spears through their cheeks had walked even further than those in Aruloor. In Mallarchipuram, after the spears had been extracted, the men were given water to drink and just sat down quietly where they had been standing, while more ash was put on their cheeks. There was no dramatic carrying away of "fainted" devotees, as there was with the *"sami"* in the huge courtyard of Aruloor's ancient Siva temple.

The place where the *alaku* are taken out—that is, where the procession and possession end—is indicative of the status of the group involved. Although the (mainly) Muthurajah Murugan procession ended in Aruloor's most prestigious temple, the Pallar procession at their Periakka festival did not even enter the Siva Temple. It merely stopped outside the entrance, and the Pallar acting-priest (Ramaiah) performed worship to the little shrine of Vakuvalamman, the village deity (*girama devatai*), outside the temple. Then it turned sharply around, ending in the Pallar street, in the temple house (*koyil vidu*) of Periakka, in front of her image.

In all cases, however, the possessions ended directly in front of the deity involved. Thus, a double unification occurred during the possession event: On the one hand, Deity (Mariyamman or Murugan) incarnated as man, thus indicating the potential unity of man and deity, while, on the other, the goal of the procession was that final moment in the temple when man met the deity face to face. While "God" came to possess man, man also went to meet "God." Woman, however, remained absent throughout.

There was no special problem in any of the three group possession-rituals I witnessed, in bringing the person out of the possessed state and back into a "normal" state. The *pusari* seemed to manage this quite easily by simply throwing sacred ash on the head of the person after the *alaku* had been removed. This is normally considered to effectively end any divine possession; only possession by *pey* is said, by some informants, to be unaffected by sacred ash. The no-longer-possessed devotee always looked intensely exhausted after the *alaku*-"wearing" experience. The priest ritually presented him with new clothes, bought by his family as a congratulatory offering. This gift-giving was emphasized by the Pallars of Mallarchipuram, but it was not given prominence in Aruloor's Siva Temple, where the Brahmin priests were far more concerned with focusing attention on the deity and on the worship that they were performing. All the items for this especially grand worship—the garlands, food offerings, incense, and other offerings—were paid for by the organizers of the procession.

I will now turn to the phenomenon of the lower-caste affiliation of virtually all forms of possession. In investigating why it is primarily the lower castes who become possessed, I will also show what Savitripatti meant when she stated that "only the Sudra" (Non-Brahmins) had the courage to wear *alaku*.

Possession and Caste

The Upper-Caste View

The last fire-walking (*ti-midi*) event in Aruloor had occurred more than fifty years earlier. In the *agrakaram* (Brahmin street), Savitripatti was one of the few old people who remembered it. A huge pit, measuring more than twenty feet in length and six feet in breadth, had been dug at the bottom of the *agrakaram,* just outside it. The pit's location was significant, indicating the permission and approval of the Brahmins, while distancing them from the pit because it was not actually in their street. Also, it stood at the road entrance to the Brahminic Siva Temple; therefore, the temple's approval was indicated as well.

This was the only occasion on which Savitripatti ever saw *ti-midi*—and she never forgot it. Normally, fire-walking is done at noon, when it is hottest, "in order to make it even more gruelling," said Siva. But the historic Aruloor fire-walking had occurred at night. Savitripatti remembered it vividly: "Praying to Draupadi, the patron-goddess of firewalkers, many, many Sudra were possessed and walked across the coals, fiery-hot in the night. It was unforgettable: I saw little children, grasping the hand of mother or father, walk across, entirely unhurt and even babies were carried across, in the arms of their mothers. Throngs of people went across, all praying, all unscathed. I was deeply impressed. No, no Brahmins walked—we lack the courage. These people, the Kudiyanar [Muthurajah] and other Sudra have far more courage than us—that's why it's only they who pierce themselves with *alaku*."

Savitripatti's assertion was certainly considered true by most Aruloor inhabitants, for her exact words were used by the Muthurajahs themselves: "We have more courage than the Brahmins! But they also added what she would certainly not have said: "We have more true devotion to God! That's where our courage comes from. The Brahmins are only words and pretence—they claim to be the most religious of all, but have you ever seen a Brahmin 'put' *alaku*? No—because they never do. They—and the Chettiars, who are like them—have no true faith in God." That was how both Muthurajahs and Pallars explained the fact that possession was essentially a lower-caste phenomenon. A Pallar woman put it this way: "We have true feeling for God so She comes to us readily. The Brahmins don't really love God, they only pretend to: It's a business proposition for them."

But the upper-caste gloss on this was very different. As Palani Chettiar said, "It's their *style* of worship, that's all. We don't believe in such an extrovert style. We believe that God is within us and that God responds to true devotion. But our style is quiet and restrained—we disapprove of throwing yourself around and losing control of yourself: there's no need for all that." Palani Chettiar was implying more than that the lower castes (*kil-jadi*) had just a different style; he was indicating that although the Chettiars (and Brahmins) chose the path of self-control, the lower castes chose the *opposite* path of the complete abandonment of control. Significantly, the body symbolism of both groups is consistent with their religious ethos: The self-control of the upper castes is displayed in their bodily immunity to penetration and possession by external beings, while the opposite is true of the lower castes. These differences correspond to the attitudes of the two groups to ritual pollution and to emotional self-control. Thus, the lower castes saw their "abandonment" as a surrendering of self to possession by God, but to the Chettiars and Brahmins, this was dangerously close to "mere" abandonment and "mere" freedom from restraint. It was dangerously close to anarchy.

Both the social position and the style of life of the communities concerned is therefore mirrored in their modes of possession. The Pallars have a comparatively more egalitarian relationship between the sexes because Pallar women support their families as much as Pallar men do. Consequently, unlike high-caste women, Pallar women were possessed in public, both in Aruloor and in Mallarchipuram. Possession, as Palani Chettiar critically implied, allows the individual to briefly throw off social restraints and norms "because he is possessed by the Goddess." This public display of otherwise "uncouth" and wild behavior is cherished by the lower castes, who normally have to behave cautiously and deferentially, even today, in the presence of their landlords and paymasters. The Muthurajahs are currently upwardly mobile, which partly explains the complete exclusion of women from their possession festival and reflects the fact that Muthurajah women are being increasingly secluded. But the Muthurajahs, though caste-Hindus and not "untouchables," rank only just above the Pallar in the village hierarchy; consequently, they, too, seemed to exult in the brief throwing-off of social bonds.

Both Chettiars and Brahmins told me that they had never heard of a caste member who had "worn" *alaku*—it was just not the "done thing." As Devayanai Chettiar, the refined and gentle wife of Aruloor's richest Chettiar, said, "Wearing *alaku* is lower-caste behaviour—that's why no Chettiar would ever do it. Yes, there may well be *Chettiars* who have been possessed by God, but this would happen quietly, with no great fuss." She had, however, heard of a young male relative who had carried *pal-kodam* (a milk-pot, to "bathe" the deity's image with, at the end) in order to obtain a son, but this was a most rare occurrence. With the Brahmins, too, I was told that *alaku*-"wearing" was *never* done "because you don't need that kind of exhibitionism if you are genuinely devoted to God." But from Devraj Aiyar, one of the two Pancangam Aiyar who ministered to the lower-castes, I learned that his son-in-law had promised to carry *pal-kavadi* (milk-pots hanging from a wooden frame) for Murugan "because his only son was dangerously ill." The boy had improved, and so his father (Devraj Aiyar's son-in-law) had fulfilled his vow by walking with lower-caste devotees in their festival procession to Murugan's shrine in his village. Uma, my Brahmin friend, was extremely surprised to learn of this and stated that it was the first case of a Brahmin carrying *pal-kavadi* that she had ever heard of. When pressed, Devraj Aiyar also admitted:

"Yes, it's very rare for Brahmins to do this, but in his village the Brahmins do carry *pal kodam* from time to time. But they would never pierce themselves with *alaku.*"

This brings me to the arguments of Fuller (1988) and Parry (forthcoming) regarding the relation between the religious ideologies of high and low castes. Fuller, finding that Brahminic religion denies that non-Brahmins have any meaningful existence in the world, argues that complementary hierarchical relationships are actually negated by the model of the Brahmins' ideal society, symbolized by the Sanskritic deities (1988: 34). He observes, "In opposition to this, village deities symbolise the hierarchical interdependence of caste. ... Thus it is not Sanskritic, but village deities—mainly worshipped by the low castes—who provide the model of and for a hierarchical world" (Fuller 1988: 35). I disagree. My arguments throughout this chapter have stressed that no such validation of hierarchic values is provided by lower-caste religion. On the contrary, through its very emphatic insistence on the primacy of religious possession and on the preeminence of devotion and "purity of heart," not purity of caste, this religious ethos implicitly challenges caste values, a challenge that becomes entirely explicit in the discourse of the enormously popular Sabarimalai pilgrimage.

Parry's examination of spirit possession and exorcism (forthcoming) comes to a conclusion that is very similar to Fuller's, for he says: "For the exorcists and the victims the whole procedure must be authenticated by the Brahman's authority. ... As with the set of ideas which accounts for who gets possessed in the first place, the hierarchical order is thus resoundingly validated by the tenets of those it demeans." In Tamilnadu, however, no Brahmin priest would even go near an exorcism of an "untouchable" who was possessed by a malign spirit. In Aruloor and very widely in Tamilnadu, Brahmin priests have nothing whatsoever to do with the exorcism of spirits afflicting the lower and the "untouchable" castes. Instead, both low caste-Hindus, such as the Muthurajahs, and "untouchables," such as the Pallars, are served by low-caste *mantiravadi* (diviners) and *udukkai*-drum beaters who specialize in the exorcism of *pey* and dealings with the spirit-world. It may be true that for much of North India, exorcisms have to be validated by Brahmin priests, but this is simply not true of the ethnography of Tamilnadu. Clearly, the positions of Brahmin priests in North and South India differ considerably in this regard. Consequently, lower-caste spirit possession and exorcism in Tamilnadu do not authenticate the hierarchical order: They form a universe that is entirely separate from the sphere of Brahmin activity.

Brahmin Possession

A Private Phenomenon. Given the Brahmin amazement at all the public forms of possession that I described to them or that they thesmselves saw (such as the Muthurajah Murugan procession, which went through the *agrakaram*) I got the impression that Brahmins never became possessed. All that the Chettiars,

Muthurajahs, and Pallars said confirmed this: They stated that they had never heard of any possessed Brahmin. The fact that all the other castes were quite convinced that Brahmins never became possessed is significant because it indicates that Brahmin possession, even though it does occur and in a group context, is a very little-known phenomenon. It is known about only by other Brahmins, not by other castes, because it is watched and encouraged and applauded by other Brahmins in what are very strictly Brahmin gatherings. But it is not a secret: When I finally realized that I had to ask about Brahmin possession, I was told about it readily.

The Dancing "Gopis." It was not until I was watching, in amazement, a Brahmin man become possessed that I realized that I must ask about Brahmin possession, despite what all the other castes had said. The occasion on which I witnessed this possession was a *"Sita Kalyanam"* (Wedding of Sita), a gathering of Brahmin men for the purpose of singing *bajan* (devotional songs). The *bajan*-singing was dramatized by making it represent the occasion of Rama and Sita's wedding (*kalyanam*), with the male *bajan*-singers representing the "female" devotees of Rama. Thus, the Brahmin men were actually impersonating women, during parts of the event, and it was while several men were dancing the roles of these God-intoxicated "women" that one of them actually became possessed. He was the most graceful dancer of all, with smooth, flowing, deliberately "feminine" movements, and, almost imperceptibly, he began dancing faster and faster, spinning round and round until he fell down. "He's possessed by God!"—in this case, Rama—it was said: His companions gently lifted him up, threw ash on his head, and made him sit down. For a long while, he remained unmoving, seated with his head bent low, as if in great weariness. Then, still slightly dazed, he joined in the singing.

There was a striking division of the sexes in that room, a hired school house in the Brahmin *agrakaram* of Mela Chintamani, in Tiruchi city. (I was in the company of my Brahmin friend Uma and her Tiruchi cousins.) The Brahmin men sat in two groups facing each other, singing the *bajans,* and impersonating female devotees. The Brahmin women sat as the audience, silently watching and occasionally softly joining in the *bajans.* So the women, relatively passive and cut off from any actual participation in the *bajan*-singing, were the audience to men who were delighting in joyous, loud, rhythmic songs of devotion: They were cast in the role of admiring audience for male religious devotion. Similarly, they were the chosen audience (all other castes being strictly excluded) for male religious possession, watching men acting women who were possessed. That is, these Brahmin men "were" God-intoxicated *gopis.* The term *"gopi,"* strictly speaking, refers only to a female devotee of the god Krishna at Vrindaban: Overcome by love for him, these women were "possessed" by him and delighted in dancing with him. By using the term *"gopi"* to describe themselves, the Brahmin men indicated that they were symbolically transformed into god-intoxicated *women.* They were also fusing the gods Rama and Krishna (both of them being earthly incarnations of Vishnu). It was in acting the part of such a "possessed" *gopi* that the "feminized" Brahmin schoolteacher actually became possessed. "This happens quite often," I was told by Uma. "It's quite normal for two or three of the dancers to become possessed. It's a wonderful sign, because it means that God has come to him." In Brahmin discourse, God was no longer "God," no longer *either* female or male, as in lower-caste speech, but strictly male. And this male God only possessed the Brahmin men who were impersonating women in front of an audience of passive Brahmin women. So here, once again, in order to become divinely possessed, *men become female* in a ritual event where women are passive onlookers.

Milton Singer's description of "the Radha-Krishna *bhajanas*" of Madras (1968) is almost identical to what went on in this *agrakaram* schoolhouse, but though he makes the Krishnavite influence plain, he entirely misses the gender significance of what occurred.

Possession Through Pollution. But not only did Brahmin men become female in order to be possessed, they also, equally remarkably, became polluted so that God might enter them. I learned about this when Uma pointed out that it was usual for Brahmin men to become possessed while dancing during "Sita Kalyanam" or "Radha Kalyanam," and at other occasions, too. She explained that, until about eight years earlier, Sita Kalyanam (or Radha Kalyanan) had been regularly performed in the Aruloor *agrakaram,* in her father's house, by this same group of Tiruchi Brahmins, which included her urban kin. "They'd have a performance exactly like this one, with all the men singing and dancing—and after the event we would provide lunch for all the men. When they'd finished eating, while the *eccil* [polluted by saliva and thus very impure] leaves were still lying there, in rows, those who'd taken vows to do so, would roll around on those *eccil* leaves. And while they rolled, they'd become possessed by God. My father and my *Periyappa* [FeB, who lived in Tiruchi] would always roll over the leaves—and they'd always become possessed. It lasted only briefly. They took the vow for various reasons—maybe one of us had been ill so they vowed to do this if we got well quickly."

As Uma explained, "To roll on *eccil* leaves is very impure. But this is an act of humility—you give yourself entirely to God, and willingly, humbly, accept impurity. This shows extreme devotion—that's why they always became possessed." Clearly, this "abandonment" to "impurity" and to God's will is closer to the so-called "Sudra" style of devotional possession than to the more normal upper-caste code of strict self-control and strict ritual purity. This is a *bakti*-style of worship, and *bakti* (devotion) has always been regarded by Brahmins as dangerously close to anarchic self-abandonment. Even so, *bakti* has always attracted Brahmins, the most famous case of *bakti* emotional excess being Chaitanya (1486–1533), who was a Bengali Brahmin.

There was yet another Brahmin style of possession, and this, too, involved rolling around on the ground. It was while at Mariyamman's greatest temple, at

Samayapuram, that I learned about this (and here, for once, the Brahmins, like the Non-Brahmins, were talking about a female God) as my Brahmin friends and I walked around the central shrine, doing *piradatcanam* (ritual circumambulation) three times. Jayanthiamma, Uma's *Periyamma* (FeBW), was with us. She said: "Many Brahmins take a vow to come here and do *piradatcanam* of this shrine, by rolling on the ground, three times around or more. Yes, women can—and have—done it, but it's usually men who do it. Normally *Sami* [God, here Mariyamman] possesses them while they roll round: It is a very blessed thing to do and brings great merit. As you can imagine, it isn't easy to roll round—it's not even easy to walk round, because of the crowds and the uneven paving." Thus, here too, possession went together with spectacular self-abnegation and with spectacular "impurity," for, as any temple-goer knows, even the cleanest temples tend to have rather dirty floors, with mysterious puddles, clots of red *vetlepakku* (betel leaf) that people have spat out, and other filth. To roll around deliberately on such a floor is to invite humiliation on oneself, but Brahmins regularly did this, when to win a boon, they vowed to the Great Goddess that they would roll around her shrine. This public act—and the simultaneous possession by Mariyamman that was claimed to accompany it—had clearly not aroused the interest of the Non-Brahmin castes, for none of them had remarked on it. But this was possibly because they were penitentially rolling around the shrine, too: This was, after all, a standard vow that was taken for many temples.

Significantly, what emerges is that for Brahmins, possession is closely related to a willing assumption of extreme impurity. No other caste thought in this manner.: The Chettiars never spoke of any such possession-through-impurity process, and no lower caste associated possession with impurity. On the contrary, in the Non-Brahmin view, possession only came to those who were in a heightened state of ritual purity. This suggests that Brahmins associate possession with "impurity," that is, what they regard as the ritual state of the lower castes, and further, that they associate purity with a self-controlled state. Therefore, to become possessed they feel that they have to deliberately incur pollution. It is important to note that this pollution is *not* similar to Edward Harper's "respect pollution" (1964), for in rolling on the banana leaves on which their kin have just eaten and on the filthy floor around Mariyamman's shrine, the Brahmins *do* incur pollution: This is not a case where "the left-overs of the high are pure for the low." This throws significant light on the Brahmin discourse regarding purity: Only the "pure" are seen as self-controlled, and the impure, consequently, must *be* controlled. This, in turn, provides self-evident legitimation for the authority of the hierarchies of both caste and gender. The circle of Brahmin logic is complete.

Other castes continue to believe in the myth that Brahmins do not become possessed. The existence of this myth and the strict privacy of Brahmin possession events suggest that the Brahmins are keen to preserve their dignified front. In Aruloor, the Telugu Brahmins are not only at the top of the ritual ladder, they are also a landed and very wealthy group, second only to the richest Chettiars on the economic ladder. The Aruloor Brahmins never behave in an uncontrolled, wild, or "possessed" manner in front of other castes nor do the Chettiars, for to behave thus is to lower oneself: It is to lose status, even if done willingly by a devotee "for God." And to lose status is the last thing Aruloor's Brahmins and Chettiars would want to do.

The Sabarimalai Pilgrim Possession and the Rejection of Caste

Spectacular spontaneous possession occurred at the ceremony where the Sabarimalai pilgrims—all male—were invested with their *iru-mudi* (literally, "two-heads"). *Iru-mudi* refers to the two bundles of belongings tied in the two large, knotted ends of a cloth, and carried on the head of a Sabarimalai pilgrim. The investiture rite happened in the Ayyanar Temple, directly in front of the image of Ayyanar because this local warrior-god is locally held to be identical with the god Ayyappan of Sabarimalai. An elderly Brahmin, a "guru" who had undertaken many pilgrimages to Sabarimalai himself, invested the male pilgrims with their ritual bundles. In December 1987, twelve pilgrims were about to undertake the journey: Most of them were of Muthurajah caste, but, very remarkably, their numbers included one young Brahmin and one Pallar. No Chettiars participated, though other lower-caste Hindus did. The presence of the Brahmin and the Pallar was not a new phenomenon: That particular young Brahmin had gone to Sabarimalai annually for six years, and another Pallar (my friend Velyudham, Siva's husband) had participated two years earlier. Velayudham had been the first "untouchable" to ever do so in Aruloor. College educated, gentle, and urbane, he was the very embodiment of the modern, upwardly mobile Pallar.

But Brahmin and Pallar participation in the event was still extraordinary, even sensational, because at the end of the ritual investiture, every pilgrim had to prostrate himself at the feet of every other pilgrim. Ritual preparation for a pilgrimage to Sabarimalai was strict (or at least it was supposed to be)—and the pilgrim-to-be was honored for the self-abnegation this involved by being addressed as *"sami"* "god," "lord") by all around him. At the end of the investiture, every *"sami"* fell at the feet of and "worshipped" every other *"sami."* This meant that not only the young Brahmin pilgrim but all the Muthurajahs and other caste-Hindus had to "worship" at the feet of Meghanathan, the Pallar participant. This was sensational because of the *tittu* they would normally incur by this act: To even go very near a Pallar would, normally, be regarded as polluting by the average Aruloor caste-Hindu. Yet this "worship," by prostrating themselves and crying *"Sami!"* (here, Lord God), was actually done to Meghanathan by every other participant—and by him to them. Thus, by viewing his fellow pilgrims "as God," the devotee ignores their caste.

Velayudham, the original Pallar participant, gave his explanation of why caste was ignored:

It's only very recently that the journey to the Sabari mountains [*malai*] has become fairly easy, as you can now go there by bus or van. It used to be a most dangerous journey—many pilgrims died, either killed by wild animals or from the hazards of the climb. So a Sabarimalai ethos developed—every pilgrim had to aid every other—and this meant that you couldn't have caste [caste restrictions] because if someone fell and you were not allowed to touch him, how could you help him? Today there's yet another reason—when you travel in a van, as most men do, you're all crushed together with no space, touching each other. You can't observe caste rules in such a context. Caste is a man-made thing—in God's eyes there's no such thing as caste.

Thus, whether for purely pragmatic reasons or partly through the influence of more transcendent notions, the Sabarimalai pilgrimage can be a caste-free enterprise. This was both astonishing and remarkable in Aruloor's caste-ridden environment, and this extraordinariness may have contributed to the intensity of emotional feeling in the twelve pilgrims, almost all of whom became briefly possessed (cf. Daniel 1984 and Kjaerholm 1986 on the egalitarianism of the pilgrims).

This possession happened to them in turn, as they sat cross-legged in front of the old Brahmin "guru," waiting for him to place the *iru-mudi* bundle on their heads. Suddenly, the pilgrim, who until then would have had his eyes focused on the smiling image of the god Ayyappan (squatting serenely before him, sculpted in sandal-paste), would cry out: "Ayyappa!" Then he would squirm or more energetically throw himself from side to side, again shouting "Ayyappa!" while friends or fellow pilgrims grabbed him. The old Brahmin would throw sacred ash on him, and the possession would subside. The pilgrim would kneel, prostrating himself to the old "guru." Then he would get up and move aside to make room for the next pilgrim. This brief possession occurred again and again, with some nine men possessed.

Nobody was surprised. "It's wonderful—it shows that the power of Ayyappan is with them and that he's pleased with them." But the old Brahmin, with his no-nonsense demeanor, looked mildly annoyed by the delays the possessions caused. Meghanathan, the Pallar pilgrim, was not possessed; perhaps he was too nervous at being so socially elevated all at once. I must add, however, that the young Brahmin pilgrim was considered a loner by others in the *agrakaram*—they did not approve at all of his joining a mixed-caste group of pilgrims each year. The *agrakaram* had its own Brahmins-only group. Five Brahmin pilgrims left for Sabarimalai two weeks after the larger, all-caste group had gone. Thus, Sabarimalai offered the opportunity to temporarily disregard caste, but it was not an opportunity that Aruloor's Brahmin men desired.

Possession and Belief

The upper castes were not very enthusiastic about the possession-practices of the lower castes, particularly their wounding of the body and spectacular *alaku*-wearing. However, no Brahmins or Chettiars ever said that they thought that the lower castes were faking their possession; rather, they evinced interest in and respect for the practices. So it is ironical that it was in the very lowest caste, the Pallars, that skepticism about possession was revealed on a mass scale. In April 1987, on Panguni Uttiram day, the Pallars celebrated their Periakka festival: The feet of all the possessed men and the sole woman (Sellaiyee, Mani's wife) involved were duly washed with water by women onlookers in the Pallar street, who fell at their feet in ritual worship. Several months later, however, when inquiring whether the festival would recur in a year's time, I was startled to be scornfully told by several Pallar women that all the possessed participants in the Periakka festival had been humbugs.

These "humbugs" included not only the man who had carried Periakka's *karagam* (sacred pot) and been possessed by the goddess herself but even the man who, possessed by the warrior-god Madurai-veeran, had stood on a knife-edge throughout the procession. At the time of the festival, I clearly remembered being told that his ability to stand for hours on a knife-edge, without cutting his feet, was "proof" of the deity's power. But now, a very different perspective was being presented: One woman said, "It's easy enough to stand on the *aruval*-edge because it's very blunt and broad and rusty. They don't sharpen it, that's the trick— they just stand on the *mottai* [blunt] edge. So it's not a miracle at all!'

In effect, these women were saying that every Pallar who had become possessed that day had faked it. "Look at Angaras, drunk every day! D'you think a *sami* would think *him* fit to possess? Of course not, not a drunken rascal like him. Yet he was 'possessed'—and we all had to bow to him!" The women argued that not a single man—and certainly not Sellaiyee, the sole woman—had been worthy of receiving a deity because all the men were drunkards or blackguards and Sellaiyee was an arrogant, conceited fraud. I was stunned because the event had been the grandest religious celebration in the Pallar street in one and a half years, and at the time, it had evoked a most enthusiastic response. The extreme skepticism and outright disbelief expressed here were, however, typical of the Pallars. They were, on all occasions, more willing to talk openly than any upper caste, whether the subject was their neighbor's sexual misdemeanors or faked religious possession.

This skepticism is a striking example of how ideas and beliefs change with context even within the same caste. In some contexts, the Pallars appeared to believe in the possession of their *sami-adi*. They had seemed to do so, for example, when they had knelt in the street in front of them. But in other contexts, they were skeptical of these possessions. Further, they did not disbelieve in possession altogether, for they had been very impressed by the possessions of those who had "worn" *alaku* at the big Murugan festival. Rather, they seemed to think that the particular possessions exhibited by their kin and neighbors, in their own street, might have been fraudulent. It is also significant that these criticisms were only voiced long after the event. Similarly, in the Three Streets, some Muthurajahs did not believe in the possessions of their institutional god-dancers either; otherwise, they would not have threatened to smash Mariyamman's *karagam* if the rival faction organized a *karagam*-festival. Yet these Muthurajahs visited temples and performed religious rites, too.

Possession and Gender

The only caste in Aruloor in which women also became regularly possessed was the low-ranking Pallar caste, yet, it was in this caste that possession was most skeptically questioned. Pallar female possession was mocked at and made fun of, though not actually to the faces of the women concerned. However, many of the Pallar women respected and believed in the possessions that occurred at the Cittirai Paurnami Murugan festival, when caste-Hindus were possessed. And, throughout the village, it was women, rather than men, who had the ritual role of offering worship by kneeling down, washing the devotees' feet, and bowing their heads to the ground in front of the possessed *alaku*-wearers. Even with the Chettiars and Brahmins, it was their women who emerged from seclusion to pour water in front of the possessed men and cool the hot road for their feet. Thus what happened, in effect, was a massive public dramatization of woman's submission to man-as-god.

Yet, with *all* the possessed males of *all* castes, the process of becoming possessed involved a striking appropriation of what, to the Tamil mind, are female characteristics: The male devotee humbly submitted, "opened" himself, and gave himself up so that the deity might "enter" him. When he was possessed by a female deity, the sexual parallel of "penetration" by the goddess became even more explicit: The goddess, exercising her *sakti* (power), entered the man. Thus, remarkably, the period of transcendent bliss (or divine possession) is, for the Tamil, a period *when man becomes female*. Only to man-as-female—submissive, open, filled with passionate devotion—does God come to possess him. In other words, only when man has rendered himself powerless can deity possess him. But man cannot surrender temporal power and control in the Tamil universe: He must remain in control. Consequently, to become man-as-female and vulnerable to possession is also, implicitly, to briefly desert one's duty as master of the temporal order. Possession is therefore only a temporary respite from his "maleness" for the devotee and from the duties this maleness imposes in the Tamil context. Further, possession is not a solitary experience: It needs a social context to stimulate and create it and to celebrate it. So the social world of a man surrounds him even while he is possessed—it honors him as a deity and then, inevitably, brings him out of possession, back to the temporal reality that he is required to control.

Possession thus reverses the Tamil "natural order" in which deities are superior to men and men are superior to women by creating, although only temporarily, a space and a time during which deities "become" men—and men "become" female. But, as noted, they do *not* become "women," for that would lower their status. It is this *symbolic androgyny* of possessed men that provides them with an immense freedom and symbolic strength, for they are both "female" *and* male as these gender constructs are understood in Tamil culture. It is this very freedom to "become female," so easily available to men, that locks Tamil women even more securely into their marginalized role because the freedom to "be male" is never allowed to them in any ritual situation. Women are allowed to be *only* "female" all the time. Even rituals performed solely by (upper-caste) women, such as *nonbu* (vows), carry the ideological message of the superior worth of men and the inferior value of women.

Thus, women are offered virtually no occasion on which they can ritually take control and dominate—in other words, be male, in the Tamil sense. It is true that during the female puberty rites, young women are represented as being goddess-like in their newfound powers of generation. They are represented, in all the Non-Brahmin castes, as being very significantly "empowered" at puberty: Procreation is the most central of the "divine female powers" that come to menarchal young women. Yet the focus of the puberty rites is on making these female powers safe for appropriation and control by men. That is why the rites take the form of a symbolic marriage, which must precede the actual marriages that these empowered women make. There is never the suggestion that women might be able to autonomously control their "divine" powers of procreation; on the contrary, the implication of the prohibitions that restrict the menstruant girl suggest that her powers are potentially dangerous both because they are so enormous and because they are entirely vulnerable to the influence of malign powers (bad planets, *dirushti, pey*). Women have "divine" generative power but are incapable of wisely directing these powers. In brief, women are the source of creative energy, but men embody the wisdom that must direct this energy.

This essentially religious conception of gender explains the paradox of Tamil possession. Women do not need to be divinely "empowered" because they naturally embody "divine" power and energy. This is made evident in Non-Brahmin belief that children come primarily from women. Women are ritually empowered in the puberty rites, in the sense that these rites celebrate and protect their *inherent,* distinctively female powers. These rites also "domesticate" their powers, rendering these menarchal young women marriageable to ordinary men. However, when men are ritually empowered through possession, being filled and energized with divine power, they, unlike women, are able to *direct* these *essentially "female" powers* as well. That is, unlike women, men, when they are "female," can represent and embody Deity in a whole and complete manner, for they are *both* Power-Energy *and* Wisdom.

Consequently, only men can be "complete." This symbolic construction of maleness closely parallels the Brahmins' representation of themselves in religious symbolism as self-sufficient and complete and not involved in dependence on lower castes: In the "Brahmanical ideal ... relationships with inferiors are denied" (Fuller 1988: 19). This ideology of male completeness is given powerful iconic form in the remarkable androgynous image of Siva Ardhanari. This icon, in which androgyny is beautifully represented, is regarded as most pleasing and satisfying in Tamil aesthetic sensibility. Consummately executed in South Indian bronze sculpture, half of Siva's body is female and half is male in this representation of the Great God. Half his face is also gently feminized. But the philosophical assumptions behind this artistic masterpiece are subtly hinted at by the fact that, though androgynous, the identity of the divine image is male. This is suggested by the slight predominance that is given to the male half of the sculptured image, and it is unambiguously stated in the name of this icon: It represents *Siva* Ardhanari, that is, the Great God "as Half-Woman." It is never described as "Parvati as Half-Man."

This ritual androgyny of *men* (for women are not allowed to be androgynous) helps explain the conundrum of the female gender of Power or *Sakti*. Because Sakti is another name for Parvati (Siva's wife and the supreme goddess of the Sanskritic pantheon) it is easy to assume that in India women are powerful and that women are symbolically viewed as intrinsically possessing more power than men. Such an assumption would find support in the fact that Sakti/Parvati is described as the "active principle" in the universe, while Siva is the "passive principle," as well as in the statement that Sakti "acts" and Siva is "still." Most convincing of all, they find, is the saying, "Siva without Sakti is *cavam* [a corpse]." However, to assume that passivity is synonymous with inferior status and activity indicates superior status is to ethnocentrically misunderstand the thrust of this particular Brahminical discourse (though there are other esoteric discourses that view Sakti/Kali as the Supreme Deity that more closely approach popular ideas about divinity in Aruloor).

The message of this Brahminical discourse is that Wisdom is "still" and "passive" and that this "stillness" is a superior mode of being to the "restlessness" of Sakti. Further, in this discourse, it is clear that Wisdom or Knowledge (*nanam*) is gendered as male and is hierarchically related to Power or Energy, which is gendered as female. Wisdom controls and directs the exuberant creativity of Power. When divinely possessed, men are both wise and powerful, male and temporarily female, too. Consequently, it is only men who can autonomously represent Divinity completely, for only men, in their possession-rites, "become androgynous" and thus "complete." And because only men can thus join Wisdom to Power, women are forever separated from Wisdom.

But the Goddess Mariyamman is not subject to this disability. One of the most striking contrasts between Brahminical religion and popular, lower-caste Non-Brahmin religion is the radical difference in their understandings of the nature of Mariyamman, the Great Goddess. Mariyamman is normally understood to be unmarried: In the Brahminical view, this automatically makes her an "angry," sexually overheated goddess who is unable to "cool" herself because she lacks a divine husband with whom to have sexual intercourse. This view is prominent in the myths of Meenakshi of Madurai (another form of Sakti/Parvati), who is described as having been angry and uncontrolled until she was subdued by and married to Sundaresvarar (Siva) (see Fuller 1980a). However, contrary to this view, in the Non-Brahmin perspective, Mariyamman *does not need a male god to control her.* For Non-Brahmins, Mariyamman is not, like Meenakshi, merely a most powerful consort of Siva. She is entirely "complete," for she is the Supreme Deity herself. In local myths, she may or may not have a husband (he is usually called Vembadian in Aruloor), but he is, in any case, entirely subordinate to her. She is the autonomous ruling power of the universe—and she is, to people in Aruloor, as infinitely wise as she is powerful. We will have no difficulty in understanding this female representation of Supreme Deity if we do not essentialize gender. For in the popular, common understanding of God in Aruloor, God/Mariyamman is female in her powers but also male in her infinite wisdom. She is supremely wise, beneficent, good, and tender—though she is also angry with sinners and destroys the wicked. She is God Herself—both female and *implicitly* male. So, she, too, is *androgynous* in gender, just as Sanskritic Divinity in its wholeness, in the unity of Siva and Sakti, is represented as being androgynous. And just as Tamil men are, when they are divinely possessed.

Thus, the preeminent iconic form of this discourse is the androgynous Deity. The Brahminical image of Siva-as-Half-Woman implicitly underlies the possession discourses of Aruloor's upwardly mobile castes. But Siva Ardhanari is replaced in the religion of lower-caste Tamils by the icon of the Great Goddess, Mariyamman, who by her *autonomous* and absolute power, implicitly shows that she unites both infinite "male" Wisdom and inexhaustible "female" Energy. In both Brahminical and lower-caste discourses, "God" is androgynous and doubly gendered. With the Brahminized groups, the stress is on God's "maleness," but what Aruloor's lower castes celebrate and sing is the "femaleness" of God.

At the coming-of-age celebration of Uma's youngest sister. Savitripatti, the girl's grand-mother, smiles in the foreground—to her left is Uma's beaming mother.

Kandan, pierced "through the chest" with Lord Murugan's spear, became the focus of devo-tion at the Aruloor festival. He exuded calm serenity, and people flocked to receive sacred ash from him.

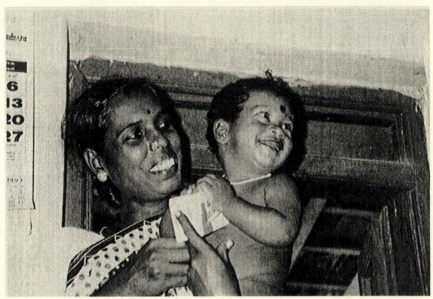

Siva and her baby boy, who survived a complicated birth. She and Velayudham gave their son the name Vettri (Victory).

At a Chettiar circling-rite *(suttradu)* during puberty celebrations. The ascetic dress and white sari of the older woman identifies her as a Chettiar widow. She is blessing the girl who is dressed in an expensive silk sari, with gold jewelry and masses of flowers.

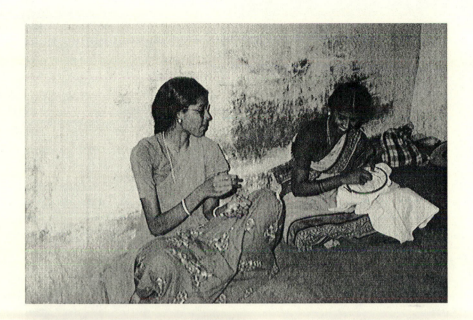

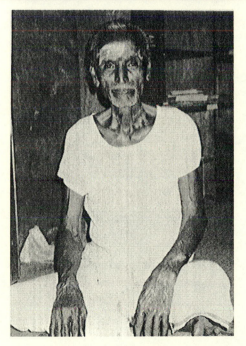

Top: Uma embroiders, sharing a joke with her younger sister. Like her grandmother, she became a close friend of mine—a friendship that has lasted.

Left: Palani Chettiar was the ritual leader of the Chettiar community. His irrepressible good humor made him a star informant of mine; he told me many devotional stories.

Grandmother Savithri ("Savitripatti") was a star informant of mine—wise, witty, and very kind. She told me and Uma a lot about Brahmin ways.

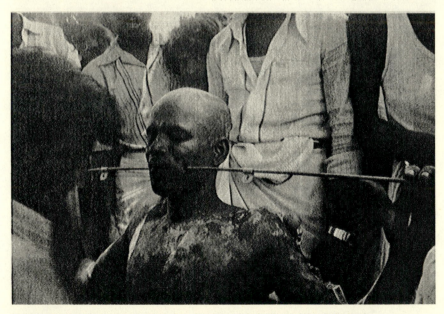

Devotee wearing a spear through his cheeks at the festival of the Pallars of Mallarchipuram. The spear is about to be removed as the procession has ended.

Devotee wearing a spear through his cheeks plus a metal frame at the festival of the Pallars of Mallarchipuram.

Siva does obeisance and pours water on the feet of a devotee at Aruloor's festival. Note the spears through the cheeks of two devotees and the fruits suspended from hooks in their flesh.

At the initiation of the Sabarimalai pilgrims, the old Brahmin guru puts sacred ash on the forehead of a possessed pilgrim to end the divine possession.

Measuring out the grain after it has been winnowed, in front of Siva's house in Periyar Street. Velayudham sits on the front step, his arm raised in conversation; Siva has her back to the camera.

Part Two

The Politics of
Everyday Life

7

"Beware, It Sticks!"
Discourses of Gender and Caste

After all, men have desire, so women should be careful.
 —Thanjayee (Pallar)

Are you a man? As a man shouldn't you exercise control over her?
 —Rajendran (Pallar)

But what, then, *is* impurity?
 —Uma (Brahmin)

Brahmin Discourse: The Sin of Menstruation

IN BRAHMIN BELIEF, to be born a woman is to show that one has sinned in one's previous life, for those who live truly virtuous lives are not reborn as women. Brahmin discourse thus connects menstruation and femaleness with *karmam* and indicates that, as with caste identity, there is a moral dimension to gender identity. The menstruating woman, like the "untouchable" and the widow, reveals the karmic "sin" of her female gender. Menstruation is explicitly designated the sign of sin in the important Brahmin ritual of Rishi Pancami. In orthodox Brahmin belief, a woman can only be purified of the sin of being a menstruating female through the complex rituals of Rishi Pancami: Only this rite can cleanse her *pavam* (sin).

It is ironic that the ideology of menstrual impurity is strongest in Brahmin discourse because today, urban Brahmin elites are in the forefront of women's emancipation. The Brahmins in Tamilnadu have gone through radical social change during this century, losing the dominant social position they held under British patronage due to the political triumph of the Anti- Brahmin Movement. Because urban Brahmin women are in the vanguard of female education and salaried employment, rural Brahmin women are confronted with very different role models in the rural and urban spheres. Only those who have experienced both worlds are likely to question the conservative values they are taught in Aruloor. This is why Uma, nineteen years old and my close Brahmin friend, was the first woman I ever heard who questioned the doctrine of female impurity.

When Uma menstruated, she was excluded from the house for three days. During this period, she was referred to as being *"duram"* (far away). She sat in the old cow-shed behind her house. Every item she touched was polluted and was ritually rinsed with water, first by her, and then again by whoever took it from her. The rinsing was merely perfunctory, but it was always done. When she was given a bucket in which to wash her clothes, she sprinkled water on it before she returned it, moving it just outside the cow-shed, and Uma's mother, before picking it up, sprinkled water on it too. These ritual gestures were so ingrained in daily life that they were hardly noticed.

Far less pleasant than Uma's airy cow-shed were the conditions in which Charumathi, the wife of a rich landlord named Raghav Aiyar, spent her menstrual days. She sat hidden behind a door because if her mother-in-law, Kalyanipatti (Grandmother Kalyani), were even to *see* her, the older woman would become polluted. This was because Kalyanipatti had performed the Rishi Pancami ritual. She explained to me that she had done it to absolve herself of the sin (*pavam*) of menstruation.

Kalyanipatti explained that this rite of worship can only be done by a woman after her menopause has ended: "After menses has stopped we wait seven years, to be quite sure that it has stopped—we must be clean. Only thereafter do we do the *pujai* [worship] for seven consecutive years. It would be a very great sin if you started bleeding once you've started performing the *pujai*." Once a woman had completed the seven-year rite, she had to protect her purity very strictly, especially where menstruating women were concerned; just seeing a menstruating woman would pollute her. This was why Kalyanipatti ordinarily only saw her daughter-in-law and her granddaughters after she had bathed, said her prayers, and eaten breakfast, "Whenever I come into the courtyard I call out and Charumathi hides herself behind that door." This game of hide-and-seek makes relations between women in a household very complicated. The ritual can therefore only be done in a rich household by an older woman who is no longer needed for daily household work. This was why Uma's grandmother, Savitripatti, had not performed the rite, for she was still very necessary to household work.

In May 1988, while I was in Aruloor, Uma was married and went to live in Chandigrah with her engineer husband. But Chandigrah was a very long way from the disused cow-shed that she had sat in, and when we both happened to return to Aruloor in December 1988, Uma's life was very different. Now she did things that were anathema to the code of the *agrakaram:* Above all, she regularly broke the menstrual taboos because she cooked for her husband and cleaned the house even while menstruating. Her grandmother strongly disapproved of this: Uma's husband should have taken over the cooking when Uma menstruated, Savitripatti declared, as the rules of ritual purity demanded.

It was at this point that Savitripatti happened to recount to us, for the purposes of my research, the story (*kadai*) ritually told during the Rishi Pancami rites. She first gave me an abbreviated version from memory but then got Uma to read it out of a compendium of rituals and ritual-stories (the *Virata Pujai Vidanam*). This version differed slightly from her own, but she said that the book was "right." Like all ritual-*kadai*, the story explains the reason for performing the ritual and extols it. Uma read it aloud: It condemned the breaking of menstrual taboos in the strongest terms, and it had an extraordinary effect on her.

In Vidharba there was a *muni* [sage] called Udankar. Hi wife was called Susila. They had a son and a daughter. They gave their daughter in marriage to a worthy groom. But a few days after the marriage she lost her husband. Unable to bear this sorrow the Brahmin sage came to live on the banks of the Ganges together with his family to teach the Vedas to disciples. His daughter spent her days serving her father.

One day, while she was sleeping, the disciples noticed that her body was crawling with worms [*pulu*] and told her mother. Her mother succeeded in removing the worms, she then took the girl to her father and asked him why worms had been crawling all over her daughter's body.

With his supernatural wisdom-insight [*nana-dirusthi*], the sage "saw" that seven lives previously his daughter had been the daughter of a Brahmin. During his lifetime, not considering her menstrual periods [*madaviday*] to be polluting [*asuttama*], she had regularly touched the pots and pans in the house. Moreover she had laughed disdainfully when she saw a friend piously do the Rishi Pancami ritual to remove the sin caused by menstrual impurity. For these reasons her body now teemed with worms. However, because of the merit [*punyam*] she had gained when she (involuntarily) witnessed the performance of that rite [*viratam*] she was now born in a Brahmin family, he said, adding that to remove this sin [*pavam*] she must perform the Rishi Pancami rites , and he explained the traditional customs [*morai*] pertaining to it. On her performing these rites, the daughter's disease [*noy*] was cured.

Therefore, particularly those women who, during their menstrual periods [*rudu*] and at other times, knowingly or unknowingly happen to act in an impure [*asuttama*] and immoral [*anacaram*] way, can remove their resulting sins [*pavangal*] and become holy and receive all blessings [*kshemangal*] if they perform this ritual.

—From the "Bavshyottira Puranam" in the *Virata Pujai Vidanam.*

Uma's reactions to this religious cautionary tale were significant. She stopped several times in midsentence to laugh, and there was both exasperation and bewilderment in her defensive laughter. According to this story—and all the norms she had been brought up with—she stood accused. She, too, had "sinned," like the unfortunate daughter whose body, in the horrific imagery of the tale, becomes that of a living corpse, teeming with worms. Closing the book, she squarely faced her grandmother and said, "There's no room for this behaviour in my life: There's no one besides me to receive guests and we have at least ten visitors—mainly my friends—every day. What d'you want me to do? Sit quietly in a corner and refuse to acknowledge them because I'm menstruating? I've no one else in the house to help. I don't even have a relative close by to help with the cooking. *I've* got to attend to guests, cook, do everything." Challenged by her indignant granddaughter to explain why she should be considered vile and impure simply for being a good wife, Savitripatti sought to be conciliatory. She loved Uma dearly, and to comfort her about the impurity that she clearly incurred, she gently said, "In God's eyes there's no such thing as impurity."

The effect on Uma was electric: Turning on her grandmother, she cried out, passionately, in total bewilderment, "But what, then, *is* impurity?" What, then, of the years during which she had sat in the cow-shed? What, then, was menstrual impurity? If God was not concerned with impurity, who was? Savitripatti was unable to answer these questions. The notion that "there is no impurity before God" is a *bakti*-influenced idea, widely influential in the religion of the lowest castes but also available to Brahmins. It is not, however, a perspective that is stressed by Brahmins in intercaste contexts, for the obvious reason that it calls their own high status into question.

I listened, in absolute fascination, aware that it was the very first time that I was hearing a woman question the "fact" of her impurity. Uma's central question showed how far she had traveled on the road that led away from the certainties of the Aruloor *agrakaram* to the questions posed by the outside world. Though she did not realize it, in questioning the legitimacy of the notion of her own female "impurity," she was questioning the upper-caste construction of both gender and caste.

Lower-Caste Discourses of Gender and Sexuality

Lower-caste discourses of sexuality are ambiguous, multiple, and contradictory—and far more varied than upper-caste discourses. Many issues, including pregnancy, contraception, "proper" fertility, and sexuality are sharply focused in the following incident and the discussions that took place around it.

The Death of Thangamma, "Mother of Gold"

Anjalai was the mother of my Muthurajah assistant, Mala. We were sitting together, discussing Muthurajah birth-rituals, when Siva unexpectedly came down the street toward us. Pallars did not normally walk through the Muthurajah street unless they had specific business there, so I knew something was up.

Siva had strange news. She said that she had deliberately come this way (it was about 9 a.m.) to see if I had come. (I felt that she was also indirectly explaining to the Muthurajahs who were present why she had entered their street.) She had to attend a funeral: A relative had died at Puthurseeli village, and she had to go there. She said, "Many others will come from our street too—maybe forty others—but *we'll* have to foot the bus-fare." When asked why, she stated, "Because they are 'his' [Velayudham's] relatives." As usual, I asked who had died, and how, but instead of the humdrum answer (old relative, of old age) that I expected, I received an astonishing reply: "The relative is a woman—she's killed herself." Again, I asked why. "Because," she answered, "she was three months pregnant at the same time as her daughter was pregnant with her baby! She killed herself out of shame [*vekkam*]!" And Siva gave Anjalai more details.

I was entirely perplexed. I asked three questions:

1. *Why* did she kill herself when she could have had an abortion quite easily?
2. What was there to be ashamed of?
3. Did they consider her to have done the right thing, or was this foolish?

And to add even more to my confusion, Anjalai laughed quite heartily as she gave her answers (she was apparently laughing at my total incomprehension), so that finally I had to ask, "But why are you laughing? Isn't the woman to be pitied?" And Anjalai replied: "She's not pitiable: She's a *fool* and she did a very foolish thing! She doesn't deserve pity at all—it's her children who deserve pity—with a drunkard father, who will look after them?" Siva seemed to be entirely in agreement with Anjalai's opinion.

Meanwhile Anjalai answered my questions:

1. "She was a fool to kill herself. Abortions used to be difficult to get and very expensive. Now they are easily had and cheap—even less than a hundred rupees! So why didn't she have an abortion, if she didn't want the child? Siva has told us that she already had six children—and a drunken husband. So what business had she to get another child?"
2. "Yes, there was something to be ashamed of—people will tease you and speak behind your back, when they hear that you're pregnant at the same time as your daughter. You *should* feel ashamed—but she was a fool to choose to kill herself!"
3. "This was a foolish and irresponsible act. This was sheer impudence [*timiru*]. Siva tells us that some of her children are quite small. Who will look after them now?"

Discussion of the death continued the next day. I was sitting with Siva on her porch, in the Pallar street, when Thanjayee came in. Thanjayee was an intelligent Pallar woman, but she had been worn down by years of hard work in the fields, illness, and bad eyesight: She wore thick glasses and squinted at you. It was 8 a.m.

She came in with one-rupee Assam Lottery tickets and wanted Siva to get the newspaper and check if her numbers had won. The first prize was Rs.100,000! No one from Aruloor had ever won. Siva told her that the draw was later that day and that the results would be in the next day's paper. With that, Thanjayee settled down on the porch to assist in our discussion.

She knew much more about the deceased woman than Siva did. From her, we learned that the woman, Thangamma, had been four months pregnant when she died. Her husband's sister's children also lived with her because both her husband's younger sister and *her* husband (HyZH) were dead (both had been in their twenties when they died). So Thangamma—her name meant "mother of gold"— had looked after her own seven children and two orphans. She was forty years old. Her eldest daughter, twenty-two years old, was married and in the ninth month of her first pregnancy. Her second child, an unmarried son of twenty, worked in a shop. Her second daughter, eighteen years old and married, was four months pregnant. The other children were a boy (thirteen), a girl (ten), another girl (six)—none of whom went to school—and a little boy of four.

Thanjayee commented: "How could she face her sons-in-law? The mother-in-law is shy of the son-in-law in any case—isn't it much worse if she is pregnant? So she should be careful not to get pregnant." The message was clear: The responsibility for successful contraception lay with women; men did not need to be careful. Thanjayee went on to put this very explicitly: "It's *we* who have to be careful—when we are sitting at rest they will pull your hand and force you to have sex. No, husbands are *not* careful, nor do they care! So if an older woman with a married daughter becomes pregnant then *she* is blamed, *not* her husband!" Siva interjected: "People consider a pregnancy the fault of the woman, never the fault of the man!" And my Muthurajah assistant, Mala, quoted a well-worn local saying: "Men can jump fifty house-walls but women cannot take even one step outside their homes!" The "fifty house-walls" referred to illegitimate sex with fifty women.

Thanjayee went on:

> She must eat local medicines [*nattu marundu*]—or go to the hospital for the English medicines, when she finds that she is pregnant. That's what Lakshmi and Sarasu, the two wives of Jagannath, keep having to do. They keep getting pregnant and have to take injections or swallow pills to induce abortions. They have to do this every few months. And when they *have* abortions—as they already have six children—their husband abuses them—he says that they are having abortions because they've been having affairs with *other* men and that's why they don't want the children. But it's *he* who's at them, demanding sex all the time—I can hear him from my house! Yes, of course he doesn't contribute towards the household expenses— he drinks all that he earns and doesn't give them even ten paise! They support the children *entirely* through their own work—and that's why they don't want to have more children. He "wants" more children, he says—because he doesn't do a thing to support them!

She continued: "Yes, it's always the *woman's* responsibility to see that she doesn't get pregnant—after all, men have desire [*asai*], so women should be careful." I objected that women feel desire too. "No, *even* if women feel desire, that's not what people say—they say *women* must go for "Family Planning" if they don't want more children—men won't go!" By "Family Planning," Thanjayee meant sterilization—this was the only contraception readily available. Mala intervened (she had worked for the local Family Planning unit briefly): "This is true— eighty per cent or more of those who go for 'Family Planning' are *women*. Men don't go. They really don't care whether the women become pregnant or not."

Three days later, news came that Thangamma had *not* killed herself after all— she had been the victim of an abortion that had gone badly wrong. She had visited a local female practitioner of herbal and traditional medicine (*nattu vaidyam*), and this woman had "cleaned out" her uterus with an herbal "stick." But though the fetus was aborted, something became stuck in the womb, it swelled up, and Thangamma became very ill. When she was finally taken to Tiruchi's General Hospital, her condition was so desperate that the hospital at first refused to take her, saying, Siva reported, "Having mucked about with your country medicines you've almost killed her—so why do you bring her here to die? We won't admit her!" Finally, they did admit her, but she remained critically ill and died on the third day. In reply to my questions, Siva said: "Why did she not go directly to the hospital? Because she wanted to keep it secret—after all, if you go the hospital you'll be seen and people will ask 'Why are you going there?' So she tried to get rid of the fetus secretly. She should have gone to the hospital, of course—they'd have performed the abortion efficiently and safely. What does her husband think? How do we know? No, it's not likely that he blames himself—it would always be considered *her* responsibility to get rid of a pregnancy."

These discussions of Thangamma's alleged suicide indicate that powerful discourses of "proper" female sexuality and "proper" fertility exist even among Pallar women, who are comparatively independent of their husbands economically. Thus, in both upper-caste and lower-caste contexts, though they are materially so different, women are controlled by powerful norms that require the subordination and self-control of their sexuality and fertility. With the lower castes, the stress is on norms controlling fertility, but with the upper castes, norms controlling sexuality are emphasized. The lower-caste norms connect with the greater sexual freedom enjoyed by Pallar women—but what Thangamma's story makes plain is that this sexual freedom is severely limited because of the lack of safe contraception. From the perspective of ordinary, impoverished Pallars, considerations of "appropriate" female behavior are quite irrelevant. These considerations only arise when a certain level of economic security is reached and women are being withdrawn from work outside the home. In short, they exist only in the context of the upwardly mobile groups in whom the desire to emulate upper-caste and upper-class norms is strong. It is among them that *"appropriate" female behavior suddenly becomes the coin of new social status for men.* The point at which women start to be withdrawn from outside work marks the division between the upwardly mobile and those below them; this is the critical juncture at which the more straightforward lower-class concern with *fertility* and survival becomes a complex upper-class preoccupation with *sexuality* and control.

The two main "contraceptive" means available to Pallar women are abortion and sterilization. Although abortion is apparently used regularly as a "contraceptive," it is seen as potentially dangerous and debilitating. Sterilization, performed in ill-equipped government hospitals (because the impoverished Pallars cannot afford private hospitals), is regarded as rather hazardous, too. Further, there is a widespread conviction, strongly held by Pallar women, that sterilization weakens a woman's body so greatly that she can never perform hard manual labor again. This is the main reason why Pallar women believe that they cannot afford to have themselves sterilized: They are convinced that they would lose their livelihood and be unable to continue their arduous agricultural work. Interestingly, professional medical opinion appears to support their view, for even at expensive private hospitals in Tiruchi city, local doctors tell women patients who have been sterilized not to carry any loads or do any heavy work for some eight months following the operation. Pallar families would be close to starvation if Pallar women stayed off work for eight months, for much of their work is very heavy manual labor.

Another reason for rejecting sterilization, given by both lower- and upper-caste women, was "men don't like it" if women are sterilized: Men find sterilized wives less sexually attractive. However, in a recent change of attitude, some Muthurajah women from upwardly mobile households had actually been encouraged by their salaried husbands to get themselves sterilized after having four (or even "only" three) children. They had done so in private hospitals. Though rare, this appeared to be an increasing trend among upwardly mobile groups in Aruloor in 1988.

Though their wives are required to "de-sex" themselves, lower-caste men are not asked to alter their sexual behavior in any way. If their wives becomes pregnant, it is the wives' "fault." Like poor Thangamma, who had looked after not only her own large brood but also orphans, women have to seek desperate remedies to terminate their pregnancies. Thanjayee summed it up: "It's *women* who should be careful. Men have desire and cannot be expected to control themselves."

This ordinary utterance leads us straight into the extraordinary complexity of Tamil discourses of sexuality. Thanjayee stated that women have to control themselves. They do this through traumatic contraceptive strategies because men cannot be expected to control themselves. Yet a completely contradictory perspective was held by some women and most men of the Pallar and other castes. In this perspective, both sexes spoke of how women have to be controlled by men and of how this is the ordained moral order, because women cannot control themselves.

This view, with its emphasis on male control of women, is strongly influenced by upper-caste mores, which it reflects. The understanding that most Pallar women had of gender relations is, however, more accurately captured by Thanjayee's view that it is *women* who must be more responsible than men in all matters.

It is Pallar men, not women, who try to invoke the upper-caste notion of a moral order of women "controlled" by men. This putative moral order—their attempt at a male-ordered world—is constituted by a set of Pallar discourses that are well illustrated in the story of Papathi's courtship. Elderly, amiable, and now partly deaf as a result of the quarrel I will describe, Papathi had suffered the loss of her only son in mysterious circumstances (possession by an evil spirit was suspected). But that was more than ten years earlier, and in 1987, the Pallar street, always rife with lively and libelous gossip, was much interested in the affair of the wooing of Papathi, now a widow of uncertain age. Papathi, who was quite well off, was a rather dotty and pleasant woman, with a squeaky voice. Siva told me that Papathi was angry with her. She explained why.

The Wooing of Papathi

Recently, Papathi's aged lover, a man from Varadampettai named Nagappa, had appeared one night, very drunk and wanting to see Papathi. But Papathi had gone to the cinema. So Siva and Velayudham, being her neighbors, had to invite him into their house and make polite conversation with him. Then, after the old drunk had fallen on the porch in a stupor, both Siva and Velayudham "escaped" by locking the house and going off for the late-night show at the cinema.

When Velayudham and Siva came back from the film, they found that Papathi was sitting on their neighbor Pandaiyee's porch. "She was looking at her lover, asleep on our porch, but she didn't dare approach him!" "Why not?" I asked. "Why didn't she take him to *her* house?" Siva exclaimed: "Good gracious, no! Kanagaraj would have *killed* him!" "Why?" I queried. "Because Papathi is his *Cinnamma* [Mother's Younger Sister]—after all, her husband has died and her son has died—so what more does she have to do? She should not behave like this. She encourages that old lover—and that old man obeys her every beck and call! No, Kanagaraj is right—and he has warned that if Papathi's lover comes here he will *kill* him! In fact Pichaiammal went and told him that the old man had come—but he didn't come to quarrel because the old man had come to *our* house. We are respected here—people know that we don't want to involve ourselves in quarrels. The old man left in the morning. And Papathi silently followed after him, at some distance—and hasn't been seen since!" "Why shouldn't she have this lover?" I argued. "She might be lonely, poor thing!" Siva retorted: "Well, if so she should go and stay in that man's house, in *his* village! Then Kanagaraj would not quarrel with her. It's because she continues to stay *here*—and carried on with the old man *here* that Kanagaraj is outraged. If she went away no one would bother any more about what she did!"

But why was Papathi's nephew so upset about the old man coming to Periyar Street? Siva explained. Nagappa, a widower, was a primary schoolteacher (*vidayar*) in his late fifties, with two fairly grown children. He had recently married his elder sister's daughter, Karupayee (in her twenties) of Periyar Street, but was, at the same time, carrying on a long-standing affair with Papathi. So Karupayee, disgusted, came back home to Periyar Street, and she remained there with her parents for one year. During that time, Nagappa continued carrying on with Papathi, visiting her in Periyar Street. It was he who asked for a divorce, on Papathi's instigation, claimed Siva. Nagappa's daughter had reached puberty recently (she was about fifteen years old), and his son, who was about twenty-two, had done an ITI (Industrial Training Institute) course.

Velayudham added: "He was crying the night he came here—though he was very drunk too!—saying that Papathi didn't want his children—but how could he reject them! Poor man! He also said that *she* is trying to have a child by him—and that they are both going to Thanjavur Medical College soon to find out about this!" Velayudham chuckled. "At her age—she's almost fifty—how would she get a child? But they have great hopes!"

While the marriage with Karupayee was breaking down, her father, Rajendran, came and quarreled with Kanagaraj. He stopped him in the road and scolded him publicly, saying, "Haven't you got any *shame* to see the way your *Cinnamma* is carrying on? Are you a *man*? As a man, shouldn't you exercise control over her? Shouldn't you discipline her and tell her how she should behave? You haven't bothered to control her and have allowed her to go free! Are you a man at all?"

Siva, who was recounting this, continued.

Many men scolded Kanagaraj. They said: "This way you're just letting your *Cinnamma* go on doing wrong while you sit quietly by! Don't you have any shame? You'd be better off dead—why don't you go and kill yourself!" In this way the men abused Kanagaraj. The whole *ur* insulted him. So, finally, about five months ago, Kanagaraj when very drunk, came and beat up Papathi, who'd asked him to just mind his own business. He beat her saying: "Do I have to kill myself because of you? Why are you behaving like this?" He beat her so severely that her ear-drum was injured and she had to go to hospital. When she returned, she said to the street leaders, "Call a meeting of the street!" [*Kuttam podanum!*] When all the men assembled [the street leaders Mani and Pechimuthu presided] it was decided that it should be publicly acknowledged that there was no longer any "connection" [relationship or kinship: *sambandam*] between Kanagaraj and Papathi: "There is no kind of relationship at all between them!" it was announced. After this Kanagaraj has only come and scolded Papathi when he's drunk: He's kept away otherwise.

Papathi had one and a half acres of *kuttakai* (sharecrop) paddy-land. This constituted considerable wealth, though she had not planted it that year (1988) because of the severe drought. She owned her small house as well as *nagai* (gold jewelry) weighing about five *pavun*. She also owned various *patram* (utensils) that she had stowed away somewhere. In short, she was quite well off. I therefore wondered if Kanagaraj's moral concern was not merely a cover for his desire to acquire control over her property. Siva, who, inexplicably sympathized with Kanagaraj, rejected this interpretation: "No, he doesn't want to inherit Papathi's property—he's got enough of his own. He's got two houses and his own half acre of banana. It's because of shame that Kanagaraj threatened to kill Nagappa—he only *threatened,* he didn't meant it. It was just to frighten him! He has no designs on Papathi's property. In fact he's told her that she can live on her wealth and use it all up—but only behave properly!" Siva may have rejected my suspicions, but Kanagaraj was Papathi's sole heir, and he would inherit her property *unless* she married Nagappa or had a child by him.

Several central concepts and roles figure in this tragicomic story. Kanagaraj's very manhood, his gendered identity, is called into question: Is he a man? For a *real* man is a man who controls and disciplines the women for whom he is "responsible." In this view, a man is responsible for the moral and sexual behavior of his wife or wives, daughters, and mother. Papathi was Mother's Younger Sister to Kanagaraj, so she was a classificatory mother to him. And not only was Kanagaraj a classificatory son to her, but he was also "responsible" for her behavior in lieu of her deceased husband and son. That was why young Karupayee's father complained to him that Papathi was breaking up the marriage of his newly wed daughter. However, in justice to Papathi (who was very badly beaten by Kanagaraj), I should point out that her affair with old Nagappa was already widely known when Karupayee's parents decided that Nagappa was a suitable spouse for their much younger daughter. They must have known about his relationship with Papathi when they arranged the wedding.

Siva claimed that "everyone" had insulted Kanagaraj and that he was therefore justified in thrashing Papathi. However, Siva's distinctly Brahminical perceptions were colored by the fact that she and Velayudham were among the very few well-off families in Periyar Street. They were at the lower end of that upwardly mobile class to which Anjalai in the Muthurajah street also belonged. To my exasperation, Siva was therefore always ready to endorse more Brahminical behavior. She was constantly criticizing the women of Periyar Street because (she said) they were "disobedient" and "did not obey their husbands" or because they refused to cook for their husbands (only occasionally) or beat their husbands (very rarely). Intelligent and sensitive as she was, she did not seem to recognize that the marital situations and working lives of her impoverished friends were radically different from her own. She herself was Tiruchi-bred, with a good high school education, and she lived comfortably and semisecluded at home. She had a gentle, intelligent, college educated, and utterly devoted husband in Velayudham. This made her position very different from that of the majority of Pallar women. Despite her criticism of Papathi's behavior, it is clear that everyone in the street did not condemn Papathi and that she had considerable support from several other women. There was certainly support for her among some of the men, too, for at their formal, all-male street meeting—the *kuttam*— they had voted that Kanagaraj should no longer have the right to exercise any authority over Papathi. In effect, she was no longer his Mother's Sister—the relationship had been terminated. Papathi was helped by the fact that she was known to have the support of Mani, one of the two street bosses. After this formal termination of kinship and of all connection (*sambandam*) between them whatsoever, Kanagaraj no longer had the "right" to beat Papathi, said Siva.

But prior to that, he *did,* for even in the comparatively egalitarian Pallar caste, men had the "right" to chastise, "discipline," and beat "their" women. The important difference between members of the upper and lower castes was that lower-caste women did not take this physical abuse quietly. Pallar women registered their anger by temporarily leaving violent husbands and going to live with their parents. If the beatings continued, the women, taking their children, extended their stays indefinitely, effectively abandoning their husbands. Largely because of the daily income that these women earned through their agricultural labor, they were readily taken back by their natal families. And for the same reason, they were likely to find second husbands quite easily.

This is quite different from the upper-caste situation, in which, due to the influence of more Brahminical norms, a woman is theoretically supposed to stay with her husband no matter how badly he treats her. It is only in these upper-caste and upper-class contexts that espouse a Brahminical discourse that the dreadful phenomenon of "bride-burning" has taken place. Avaricious families have taken to murdering their new daughters-in-law (by burning them) so that their sons can make second marriages in order to gain more "dowry" wealth. But such murders are still far rarer in Tamilnadu than in North India. This is because the Tamil Non-Brahmin paradigm of the *right* of married women to the continued protection of their natal kin, particularly their brothers, is widely influential. It has traditionally been the most powerful kinship discourse in this part of Tamilnadu, though it is weakening today.

Discourses Regarding "Untouchable" Impurity

"Reservations" (reserved places) for "untouchables" in higher education and, particularly, in salaried government jobs have, in Aruloor, created an entirely misplaced resentment against the impoverished Pallars, who never get even remotely near receiving these benefits. The change in the official status of the Pallars from "ex-untouchables" to "Scheduled Castes" was fiercely resented by the Muthurajahs, who were clearly worried by the possible rise of those who were just below them in the caste hierarchy. Consequently, Muthurajahs often made the Pallars the scapegoats for everything, including the drought that was in its third year in 1987. The drought continued, some of them claimed, solely due to the Almighty's displeasure with human—and especially "untouchable"—insubordination. Anjalai, my articulate Muthurajah friend, put it emphatically:

> All these problems have arisen because today people have chosen to play God [*Sami*]. They think they can make what rules they please, change what they please. Gandhi did a criminal thing in allowing the untouchables to enter the temples—this is an outrage against God. God made the rule that no untouchables should enter the temples—and none did. But today they do—so the temples are polluted [*tittu*] and God is angry. That's why He has sent drought upon us. It is said that when people are good there is rain, because virtue pleases God and He gives us the rain we need: This drought is a sign of His anger. ... The *talttapatta* [untouchables] should be given their own temples and kept separate from us. Only then will it rain again, as it used to!

Anjalai's diatribe essentially expressed Muthurajah economic anxieties and frustrations; interestingly, it also echoes Brahminical ideology—such as Dharmasastra—that claims God punishes social disorder with drought.

Pallar Rejections of Ritual Impurity

Case 1: The Battle for Right of Way

Pallars actively rejected the constraints imposed upon them. They did so most dramatically in the 1960s in a violent confrontation with the Muthurajahs to secure the right to walk down the Muthurajah street to the Pallar's new cremation ground. Previously, Pallars of Periyar Street had buried their dead; however, cremation is of much higher status than burial.

The Pallar street was very close to the Muthurajah street. Many Muthurajahs were humble agriculturists and very low on the caste ladder, yet, unlike the Pallars, they were caste-Hindus. The Pallars saw this as entirely unfair. Why were they labeled as "untouchable," they asked, when the Muthurajahs, who were agricultural laborers like them, were accorded caste-Hindu status? The Muthurajahs would have countered Pallar claims to "clean-caste" status by pointing out that the Pallars were the traditional funeral servants of the Asari (Craftsman) caste. Though this was not their primary caste occupation, this involvement in "polluting" work was enough to make them "untouchable"—or so the Muthurajah argument ran. A keen competitiveness between the two castes existed, especially since only twenty years earlier, many Muthurajahs had been just as impoverished as the Pallars. The Pallars, though poorer, clearly had no awe of their neighbors.

In the 1960s, encouraged by E. V. Ramaswami Naicker's call for a casteless society (which was the ruling DMK government's official rhetoric, too), the Pallars had demanded and at last been granted (by subdistrict level officials) a cremation ground for their dead. Previously, they had had to bury their dead in an area that was very difficult to reach, especially in the monsoon season. But to reach the new cremation ground, the Pallars had to walk down what, until then, had been strictly a Muthurajah side street.

Problems arose after the death of an old man in the Pallar street, for when his funeral cortege was ready to proceed to the new cremation ground, the Muthurajahs refused to let it pass through their side street. For almost a day, the body lay rotting in its bier. Infuriated, the Pallar men, armed with their farming sickles, knives, and spears, attacked the well-prepared Muthurajah men. In the ensuing fight, some blood was spilled, but no one was seriously injured. However, the Pallars won the day because in the negotiations that followed, the Muthurajahs finally agreed to allow Pallar funeral processions to pass through their side street from that day forward.

Case 2: "Our Blood Is as Red as Theirs!"

Poor, uneducated Pallars, who constituted the large majority of Pallars, had learned not to publicly question upper-caste authority, but even they rejected the pretensions of their caste-Hindu neighbors, the Muthurajahs. Ambal, a gray-haired woman whose pleasant face was tanned dark by the sun, was a perceptive and articulate Pallar in her late sixties. She roundly rejected the Muthurajah claim that they were superior to the Pallars, unconsciously echoing Shakespeare's Shylock when she eloquently demanded, "Aren't our veins full of blood that is as red as theirs? In what way are they our superiors?" ("If you prick us, do we not bleed?") Thus, even illiterate older people like Ambal rejected the upper-caste constructions of Pallars as ritually impure and inferior, at least in relation to the Muthurajahs. The few urbanized, college-educated, young Pallar men, on the other hand, rejected not only their own alleged impurity but the entire legitimation of caste hierarchy that was premised on it. Velayudham and his friends recognized that their "untouchable" identity was foisted on them as part of upper-caste strategies of domination.

Case 3: "Beware, It Sticks!"

Mala, my Muthurajah research assistant, happened to have a nine-year-old Muthurajah girl, her neighbor, with her one day when we were talking to women in the Pallar street. A young Pallar man, on his way past, accidentally brushed against her, and the nine-year-old cringed. Noticing, instead of being offended, he laughed, saying teasingly to her, "Beware, it sticks!" (*"Batram, ottikkaradu!"*). "It," of course, was ritual impurity. This genial and humorous attitude on the part of Pallars when faced with the reaction of others to their supposed pollution, is very significant, for their ability to make ironic jokes about "impurity" indicates that Pallars can laugh at the absurdity of the very attitudes that seek to demean them.

The Pallars observed Muthurajah behavior at close quarters daily, for the Muthurajah streets bordered on Periyar Street. Certain Pallar men also drank liquor and ate pork together with certain Muthurajah men, although both groups were described as "dissolute" in their respective streets. Nonetheless, this meant that the Pallars knew that Muthurajah men regularly broke the purity rules that forbade the consumption of liquor and pork. So, whatever claims the Muthurajahs liked to make, the Pallars knew that they themselves were as good as their neighbors.

Both in religious orientation and in everyday discourse , the Pallars showed deep skepticism toward upper-caste values, characterizing them as hypocritical and permeated by self-interest. They had many stories of Brahmin duplicity, hypocrisy, and greed and, in private, made sure that I knew about the affairs that wealthy Brahmins and Chettiars were having with Pallar women. They deeply resented the rude way in which their upper-caste employers (including Muthurajahs) habitually addressed them, using the condescending forms *"ni"* and *"da"* instead of *"ningal,"* the polite form for "you." A favorite proverb, which was regarded as wittily apt, asked, "If you meet a Brahmin and a snake, which should you kill first?" The answer was evident in their chuckles.

Consensual Versus Competing Discourses

Louis Dumont (1970) and Michael Moffatt (1979) have argued that an "encompassing" and "consensual" Hindu discourse prevails throughout the subcontinent. They claim that ritual purity is the central value of all castes and that purity and pollution are the overriding concerns of all Hindus. Dumont says: "It is by implicit reference to this opposition [between pure and impure] that the society of castes *appears consistent and rational* to those who live in it" (1970: 44, emphasis added). Dumont is supported by Moffatt (1979), who claims that purity has the same central place in the lives of Tamil "untouchables" as it does in the lives of the upper castes. He says: "The cultural system of Indian Untouchables does not distinctively question or revalue the dominant social order. ... The present argument is for fundamental cultural consensus from the top to the bottom of a local caste hierarchy" (Moffatt 1979: 3). He adds: "The present analysis of cultural consensus among the very low castes ... is compatible with Dumont's assumption of ideological homogeneity throughout the caste order" (Moffat 1979: 298).

Moffat argues that if "untouchables" "replicate" the caste structure by treating their own service castes as lower than themselves, this proves they consensually share the dominant castes' concern with ritual purity. Such so-called replication exists in Aruloor, too; that is, the Pallars also have Washermen and Barbers who belong to inferior service castes with which the Pallars do not marry. The Pallars do not allow these Washermen or Barbers to enter their homes. But this is not evidence of any "fundamental" interest in ritual purity. On the contrary, this has much to do with making a claim to social status. The Pallars are merely treating their service castes in exactly the same way as other castes treat theirs. They are following conventional social behavior.

Recent scholarship has strongly rejected Moffat's Dumontean claims of "fundamental cultural consensus." This is the case with David Lorenzen's account of "untouchable" religious groups (1987) and with Shalini Randeria's analysis of the self-perceptions of "untouchable" groups in Gujarat (1989). Robert Deliege's findings also support a more multivocal view (1988, 1992).

Randeria, like Moffat, finds a hierarchy of "untouchable" castes in Gujarat, but she emphatically rejects Moffatt's claim that this proves an "underlying cultural consensus" (1989: 188) and rightly states that it is *coercive power* that protects upper-caste status: "The hierarchical order is based on an exercise of power rather than on value consensus" (1989: 189). As she says "Acceptance [of the upper-caste discourse on untouchability] is limited to the categories used by each caste to define the other, and *does not extend to its own self-representation.* ... Each untouchable caste's self-image is strikingly different from its image of the other" (Randeria 1989: 188, emphasis added). She is entirely right: The fact that the Pallars might see other "lower" castes as unclean does not mean that they see *themselves* as impure.

The historical dimension of changes in "untouchable" consciousness is of great importance in Tamilnadu. "Periyar"'s (Ramaswami Naicker's) Anti-Brahmin Movement was extremely influential in politicizing "untouchables" through its call for a castefree society. In Aruloor today, only a tiny minority are politicized; a minority that consists of the college-educated Pallar and Christian Paraiyar men who are imbued with egalitarian values primarily learned from "Periyar," the Dravida Kazhagam party, and the DMK party. Of them, it can be said that they discern, quite clearly, the answer to Uma's question: "But what, then, *is* impurity?" However, this is also true, though less explicitly, of all Pallars. Through their everyday resistance to upper-caste exploitation, they show that they, too, can see that other worlds and other possibilities exist.

Part Three

Gender and Production Politics

8

Pauperizing the Rural Poor: Landlessness in Aruloor

> We refused to return it. We'd planted banana on it. They registered a police complaint against us. They are very rich you know. Two lorries of policemen came and they went to the fields and cut down all the banana saplings. No one went near when the police cut down our banana saplings—we knew the police would beat us up if we did. We stood on the road and watched—silently.
>
> —Valliammai (Pallar)

ARULOOR LIES ON THE western edge of the Kaveri Delta, the traditional "rice bowl" of India. For centuries, this area of Tiruchi District and most of Thanjavur District (which lies to the east, on the Bay of Bengal) has been the main rice-growing area of the Tamil-speaking region. Historically, paddy cultivation here has depended on the channel irrigation of water from the Kaveri River. The Panguni, a small river, flows through Aruloor, and the Koolai River flows south of it. The Panguni comes from the Kollidam (Coleroon), which is a branch of the Kaveri and is dry for half the year. The Koolai, also small, is a perennial stream. The monsoon season, extending from October to December, usually brings heavy rains that provide welcome additional water in an area that is otherwise entirely dependent on channel irrigation. This irrigation used to be reliable, thus earning these irrigated areas the name "wetlands" (*nanjai*), in contrast to the "drylands" (*punjai*) that were fed by tank and rain.

In recent years, however, due to climatic changes that are probably connected with deforestation (MIDS 1988: 252–253), the monsoon has failed for several years in succession, so that now even the "wet" paddy-growing areas suffer from a cyclical water shortage. There is insufficient water in the Kaveri, and not infrequently, the monsoon fails. Consequently, in the Lalgudi Taluk area (as in much of Tamilnadu), every farmer who can afford it has sunk bore wells to raise water to

181

the surface for his paddy-fields. Despite various government subsidies (especially for electricity, where it is available), irrigating with bore wells is expensive, so this has increased the costs of cultivation and driven marginal farmers into giving up tenancies or selling their land. This has also had a disastrous ecological effect because the overexploitation of groundwater, due to very widespread drilling, has caused the water table to fall dangerously (MIDS 1988: 180–182, 186).

Further, as the MIDS economic survey notes, "groundwater irrigation has tended to worsen already sharp inequalities in the agrarian structure" (1988: 182). This is true of Aruloor, where it is the rich farmers—the Chettiars, the Brahmins, and some Muthurajahs—who have expanded their already large holdings while smallholders have had to sell. The costs of irrigation to the farmer have greatly increased statewide since the 1960s, when the "pumpset revolution" started. Because large farmers had the capital necessary to invest in wells and pump-sets and smaller farmers did not, those smaller farmers (in Aruloor and elsewhere) have had to rent pump-sets from their wealthy neighbors. Thus, "in the hands of large farmers with sizeable holdings, pumpsets have become valuable surplus-generating assets" (MIDS 1988: 182). "The changing economics of agriculture has driven many small farmers out of business. Informants claimed that there were far more smallholders in Aruloor in the 1940s and 1950s, and statistics on landholdings among the Pallar bear this out.

A continuing debate focuses on whether there is increasing proletarianization of the rural poor. In his review of trends of change in agriculture, John Harriss (1992) has pointed out that there are strong arguments and detailed evidence on both sides. He concludes: "The micro-studies really make the point that all-India, or even 'all-Tamil Nadu', or 'al-Maharashtra' generalisations are bound to be misleading. ... But it is at least possible to conclude that the available data do not support the view that the process of dispossession/depeasantisation and proletarianisation has been taking place universally" (Harriss 1992: 195). This seems right, for generalizations are misleading, but even those who argue that proletarianization is not widespread also present evidence to the contrary.

Gail Omvedt has argued vigorously that those who see "the growth of capitalism as leading to differentiation in agriculture resulting in the formation of a 'capitalist farmer' class exploiting a growing 'proletarianized' agricultural labor class are trapped in an obsolete "traditional Marxist" conception (1988: 21). She rejects census statistics on the increase of agricultural laborer households as being misleading, yet her own choice of National Sample Survey (NSS) statistics proclaims an emphatic all-India rise in this category, from 25.9 percent of all rural households in 1974–1975 to 29.9 percent in 1977–1978 (Omvedt 1988: 18). This is a substantial increase of 4 percent of the total rural population in only three years. And yet, strangely, Omvedt tries to minimize the importance of these statistics by describing them as only "a modest rise" (1988: 18).

Terry Byres (1981), on the other hand, in an important early article, showed that "partial proletarianisation" was well under way in areas of northwest India using new agricultural technology such as high-yielding varieties (HYVs). Here, I would argue that such partial proletarianization is also clearly evident in the paddy-growing south, particularly in eastern Tiruchi District in Tamilnadu, the source of my data.

Women and men from the low-ranking Pallar caste constitute the main labor force in south Aruloor. I contend that the majority of Pallars have become steadily more proletarianized and the landless Pallars risk becoming pauperized today. There has been a staggering fall in their landholdings over the last thirty years, and their inability to find other nonagricultural sources of employment has meant a radical impoverishment. On the other hand, the middle-ranking Muthurajahs who live in the next street from the Pallars have not only managed to hold on to their small plots but also to increase their holdings and to enter salaried employment. This provides strong support for my argument that the fact that proletarianization is partial has a great deal to do with the options available to the different castes. Middle-ranking castes, such as the Muthurajahs, have benefited more from land legislation than the Pallars, not purely because they were better off than the Pallars but also because of the enormous social stigma that even in the 1990s attaches to "untouchables" in rural Tamilnadu, limiting their options in every field. Partly because educated "untouchable" Pallars still find it so difficult to get jobs, there continues to be very limited interest in sending Pallar children to school. But this is also, of course, because Pallar families tend to be very poor and therefore need the household services and the incomes of their children. As a result, very few Pallar children finish even primary school.

I will first discuss the various types of landholding in Aruloor. Then I will survey the course of legislation relating to land reform and discuss relevant Pallar case histories. Finally, I will evaluate the impact on the Pallar community of both land reform legislation and caste discrimination in the specific context of statistics on landholding through the last thirty years. These statistics show a striking difference between the Pallar and Muthurajah castes. They also underline the dire predicament of Pallar landless laborers and marginal peasants today.

Kinds of Land Tenure in Aruloor

There are two major forms of landholding in Aruloor, one of which does not involve ownership but which, at least today, gives the registered holder a control that cannot be easily taken away as long as he fulfills the obligations it entails. (I use "he" because land is still generally held in the man's name: According to custom, sons, not daughters, inherit land.) Informants did not initially differentiate between the two kinds of landholding but simply spoke of holding a certain

amount of land, implying that both types of control were subsumed under the notion of the right to cultivate that land. The two types of holding are distinct, however: They are (1) land that is owned (*sondam*); and (2) land that is held on a
sharecropping tenancy (either a *kuttakai* lease or a *varam* lease). Most land in
Aruloor fell into these two categories, but a minor third category existed—mortgaged land (*otti*).

Sondam (Land That Is Owned)

Legally owned land (*sondam*) is a construct of British law. David Ludden notes
that this concept did not exist in the Tamil land in pre-British times, when property right was, instead, embodied in two principles, namely, *pangu* and *pattam.*
He says, "Pangu means 'share.' Rights founded on the pangu principle accrue to
members of a group, as in the paradigmatic case of family property. Pattam means
'title.' Rights founded on the pattam principle accrue to a person as the recipient
of a title from higher authority, be it king or god or both" (Ludden 1985: 165).
The term *"pangu"* ("share") is closely connected to the term *"pankali"* ("sharers"), referring to those who constitute the male lineage (patrilineage) in the
Tamil kinship system in Aruloor. This implies that women had no traditional
rights in family property, for men were the primary constituents of the *pankali.*

Kuttakai (Fixed-Rent Sharecrop Tenancy)

"Kuttakai" ("sharecropped land") is a complex category because its terms are
variable. It has been variously defined in the literature as "fixed-payment sharecropping" (Mencher 1978: 298) and as "fixed rent land tenure" (Gough 1989:
556). The first definition is better because it indicates clearly that this rent is always paid in kind. This fixed-payment sharecrop is negotiable, depending on the
quality of the land and the relationship between landlord and lessee. But for
paddy-land in the Aruloor area, it was normally fixed at 16 *kalam* of paddy per
kani (a *kalam* equals 12 *marakkal,* or half a bag of paddy and weighs about 28.1
kilograms. A *kani,* as Mencher points out, is "a measure of land, varying in different localities" (1978: 298): In Aruloor, informants understood it to mean an acre
of land. Their standard computation was that a *kani* of paddy-land (wetland) of
standard quality gave a harvest of 40 *kalam* of paddy. Since the normal rate of
kuttakai sharecrop in the area was 16 *kalam* per harvest (per *kani* or acre), this
meant that the fixed rate worked out to 40 percent of a 40-*kalam* harvest. This exorbitant rate of fixed rent was made more bearable for those who were able to get
a higher yield from their land, for some *kuttakai* tenants managed to get 60 *kalam*
per *kani,* thus reducing their rent to 26 percent of the harvest. Both Muthurajah
and Pallar tenants explained that they therefore put all their efforts into securing
the largest possible yield from their land, secure in the knowledge that any profit
(any increase on 16 *kalam*) was their own. Consequently, they stated, that they

strongly preferred the fixed-rent sharecrop system of *kuttakai* to the fixed-percentage sharecrop system called *varam*.

Varam is nonexistent in the Aruloor area today but has been documented for other areas, such as Thanjavur (Gough 1981, 1989) and Chingleput (Mencher 1978). However, *varam* did exist in Aruloor some decades ago, when it varied from one-third of the crop to 50 percent. As with *kuttakai,* the tenant supplied all inputs, such as seed, fertilizers and pesticides, and all labor. The landlord paid only the land revenue. Marshall Bouton reports the decline and extinction of *varam* in Thanjavur, too, noting that the period "beginning in the late 1940s and continuing to the present, witnessed the almost total disappearance of both *varam* and *pannai* [attached labor] cultivation, both of which were replaced by *kuttagai* tenancy and/or cultivation through hired casual [daily wage] labor. The main impetus to this change was the threat, and later the actual implementation, of tenancy reforms" (1985: 183–184). This parallels what happened in Aruloor and for the same reason: The initiative was taken by the landlords, especially the out-migrating Brahmin *mirasadars* (landlords), who found it easier to collect a fixed rent rather than a proportional rent because the latter required far closer supervision of the harvest.

Bouton observes that a *kuttakai* tenancy was "less remunerative" than *varam* for the landlord, though more practical (1985: 185). K. B. Sivaswamy points out that being a *varam* tenant was very similar to being a *pannaiyal* (attached laborer), for *varam* was "nothing but a device to pay a tenant no more than the wage of a *pannaiyal* ... with the advantage [to the landlord] of reducing it in proportion to the yield" (1948: 52). This was the perception of Aruloor tenants as well, who strongly preferred the fixed-rent *kuttakai* system to the percentage *varam* system. According to both Pallar and Muthurajah small tenants, a *varam* system of tenure discouraged effort because, as they put it, if you produced a lot extra, you had to give an *increased* share of your profit to the landlord. The *kuttakai* system encouraged them to work much harder on their land, they claimed.

Interestingly, this preference for fixed-rent tenure is exactly contrary to that reported by James Scott (1976). From his survey of peasant tenancy preferences in Southeast Asia, he concludes that "fixed rents—in cash or kind—would, in safety-first terms, be the most onerous (Scott 1976: 46). This was because evidence showed that "peasants in many parts of lowland Southeast Asia judged the fairness of tenure systems according to how reliable they were in subsistence terms" (Scott 1976: 47). Therefore, Scott argues, "both the patterns of choice and the values peasants brought to bear on that [tenancy] choice betray a constant preoccupation with subsistence risks" (1976: 50).

Significantly, the preference of Aruloor's small tenants for fixed-rent tenancies suggests that they have been reasonably sure of a subsistence income from their land in the past. This certainty of at least a minimal income derives from the fact that Aruloor lies in the fertile Kaveri Delta area, where the fields are largely wet-lands (*nanjai*) that are channel irrigated and that traditionally gave large yields. Further, though the *kuttakai* fixed rent is supposed to be 16 *kalam* per acre, very few tenants actually pay this. I was told by small tenants that most of them told their landlords their yields were considerably smaller than they actually were and that they consequently paid as little rent as possible. When the harvest was bad, no rent was paid. Recent legislation made this legal, though in earlier decades, this had provided reason enough for the landlord to throw the tenant off his land. Tenants both small and large had made the most of this legislation, and conse-quently, rents on temple-lands, particularly, remained almost entirely unpaid be-cause the temples could not extract rent unless they took their tenants to court. Aruloor's Pancangam Brahmin priest complained bitterly to me in 1988 that the ancient Siva Temple was virtually penniless, even though it owned vast lands, be-cause no tenants paid rent. Significantly, virtually all these temple-tenants were large tenants.

Otti (Usufructuary Mortgage)

The last category of landholding prevalent in Aruloor is *otti,* or usufructuary mortgage. Venkatesh Athreya, Goran Djurfeldt, and Steffan Lindberg catego-rized usufructuary mortgage as belonging to the "unofficial credit market" when noting its prevalence in Tiruchi District (1987: 150). By a written agreement, land is handed over by mortgagor to mortgagee in return for a specified loan of money. The mortgagor is often not the owner but merely the *kuttakai* tenant of the land. This poses no problem, for *kuttakai* land is universally treated by a ten-ant as his own land and is readily subleased. When mortgaged, the *kuttakai* land is treated by the mortgagee as his own land, he farms it and pays the *kuttakai* rent for the period of the mortgage. What he earns from the land, after the payment of rent, is his own. At the end of the stipulated period, he is expected to surrender the lease on receipt of his loan. His income from the land is considered his *otti* lit-erally, interest on a loan. However, the borrower quite often is not able to repay the loan on time. This is to the advantage of the mortgagee, who, for the relatively small outlay of the initial loan, has the right to continue to cultivate the mort-gaged land. When the borrower is finally able to repay the loan (in a lump sum) and demand his land back, the lender is very often loath to oblige, and a court case may result. If the borrower fails to repay the loan, the land effectively becomes the property of the mortgagee. It was popularly felt that even if repayment was de-layed, the land ought to revert to the mortgagor when the loan was paid off. But if ten years or more had passed, most of my informants who were small tenants felt that the land then belonged to the mortgagee.

The chief reasons for mortgaging land vary. It is done, for example because a marginal cultivator finds that it is uneconomical to plough his land or because a family is in debt. Land is also "given in *otti*" (mortgaged) because the farmer urgently needs cash for some reason. This was the situation with one Muthurajah family, whose case (described in the following section) illustrates the current trend toward cash-cropping.

Case 1: Anjalai's Mortgage

Anjalai, the mother of my Muthurajah assistant, was a widow. She held 1.25 acres of paddy-land on a *kuttakai* lease from its owner, the wealthy "Penang" Reddiar, a Reddiar from Tiruvanaikovil (Srirangam). Anjalai had mortgaged this land in 1984 to Meena, a well-off Pallar woman of neighboring Periyar Street. The mortgage was for Rs.5,000, to be repaid after three years in 1987. But in 1987, Anjalai did not have the money, and so Meena's family continued to cultivate the land. In 1988, however, Karuna Pullai of Varakaneri, Tiruchi city, the agent of a big banana merchant, offered Anjalai Rs.6,000, cash down, for a one-year lease of the land. Anjalai agreed at once, intending to pay Meena her Rs.5,000 out of the Rs.6,000 and thus retrieve her land from mortgage. But Karuna Pullai suddenly decided that the land was too far away from the other fields he had taken on lease and dropped his offer to Rs.3,000.

Meanwhile, Meena came up with a counteroffer. For the past four years, her family had grown paddy on the mortgaged land, but now—like many others— they wanted to plant banana. Their fields were very close to Anjalai's fields, which was why they were particularly keen on continuing to lease her land. So Meena upped the banana agent's offer and proposed to pay Rs.5,000 per annum on a two-year lease. If Anjalai agreed to these terms, her mortgage would be canceled automatically since this equaled one year's rent. Further, she could now look forward to actually receiving Rs.5,000 the following year. Anjalai lost no time in agreeing, and members of the Pallar family were equally happy because banana was becoming an extremely profitable crop in the Aruloor wetlands. As Athreya, Djurfeldt, and Lindberg point out, banana gives "a net profit per acre and year which is more than double that for paddy" (1987: 182).

In this discussion, "small" tenants and landholders are considered to be those who hold up to two acres of land. Such agriculturists regularly participate in wage-labor in order to earn a subsistence income, and therefore, they closely resemble proletarian landless laborers. Informants from this category (mainly Pallars and Muthurajahs) uniformly claimed that their landholdings only provided them with food (*sappadu*) and that to pay for other expenses, they had to seek casual wage work. Those in the "middle" peasantry (tenants and owners), a very differentiated group, hold between two and thirty acres. "Large" peasants (both tenants and owners) and "large" landlords constitute the third class. The former generally supervise work themselves; the latter generally delegate management. Capitalist farmers belong to this group, which consists of those with landholdings of more than thirty acres. These divisions are very rough, because class does not depend solely on agricultural income or on size of landholding but also on productivity, on the kinds of crops planted, and, importantly, on other nonagricultural sources of income (Patnaik 1987, and Athreya, Djurfeldt, and Lindberg, 1987).

Land Reform Legislation

The disastrous drought that continued through 1987 and 1988 would have ruined the small tenants of Aruloor if landlords had still been able to evict them for being unable to pay their *kuttakai* rent. Fortunately for these tenants, legislation had been enacted in 1978 protecting their tenancies in the event of nonpayment due to natural disasters. However, most land reform legislation enacted in the preceding decades by the Tamilnadu government, though ostensibly intended to bring about a more equitable distribution of land, had done little for the poor.

The channel-irrigated lands around Aruloor have much in common with the paddy-growing areas of Thanjavur District described by Gough (1989). Taking 1950 as her baseline, Gough states that in that year, landlords and rich and middle peasants formed 43.4 percent of agriculturists, poor peasants formed 22.2 percent, and the "remaining 34.4 percent of the agriculturists were primarily laborers owning little or no land" (1989: 20). In 1950, *kuttakai* tenants "usually paid about three-fifths or more of the net crop as rent after meeting their own cultivation expenses" (Gough 1989: 20). In 1955, the Madras Tenants Protection Act was passed to protect tenants from eviction. It "forbade any landlord to evict a cultivating tenant unless he failed to pay rent" (Gough 1989: 22). However, both before and after the Act was passed, landlords started evicting small tenants, fearing that future legislation would further strengthen the tenants' position. These small and marginal tenants had no redress because they had held their lands through verbal contracts and depended on the landlord's goodwill. Then in 1956, the Madras Cultivating Tenants (Payment of Fair Rent) Act was passed. This concerned the fixing of rents and "reduced the cultivating tenant's rent from about 60 percent to 40 percent of the gross crop of wet land" (Gough 1989: 22). In Aruloor, only the largest tenants, because they depended on the goodwill of the landowner, continued to have little say about the rent demanded from them.

In 1961, the Madras Land Reforms (Fixation of Ceiling on Land) Act was passed. This "limited land ownership in normal circumstances to 30 standard acres for a family of up to five members, 5 more standard acres being added for each additional member. A standard acre was defined as an acre of land paying revenue ... of Rs 10 or more per year. ... A large number of partial or total exemptions from this act were stipulated, however" (Gough 1989: 22). To circumvent the Land Ceiling Act, all sorts of tricks and subterfuges were adopted by those with excess land in Aruloor, especially the trick of *"benami"* holdings. The term meant that they evaded the law "by showing excess land under other names such as those of friends, relatives and attached labourers" (MIDS 1988: 141). This occurred on a large scale in Aruloor, with impoverished Muthurajahs suddenly made the "owners" of five acres of land each, temporarily bestowed on them by their Brahmin masters or by their own rich kin. Brahmin landlords did not have enough kin to whom they could "nominate" their extensive land, and so they turned to trusted Pallar attached laborers (*pannaiyal*). The later 1969 Record of Tenancy Act meant, however, that they took back these "ownership" rights in a hurry because after 1969, the nominal holders could have claimed their nominal rights as real ones. Several long-lasting Muthurajah quarrels (still continuing in 1988) resulted between kin when land titles were demanded back by rich kin in the 1960s. The Pallars had several stories of *benami* holdings that were first put in their name by Brahmin landlords and thereafter withdrawn. I will cite two cases.

Case 2: *Benami* Holdings—Pechiyai

Pechiyai, an older woman, described how a Brahmin landlord registered five acres of his land in her father-in-law's name: "That was when the law came that you couldn't hold more than five acres—that's why he gave it as *kuttakai* to us. We planted it for one year, but then he gave it to someone else and the following year he took it back to cultivate himself." In this case, the Pallar involved was not *pannaiyal* of the landlord but someone who worked for him regularly. Though the land was (briefly) registered in their name, Pechiyai's family members regarded it as a temporary tenancy. This particular landlord had been the biggest of the Brahmin *mirasadars*—and he still was in 1988. Pechiyai's household number is 12 in Table 8.1 (Pallar landholdings).

Case 3: *Benami* Holdings—Kannagi

Kannagi and her husband had worked for a major Brahmin landlord, Visu Aiyar of neighboring Pinnavasal village, as attached laborers. She said, "We got one acre *kuttakai* from Visu Aiyar. This was when the law came that those who had more than 5 acres should give the government the land. They gave Nagaras [Muthurajah] 1 acre, Krishna [Muthurajah] 1 acre, Kooloo [Muthurajah] 5 acres, Malliha [Pallar] 1 acre and Angamuthu [her husband] 1 acre. But after one year, without telling us they took back the fields. At this a major village quarrel developed." But though the Muthurajahs and Pallars argued with the Brahmins, Kannagi and her husband lost the land—the only land they had ever held (they are Household 9 in Table 8.1).

Mencher (like Gough) points out that the large number of exemptions stipulated in the Act itself provided the means of easily evading the law (1978: 117–123). Seasoned researcher as she was, she found that "collecting such data [on landholdings] was the hardest piece of research work I ever attempted" and that even with the most painstaking work, she "could not account for somewhere between 10 per cent and 30 per cent of the village lands," presumably because this information "was simply left out" of the register (Mencher 1978: 117). This

TABLE 8.1   Pallar Landholdings Through Thirty Years (in *kani*)

Household number	1958 S[a]	1958 K[b]	1968 S	1968 K	1978 S	1978 K	1983 S	1983 K	1988 S	1988 K
1	—	2	—	—	—	—	—	.75	—	.75
2	—	2	—	—	—	—	—	.35	—	.35
3	—	2	—	2	.5	—	.5	—.	.5	—
4	6	—	6	—	2	—	1.5	—	—	—
5	—	3	—	3	—	2	—	.75	—	.75
6	—	10	—	—	—	—	—	—	—	—
7	—	3	—	3	—	.75	—	.75	—	—
8	—	2.5	—	2.5	—	.25	—	.25	—	.25
9	—	—	—	1	—	1	—	—	—	—
10	—	2	1.25	.75	1.25	.75	1.25	.75	1.25	.75
11	—	5.5	—	4	—	2.75	—	2.1	—	—
12	—	5	—	—	—	—	—	.75	—	.75
13	—	1	—	1	—	1	—	—	—	—
14	.75	1	.5	1	—	1.5	—	1.5	—	1.5
15	1.25	—	.5	—	.11	—	.11	—	—	—
16	—	4	—	4	—	1	—	—	—	—
17	—	2	—	.75	—	.75	—	.75	—	.5
18	1.5	2	1.5	2	1.5	2	1	2	1.5	2
19	—	—	—	—	—	—	.5	.5	.5	.5
20	—	.75	—	.75	—	—	—	—	—	—
21	—	.75	—	.75	2.25	.75	2.25	.75	2	1
22	1.5	—	.75	2.25	—	1.5	—	.75	—	—
23	—	—	1	—	2	—	3	—	3	—
24	—	4.5	—	4.5	—	—	—	—	—	—
25	—	1.75	—	1.75	—	—	—	—	—	—
26	—	2.5	—	2.5	—	.75	—	—	—	—
27	2	2	—	—	—	—	—	—	—	—
28	.25	—	.25	—	—	—	—	—	—	—
29	—	1	—	1	—	1.5	—	1.5	—	1.5
30	.5	—	—	2.75	—	2.75	—	1	—	1
31	—	—	—	—	—	—	—	.5	—	—
32	—	1.5	—	1.5	—	1.5	—	1.5	—	1.5
Sondam	13.75		11.75		9.61		10.11		8.75	
Kuttahai		61.75		42.75		22.5		17.20		13.10

[a]S: Sondam.
[b]K: Kuttahai.
All dates are approximate.

helps explain why large landlords could simply take their land back, for they soon
learned a variety of ways in which to conceal ownership.

The 1969 Tamilnadu Agricultural Lands Record of Tenancy Rights Act was an
attempt to change this. Here, "cultivating tenants were theoretically given further
protection … Each tenant received a document confirming his tenancy. Tenants
holding documents were thus in theory enabled to uphold in court their claims to

cultivate and to pay fair rent" (Gough 1989: 23–24). In Aruloor, leases had traditionally been agreed upon verbally. But despite the Act, very few small tenants had received documents even nineteen years later, by 1987, because the landowners refused to register their names. This meant that most small tenants had no legal tenancy rights to the land they tilled and could therefore be easily evicted. It was the larger tenants (of middle-caste rank, e.g., Muthurajahs and Veerakodi Vellalars) who insisted on and received documents because they could threaten to take the landlord to court. Further, the Act, being so weakly implemented, had a deeply retrogressive effect: The large landlords evicted many small tenants of long standing so that they could not press their claims, and for the same reason, they began to switch tenancies on a yearly basis among different small tenants. Lower-caste tenants (particularly Pallars) suffered the most, with many losing their tenancies entirely. Gough records very similar results in neighboring Thanjavur (1989: 44–48). Those small tenants who did succeed in registering their tenancy benefited greatly because (as Valliammai's case, which I will discuss, indicates) they were able to take the landlord to court when he tried to evict them. The law today requires that if landowners want to evict registered tenants, they must pay up to one-third of the value of the land as compensation. But because most remaining small tenants in Aruloor still hold unregistered tenancies, they continue to be at the mercy of the landlords.

Byres is quite right, therefore, in his evaluation of land legislation: "By far the greatest beneficiaries of ... land reform, were the rich peasants. ... They were stabilised as independent proprietors, and were on the way to becoming, in many areas of India, the new dominant class in the emerging agrarian structure. *Legislation, to the extent that it was successful, extended protection not to all tenants, but to the upper layers of the tenantry*" (1981: 423, emphasis added).

The Pallars certainly have not gained but have suffered from land reform legislation, particularly through their eviction from their *kuttakai* holdings when the landlords resumed their leased-out lands in order to enlarge their holdings. The HYVs and the new agricultural technology of the "green revolution" gave large-scale farming the highest outputs. Thus, there were two strong imperatives for the resumption of land, for there was both "fear of future land reform" and the desire "to secure as much land for personal cultivation as possible" (Byres 1981: 424).

Statistics on resumption of land from small Pallar tenants are strikingly high. In a random sample of thirty-two Pallar households (see Table 8.1), land was resumed by the landlord (usually Brahmin or Chettiar) in ten cases—a proportion of almost one-third. I will discuss some of these cases more specifically.

Case 4: Resumption of Land—Manakayee

Manakayee, a member of Household 7, was very aged in 1988. Twenty-five years earlier, her family had held three acres of *kuttakai* land from the Siva Temple. But the temple took the land back and redistributed the acreage among three well-off

Muthurajah tenants. This is, therefore, also an instance of the tenant-switching that occurred on a large scale, with a marked shift of tenancies from poor to rich tenants. Byres emphasizes the importance of this phenomenon, observing, "The poor peasantry has lost an increasing share of the operated area to rich peasants" (1981: 430).

Case 5: Resumption of Land—Rengammal

Rengammal, a Pallar widow of Household 13, had been a small tenant in 1969. She said: "We had a quarter acre of *kuttakai* from Ratnam Aiyar [a Brahmin landlord] and a three-quarter acre *kuttakai* from Murugan Chettiar when my husband was alive. When my husband died—my son was only ten years old—the two landlords both claimed that we'd not paid the *kuttakai* properly and that therefore they were taking the land back. This was not true: We had paid it all. But they both cheated us by writing that we were voluntarily *giving* back the lands to 'pay for' the *kuttakai*. They took my signature on two pieces of paper, but as I can't read I didn't know what I was signing. I was paid Rs.250 by the Chettiar. The Aiyar [Brahmin] gave his land to Poosari [a Pallar] who'd encouraged me to sign. So now I have no land at all." Poosari had worked as *pannaiyal* (attached laborer) to the Brahmin landlord and had, she claimed, participated in the deception of Rengammal.

Case 6: Resumption of Land—Valliammai

Valliammai benefited greatly from the fact that the 1969 Record of Tenancy Rights Act existed, even though her family (Household 3) had no written lease. They had held the land for more than forty years by the mid-1970s, yet they were vulnerable to eviction. The brutal display of police force in defense of the Brahmin landlord's claim is very striking in her simple account. Valliammai said: "We had had two acres *kuttakai* from Sekhar Aiyar for many years—from about 1930. Then about ten years ago [around 1975] they asked for the land back." At this point, other Pallars interjected that this was because the landlords had been frightened by the then Chief Minister's proposed legislation to give land to the tiller. [No such legislation was ever passed.] Valliammai continued:

> We refused to return it. We'd planted banana on it. They registered a police complaint against us. They are very rich you know. Two lorries of policemen came and they went to the fields and cut down all the banana saplings. No one went near when the police cut down our banana saplings—we knew the police would beat us up if we did. We stood on the road and watched—silently. But we filed a case against them at once. In the interim I, my son and Gopal, my elder brother [Valliammai was a widow], were all advised by the street to remain in the house as otherwise we'd probably be beaten and forced into signing a paper saying that we had no rights to the land. The court ruled in our favour. Sekhar Aiyar at once appealed to Madras High Court,

so the case went there. We won again there: "You may transplant the field!" they said. Then, without fear, we transplanted paddy in it. Then the Aiyar [the Brahmin landlord] said to us, "Let bygones be bygones—I'll pay you for the fields." And he gave us Rs.15,000 to resign our right. But he thereafter *harvested* the paddy we'd planted. This was very wrong of him—but we let it go, saying, "There's no need to quarrel any further!"

If Valliammai had refused the Brahmin landlord's offer of Rs.15,000 in 1978 and held on to her tenancy, he would have had to pay her around Rs.40,000 as compensation in 1987. This was because by then, a landlord had to compensate a registered tenant with one-third the value of the leased land if he wished to evict that tenant. One acre of good paddy-land in the Aruloor area sold for between Rs.50,000 and Rs.60,000 in 1987–1988, so a registered tenant was legally entitled to between Rs.15,000 and Rs.20,000 and could hope to actually receive between Rs.10,000 and Rs.18,000. This was an enormous sum of money to the average Pallar and Muthurajah small tenant. Papathi benefited from this protection in 1988.

Case 7: Resumption of Land—Papathi

Papathi, whose love affair was described in the last chapter, was a widow. She did well, for she received Rs.30,000 in 1988 from her landlord, the wealthy Muthurajah widow Lohambal of Pathukattu Street, on surrendering her *kuttakai* lease of one and a half acres. This was less than the stipulated one-third, but everyone in the Pallar street thought that Papathi had done extremely well out of it. From this money, however, Papathi had to give a "gift" of Rs. 1,000 to Pechimuthu, the Pallar Ward Member (of the Panchayat) for his unspecified "assistance" in the matter. He was the powerful Pallar street leader who also held the influential post of Vice President of Aruloor Town Panchayat.

In 1970, the Land Ceiling Act was amended to reduce the maximum holding for a family of five members from thirty to fifteen standard acres. But once again, many exemptions existed in the law, and the large landlords had no difficulty in continuing to hold on to their lands. Gough notes the same for Thanjavur, observing that *benami* transactions were so widespread that most of Thanjavur's major landlords held on to large parts of their estate throughout the 1970s (1989: 41). However, the Tenancy Relief Ordinances promulgated from 1978 onward provided some protection to small tenants, for they stated that tenants in areas affected by natural disasters were exempt from eviction if they failed to pay their rent (Gough 1989: 24). This was increasingly important in Aruloor since the continuing drought that started in 1984 ruined the *kar* paddy harvest in 1987 and 1988. The *kar* paddy is the secondary (dry season) crop; it contrasts with the *samba* paddy, which is the main crop, grown in the monsoon season.

The final piece of legislation I will note here is the 1979 amendment of the law regarding tenants' rent. This stated that "cultivating tenants need pay as rent only

25 per cent of their normal gross produce" (Gough 1989: 24). Given that small tenants still did not have written leases, this had little effect: They simply continued to pay the required 16 *kalam* per acre, though this was, in effect, a 40 percent rate (computed on a 40-*kalam* yield). But due to the drought, few tenants were paying regular rent anyway in 1987 and 1988.

The Implications of the Land Reforms and of Caste for Landlessness

The Results of the Land Reforms

The effect of these land reforms on the confiscation and redistribution of agricultural land was nugatory. Gough puts it very clear: "What of the results of this long series of land reforms? To put it mildly, they were very imperfectly implemented" (1989: 24). She points out that by the mid-1970s "only about 2.7 per cent of Tamilnadu's ... cultivated land was distributed by the government to needy families," but of this, "only about 0.5 per cent ... was actually confiscated from bigger owners" for "most of it was government owned waste land" (Gough 1989: 25).

The important MIDS survey comes to the same conclusion, noting that the NSS Report on Land Holdings of 1982 indicates that Tamilnadu had one of the highest percentages of landless households in the nation, at 19.13, second to Maharashtra, which had 21.24. According to the survey, this reflects badly "on the effectiveness with which the land ceiling legislation has been implemented in the State" (MIDS 1988: 143–144).

The survey also refers to the Tamilnadu census reports for 1961, 1971, and 1981 on the changing occupational profile of the population. These census data support the trend noted in my microsurvey of Pallar landholdings, namely, that from 1958 to 1988, small tenants and marginal peasants increasingly lost their lands and became agricultural laborers (see Table 8.2 on the occupational profile of rural Tamilnadu). However, Harriss has questioned the value of using census data in cross-decade comparisons because definitions of occupational status have varied from census round to census round (1992: 192; see also Omvedt 1988: 18). But Harriss accepts that the more reliable NSS data also show an increase in the incidence of agricultural labor households (see the NSS statistics quoted in Omvedt 1988), though he argues that NSS data on land ownership "clearly indicate that the incidence of landlessness *declined* between the mid-1950s and the early 1970s" (1992: 192). My Pallar data do not support this: They indicate a clear pattern of the proletarianization of small tenants and marginal peasants, the majority of whom have been transformed not only into agricultural laborers who are mainly dependent on wage-labor but also, in sixteen of thirty-two cases, into *landless* agricultural laborers. This sample shows a dramatic decline of 50 percent of smallholding Pallar households into landlessness and penury.

TABLE 8.2   Occupational Profile in Rural Tamilnadu, 1961, 1971, and 1981

	1961	*1971*	*1981*
All main workers	100.00	100.00	100.00
Cultivators	51.0	40.0	38.4
Agricultural laborers	21.8	38.1	39.9
Household industry workers	6.7	3.7	4.1
Other workers	20.5	18.0	17.6

Source: Census reports quoted in MIDS 1988: 144.

Eviction from unprotected tenancies has been a major reason for this proletarianization. The economic condition of these landless Pallars who are solely dependent on casual wages has been further exacerbated by soaring inflation (see MIDS 1988) and population pressure. Thus, a process of the pauperization of the landless poor is indeed under way here.

Gough notes that conditions in Thanjavur were even worse than the statewide statistics suggested (indicated in Table 8.2). The decennial census figures for Thanjavur showed that in 1951, agricultural laborers were 40.4 percent of the agricultural workforce, but in 1961, they were 47.4 percent; in 1971, they were 59.1 percent; and by 1980, they had leaped to 65.0 percent (1989:45). These figures are quite relevant to Aruloor because of Thanjavur's similar agricultural situation. They offer, on a much wider scale, evidence of the same proletarianization noted in the Pallar street.

In Aruloor as elsewhere, the largest landlords did sell some land in order to avoid prosecution. They generally sold it to the large tenants who had cultivated it. Thus, in the 1960s and 1970s, those tenants who had possessed the money were able to buy land. Newly educated, salaried, upwardly mobile castes, such as Aruloor's Muthurajahs, benefited. These middle-ranking castes greatly increased their holdings and became part of the landowning class, while many Brahmin landlords sold out altogether. These changes, closely connected with the political support the upwardly mobile middle castes received from the Anti-Brahmin Movement, established a new dominant class in rural Tamilnadu. Gough describes this trend in Thanjavur in the 1970s, where the "dominant agricultural class ... came from people of middle caste rank ... to a greater extent than in 1951" (1989: 45). Vast estates, like those of Aruloor's richest Chettiars, continued to exist, however, alongside the new rich peasant hierarchy. Indeed, as the occupational profile of the census reports indicates (Table 8.2), landownership was actually concentrated in fewer hands in 1981 than in 1961.

Landlessness, Poverty, and Caste

The pauperization of the landless Pallars has occurred partly because no other sources of income have become available to them. This is in sharp contrast to those Muthurajahs who have become landless in the neighboring street. A random sample of landholdings in the Muthurajah street indicated that out of thirty-two households, only five were landless—and that every one of these five households had a significant nonagricultural source of income.

1. one household had a small shop;
2. another had two shops in Aruloor;
3. in the third, the husband earned a "good income" (around Rs.1,500 per month) as a cattle broker;
4. in the fourth, the family had a small gemstone workshop in the home and made about Rs.50 per day (Rs.1,500 per month); and
5. members of the fifth household polished vessels and also made around Rs.50 per day (Rs.1,500 per month).

This is amazingly different from the plight of the landless Pallars. Of the thirty-two Pallar households, sixteen are landless today (see Table 8.1) Of these sixteen, only one family (number 7) has a source of income other than casual agricultural labor, and this is merely the tiny pension paid following the death of a son while in government service. This raises the question of whether there is a strong causal correlation between caste and poverty or landlessness.

Historical evidence demonstrates clearly that there has been a strong correlation between caste and landlessness. "Untouchable" landless laborers, through the centuries, have been preserved as a landless group. Pallar informants were well aware of this and stated that this was because customary law did not allow them to hold land, simply because they were defined as "untouchable." Historically, the so-called untouchable castes were agrestic slaves, and as slaves, they were not allowed to hold property. Dharma Kumar documents their slave status (1965: 189–191), as does Gough (1981, 1989), and Mridula Mukherjee confirms that "untouchables" were "debarred ... from owning land" (1988: 2117). Irfan Habib, too, notes that they were "excluded from the village and prevented from holding land" (1983: 39–40). Consequently, these castes were legally constituted as landless, a most remarkable fact in a context in which competition for land has been extreme. Only recently, in this century, did the situation change in Aruloor, when many Pallars acquired small tenancies and also the ownership of small plots of land, especially from the very large landowners for whom they worked as attached laborers.

But the correlation between caste and landlessness had a further implication. Why have only landless Muthurajahs found alternate nonagricultural incomes, and why have the Pallars not done so, too? The answer is complex but essentially has two aspects to it, one economic and one status-related. Economically speaking, the answer is that the landless Pallars are *so* poor that they lack the capital to set up, say, a gemstone workshop. But economics cannot be divorced from notions of status and from the cultural context in which both economics and status exist. Very significantly, rural Pallars also lack the social standing and the social connections that would encourage others to lend them capital and to be their customers. Untouchability is still believed in, in the village: The impoverished Pallars are still seen as "polluted."

Though the very nature of caste is changing in response to rapid change in the rural environment, caste discrimination against "untouchables" still persists. This means that Pallar children meet discrimination at school and that young Pallar men and women meet it in their search for jobs outside agriculture. In this context—the real world as opposed to political fantasy—"reservations" and being on "Scheduled Caste lists" mean remarkably little. After all, when almost no Pallar child in Aruloor gets even a secondary education, what is the relevance of the fact that reserved places supposedly exist for "untouchable" castes in higher education and in government jobs? They remain a mirage, creating envy and resentment in the upper castes in Aruloor and failing to benefit the Pallars themselves. If a genuine political will existed to help the Scheduled Castes, how about starting by guaranteeing a good primary education to every "untouchable" child? This would require creches for the infant siblings whom Pallar children look after. It would require that their laborer parents be paid a living wage and not be forced to rely on the wages of their children for survival. It would therefore require genuine political will. But as far as the "untouchable" landless and near-landless are concerned, such a political will has never been exerted on their behalf by any government.

The rights of peasants (especially rich peasants) are protected in Tamilnadu today. But the rights and interests of landless laborers and marginal peasants, who depend on casual wage-labor and who are the most vulnerable group of all, have never been protected by legislation. That is why their economic condition has continued to deteriorate, especially in inflationary circumstances. Even economists and other social scientists have tended to ignore the landless and the near-landless, focusing instead on "the peasant." Harriss rightly observes: "The focus in research on 'small farmers' and MVs [modern varieties] was misplaced, given that the rural poor in South Asia are predominantly those dependent upon casual wage labour. ... *An extremely important but very little recognised fact about poverty in India is that poor people are not primarily 'small farmers' but those dependent upon irregular and unreliable wage incomes*" (1992: 200, 199, emphasis added).

There is an urgent need for more research on these poorest rural people who are dependent on casual wage-labor. If their condition is deteriorating, it cannot be complacently argued that genuine rural development is occurring simply because the middle peasantry is becoming more secure. These data from Aruloor also indicate the urgent need for the diversification of employment opportunities in rural areas so that nonagricultural employment is available to those who are being squeezed out of casual agricultural wage-labor. Planners, social scientists, and donor organizations all claim that they wish to assist the poorest. If so, it is high time that they turned their attention to landless laborers and marginal peasants, especially those of the lowest castes—before it is too late.

9

Every Blade of Green:
Landless Women Laborers,
Production, and Reproduction

He's given me nothing: he spends it all on drink! And he's drunk half the time. He only comes home to eat and sleep.

—**Pallar woman worker**

RECENT RESEARCH REGARDING women's economic contribution and modes of conceptualizing it has found not only a strong tendency on the part of men to minimize their wives' contribution but also that women themselves are often socially conditioned to undervalue and underreport their own work (Bruce and Dwyer 1988: 15). Even when women make a major economic contribution, this is often not socially recognized and therefore not enumerated in economic surveys. This may be why the major involvement of lower-caste landless laborer women in agricultural work in South India has largely gone unrecognized. This "social blindness" has been shared by social scientists to a surprising degree, so that, for instance, even feminist researchers assume that it is primarily in Africa, rather than Asia, that one finds a high "visibility of women in key economic activities" and a startling "explicitness of differential male and female income streams within the household" (Bruce and Dwyer 1988: 12). However, both these phenomena equally characterize landless women laborers in Tamilnadu, so Asia is not so distant from Africa after all. We have yet to recognize the enormous diversity of socioeconomic and cultural patterns within the area we call "South Asia."

In this chapter, I will discuss key aspects of the economic contribution of the Pallar women of south Aruloor. There were around 110 Pallar households in the Pallar *ur* (street/residential area) (Periyar Street and Kamaraj Colony) in 1987–

1988. Most families were landless, and many were very poor. Almost all were dependent on agricultural wage-labor for a living.

Remarkably, it is Pallar women who today form the major part of the agricultural labor force in the area. Even more remarkably, they contribute a far larger share of their incomes to the household than their husbands do, and they do so far more regularly. For this reason, I will argue that their labor and their earnings are crucial to the survival of their families. These women are major providers and breadwinners. This fact is implicitly recognized and positively valued in Pallar culture, which takes a very different view from upper caste culture, which denigrates manual labor and especially the participation of women in such labor. Further, this work has not been recognized by policymakers and planners.

The first part of this chapter describes the double burden of women; the second draws on Joan Mencher's research and compares it with my own findings. In the third part, I will discuss changes in the work participation of women and men that have led to a "feminization" of agricultural labor in the area. I will also briefly compare Gillian Hart's observations on Muda with the situation in Aruloor. The chapter's fourth section describes the sexual division of labor, and the fifth discusses gender-differentiated payments in agriculture. In the final section, I will return to the issue of differential contributions to the household and its implications.

Recruitment to and Organization of Domestic Labor

The Double Burden of Pallar Women

The Pallar woman plays the role of breadwinner in addition to doing all the household work. Pallar men do not normally assist women in these tasks. Thus, the typical Pallar woman is up by 7 a.m. and off to the fields after breakfasting on cold rice porridge (*kanji*) by 7:30 a.m. It takes half an hour, on average, to get to the field site. From 8 a.m. to noon, she and the other women in her "coolie" group labor, for example, at weeding or transporting manure or soil. At noon, they ought to break off, but because of the scarcity of work, it has become common (since October 1987) for employers to demand that laborers work an extra hour, until 1 p.m., for the same wages (Rs.5).

When she returns home, the Pallar woman washes dishes and eats some more cold *kanji*. Most Pallar families can afford only one main meal a day, and this she cooks in the late afternoon or evening. She spends the afternoon doing other household tasks such as washing clothes, cleaning the house, and caring for young children. She has her bath in the river, and she might rest if she has no other housework. In the evening, the women of neighboring houses sit together on their front steps or right in the middle of the street and chat. After the meal, which is eaten quite late (at about 9 p.m.), everyone goes to bed, by about 10 p.m. During the continuing drought, all bathing and washing of kitchen utensils, clothes, and children became a very difficult task because there was no water in Aruloor's river or in the street pumps. The women had to trudge out to the fields to find a pump-set from which water was flowing. So the relatively leisurely afternoons I describe seldom occurred then, nor did they exist during the busy months of full employment. When transplanting of the *samba* paddy crop occurred (in October and November) and when the *samba* harvest took place (mid-January to mid-March), many women only entered their homes at night to eat and sleep, utterly exhausted from ten or twelve hours of intensive labor. This was when extra domestic help was most essential, primarily to provide child care and, secondly, to cook and do the housework. As a result, virtually no female child attended school during these months because her labor was needed at home.

Female Child Labor

Female child labor is a crucial aspect of the Pallar domestic economy. Homes with daughters count themselves lucky because this frees the Pallar mother for wage-work. When there are young children to be cared for and there is no daughter, the logical alternative is followed: The eldest son is withdrawn from school. This is unusual, however, and I came across only two such cases. In one, twelve-year-old Prakash, a very bright boy, looked after his three younger brothers, including a baby. In the other (Rajalakshmi's household), her five-year-old son was left to "look after" the baby when both parents were at work at transplanting and at harvest times. Clearly, this was a desperate and most unsatisfactory arrangement because the little boy could hardly look after himself, but Rajalakshmi's husband could find little work, and in order for them to survive, she had to abandon her young children for the day.

There are 104 independent households (with independent hearths and separate budgets) in the two Pallar streets. In these households, there were a total of 127 working females in October 1987. By working females, I mean both women engaged in agricultural wage-labor and female children engaged on a full-time basis in essential household work, which allowed the mother to go for fieldwork. In some 12 of the 104 households, women did not do agricultural labor on a regular basis (or at all) either because they belonged to the very few "better-off" households or because there was no one else to look after their babies. The ages of the 127 working females drawn from 92 households ranged from six (young Amudha, who grazed goats all day) to seventy (Avati, who, though old and toothless, was still spirited and hard-working; she regularly worked on her own field, for which she hired and supervised labor as well).

I classify females aged fifteen and under as children. Based on this, there are 18 female children engaged in full-time subsistence labor. The older ones (age twelve and above) are deliberately dressed up in half-saris to convince the employers that they are "adult" females past puberty, and they are taken along by their mothers for daily labor. This deception is necessary because only women past puberty are allowed to do wage-work. Also, there is no "child" wage: All females earn the same adult wage. A very few—including a little trio of bosom-friends (twelve-year-old Sumathi, eleven-year-old Gowri, and eleven-year-old Santhi)—went to school in 1988, despite the remonstrations of their mothers and other kin *not* to do so. They will soon have to drop out entirely, even though all three would like to continue their education. Their life is one of a double burden, too: They spend all day at school and then must do all the household work (cooking, washing, sweeping, and so on) when they get home.

When not engaged in wage-work or domestic work, a young girl is sent to cut grass for sale as cattle fodder. The task takes several hours because grass has become difficult to find due to the drought, but it is considered light work. It is therefore the particular occupation of old Pallar women who are no longer allowed to join the work-groups because they are too slow. These women support themselves by selling small bundles of fodder.

In Table 9.1, I list the names, ages, level of schooling, and primary work done by these 18 young girls. Remarkably few (5) are still in school, and those who are will certainly drop out by age thirteen or fourteen simply because their mothers will need their labor, especially for additional wage-labor. I also list the names of their mothers. The redoubtable Sarusu is assisted by her twelve-year-old daughter Latha, who runs the home and cooks for the family; Sarusu's younger daughter assists in domestic work when she is not grazing goats. Finally, I include the marital status of the mother. Two of the women, Sarusu and Muruvayee, have been deserted by their husbands, who live in the same street but with other women. Six of the women are widows though they are quite young, an unusually high percentage compared to the upper castes but typical of the Pallar average because so many Pallar men die in middle age, apparently from complications resulting from excessive drinking and poor nutrition. All the poorest groups in Aruloor suffer from poor nutrition.

Pallar households tend to be nuclear rather than joint. In Aruloor, the poorest households tend to be nuclear, and the richest (Chettiars and Brahmins) tend to be extended households. Thus, unlike women in the wealthy Brahmin or Chettiar households, Pallar women of the older generation are not part of a young couple's household unit, nor are these women—typically, the mothers of the men since residence is virilocal—supported by the younger generation. In the harsh economic world that the Pallars inhabit, individuals are encouraged to be as economically independent as possible; dependence is not encouraged and is often not even possible. Thus, the Pallar woman (unlike women in the upper castes) cannot turn for help with child care to women of the older generation, either in her own or neighboring houses, because these older women are usually not at home. They

TABLE 9.1   Female Child Labor

Name	Age	Education	Type of Work Done	Mother's name	Mother's Marital Status Ma	W	D
Papathi	12	—	Agri labor, cg	Ilanjiyam	—	W	—
Gowri	11	6	Domestic work	Periavuti	—	W	—
Sarasu	11	6	Domestic work	Govindam.	—	W	—
Selvi	15	—	Agri labor	Amusu	Ma	—	—
Kannagi	14	—	Agri labor	(only B)	—	—	—
Latha	12	5	Domestic work	Sarusu	—	—	D
Manjula	8	—	Grazing goats	"	—	—	"
Kannagi	15	—	Agri labor	Lakshmi	Ma	—	—
Amudha	6	—	Grazing goats	"	"	—	—
Anjalai	13	—	Agri labor	Marudam.	Ma	—	—
Sumathi	12	—	Agri labor	Muruvay.	—	—	D
Devika	13	—	Agri labor	Anjalai	Ma	—	—
Sasikala	12	—	Agri labor	Poongothai	Ma	—	—
Podum	10	—	Grazing goats	Lingamma	Ma	—	—
Sumathi	11	6	Domestic work	Kamakshi	Ma	—	—
Santhi	11	5	Domestic work	Dhanam	—	W	—
Lakshmi	12	—	Agri labor, cg	Ramaiyee	—	W	—
Santhi	10	—	Grazing goats	Gomathi	—	W	—

Key: Agri: Agricultural
      cg: cutting grass
      Edn: education
      M: Mother
      B: Brother
      Ma: Married
      W: Widowed
      D: Deserted

are working to support themselves, either by cutting grass or in some other in-come-earning job (even daily wage-work, if they are not too old). This is why working mothers only have the younger generation to turn to, and this, in the Tamil cultural context, means *female* children because young males are not drawn into household work. Consequently, girls of eleven and twelve become full-time surrogate mothers: They do all the housework and child care and also participate in wage-labor when possible. In a sense, they are also surrogate wives because they cook the food that their fathers eat. If a woman is both widowed and incapaci-tated, a very young daughter might become her sole support. Generally, because the Pallar woman is so often the main breadwinner of her family, when she cannot work due to advanced pregnancy or illness, her eldest daughter steps in as family provider, sometimes helping, by her wage, to feed a family of six or seven mem-bers (as in the case of Sasikala, which I will discuss). To understand more closely the extent to which Pallar families depended on female children, I will cite five cases.

Case 1: Sasikala. Sasikala's mother, Poongothai, had done wage-work daily, but in March 1988, being heavily pregnant and very close to delivery, she found it impossible to continue. Sasikala's father, Sundarchami, worked at a rice mill in Aruloor, where the Chettiar owner paid him a pittance, less than Rs.150 per month. Sundarchami was also *tanni-paccaravar* (irrigation supervisor) to this Chettiar. Sasikala, who in 1988 was about twelve, dropped out of school when she was about nine years old to look after her four younger siblings while her mother was at work. She cooked, kept house, and also cut grass for sale. Sundarchami's Rs.150 disappeared very quickly in family expenses, so for the rest of each month, it was solely Poongothai who supported them. When Poongothai was unable to work (especially after a delayed and difficult delivery), it was young Sasikala who largely supported the entire family on her agricultural wage of Rs.5 per day. Because her mother was very weak and ill for three weeks, Sasikala also cooked. Thus, this twelve-year-old was already well grounded in her role as an "adult" Pallar woman, cooking in the evenings and laboring in the fields by day.

Case 2: Anjalai. Anjalai's father, Palani, is a smooth-tongued cattle broker who occasionally makes some money but spends it all on himself, according to his wife, Marudambal. Marudambal (one of my most articulate and perceptive informants) was in poor health for five years and therefore stopped going for fieldwork entirely. Even for harvest work, which is enormously difficult and which a wife and husband normally do jointly, it is Palani and frail-looking, thirteen-year-old Anjalai who go, not Marudambal. Anjalai goes for daily wage-work (wrapped in a half-sari, pretending to be adult; she reached puberty only in May 1988), and since her father contributes virtually nothing but expects to be fed at home, she has been the family's sole provider for the past year. She is the only child. The question arises as to what Palani and Marudambal will do when Anjalai is married, which is normally within two years of becoming sexually mature.

Case 3: Selvi. Selvi's case is similar to Anjalai's. When Selvi got married, there was no one to support her widowed mother, Thanjayee, because Selvi (like Anjalai) was an only daughter. Thanjayee (like Marudambal) had been unable to work regularly for several years due to continuing ill health and migraines. So Selvi started wage-work at age eleven. In 1987, at seventeen, Selvi got married to a young mason who lived in the same street. She continued doing fieldwork, as all married Pallar women do, but because she was married, she could not give her entire earnings to her mother. However, she gives her mother a considerable part of their earnings regularly, and Thanjayee survives on this and on the agricultural produce that her own very aged father brings for her occasionally from her natal *oor*. (Selvi is not listed in Table 9.1 because she was no longer a child in 1988, being eighteen years old.)

Case 4: Sarasu. Sarasu (aged eleven) dropped out of school in February 1988 because she started doing harvest work with her elder brother. She lived with her frail, sick mother, Govindammal. Govindammal was too weak for fieldwork, and so she and Sarasu regularly cut grass for sale. Sarasu's elder brother, Madhi, lives separately with his wife Kalyani. Sarasu reported that Madhi had told her, "Don't go to school anymore—it's a waste of time. Stay home and do something useful. What's the point of going to school? Is it going to help you in any way? Better if you go for fieldwork and help Mother to get some money." Sarasu, like most Aruloor children, was very little enthused by the education she received in school, and it was perfectly clear that she was happy to stop. Having spent three months in Aruloor's schools myself, I could well understand why.

Case 5: Santhi. This tiny girl looked eight years old but was supposed to be ten. I almost never saw her because she was always working, usually grazing the goats of a kinsman. Gomathi, her mother, was a destitute widow who, after the death of her husband, had left her marital *ur* to return to Aruloor, her natal *ur.* She had not even a house of her own and could not afford to rent one, so she and young Santhi slept and cooked on the veranda of the goat-owning kinsman's house. Gomathi went for fieldwork and cut grass, and Santhi grazed goats, so both of them were away all day. Because Gomathi had a "weak heart," she could not carry a head-load of paddy at harvest, which unfortunately excluded her from the most profitable work of all. She could only glean paddy from the fields after the harvesters had left.

These five cases show how the full-time employment of female children in subsistence activities and in wage-labor constitutes a central strategy of Pallar survival. There is little knowledge or concern about the dire straits in which the Pallars live among the schoolteachers who "educate" their young. Their view was as follows: "Pallar parents are irresponsible. They don't bother to send their kids to school and when the kids don't come their parents say nothing. They are the worst community as far as education goes—they have no interest in it at all." But the Pallars' "lack of interest" is obviously related to their extremely precarious economic situation, in which their children are essential as surrogate mothers and as extra wage-labor. Those very few, very exceptional Pallar mothers who did keep their children in school were left wondering if they had made a great mistake. Thus, Lingamma, wise and witty and with visionary ambitions for her children, educated Kennedy, her seventeen-year-old son, right up to the final high school exam (which he failed, together with the great majority of Aruloor's caste-Hindu school dropouts). But a year after leaving school, Kennedy (a fine young many of considerable ability) was still unemployed because Lingamma, with her daily income of Rs.5, could not afford the *lanjam* (bribe) of Rs.2,000 that was being asked for the bus conductor's job that he was qualified for. Small wonder that parents—and not just Pallar parents—were losing their faith in education. As I noted in the last chapter, the reservation of places in higher education and of government jobs is a farce for the Pallars because they are so entrapped in a cycle of poverty and deprivation that their children normally never even complete primary school. Instead, these children remain engaged in wage-labor.

Differential Wage-Contributions to the Household

In October 1987, Siva and I initiated a daily census in which we asked every woman in the two Pallar streets (Periyar Street and Kamaraj Colony) what work (both domestic/subsistence and waged) she had done, how much she had earned, and how much her husband had contributed from his wages. This daily census continued until the last week of May 1988. It provided overwhelming evidence for the claim that Pallar women had been making all along, namely, that their husbands gave them little of what they earned, sometimes less than half, and that the women themselves normally gave their entire wages toward supporting their families.

Pallar men do contribute to their households but on a fairly irregular basis. Their wives normally had no idea how much their husbands had earned that day because the men did not tell them; that is why our survey only listed husbands' contributions and could not detail husband's earnings. Given that it is women who contribute virtually their entire earnings on a wholly regular basis, it is arguably they and not their husbands who are the family's main support. But though Pallar men's contributions to domestic income were limited and irregular, they did not hesitate to demand that they be fed every day. This discrepancy between the contribution made by men to the domestic economy and their consumption of the domestic product was a central reason for quarrels between women and men. As a sign of their frustration or because of genuinely inadequate food provisions, women sometimes refused to cook or literally could not cook for their husbands. This situation normally resulted in physical violence by the husband, who was quite often drunk.

I will provide two samples from the census of earnings and contributions in October 1987 to illustrate the difference between lean and good times and between the contributions made by women and men. The first sample is of four days in early October just before water was released into Aruloor's Panguni River. No water meant no work, so during these days, as in the preceding weeks, very few women and men found jobs, and earnings were low (see Table 9.2). As Siva and I went on our census round, the women would bitterly say: "You ask did we go for work today! Where is the work? *Then* we'll tell you about work!"

The highest female earning in these lean days, between October 2 and October 5, 1987, was Rs.9, the daily wage of Rajamba, a skilled worker in her mid-fifties. However, she earned this not in Aruloor but by commuting daily by bus to paddyfields near Srirangam, where she spent eight hours doing transplanting work per day. The fields belonged to the relatives of a wealthy Muthurajah widow (of the Muthurajah Three Streets in Aruloor) for whom Rajambal's husband was irrigation supervisor.

The highest contributions from men (Rs.50 on both October 4 and 5) were exceptional. In both cases, the money was given for the specific purpose of buying parboiled rice (*pulungal arisi*) from the government ration shop, where it appeared on October 4. On both days, only a single contribution of Rs.50 was made by one man toward buying rice, and the great majority of women had to buy the family's ration solely out of their own earnings. Lohambal, a widow, had to pawn her kitchen pots, including her large stainless steel *kodam* (water pot) to get Rs.60 with which to buy rice. The ration shop's rice is of poor quality, but the Pallars have to buy it because it is considerably cheaper than rice in the open market. Thus, the Pallars whose labor actually produces the finest rice in Tamilnadu, have to live on the worst rice the state produces—the irony is striking and not unnoticed by them.

There are normally two paddy crops a year in this area of Lalgudi Taluk, which has traditionally been part of the "rice bowl" of South India, well watered by the tributaries of the Kaveri River. The first crop, the *kar,* is grown between July and September, while the second, main crop, the *samba,* which is of better quality, takes longer to grow—it is normally grown between October and January-February. However, a long-running drought that was in its fourth year in 1987 had had dire consequences, and for the fourth year in a row, the *kar* crop failed due to lack of water. So, as Table 9.2 indicates, in the first week of October 1987, only a few laborers found work harvesting the *kar* crop, for there was so little to harvest. Normally, payment for agricultural work is made in cash; only paddy harvest work is paid in paddy.

Paddy contributions from men (in both Tables 9.2 and 9.3) are markedly lower than those from women because many Pallar men sold their paddy for cash to buy liquor. Women never did: This harvested paddy provided rice of a quality far superior to the government ration shop's rice, which is why Pallar women treasured the harvest paddy—as, indeed, did everyone in Aruloor who had access to it. I was constantly told that shop-bought rice was never as tasty as the home-produced variety.

Table 9.3 indicates how dramatically earnings and numbers of women and men employed increased within four days of the first appearance of the prayed-for, longed-for water. The number of women in wage-work more than doubled between October 5 and October 12 (rising from 37 to 83), and the number of men who contributed to the household doubled (rising from 14 to 28). But as always, some men continued to give nothing at all in household contribution. Although the amount of cash earned by women more than tripled (going up from Rs.109 to Rs.336), the amount contributed by men only doubled (from Rs.132 to Rs.288).

In our daily census, we were often told that the husband had earned a wage that day but had contributed nothing. Our questions often elicited a reply like the following: "He's given me nothing: He spends it all on drink! And he's drunk half

TABLE 9.2   Female Earnings and Male Contributions Under Drought Conditions

1987 Date	Women's earnings					Men's contributions				
	Number of W	Cash High (Rs)	Cash Low (Rs)	Cash Total (Rs)	Paddy Total (Mar)	Number of M	Cash High (Rs)	Cash Low (Rs)	Cash Total (Rs)	Paddy Total (Mar)
October 2	28	8	0.50	122	—	13	35	0.60	152	—
October 3	27	9	1.00	109	3	10	35	5.00	132	—
October 4	44	9	1.00	173	6	13	50	5.00	219	—
October 5	37	9	1.00	147	3	14	50	5.00	189	4

Key: W: Women
  M: Men
  Mar: Marakkal
  High: Highest single wage/contribution
  Low: Lowest single wage/contribution
  —: Men tended to sell their paddy for cash to buy liquor

the time. He only comes home to eat and sleep." Many women were deeply frustrated by such behavior.

The pattern of contributions to the domestic budget from women and men in Table 9.2 indicates that between October 2 and 5, men's total contributions exceeded women's total earnings every day. This is because men's wages are much higher than women's. For this reason, even though only some men made contributions and almost none gave his entire earnings, women's wages were so low in comparison that they added up to less. Between October 10 and 13, however, this pattern changed (see Table 9.3) because, with the coming of riverwater, the transplantation of the *samba* paddy crop swung into action. Consequently, during these transplanting days women's earnings exceeded men's contributions daily. Both female earnings and male contributions increased in the following weeks when there was virtually full employment for both sexes. Full employment only exists during the months of transplanting and the months of harvest, when demand for labor is at its peak.

Significantly, although male contributions never included the wages of a male child because young boys did not participate in adult male wage-labor, female earnings regularly included the wages of female children who often participated in adult wage-labor and were paid the adult female wage.

Pallar women in Aruloor contributed virtually 100 percent of their earnings to the household, in sharp contrast to Pallar men. They saw nothing extraordinary in this, and it appears that Pallar women in the neighboring villages of Nannikal and Pettupatti did likewise. Indeed, the extensive research of Joan Mencher on landless agricultural laborer households (1985, 1988) suggests that this differential pattern of high contributions from women earners and low contributions from men earners is typical and widespread not only in Tamilnadu but also in the neighboring southern state of Kerala and elsewhere.

TABLE 9.3   Female Earnings and Male Contributions When Water Supply Is Adequate

1987 Date	Women's earnings					Men's contributions				
	Number of W	Cash High (Rs)	Cash Low (Rs)	Cash Total (Rs)	Paddy Total (Mar)	Number of M	Cash High (Rs)	Cash Low (Rs)	Cash Total (Rs)	Paddy Total (Mar)
October 10	68	9	1	281	4	25	35	5	221	2
October 11	80	5	1	303	7	25	10	5	211	2
October 12	83	8	1	323	8	28	35	5	274	—
October 13	76	8	2	336	10	27	35	5	288	—

Key: W: Women
   M: Men
   Mar: Marakkal
   High: Highest single wage/contribution
   Low: Lowest single wage/contribution
   —: Men tended to sell their paddy for cash to buy liquor

Mencher discusses her detailed surveys of rural landless laboring households in Tamilnadu, Kerala, West Bengal, and elsewhere in several articles (See Mencher 1980, 1985, 1988; Mencher and Saradamoni 1982; Mencher, Saradamoni, and Panicker 1977). Her data on landless households detail the share of earned income contributed to the household by wives and husbands and very clearly shows that women contribute a much larger percentage of their incomes. Her findings (1985: 362–363) for the Tamilnadu districts that neighbor Tiruchi District show that:

1. in Thanjavur, wives contributed 99 percent, husbands 77 percent
2. in South Arcot (Area 1), wives contributed 99 percent, husbands 77 percent
3. in South Arcot (Area 2), wives contributed 96 percent, husbands 71 percent

Mencher comments: "What is most significant in these figures is that in every case, the proportion of income contributed by wage-earning women to the household is far higher than that of their earning husbands" (1985: 365). She therefore concludes that policy planners and governments must "pay more attention to female income. The contribution of our female informants is crucial for family survival, even in households where there are working males" (Mencher 1985: 366). My data from Aruloor entirely support these conclusions.

Pallar Men and Technological Change

On the one hand, it was true that Pallar women often spoke of the problems caused by excessive male drinking and that violence against women was a visible phenomenon in the Pallar street. On the other hand, there were good reasons why

Pallar men might feel frustrated and depressed and therefore have recourse to alcohol. Among contributory causes, the central one was probably the impact of technological change.

C. P. Chandrasekhar (1993) has pointed out that researchers who study rural populations need to be clear about what phase of agricultural development they are in at that point. He has noted that an area that has reached a peak of Green Revolution development makes intensive use of HYVs of seeds, fertilizers, and pesticides and invests in improved irrigation; during this phase, there is an increased demand for labor due to intensive cropping. However, Chandrasekhar notes, this phase of the Green Revolution is generally followed by a quite separate phase of mechanization, in which agricultural labor is displaced and labor demand falls. This appears to be the phase that agriculture in Aruloor is in at present. Within the short period of about fifteen years, ploughing in Aruloor has been almost entirely mechanized. Haruka Yanagisawa (1984) has noted that there was no mechanization of ploughing at all in Appadurai and Mela Valadi (villages fairly close to Aruloor) in 1979 when he carried out fieldwork there. Thus, a dramatic change has occurred in male agricultural employment in the area within a very short space of time.

Ploughing was traditionally the male activity par excellence, and consequently, Pallar men have, within the last decade, suddenly been stripped of their major agricultural task. Virtually no other task has been mechanized, however, in sharp contrast to the mechanization that has revolutionized wheat farming in the Punjab. No female task has been touched by mechanization so far, possibly because the very low wages that are paid to women laborers make the mechanization of female tasks unnecessary and uneconomic—at present. However, Mencher has noted with some degree of alarm: "At a conference on women and rice cultivation in 1982 at the International Rice Research Institute, descriptions were presented of ... labor-saving innovations, such a herbicides (to eliminate weeding), hand-operated transplanting equipment (which would reduce the number of women needed to transplant by a factor of six), and very simple harvesting equipment. ... It is possible that these innovations will come soon to Tamil Nadu and Kerala. Such changes, blind to gender dynamics in income processes and to the class structure of the society, have the potential to do profound damage to large numbers of households" (1988: 99–100). This prediction holds true for Pallar households in Aruloor: Mencher's alarm is well justified.

Traditionally, ploughing up paddy-fields prior to transplanting was a central occupation of Pallar males, who received comparatively high wages at Rs.15 a "furrow" (*er*) for this specialized task. An acre of paddy-field required eight furrows to turn the soil, four lengthwise and four breadthwise. The job was usually done by four teams of oxen. As a result four men were involved, and each earned Rs.30 for a job that took three to four hours. This meant that the landholder paid Rs.120 to plough a field. Today, however, a small, mechanized power-driller called a "hand-tractor" ("*kai*-tractor" in Tamil) can plough a field at less cost

(Rs. 90 to Rs.100), directed by one man who walks behind, holding it. Small trac-
tors have also come on the scene, further undercutting the cost of traditional
ploughing. In the space of fifteen years, then, a great change has occurred, for
about 90 percent of ploughing in Aruloor is mechanized today, according to the
estimates of Pallar informants. In this way, Pallar men have lost their most profitable job.

Though Pallar men have faced steadily decreasing opportunities for work, unlike Pallar women, they do not readily cross the sexual division of labor in order to
take up "female" work because they would lose status if they did. However, the
fact that young Pallar boys are not drafted into adult male labor also suggests that
there is far less demand for male agricultural labor in the area today.

Transplanting, however, has not been mechanized, nor has weeding; consequently, more "female" work than "male" work is now available in paddy cultivation. Pallar women have more work available to them than men, not only in the
cultivation of paddy but also with regard to sugarcane and banana. This "feminization" of agricultural labor is a striking feature of work in Aruloor today, but it is
not a unique phenomenon, for it has been well documented in other areas, too. In
Vadamalaipuram in Ramanathapuram District, for example, Venkatesh Athreya
notes that though the average total of days of employment for men was 200, for
women it was 215 (1984: 96). He continues: "The decline in average casual employment for male workers from eight months to 200 days appears to be related to
the tractorisation of much of ploughing work. The significant increase in average
duration of female casual employment between 1958 and 1983 appears to be the
outcome of more intensive cropping and higher yields arising therefrom"
(Athreya 1984: 96). The Vadamalaipuram employment situation therefore closely
resembles that in Aruloor—and for the same reasons.

The fact that Pallar women are far more independent from their men than
women of higher castes may be another reason for the apparent frustration and
lack of morale among many Pallar men. Whether they want to or not, unlike men
of higher castes, they are forced to occasionally depend on the wages of their
wives, given that Pallar women are more steadily employed. This suggests that a
deep contradiction exists between the ideal self-image of Pallar men and reality:
They like to see themselves as authoritative and in control, but in fact, they have to
regularly depend on their wives' incomes. This may contribute to their depression
and frequent drunkenness.

This situation also exacerbates the tendencies induced by men's socialization as
children. If such a rigid sexual division of labor did not exist between "female"
and "male" tasks, boys could perhaps be socialized into light "female" wage-
work as easily as girls are. However, the sexual division of labor is unlikely to
crumble easily, not only because of the strength of cultural tradition but also because there is too little work available even for the women.

The Sexual Division of Labor

The sexual division of agricultural work in Aruloor is a cultural construction, but like all successful cultural constructions, it has assumed the appearance of "God-given" fact and is regarded as natural and dictated by human biology.

The central sexual divide in agricultural labor was between activities like sowing and ploughing, which were defined as "male" activities, and activities like carrying and weeding, which were seen as "female." Tamil cultural rationale defined all digging with the large hoe (*mamti,* from *"manvetti"*: "breaking the soil") and ploughing as "male" labor. A fairly explicit symbolic parallel was set up between Tamil ideas of sexual intercourse and procreation, on the one hand, and agricultural activities, on the other. A typical image of sexual intercourse (particularly strong in upper-caste discourse) was that of the male "seed" that entered the female's "field" to germinate and develop into a baby. Thus, the "sowing of seed" both in sexual intercourse and in agriculture was seen as a quintessentially male activity. Digging or the "breaking of earth" (*"manvetti"*) was a similar activity, identified with the invasive male, while the female was identified with the dormant but nurturing earth. Though Pallar informants stated that digging was a "male" activity, an exception was made for the "digging of weeds" (*"kalekottradu"*) for certain crops (especially banana and sugarcane); this was defined as a "female" task. The rationale was that such weed-digging did not involve the use of the large hoe, so it was not really "breaking the earth" and was therefore not a "male" activity.

With women's work, a parallel between what is viewed as "biologically female" and as appropriate agricultural work is quite explicit: Pregnant women carry their babies for ten lunar months before delivery, and after childbirth, they carry and suckle their babies for many more months. Therefore, carrying is seen as a peculiarly "female" task. Further, to carry an object for someone expresses the inferiority of the bearer to the person whose burden she bears; carrying a burden is typically the task of a social inferior. Here it is not sexual hierarchy but social hierarchy that is enacted. In Tamil society women are the inferiors and the "servants" of men, hence, in agricultural activities in Aruloor, it was primarily women who bore burdens.

These ideas were reflected in daily life and on ceremonial occasions, too. In ritual processions, it was women who carried the burdens of ritual gifts (*sir*) on their heads, while men normally carried nothing at all. If a man—of any caste—had to carry something, he carried it in his hands, on his shoulder, or on his back, never on his head. To do so was to carry something "like a woman" (that is, like an inferior) and thus to provoke derision. There were a few exceptions to this general rule, however, given that it was felt that the easiest way to carry heavy loads was on the head. So at the paddy harvest, both women and men carried their immensely heavy loads of paddy on their heads. At the banana harvest, too, the *tar* (banana clusters), which were extremely heavy, were carried on the head by both sexes.

In these ways, the agricultural labor connected with Aruloor's three main crops of paddy, banana, and sugarcane was sexually divided so that all carrying, weeding, and transplanting were "female" jobs, and digging (with the large hoe) and ploughing were solely "male." In harvest work, which required both sexes, some tasks were performed jointly, and others were segregated. Very significantly, as a general rule, jobs that carry higher status are "male" jobs. Consequently, paddy harvest work is sexually divided so that sieving and winnowing, which are very tedious jobs, are "female," whereas the important but easy task of finally measuring the grain is strictly "male." All male jobs are always paid considerably more than female jobs.

These are the general principles on which agricultural work is sexually divided. Gender boundaries are normally not transgressed; ploughing, especially, is entirely taboo for women. I learned (after assiduous inquiry) of only one widowed Pallar woman in a distant village (Pichandarkoil)who had chosen to plough her own fields because her male kin demanded excessive payment to do so. She had been virtually ostracized by her community for appropriating this male prerogative. Pallar informants in Aruloor who heard of her were amazed at her daring.

With the sole exception of ploughing, however, women actually can and do perform "male" jobs in the privacy of their family farms. Thus, *when no male wage is at stake,* Pallar men are perfectly happy to let women perform "male" labor. Further, due to the continuing drought in Tamilnadu and the consequent shortage of agricultural work (which depends on water), Pallar women occasionally crossed the gender divide and performed "male" jobs if Pallar men did not take them up. My Pallar informants reported a team of Pallar women from another village doing heavy *mamti* (digging) work—"male" work—in that village, and in Aruloor itself, women occasionally did "male" digging jobs if they became available. But despite the dire straits their families were in, unemployed Pallar men never took up "female" jobs: They preferred to depend on their wives' wages. Also, they would have lost face if they had performed "female" tasks. So the crossing of boundaries in the sexual division of work occurred in one direction only, with women crossing to "male" jobs whenever these became available.

The division of agricultural tasks by age did not formally exist in Aruloor because all jobs were defined as adult jobs and paid an adult wage. Those who were too young or too old for the rigors of fieldwork were automatically excluded from it. It was mainly in domestic labor that children (particularly female children) participated. But young girls eleven and older were regularly recruited into adult wage-labor by their female kin and dressed up like adult women in saris. Those Pallar women who were too old for wage-labor cut grass for sale as fodder or grazed goats. They never sat idly at home because they had to support themselves. Among the impoverished Pallars, there were no joint families, only nuclear households.

Payment for Agricultural Work

The most distinctive feature of agricultural wages—apart from their meagerness—is the huge degree of sexual differentiation involved. For daily work, which consisted of four hours of field labor from 8 a.m. to noon, women were paid Rs.4 before October 1987 and Rs.5 thereafter (having successfully negotiated a higher wage). For a similar four hours daily work, men were paid Rs.10. In other words, men were not just paid more, they received more than *double* the female wage. However, my Pallar informants felt that there were various reasons for this. On the one hand, both women and men agreed that men should be paid more "because their work was harder"; on the other hand, it was generally felt that it would be deeply humiliating for a man if he was paid the same wage as a woman for the same work. Therefore, a differential had to be observed simply to secure the superior status of the man. Indeed, we will see how (male) employers willingly gave a "gift" of extra payment to men but never to women.

It is extremely interesting that most women—at least formally—endorsed the idea that male work was paid more because it was "harder"—particularly since this assumption was obviously often not true. Digging the earth ("male" work) might appear to be harder than carrying soil ("female" work), but because the two jobs are paced very differently, digging is not necessarily more exhausting. For instance, when a field has to be leveled, two men might be hired to dig out the earth, which is then carried (in baskets on the head) by a team of eight women to the site that has to be raised. The men dig a little then rest, but the women have to carry their baskets to and fro almost unceasingly, often under a blazing sun. In these circumstances men's work does not appear harder, but the men get Rs.10 each, and the women get only Rs.5 each. Nonetheless, the women do not complain about this.

On the other hand, they did complain about and deeply resent the ways in which Pallar men regularly exploited their wage-labor. This happened in the context of contract (or piece-rate) work, for which Pallar men regularly recruited Pallar women who were often their own kinswomen or even their own wives. If a mixed-sex group was required for a contract job, it was automatically the men who appropriated the position of authority, recruited the workers, and negotiated the deal. Men took charge because they normally did so in any mixed-sex social interaction. Contract work differs from fixed-wage work in being much more highly paid. However, this higher pay never reached the women because men "talked" the contract. That is, the men negotiated the higher wage per worker with the employer but then kept this wage a secret from the women and instead paid them at the daily work time-rate (Rs.5), even though the women were working longer hours and faster. If far more than the standard four hours of daily labor was required, the women workers were paid a little more but still much less than what the men paid themselves. I was told that if the women were paid Rs.8 each, then one could be sure that the men were getting at least Rs.20 each. Because

women knew that they were being exploited in this way, they preferred to negotiate their contract work themselves, in separate all-female work-groups: This was
increasingly done. Contract work used to be far rarer than daily work in Aruloor
(and elsewhere in Tiruchi District: See Athreya, Djurfeldt, and Lindberg 1990:
139–146), but today, it is more and more common. There has been a corresponding increase in the frequency with which women negotiate their own contract
work, in order to eliminate men and their special cut altogether.

So exploitation does not exist only between high-caste employers and low-
caste laborers; it also often exists between Pallar men acting as proxy employers
and the Pallar women they recruit. It is intriguing that in these wage-labor contexts, the exploitation of Pallar women's labor by Pallar men, though a central fact
of domestic life, is not accepted or tolerated by women in the sphere of work. This
suggests that Pallar women feel that the values of the workplace are different from
those of the home. They are apparently willing to tolerate domestic exploitation
of their labor because this is legitimized by a whole constellation of Pallar cultural
imperatives that define their roles as women and mothers. But these cultural
norms also emphasize their role as providers for their children: This sets up a sharp
contradiction when the men they are required to respect as their husbands become their exploitative proxy employers. Outright conflict with husbands over
wages is avoided by not entering into their employment: All-female contract work
groups are one answer that women have found.

When the boundaries of the sexual division of labor are crossed, it is generally
by women who take up vacant "male" jobs. This appears to be because the responsibility of providing for their children is felt much more keenly by women
than by men. However, on those rare occasions when a woman performs waged
"male" labor, she is not paid a male daily work-wage (Rs.10). Instead, though she
has done a man's job, she gets a woman's daily work-wage (Rs.4). Thus, when
Bathma, a strong young woman of about twenty-five, did a "male" digging job
with the large hoe one day, she was paid only Rs.4, not Rs.10. But she was not ag-
grieved. When my assistant and I asked her what she thought about it, she simply
said that she had known from the first that she would not be paid a man's wage.
So, even for waged "male" work, a woman is paid less than a man, and she accepts
this as normal.

The literature on Tamil paddy agriculture has claimed that there is one set of
tasks for which women and men are paid exactly the same—namely, harvest work
(Saradamoni and Saradamoni; 1987; Mencher 1982). This however, is not the
case in Aruloor, where I too, was told that there was exactly equal pay for both
sexes for harvest work but found that this was, in fact, not quite true.

On two occasions during harvest work, total pay for women and men differs.
The first occurs when the paddy has been threshed (by both women and men),
measured out, and poured into sacks. The women laborers then leave for home to
cook dinner, while their male harvest partners (fathers, husbands, brothers, or

sons) collect their share of the paddy "wage." The men then load the paddy sacks onto a cart or carry them into the owner's house (if the threshing has occurred on his doorstep). At this point, they are always awarded an extra "gift" of paddy for the job; they typically sell this paddy immediately and spend the money on drink before going home. It is said that they are paid more than the women for the extra job of loading or carrying. If this is true (which is arguable), the extra pay may be justified in this case.

However, the second event at which men are paid more (by their male employers) is particularly striking because they do no extra work at all. This happens on the following day, when the final task of threshing the hay (to glean the remaining grain) is done. The hay is first trampled by cattle, and then the grain is sieved and winnowed by women. Here, it is glaringly obvious that it is the women, not the men, who deserve the extra pay, for it is the women who labor for hours while the men just sit around or sleep. On one occasion in the Pallar street, after the employer had given the men the expected gift, I heard one of the women say, ironically, to the man who was receiving it, " *We've* done all the work, but *you're* getting the extra pay! Won't you give us some of it?" The man was not a whit embarrassed: He totally ignored her and, without pause, proceeded to sell the paddy on the spot for liquor money. Thus, it seems that even when no differential wage is clearly justified, it is deliberately paid though a "gift" to male laborers by their employers.

This extra pay might, on the one hand, be seen as ostensibly protecting the higher status of Pallar men: That is, it protects them from the indignity of being paid the same as women. But on the other hand, it subtly underlines the implicit co-option of Pallar men into the system of patronage dominated by upper-caste male employers. Employers are virtually always men, which is inevitable in a patriarchal society in which both authority and property are vested in males. The extra gift that male employers give male workers also serves to emphasize the indebtedness of Pallar men to their masters. The bonds of patronage that exist between upper-caste employers and Pallar men are ancient. Today, they are most clearly embodied in the fact that Pallar irrigation supervisors (*tannipaccaravar*) are virtually all men. This position, the only agricultural salaried job that is available, is virtually reserved for men: It is the modern incarnation of the ancient job of *pannaiyal,* the bonded farm servant, who was also male. Women were traditionally excluded from being *pannaiyal* in their own right. They could only share in this work if they were married to the farm servant.

Now, however, the situation is more complex. In a formal sense, the marginality of women workers appears to continue, for almost all irrigation supervisors are still men. But actually, things are changing. Most Pallar men used to be *pannaiyal,* but in recent times, only a few have retained jobs as irrigation overseers. Meanwhile, the feminization of labor has meant that employers actually depend more on women workers than on men to get the work done. Therefore, though Pallar women have been and continue to be excluded from the male system of work-patronage, they are simultaneously in a stronger bargaining position than Pallar men because it is their labor that is in greater demand. In such a context, women workers are likely to resist exploitation by employers more staunchly than men to, and this is, indeed, the case in Aruloor, as is attested by the fact that in 1987, agricultural wages were pushed up through a strike initiated by the women's work groups.

Gillian Hart makes a very important observation when she notes that in Muda in rural Malaysia, the greater ability of women workers to organize collectively (as compared to that of men) was, among other factors, related to their exclusion from a system of male patronage (1991: 114–115). The Pallar women of Aruloor provide an example of the superior organizing ability of women workers as compared to male workers in a Tamil context, in which women laborers receive none of the favors that their male counterparts receive. Gender relations in agricultural production in Aruloor thus show several remarkable points of similarity with the situation described by Hart.

The Profits of Production and Ideologies of Reproduction

In conclusion, I will turn to the relationship between capitalist agricultural production and reproduction in the subsistence sphere. Though small-scale agricultural production in Tiruchi District was becoming increasingly unprofitable in 1987 and 1988 due to the continuing drought, large-scale farming remained profitable. For several decades, large-scale agricultural production in the Tiruchi and Thanjavur area had been turning into an agribusiness in which the agricultural producer was a capitalist entrepreneur who employed an increasingly proletarianized labor force (see Gough 1981, 1989 for a detailed analysis).

All transplanting work in the Aruloor area is done by Pallar women: Indeed, every blade of green in the paddy-fields was planted by the hand of a Pallar woman. The relations of reproduction of the Pallar household depend on the recruitment of Pallar women to the fields and of Pallar women and female children to the household. And only the co-opting of female children as surrogate mothers allows women with young children to participate in full-time agricultural work. The supply of work available to Pallar men has steadily fallen. Given that the wages of both women and men are very low and that men normally give only part of their earnings to their households, the earnings of Pallar women and the unwaged work of both women and female children are absolutely essential to Pallar subsistence. Ironically, they are equally essential to the capitalist agrarian economy.

The crucial point is that the profitability of agricultural production is based not only on the recruitment of Pallar men at very low wages but also—and even more so—on the recruitment of Pallar women at even lower wages and of female children at no wages at all. On the one hand, the unwaged labor of women and young girls maintains and reproduces the Pallar household; on the other hand, the meager wages of Pallar women and men together maintain the profits made by the large landholders and agrarian entrepreneurs. In short, the unwaged household labor of Pallar women and female children subsidizes the profits of capitalist farming.

Because supply exceeds demand in the rural agricultural labor market, wages in Aruloor stay low (well below the minimum wages enshrined in government legislation), and profits stay comparatively high. The shift toward cash crops (especially banana; see Athreya 1984: 70) has resulted in Pallar and other landless laborer groups earning decreasing supplies of paddy. Mechanization has decreased male work, but precisely because female labor is so cheap, there is, at present, not much incentive to mechanize further. Low wages and scarce work have trapped the Pallars in a cycle of deprivation in which children are recruited to household work and wage-work and therefore have virtually no chance to get an education. The Pallars have been steadily impoverished and almost pauperized over the last few decades, and if better-paid jobs became available to them elsewhere, they would probably migrate. However, with no such possibility in sight at present, they remain where they are and continue to subsidize the profits of capitalist agriculture.

The differential employment prospects and the contribution to the household of Pallar women and men makes it clear, however, that the burden of family survival falls much more heavily on the shoulders of women. It is their unstinting contribution of their entire earned incomes to the family budget that keeps their families from destitution. As Mencher (1988) has warned, if the enormous contribution of landless laborer women to family income is not recognized and if their agricultural work is taken away from them through state-subsidized innovations in technology, the results could be disastrous. Policymakers and planners must take due note: Those hands that plant the green blades in South India's paddyfields are hands that, to adapt the Chinese proverb, "hold up more than half the sky."

10

Discipline and Control: Labor Contracts and Rural Female Labor

Who does that woman think she is? Is she queen of this country? The Chettiar's wife?
Does she own that field? Let that whore watch what she says! Is only she to eat—and
the rest of us to starve? She wants *more* work and *fewer* workers so that she can get
the highest wages! And the rest of us can just starve!

  —Kalyani (Pallar)

WHY ARE SOME LABOR contracts negotiable and others not? Is there
"collusion" between laborers? And if so, what effect does that have on labor
contracts? Current changes in the mode of employment of agricultural labor in
Tamilnadu provide some clues to these important questions.

I argue that the steady increase in the use of piece-rate contract labor instead of
daily wages labor signals two major changes in the mode of employment. The first
change is in the relationship between laborers and employers; in which we find
that the traditional rights of workers and the customary obligations of employers
are giving way to a more blatant exploitation of the workforce. The second change
is in the relationship between laborers and their work: A subtle internalization of
discipline is evident, suggesting that employers' control of workers is now manifested in workers' self-discipline. This new work-discipline is both a sign of "modernity" in its impersonalized control of laborers and an indication of the growing
vulnerability of laborers. The following discussion is focused on the work of the
Pallar women.

218

Changes in the Mode of Employment

Kinds of Labor Contracts

As in most of rural India, there are three broad categories of casual labor contracts in Aruloor, namely, daily wages work (or time-rate work), piece-rate work (locally termed "talked-about" or "contract" work), and harvest work. Jean Dreze and Anindita Mukherjee point out that "the co-existence of daily wage, piece rate and harvest share contracts ... appears in most microstudies" (1989: 249). The first two categories of work are paid in cash, and harvest work is paid in kind. Traditionally, rice was the main crop in this "wet-soil" area, irrigated by tributaries of the Kaveri River. For the landless laborers of Aruloor, harvest payments of paddy have undoubtedly constituted their largest earnings because their value exceeds the low wages earned through daily wages labor. Dreze and Mukherjee similarly note that during harvest, workers in western Uttar Pradesh "earn far more per day than they do during the rest of the year" (1989: 243).

However, the two main kinds of casual labor in Aruloor are: (1) daily wages or hour-rate (or time-rate) work, and (2) piece-rate work, which is locally termed *"pesigitta vele,"* or "contract" work.

"Pesigitta vele" literally means "talked-about work" and implies work for which the rates have been discussed or bargained. Informants often used the English word "contract" to translate *"pesigitta"* and they also Tamilized it, regularly speaking of *"contract-vele."* They stated that this was a relatively recent form of labor contract in Aruloor but that its use was increasing very rapidly.

The term that Pallar women commonly used for daily wages work was *"senjaya vele."* This appears to be their colloquial form of the words *"senja vele,"* which simply mean "work done." They also—more rarely—used the term *"kuli vele"* for daily wages work: It implies hard manual labor. The term *"kuli"* means "daily wages," so Pallar women would often speak of the *"kuli"* they had earned that day. Daily wages work remains the most common kind of agricultural work. Pallar women also spoke of the *"kuli"* paid for a piece-rate "contract" job that was finished in one day. But "contract" or piece-rate work normally takes more than one day to complete, and so a different term was used for its payment, namely, *"panam"* (money).

Daily Wages Work

It is a significant characteristic of this labor market that small and marginal tenants also work as casual laborers, for their holdings require little work. Consequently, they understand the concerns of landless laborers well because they share them to a large degree. They also know the tricks of the trade of landless laborers, particularly regarding daily wages work.

Daily wages work, traditionally the commonest form of labor contract, means that the laborer is paid a fixed wage for a fixed number of hours of work. Typically, such work consists, for female laborers, of jobs like weeding paddy, weeding banana, and carrying manure to the fields. The period of work is generally from 8 a.m. to noon. This four-hour session is considered a day's work, and the laborers are exhausted when it ends.

Because they are paid by the hour and because work is scarce, the women believe it is in their interest to drag out a job for as long as possible, for this results in more employment. Weeding one acre of paddy normally takes a team of eight women two or three days, but they generally try to stretch the work to four days. Because employers know that laborers are always trying to delay the completion of daily wages work, they usually supervise them. One female employer compared hour-rate work with piece-rate work in this way: "Because it's daily wages work you *have* to be by them, otherwise they don't work—they just stand around and talk or work very, very slowly. You have to be there, standing above them, nagging at them. Contract work causes no such problems—they work fast and finish the job—because they know they won't get more by dragging it out."

Sometimes, supervision is not exercised by the landholder. Instead, authority is vested in the Pallar woman who was responsible for recruiting the others in the work-group. Given that the normal period necessary to complete a task is well known, the recruiter is held responsible by the employer if completion is unreasonably delayed, and he is not rehired. (Relations of patronage and control between employers, recruiters, and laborers will be examined later.) Significantly, Pallar women generally considered daily wages work to be more advantageous to the laborer and less so to the employer. I will examine this perception in my discussion of negotiable contracts.

Piece-Rate Contract Work

If hour-rate daily wages work is considered less profitable to the employer, the reverse is true with contract work (*pesigitta vele*). With piece-rate contract work, the need for supervision is considered to vanish altogether, for what is required is the satisfactory completion of a piece of work no matter how long it takes. Regardless of how many or how few days the job takes, an agreed payment is made. Thus, it is in the laborers' interest to finish the job as quickly as possible. Given that a minimum standard of work is demanded, Pallar women know that if they try to rush a job, the employer can always insist on its satisfactory completion before paying them.

Labor Exchange

Among the poorer smallholders, such as Muthurajahs and Pallars, a system of labor-exchange traditionally existed, involving no monetary payments at all. It existed primarily between kin and solely within the same caste. When a smallholder needed labor, it was provided by other members of the same caste, and the smallholder's family reciprocated by working for them when they needed labor. However, labor-exchange has fallen into disuse. In fact, all daily wage laborers have been paid in cash for more than thirty years now.

Casualization of Work

Because other forms of employment are not available, marginal landholders turn to casual labor. Further, there has been a drift of tied labor to the ranks of casual labor in the last few decades. Today, there are hardly any *pannaiyal* (tied or bonded) farm servants left in Aruloor, whereas thirty years ago, there were many, with the Pallars represented strongly among their numbers. These *pannaiyal* acted as agents and supervisors for their employers, and they held land from them, too. But the tied labor system began to disintegrate in Aruloor when owners started taking back their holdings from their *pannaiyal*-tenants in the 1950s because of their fear that the Tamilnadu government's land reform legislation would strengthen the rights of tenants (see Chapter 8 and Gough 1989: 20–24).

Ironically, both in Aruloor and in other parts of Tamilnadu, some landless agricultural laborers now regret the passing of the system of bonded labor because they regard it as having provided a measure of job security that they now entirely lack. This situation stems from the context in which landless laborers find themselves: Alternative and better-paid employment is not available to them, and there is an abundance of labor. Hence, V. K. Ramachandran (1990) has noted laborers' readiness to enter into tied-labor status in Cumbum Valley. Only one Pallar *pannaiyal* was left in Periyar Street (the Pallar street) in 1987. Attitudes toward him varied. Some Pallars felt he was demeaned by his job, but he was envied by others for his "tenured" job, even though it paid little.

The casualization of labor that I have noted is part of a wider trend in which employers in the Aruloor area have been gradually shedding their traditional obligations even to their casual laborers. Siva described what was happening: "About two years ago, everybody—even those with only a quarter acre—would provide lunch at 4 pm at the end of transplanting for all the women. But today nobody provides this lunch—not for the last two years." She added that this was due to the continuing drought: Landholders were now harvesting only one rice crop (the *samba*), not two.

However, it seems very unlikely that the meal will be provided once again even if crops improve. This is because all traditional prestations and gifts from employers to workers and from the wealthy to the poor are declining. For example, food is no longer provided for the impoverished lowest castes at the end of the grand household ceremonies of the middle and upper castes.

Even those jobs that replicate the *pannaiyal's* job are now paid by the month and offer little job security. The *tannipaccaravar* (water irrigator or irrigation supervisor) performs one of the major jobs of the erstwhile *pannaiyal*: He has to walk around his employer's planted fields every day to see that the water is flowing in the irrigation channels, and he has to build them up or dam them as necessary (cf. Athreya, Djurfeldt, and Lindberg's discussion of *nirpaichi*, 1990: 147). Several landless Pallar men were irrigation supervisors to higher-caste employers in 1987, and so were two Pallar women. However, though they can be fired at any time, most irrigation supervisors continue to hold their jobs over several years. The great benefit their position offers is that they also act as recruiters for work on their employer's fields. As I will describe, this is a major source of power and influence within the Pallar community.

Recruitment and Organization of Female Waged Labor

South of the Panguni River, which divides Aruloor, Pallar women monopolize the task of transplanting paddy. Transplanting is piece-rate work, but it is not bargained for; like daily wages work, it has a standard scale of pay, which in January 1987 stood at Rs.100 per acre. Transplanting requires specialized skill and is recognized by women of other castes to be the particular skill of Pallar women. Other work, especially daily work such as weeding or carrying manure, is more easily done by women who participate in agricultural work only irregularly. This is the case with poor women from the Muthurajah, Pathmasaliar, and Christian Paraiyar castes north of the river. However, because they work for employers who also live north of the river (especially the Chettiar landlords), there is no conflict of interests between these women and the Pallar women south of the river. I will discuss the segmentation of the female labor market and of wage rates between north and south Aruloor in detail in the next chapter.

Because the Pallar women and men of Periyar Street constitute the regular agricultural workforce of those landholders who live south of the Panguni, they both see themselves and are seen as controlling the recruitment of labor in this area. Pallar women therefore claimed that if a landlord were to dare to recruit cheaper labor from elsewhere and import this labor into his fields, they would disrupt such work because the landlord was morally obliged to employ *them,* the members of his regular workforce. Similarly, a landlord would expect that the Pallars would work for him whenever he needed them. However, when labor demand peaks—as it does seasonally for transplanting (October-November for the *samba* paddy crop) and for the *samba* paddy harvest (January-February)—this "closed shop" policy is relaxed. This is particularly true at harvest time, when both Pallar women and Pallar men seek work outside Aruloor as well and tolerate the presence of migrant harvest laborers.

Pallar women performed virtually all their work in work-groups or teams, both for daily wages work and for piece-rate contract work. They almost never allowed women of other castes to join these work-groups. The only occasion when I saw this happen was at the paddy harvest in February 1988 when two poor Odaiyar (caste-Hindu) women, a mother and her married daughter, were allowed to join a harvest-gang. However, harvest work was exceptional in that the demand for labor normally far exceeded its supply; consequently, allowing two extra hands to join in was not a problem. It is extremely unlikely, however, that these Odaiyar women would have been allowed by the Pallar women to participate in daily wages work with them. They were permitted to join because they claimed they were destitute migrants and because they had won the favor of the Pallar women by providing the regular sale of cooked snacks in Periyar Street every morning. Muthurajah women were never allowed to join in the Pallar work-groups or at harvest time. So, at harvest, the poorer Muthurajah women and men would create their own mixed-sex work-groups. They worked quite separately from the Pallars, in other fields.

Recruitment to Daily Wages Work

Recruitment and organization differ sharply for daily wages work, on the one hand, and contract work (piece-rate work), on the other. For daily wages work, it may or may not be a local Pallar woman who tells the others about the availability of work, for the caste-Hindu landholder or, more usually, his irrigation supervisor may come directly to the Pallar street to recruit labor. As noted, the irrigation supervisor is often of Pallar caste and is generally used by the landholder as his agent and labor recruiter. More precisely, this man recruits male labor, and his wife recruits female labor.

The Pallar word meaning "to recruit to work" is simply translated as "to call" (*"kuppiddu"*: "call"). Therefore, the woman or man who recruits others to work is simply referred to as "the one who 'calls' others." This Tamil word is an exact parallel to the Hindi term used in Uttar Pradesh: "The local term for offering employment to labourers is simply *bulaanaa* which literally means 'calling' or 'fetching,'" as Dreze and Mukherjee note (1989: 240). They rightly point out one implication of the term—that no wage bargaining ensues where laborers are "called" to daily wages work. But, as we will see, the same term is used for recruitment to piece-rate work as well, where bargaining is of the essence. Hence, at least in Tamilnadu, the term does not connote solely a fixed-wages context.

Considerable powers of patronage belong to the Pallar woman who acts as recruiter because when labor means food and survival, the one who provides labor has power and influence. However, the strongly egalitarian tendencies of Pallar society have limited the development of positions of leadership among the recruiters, and the fact that many different women act as recruiters lessens the power of the position.

Recruiting for daily wages work is normally done in the early morning, when news of the day's jobs comes to the street either from caste-Hindus, Pallar irrigation supervisors, or their wives. Any Pallar woman can be a recruiter; all she needs is knowledge of the existence of a particular job for that day.

Theoretically, for daily wages work, an employer does not mind how many women volunteer for a job by presenting themselves at the concerned field because the more workers there are, the more quickly the job will be done. Actually, however, there are sometimes restrictions on the number who can be employed. The landholder may choose to restrict numbers because he has to give a full daily wage (Rs.5 after mid-October 1987) to all the women who work, no matter how quickly they finish the job.

In daily wages work, it may appear that *individual* Pallar women seek work, for each woman volunteers for work at the worksite: No team is formed beforehand. However, here, too, a sense of collective interests is present because all the women who come know each other and live on the same street, and they only allow other Pallar women to present themselves for work. No Muthurajah woman would even bother to try for daily wages work in south Saruloor because she would know that she would be rejected out of hand by the Pallar women. Further, *all* Pallar women, including those who are old and slow or young and incompetent, are readily allowed to join the group because their limitations can only drag out the job to the next day, which is entirely beneficial (to the workers) since it provides them with another day's work. Thus, both Pallar women's self-interest and their collective interests are served well by daily wages work.

Recruitment to Piece-Rate Contract Work

Contract or piece-rate work is much sought after because, though it demands much harder work at a faster pace, the pay is much higher than that for time-rate work. In addition, recruitment to piece-rate contract work is very different from that for time-rate work because the work-group is constituted not at the work site itself, through ad hoc membership, but in advance, among the Pallar women, before going to the field. A far tighter control over recruitment exists, and the influence of the recruiters—the woman who "calls" the others for work—is correspondingly greater. She is not normally referred to by any special term in Aruloor, but my Pallar informants agreed that the term *"kottukari"* could be applied to her. This is the term—particularly in its male form, as *"kothukarar"*—that Athreya, Djurfeldt, and Lindberg report for the leader of the piece-rate work-group in western Tiruchi District (1990: 142). Significantly, they also point out that the term *"kothu"* means "contract" (1990: 318), indicating that piece-rate work is perceived as distinctively "contractual" work in western Tiruchi District, just as it is in Aruloor.

Informants claimed that work-groups had no leaders and that though a particular woman happened to call the group for work, she was not considered its leader in any respect. When the job was done anyone could collect payment from the employer that evening or the next day; the recruiter did not have to do so. What all my female informants emphasized was the democratic ethos of the Pallar women's team: It had no hierarchy, they claimed, and the recruiter gained no special privileges at all, for she collected exactly the same wage as the other women.

However, with time, my closer familiarity with the Pallar women made it obvious to me that this emphasis on absolute equality was more ideology than fact. Actually, the recruiter did benefit greatly from being the one who constituted the group because she had a greater say than anyone else on who became part of it. Since she distributed jobs, her powers of patronage were considerable, and if, like the redoubtable Sarusu, she regularly recruited laborers, then her influence was great. This was because a recruiter like Sarusu was perceived to have the ability to offer almost continuous employment, and so the women she recruited did not question her actions. She regularly recruited her own prepubescent daughter for contract work in order to get an extra wage, even though the young girl worked very slowly. But none of her work-group dared to complain, even though they themselves had to work harder to make up for the incompetence of Sarasu's daughter.

Young and Old

When prepuberal girls were recruited, this was normally solely for light daily wages work, such as carrying manure or weeding. They were very seldom employed in contract work, such as transplanting, because these were tasks where speed and skill are essential and where the inexperience of the young girl would slow down and annoy the entire group. For exactly the same reason, old women who could no longer work fast were normally never included in contract labor work-groups. At best, they were allowed to participate in daily wages work. However, as in the case of Sarusu's daughter, young girls and old women were sometimes allowed to join a contract work-group when a kinswoman or kinsman organized it.

Alamelu, an elderly widow who was piteously thin, told me: "I went to Lalgudi today to pull out seedlings—but there was no work. They had enough people." This was at the end of November when some transplanting work was still going on. Having pulled the paddy seedlings out of their nursery, the women transplanted them in the fields the next day. Siva explained:

> These days the women leave very early for the fields, even by 5 am, while it's still dark. By the time they get to the field it's a little light and they start work at once— pulling out the seedlings and tying them in bunches. This way they corner the job— and those who come later are not allowed to join in. So Alamelu probably turned up a bit late—and these days that's fatal because the other women don't allow you to join in. They do this because this way you can earn more— the fewer workers there are, the more you get because you're paid a fixed rate—Rs.110 for one acre. So if

there's twenty of you, you get only Rs.5.50 each—but if there's just ten of you, you get Rs.11 each! That's a lot—so the women try to keep others out.

Athreya, Djurfeldt, and Lindberg (1990: 145) have suggested, following Hart (1986), that the exclusion of incompetent, slow, disabled, and inferior workers from work-groups identifies this process as what Hart termed an "exclusionary labour arrangement." This is because the manner in which work-groups are organized "excludes a number of potential wage workers from sharing in a given quantity of employment opportunities" (Athreya, Djurfeldt, and Lindberg 1990: 145). It is quite true that the constitution of contract work-groups excludes many categories of less-capable workers (as I will show).

However, in adopting Hart's characterization of employment trends in rural Java without qualification, Athreya, Djurfeldt, and Lindberg appear to have overlooked a major difference between Hart's Javanese context and their own. They describe two types of work-groups in western Tiruchi District: (1) "gangs" organized by labor contractors, and (2) "gangs" organized "fraternally" (1990: 142–143). In Aruloor, only the latter type of work-team exists—a so-called sororal group organized by an ordinary Pallar woman who shares equally in the work. In Java, only the former type of work-group is discussed by Hart, who points out how *employers* recruit laborers in an exclusionary manner, favoring some workers and excluding others (1986). The point I wish to make is that in the Pallar women's work-groups (and Athreya, Djurfeldt, and Lindberg's "fraternal" work-groups) "exclusionary practices" are practiced *by workers* against other (less competent) workers. This is extremely significant, as I will show later in this chapter.

Sarusu was the recruiter par excellence for female contract work because she—untypically—held the "male" job of irrigation supervisor for Sundaresan, a Muthurajah who hired laborers not only for his own fields but also for other landholders. Being Sundaresan's agent, she could almost always provide work, and so her work-group exhibited the most constant membership. Most other work-groups had temporary, fluctuating memberships, for when a job was done, a woman often joined another group. Only those groups in which the recruiter was able to provide regular work, through her excellent contacts with landholders or through her husband's good contacts, had a fairly stable membership. None had as constant and loyal a membership as Sarusu's team of women, precisely because she literally fought—as we will see—to get work.

Contract Work and Collective Interests

In contract work, collective interests—narrowed to the interests of the work-group—are taken much further than in daily labor. Here, the team is regularly formed beforehand, in the Pallar street, and usually in secret, for the women do not wish to antagonize others who are left out. The team limits its numbers because the women want to maximize their earnings: Each woman earns an equal share of the sum stipulated in the verbal contract. More workers mean less pay, so the women deliberately choose to remain a smaller group than the optimum; this means harder work and longer hours for them, but the higher share of pay makes this desirable. But because work is scarce—and this crucially determines production relations—each work-team is implicitly in competition with every other work-team within the Pallar street.

The Constitution of Contract Work-Groups

Though the membership of work-teams fluctuated, there were certain broad patterns discernible in membership, particularly the fact that women who lived very close to each other tended to coalesce in a group. Rajalakshmi, who was unusual in having a high school education and being from Tiruchi city, explained what the criteria for membership were. I had asked if women preferred to recruit their own kin. She replied, "No, we don't. What's important is that the woman should be a good worker—she must be fast, because if she's slow she'll delay us all. So we don't take anyone who's old—because the old women have become slow—and we don't allow anyone very young because they don't know how to do it. And yes—if she's called me for work, then that's a good reason to call her too." I asked if kinship was not important. "Only a little," she replied. "If she's fulfilled our criteria we take her—if she's also kin that will help her a little, but not much." This, however, is not entirely true, for kinship is clearly of great importance to Pallars.

Another factor, proximate residence, is of great importance as well. Rajalakshmi explained why: "You've got to rush off for work early in the morning and can't spend time going to houses further away. So you call the other women for work very discreetly. If you wake the others they'll want to come too and when you refuse them they'll get angry and abuse you. So we take close neighbours: we wake them quickly and go off, with no fuss." The discretion required in calling others for work is important, and for this reason, the recruiter usually keeps the job secret, telling only those women whom she wants on her team. Such discretion is essential not only to avoid ill feeling but also (informants said) to avoid the danger of *dirushti*, the evil eye, which is caused by envy.

Some women claimed that in their work-groups, decisions about new members were taken jointly by the group and not unilaterally by the original recruiter. They stressed that women moved from one work-group to another merely as a matter of convenience. Thus, A moved from B's group to C's because C had a better-paying contract for the next day's transplanting or because A could not go to work with B's group for one day. Absence for even one day could mean that a woman was not allowed to rejoin her group, even if her absence was due to illness, not deserting to another group. Young Kannagi, smiling but upset, made a sad joke about it: "I wasn't able to go with them for two days because I was sick. Now they won't let me rejoin. They've rejected me just like a monkey-mother who rejects her baby because it fell to the ground!"

This suggests that for Pallar women, work is strictly business with no considerations of kinship or friendship intervening, as Rajalakshmi contended. But this is not an accurate picture because kinship actually plays an important role in the selection of workers by a recruiter. The first women whom she employs are usually her own close kin: This is clear from the actual constitution of the teams because sisters, co-wives, mothers-in-law, and daughters-in-law are always in the same groups. Kin tend to live next door to each other, which might explain why my informants stressed proximity of residence rather than kinship.

In theory, the Pallar women gave salience to a meritocratic ideology, rather than stressing kinship. This ideology seems to serve two purposes: On the one hand, it makes it seem just and reasonable that "incompetent" workers are not allowed to join work-teams. On the other hand, this stress on competence disguises the fact that some of the team-members are there solely because of kinship considerations.

The Struggle for Work

Sarusu clearly emerged as the most important leader of the work-groups—a tirelessly hard-working woman who, during the months of transplanting, was gone for work from 6 a.m. to 6 p.m. every day. However, several Pallars, both women and men, were antagonized by her. They tended to portray her as domineering, unwomanly, and "like a man" because of her unrelenting pursuit of higher wages for herself and her team, even when this meant lower wages for others. But her doggedness and aggressive pursuit of employment ensured that her group almost always had work, even when no other did.

Hart notes a very similar phenomenon when quoting Boedhisantoso's description of how privileged workers were regarded: "The holder [of an exclusive right to harvest] may suffer from social isolation ... by being condemned as greedy or anti-social by his fellow villagers, who are themselves fighting for their day-to-day livelihood from limited opportunities to work" (Boedhisantoso 1976: 24, quoted in Hart 1986: 690). This reverberates strongly with the way Sarusu was perceived and with the two conflicts I shall now describe.

Both conflicts were associated with and blamed on Sarusu. The period between January 1987 and June 1988 was a time of immense hardship for the Pallars because in 1987, the monsoon failed for the third year and the widespread drought was acute. Agricultural work was very scarce, and the competition for work between Pallars was exacerbated. In both conflicts, the prevailing opinion was that Sarusu and her work-group had broken the unwritten laws that dictated, first, that no restrictive practices should be allowed in the recruitment of harvest labor and, second, that no one should seek an unfair advantage in getting a job.

Sarusu's group broke the latter norm by offering a bribe of Rs.50 to Mani, the Muthurajah irrigation supervisor of the largest Brahmin landlord. In return, Mani was to give to their group all the transplanting work on five acres of paddy-land owned by Venkat Aiyar. The other women in Periyar Street were outraged when the story of the bribe became known and angrily exclaimed that they knew that bribe-giving pervaded all other areas of life but had never before heard of a bribe being given for an agricultural job. Old Ramaiyee had actually given the bribe, probably under orders from Sarusu. Recrimination poured down on her head: "Ramaiyee and her group should be ashamed! Do they want to start a new fashion, where we all starve ourselves further, in order to bribe the irrigation supervisor?"

The second conflict, which occurred during the *kar* harvest in September 1987, was far more serious. Because of the acute shortage of water, only the wealthiest landholders, who owned diesel pump-sets, had been able to plant the *kar* crop. As a result, there was great anxiety among the Pallar to get what little harvest work was available. Sarusu's refusal, at this time of acute need, to allow other Pallar men and women to join in harvesting a field that "her" women and men were reaping consequently caused an enormous furor because it went against custom, which allowed anyone who was strong enough to carry the immensely heavy head-loads of paddy to join in the harvesting. Interestingly, Hart notes that in Java, "the open harvest, in which all who wish to participate are paid a share of the paddy they reap, is commonly regarded as the archetypical 'poverty-sharing' institution" (1986: 686). This was certainly how the harvest was regarded in Aruloor, which explains why Sarusu's behavior provoked such anger.

Two fields belonging to a rich Chettiar were to be harvested. When other Pallars entered the field where her group was already working, Sarusu shouted that they should get out of "her" field and go work in the next. Her argument was that her team had been reaping for half an hour before the other harvesters arrived and therefore had done more work than the others. So she demanded that the paddy reaped in "her" field should be bundled, threshed, and paid for separately by the Chettiar. Since Sarusu's group was small, it was obvious that it would receive far more paddy per head than the later, much larger group. But when her team put their case to the Chettiar's manager—himself a Chettiar—who stood, tall and fat, at the threshing-floor, he refused pointblank and said he would allow no division: All the paddy would be bundled, threshed, and paid for as one harvest. If they did not agree, they could leave right away, he said, and he would get other harvesters. Because he could have done so easily, Sarusu was forced to meekly accept this edict.

But tempers were still at boiling point when the harvesters returned to Periyar Street. Kalyani, known for her forthright speech, denounced Sarusu (in absentia) in the middle of the street. "Who does that woman think she is?" yelled Kalyani. "Is she queen of this country? The Chettiar's wife? Does she own that field? Let that whore watch what she says! Is only she to eat—and the rest of us starve? She wants *more* work and *fewer* workers so that she can get the highest wages! And the rest of us can just starve!" Kalyani clearly voiced the sentiments of many others who felt that Sarusu often broke the cardinal rule of at least a modicum of sharing. Everyone recognized that work-groups competed with each other but not to this degree. Kennedy's mother, Lingamma, commented both generously and perceptively in her humorous way, "That Sarusu! She's not afraid of anyone, is she? She's a *man,* really, in her courage!" This grudging admiration must have tempered the envy that many others felt, because through Sarusu's initiative her team always had work.

Workers' Awareness of Collective Interests

Though no one in the street explicitly commented on the sad fact that the Pallars were fighting each other instead of their exploitative employers, it is clear that an implicit consensus existed to that effect. In both the quarrels just described, the common theme was a plea: "Are we going to compete so ruthlessly that we all starve ourselves further?" Everyone recognized the fact that unless the Pallars stuck together, they would simply be even more grossly exploited. This recognition was given concrete shape in the absolute unity of the Pallar women when demanding higher wage rates.

Ashok Rudra has argued that agricultural workers have little awareness of their own best interests. He says: "Even labourers belonging to the same village do not reveal any capability of acting in a collective fashion. Even in the villages where there were strikes they were precipitate actions without any collective bargaining; that is to say, they were in the nature of wild-cat strikes typical of undeveloped working-class consciousness" (Rudra 1984: 260). This comment, however, does not apply to the Pallar women whose work-teams constantly acted collectively and whose strikes were always backed up by collective action. That is why, though the women's work-teams did compete with each other for work, they can, indeed, be seen as constituting "a *proto-union* form of organization," as Athreya, Djurfeldt, and Lindberg have so rightly noted (1990: 145).

The data from Aruloor therefore present us with a striking paradox: Pallar women workers are quite conscious of their common economic interests and are therefore wiling to see their internal conflicts as secondary and their struggles with their employers as primary—when occasion demands it. Yet their loyalties do not traverse caste-street and kinship boundaries—because production relations themselves are organized along the axes of kinship and caste. Their exclusion of other castes clearly divides the village labor force, while their exclusionary practices regarding other Pallar workers weaken Pallar solidarity. In short, "micro" competition for work between Pallars weakens their "macro" solidarity as a class, even though it does not entirely undermine it.

Finally, a brief note on terminology is needed here. If the Pallar women unite collectively, as they clearly and regularly do, is this rightly termed "collusion?" This term, commonly used in the literature (see Dreze and Mukherjee 1989: 246, 251), is defined by the *Shorter Oxford English Dictionary* as "secret agreement or understanding for purposes of trickery or fraud; deceit, fraud, trickery" (Onions 1973: 369). Surely, the negative connotation of the term makes it entirely inappropriate to use this word to describe the solidarity and mutuality of the Pallar women.

The Move to Negotiable Contracts

Though Athreya, Djurfeldt, and Lindberg have noted the great increase in the use of piece-rate contract labor and of the work-teams who performed this work (1990: 145–146), they have contented themselves with examining its implications as an exclusionary labor arrangement (discussed earlier). Here, I would like to suggest that the spread of contract labor has further implications.

As the Pallar women pointed out, daily wages work benefits workers because they can be lazy and yet earn their hour-rate wage. Dreze and Mukherjee point out that daily wages are remarkably rigid (1989: 259); in the next chapter, I will discuss the manner in which the solidarity and resistance of Pallar women maintains the "stickiness downwards" of daily wages, despite the constant desire of employers to pay less. The crucial point about daily wages is that they are nonnegotiable, which is why subsistence theories of wages are particularly suitable in explaining them. As Dreze and Mukherjee show, such theories "consider real wages to be determined by norms or forces largely extraneous to labour market conditions. ... Examples of such norms are ... common moral perceptions of what constitutes a 'fair wage' ... traditional 'rights'" (1989: 253). Common moral perceptions of "fairness" and laborers' "rights" are precisely what are disappearing today— though it must be questioned whether "common" and consensual norms ever did exist in the Indian village. Rather, the employers' views of laborers' rights (which are unlikely to have coincided with the laborers' own views on them) have traditionally prevailed, and it is these perceptions that are changing today. There is not space here for an analysis of why these changes are occurring: What needs to be stressed, however, is that the relationship between laborers and employers is becoming more nakedly exploitative, for the traditional rights of workers disappear as soon as they lose their usefulness to employers. Thus, Dreze and Mukherjee note that "traditional patron-client relationships have disappeared ... a clear trend exists towards the 'casualisation' of labour transactions" (1989: 244).

Discipline and Control

Against this background, two sets of correlated changes emerge in Aruloor. On the one hand, there is a steady decline in nonnegotiable labor contracts, typically in the form of daily wages labor, together with a decline in employers' obligations to workers. On the other hand, there is the steady increase in piece-rate labor contracts, whose crucial characteristic is that they are negotiable. But the labor market of Aruloor ensures that this negotiability is entirely to the benefit of employers, for there is a large surplus of labor.

Piece-rate work, as already noted, is viewed by Aruloor employers as a boon, because they claim that it removes the need for supervision. But because workers recognize that they are fortunate to have work at all and since quality control is exercised by employers, the workers themselves have to institute a regimen of supervision under which they are forced to supervise themselves. This internalization of discipline, subtle though it is, signals a powerful extension of the employers' control of the workforce. Thus, not only do ordinary Pallar women recruit work-teams but they discipline them as well. This new process of self-discipline, which the worker imposes on herself with the employer now invisible, is, I suggest, a sign of the "modernizing" of production relations (cf. Foucault 1987). This is because in the old regimen, laborers were violently punished by their employers for infringing work rules. Today, a less spectacular but more insidious system of social control exists, for though the chronic insecurity of landless laborers instills fear in them, the "privilege" of belonging to work-teams makes them value their work greatly, thus ensuring "not only an adequate labour force, but also a hard-working and docile one" (Hart 1986: 689). All the signs indicate that landless laborers are at risk. Given that Pallar women tend to be major breadwinners for their families, it is entire communities who are being steadily impoverished while they, ironically, are forced to participate in disciplining and controlling themselves.

11

Mutuality and Competition: Women Landless Laborers and Wage Rates

Those fields bear crops through *our* sweat and toil. But *they're* the ones who get all the profit!

—Marudambal (Pallar)

IN HIS REVIEW "Does the depressor still work?: Agrarian structure and development in India" (1992), John Harriss points out that wage rates in rural labor markets are characterized by a "stickiness downwards." Further, he observes that this characteristic is associated with the fragmentation of rural labor markets so that different wage rates obtain for the same tasks even in villages that are very close to each other. He notes that, among others, Ashok Rudra (1984) has stated that these phenomena cannot be adequately explained in terms of either neoclassical economics or Marxist theory. I will start my analysis by focusing on Rudra's important article, suggesting that although his explanatory model is illuminating and valid for his Bengali data, it does not fit so well with data from Aruloor. Thus, it cannot provide us with a satisfactory pan-Indian model. This is partly because social and cultural factors are so important, complex, and varied, which is why I will argue that detailed, microlevel sociocultural data must be an essential part of any model that seeks to explain these important features of rural labor markets.

My data from Aruloor suggest that a complex and contradictory situation exists in this part of rural Tamilnadu. Though there is no villagewide ethos of collective self-interest that cuts through caste loyalties, there *is* an awareness among the Pallar women of where their collective interests lie (this finding agrees with that of Athreya, Djurfeldt, and Lindberg 1990). In discussing this Tamil social context, I will briefly mention the caste context of Aruloor, where caste-segregated streets still exist. I will also note the strong localization of identity that divides even caste-groups and point out its relevance for the segmentation of wage rates. Discussions of wage rates in India have so far had little to say about female labor, partly because women's participation in labor has been very low in the areas researched (e.g., Rudra 1984: 258; Dreze and Mukherjee 1989). However, even where female participation is high, it has not been the primary focus (Athreya, Djurfeldt, and Lindberg 1990).

Rudra's Model

Rudra's explanatory model assumes a self-contained village society that is "composed of two parts" (1984: 252): laborers and property owners. This is perhaps insufficient because an all-India model should surely also take due account of the complex phenomenon of caste. Further, the important contemporary phenomenon of the development of class stratification within endogamous caste groups cannot even be approached in a model that ignores caste.

His model makes several major assumptions about pan-Indian village society, as follows:

1. Rudra appears to assume that the "ideological forces" that mold values, norms, and culture are identical for all groups, no matter what their position in relations of production. This implies that culture and tradition are single, unitary, and homogeneous entities, whose values are consensually shared by all groups within a village. Rudra's model is thus somewhat reminiscent of Dumont's view of Indian society as essentially consensual (1970). But recent anthropological studies that take account of lower-caste views have rigorously questioned this perspective (Randeria 1989; Deliege 1988, 1992). I, too, have argued throughout this book that the cultural discourses of lower-caste groups in Aruloor have distinctively different values and norms than those of the upper castes: There is no single, consensual villagewide culture in Aruloor.

2. In Rudra's model, isolation and self-sufficiency characterize the Indian village, and production relations are similarly "self-contained and isolated." However, my data, discussed later, show that agricultural labor in Aruloor is not isolate, nor are production relations limited to the village; the data of Athreya, Djurfeldt, and Lindberg (1990) support my findings.

3. In Rudra's model, employer-worker relations exhibit a "patron-client type of relationship ... of mutual though necessarily unequal dependence" (1984: 253–254). This paternalistic relationship "pervades the entire social life of the village community" (1984: 254). In this world of village mutuality, the laborers' "potential of labour power [is] always at the disposal of the village society" (1984: 254).

This model, though suggestive, overemphasizes villagewide complementarity and consensus, I believe. Though such mutuality is, indeed, viewed as an ideal by *employers* in Aruloor, it does not actually characterize employer-worker relations. Rudra suggests that in the patron-client relationship found between employers and agricultural workers in Bengal, each side regularly extends preferential treatment to the other (1984: 262). But such a patron-client relationship does not characterize the production relations prevalent in Aruloor. In this part of Tamilnadu, production relations between workers and employers appear to be much closer to a hardheaded, "businesslike" norm: The employers' central concern increasingly is profit, and the workers have a difficult time making ends meet. Here, employers generally view workers as lazy shirkers who do not deserve even the wages they get; workers believe employers are constantly seeking to exploit them.

4. Rudra's model posits an intimate world in which the employers' personal knowledge of laborers forms the basis of all economic exchanges between individual employers and individual laborers; every property owner "knows the laborers individually" (1984: 253). He emphasizes that "such *personal knowledge* is a *privilege* of people who are *close neighbors*, whereas it is not practical between people who live far apart from each other" in accounting for the localization of the production relations he finds (1984: 254, emphases added). His model (based on Bengali data) assumes social conditions that appear to be strikingly different from those existing in Tamilnadu. Although Rudra does not describe in detail the relevant Bengali pattern of residential location, it appears to lack the very distinct residential segregation that still exists in Tamilnadu between the laboring "untouchable" castes and caste-Hindu employers and landowners. Symbolic space is extremely important in Aruloor, with the result that laborers and employers are very far from "close neighbors." Indeed, Aruloor and other villages in Lalgudi Taluk are apparently exceptional, in that the "untouchable" streets in these Tiruchi villages are, in fact, much closer to (lower) caste-Hindu streets than in other Tamil villages. Very often in Tamilnadu, the "untouchable" castes are totally segregated, being forced to live in an entirely separate village that lies at some distance from the so-called "main" village of the caste-Hindus (cf. Moffatt 1979).

Further—and very importantly—production relations in Aruloor were often *not* directly between individual laborers and employers. Wealthy employers of Brahmin and Chettiar caste never approached the "untouchable" Pallar street; instead, they used Pallar agents or Pallar "middlewomen" (and middlemen) to recruit labor. The street was universally considered extremely polluting by caste-Hindus, due to the supposed ritual impurity that would affect them if they entered it. Although other employers of middle-ranking castes (Muthurajahs, Veerakodi Vellalars, Pathmasaliyars) regularly came to the street to recruit Pallar labor, they, too, preferred to use Pallar agents if they could afford this. Thus, production relations in Aruloor were often mediated through Pallar recruiters.

Rudra states that it is because of the importance of employers' personal knowledge of workers' abilities that "the laborers and employers entering into production relations belong to the same village" (1984: 254–255). This does not always follow in Aruloor because production relations are, in fact, not always limited to the same village. Pallar women (and men) take work wherever they can get it, not solely in Aruloor but in surrounding villages as well. This happens especially in times of high labor demand—for example, during paddy transplantation and paddy harvest—when the workforces of their own villages have more than enough work to do. Important confirmation of such labor mobility is provided by Athreya, Djurfeldt, and Lindberg, who have documented that there is and has traditionally been considerable mobility of work "gangs" in this part of Tamilnadu (1990: 143–145).

As far as Aruloor is concerned, Rudra is largely correct in his explanation of why labor and wage rates are segmented. That is, he is largely right when he points out that "labourers do not allow labourers from the neighbouring villages to come in" (1984: 259). However, in the Aruloor area, this was never an absolute rule because the Pallar workers allowed free entry of outside labor during those peak seasons when work was plentiful. In consonance with Rudra, Pallar women did claim that the landholders south of the Panguni River were careful not to alienate Pallar laborers by importing cheaper labor from outside because they knew that they had to rely on the Pallars for daily work in the long run. But both migrant labor and outside labor from surrounding villages were hired in Aruloor for harvest work, and the Pallars were not worried by this.

Similarly, Rudra is partially right when he says, "There is an understanding among labourers of adjacent villages that they would not enter in to each other's territories" (1984: 259). Once again, this is true when work is scarce but not otherwise. What is very significant about Rudra's findings is that they suggest that there is a certain degree of solidarity between workers even across villages; interestingly, however, Rudra rejects this conclusion for a different interpretation. He posits, instead, a model of reciprocity between employers and workers, under which employers "reciprocate" the loyalty of workers: "As labourers do not go out to other villages for work employers reciprocate by not employing labourers from other villages, lest village labourers be not available during busy periods" (1984: 259). In the Aruloor area, on the contrary, only a model of very strong mutuality between workers of the same caste-street and, secondarily, a much weaker mutuality between same-caste workers in different villages can explain the segmentation of labor. It was quite clear from the discussions of Pallar women that just as they strongly resented outside women workers taking jobs in Aruloor when work was scarce, so, too, they respected the interests of women workers in other villages and generally did not trespass on their work areas at such times. It is important to note that female agricultural laborers in this area are virtually all Pallar ("untouchable") caste, so the women workers in surrounding villages were generally also of Pallar caste and were sometimes kinswomen. Thus, very significantly, kinship and caste loyalties were a crucial part of Pallar women's sensitivity to the domains of other women workers.

These intervillage kinship networks are of great importance because they are a major channel both for the communication of news about jobs and for access to these jobs. During seasons of high labor demand, it is often female Pallar kin in other villages who call Aruloor's Pallar women to come for work. And, importantly, this is also the route by which wage rises in one village are communicated to women workers in nearby villages. The findings of Athreya, Djurfeldt, and Lindberg (1990) lend support to a model of solidarity between workers (at least for this part of Tamilnadu) because, in addition to noting the mobility of work-groups between villages, they also find that "solidarity between groups was stressed" (1990: 145). The parallel that they draw between work-groups and trade unions (1990: 145) is very apt because there are "closed shops" (of agricultural laborers) in the various villages that are only open when labor-demand peaks. Not only does respect for each others' work domains mean that conflict is avoided, it also has the effect of *restricting the supply* of labor and thus maintaining wage levels. Thus, the worker-controlled segmentation of the labor market also works to maintain the "stickiness downwards" of wages.

Interestingly, in contrast to his 1984 model, a later study that Rudra coauthored with Pranab Bardhan notes a far greater degree of labor mobility in Bengali villages (Bardhan and Rudra 1986).

5. Based on his assumption that production relations are limited to the same village, Rudra makes four subsidiary assumptions:

> "Labourers cannot maximize their income by working for employers paying the highest wages in an area which is within the reach of labourers" (1984: 256).
>
> "Employers cannot maximize their profit by employing labourers at the lowest wages available in an area from where labourers can reach the village" (1984: 256–257).
>
> "Better labourers cannot earn more than their inferior colleagues in the same village as a function of their higher productivity" (1984: 257).
>
> "Employers cannot lower their costs by paying lower wages to labourers with lower productivity" (1984: 257).

My data from Aruloor and those of Athreya, Djurfelt, and Lindberg (1990) suggest a rather different scenario in parts of Tiruchi District. This is because of the system of contract labor, which is becoming increasingly important and which is monopolized by the most competent workers. The results of the contract labor system are that (1) better workers can earn more than inferior ones, and (2) employers therefore do lower their costs as inferior workers are relegated to lower-paid daily labor jobs.

For this reason, Rudra's last two assumptions do not hold in the Tiruchi context. Meanwhile, his first two assumptions are apparently based on the view that any area that is physically within reach of laborers is open to them. However, intervillage kinship and caste solidarity and the "closed-shop" system of workers means that spatial proximity, though important, becomes secondary: From a year-round perspective, access essentially depends on the seasonal demand for labor in the village concerned.

6. Rudra assumes that consumption loans extended by employers to workers are of crucial importance because a property owner is "the sole source for all the assistance that [a laborer] requires" (1984: 253). He says, "Labourers do not go to other villages for fear of losing the benefits of consumption loans and other help from village employers" (1984: 259). Such loans typically take the form of a credit-labor interlinkage, in which a loan is repaid in labor during the peak season. Such credit-labor interlinkages do not appear to exist in Aruloor, nor do they prevail in the area of Tiruchi District studied by Athreya, Djurfeldt, and Lindberg, though the latter do note the exceptional cases (1990: 138–139). Further, Dreze and Mukherjee have found that even in North India, the incidence of such institutionalized credit-labor interlinkages has declined sharply: They did not exist in the western Uttar Pradesh area studied by them (1989: 257). One reason for the apparent lack of credit-labor interlinkages in Tiruchi District noted by Atreya, Djurfeldt, and Lindberg (1990) and by me may be the wide availability of credit facilities extended by government-supported credit cooperatives. However, in Aruloor, these facilities did not reach the very poorest. They had to continue to take loans, lent at exorbitant rates of interest, from moneylenders and neighbors. Only those who had collateral—and, often "connections"—were able to get co-op credit. Further, Athreya, Djurfeldt, and Lindberg note that credit facilities have been overextended by government institutions and that there has been defaulting on a massive scale (1990: 270), so the institutional credit situation is currently uncertain.

7. In Rudra's model, seasonal wage rises are isolated, village-bounded events, which do not spread to neighboring villages: "If there was any kind of mobility of labour between neighboring villages it could not have happened that there would be seasonal wage-rise affecting some of them whereas some others would be left untouched" (1984: 260). But in Aruloor and its environs, a seasonal wage rise in one village typically *did* affect wage rates in surrounding villages, though differential rates continued to exist. This was dramatically exemplified in October 1987 when both daily money wages and piece-rate contract wages rose first in Pettupatti village, then in south Aruloor, and thereafter in north Aruloor and Nannikal village, in a "wave" of wage rises that traveled from south to north. Significantly, there appears to be a correlation between proximity to the urban sector

and higher wages, for the highest agricultural wage rates were paid in the village closest to Lalgudi town (Pettupatti), and the lowest rates were paid in the areas farthest from it (north Aruloor and Nannikal village). Thus, in this regard, Rudra's model provides a fascinating contrast to the Aruloor context. We have much to learn from the important differences between these Bengali and Tamil contexts.

The Socioeconomic Context

Localization of Identity

The Brahmin street of Aruloor lay south of the Panguni River; the Chettiars all lived north of it (see Figure 1.2). But the Muthurajahs were spread through several streets both north and south of the river, and the two streets of Pallars were similarly placed on both sides of the river. It is well known that caste identity is still very strongly felt in rural Tamilnadu, but in Aruloor, it emerged that even this loyalty gave way before yet another division, namely, a striking localization of identity.

This existed among both Muthurajahs and Pallars. For instance, each of the Muthurajah areas saw itself as having a social identity that was separate from that of other Muthurajah areas. The Muthurajahs of the Three Streets area south of the river saw themselves as a self-contained group: Their daily social intercourse was with their neighbors and close kin within those streets. They consequently had little to do on a daily basis with the Muthurajah community centered on Ayyanar Temple Street, which lay to the north just across the river, and they often spoke very disparagingly of those Muthurajahs as "dirty," "promiscuous," and "of bad habits." However, the central fault of the Ayyanar Temple Muthurajahs appeared to be simply the fact that they were much poorer than most of the Muthurajahs of the Three Streets. The latter (the "southern" Muthurajahs) included several salaried, upwardly mobile men; the former (the "northern" Muthurajahs) were primarily landless laborers, often as poor as the Pallars. Though the Three Streets Muthurajahs were reluctant to socialize and identify with the Muthurajahs of Ayyanar Temple Street, the two groups did attend each others' marriages and major celebrations.

The remarkable fact that two street-based communities perceive themselves as different communities, despite the fact that they have kinship links and are part of the same endogamous caste in the same village, must be explained. There appear to be two reasons for this perception. First, because the two communities have lived separately, they seem to have constituted de facto units of endogamy over time. There is comparatively little intermarriage between the two groups today. Second and crucially, growing class differentiation within the Muthurajah caste has meant that the lower economic status of the Ayyanar Temple Muthurajahs has further discouraged marriage alliances between the two groups. "Southern" Muthurajah informants commented: "Many marriages took place [between the two streets] thirty years ago. But now very few occur. Boys prefer to marry girls from outside and so do the girls." These preferences, they explained, were primarily due to the new differentiation between the two streets in terms of education and wealth. This points to the increasing tendency (in all castes) to seek marriage with caste-members of the same economic class, even if they come from "outside," rather than with kin, as was the traditional custom.

In exactly the same way as the Muthurajahs who lived south of the Panguni, the "southern" Pallars of Periyar Street also showed little interest in the Pallars of Tiruvalluvar Street (in Nannikal village) north of the Panguni. Once again, informants stated that growing economic differentiation between the two streets lay behind their de facto endogamy and the increasing social distance between them. Tiruvalluvar Street Pallars were considerably poorer than those of Periyar Street, partly because the Pallars to the south of the Panguni received better wages for their agricultural labor. This unusual situation of a segmentation of agricultural wage rates within the same village will be examined later. Its effect was to further increase the economic differentiation that already existed between agricultural laborers (of both caste-Hindu and "untouchable" castes) on the two sides of the Panguni River.

Space is a very potent symbol in Hindu life, and symbolic acts of exclusion and inclusion are important markers of identity. The very fact that, even today, Aruloor is largely organized in caste-streets indicates that members of a caste still strongly prefer to live together. Kinship continues to be very positively regarded; indeed, family and kin are considered among the highest goods of life. This kinship discourse accounts for the universal desire, evident in all castes, to live surrounded by close kin.

The Impact of Chronic Drought

There was a steep fall in agricultural production in Lalgudi Taluk from around 1983 due to a severe drought: The fields around Aruloor that had regularly produced two rice crops a year (both the *kar* and *samba* crops) now produced only one crop per year (the *samba*). During my fieldwork period (January 1987 to May 1988), this drought continued unabated, and its painful effects were plain: Instead of busy agricultural activity in the period from July to October, there were scorched fields. This left only the *samba* rice crop period, from October to January. Consequently, there was a chronic shortage of work for the Pallars, both women and men, except at the work-peaks of transplanting and harvesting. Thus, throughout September, the Pallar women would bitterly say to Siva and me, "Why do you come and ask us what work we have done? Where is the work? Come back when there is water in the river, then we'll have something to say." Water that in predrought years had regularly arrived in Aruloor's Panguni River in July, only appeared in early October during 1987. This water created work in an almost magical manner: The number of Pallar women in daily wages work immediately tripled, rising from around 28 to 83. This indicates the grave implications of the continuing drought: In both 1987 and 1988, during the eight months of the year when there was no water, a large proportion of the workforce was left idle, without income and edging closer to destitution.

The Process of Wage Negotiations

In Rudra's model, when accepting a certain wage rate, workers "have no consultations over the matter with labourers of other villages, even neighbouring ones" (1984: 262–263). This was not true for Aruloor, where the Pallar women heard about the wage rises of Pallar kinswomen in the villages to the south and discussed these rises with those women, thereafter demanding similar rates in Aruloor. The villages south of Aruloor (Pettupatti, Mela Valadi) had a steadier source of water, more work, and therefore a stronger demand for labor throughout the year, even in 1987–1988. Both female and male workers were therefore able to demand higher wages in these areas first.

Remarkably, Rudra sees the process of wage rise as being initiated by employers at all times. He says, "Even labourers belonging to the same village do not reveal any capability of acting in a collective fashion. Even in the villages where there were strikes they were precipitate actions without any collective bargaining" (Rudra 1984: 260). His footnote to this passage mentions that in thirty villages, the wage rise came about through the *unilateral* action of the employers who announced a raise: "In most of them there was not even any collective bargaining or negotiations" (Rudra 1984: 260). He says "Labourers expressed their dissatisfactions separately and individually to their respective employers. The employers being more conscious of their own class interests pre-empted the labourers getting together and acting collectively" (1984: 261).

This is remarkably different from the Aruloor context, in which it was unheard of for employers to volunteer a wage rise. Every increase had to be extracted from employers with the greatest difficulty, and when they gave in, it was with very bad grace. A uniform, distinctive extractive strategy emerges from the recent fieldwork of Dreze and Mukherjee in western Uttar Pradesh (1989); Athreya, Djurfeldt, and Lindberg in western Tiruchi District (1990); and my own fieldwork in Aruloor (in eastern Tiruchi District). In this simple strategy, agricultural workers never demanded a raise when work was slack but only when there was a very high demand for labor. During peaks of labor-demand, when employers were competing with each other to get laborers to perform agricultural tasks that could not be delayed, laborers struck work and made their demands.

In paddy cultivation—still of crucial importance in the Aruloor area in 1987–1988—the demand for labor peaked during the transplanting season (October-November) and at the *samba* harvest (January-February). However, of the two peaks, it was the transplanting season that was particularly opportune for bargaining for higher wages because laborers did not stand to lose a share of the harvest if they refused to work. Further, this was when the demand for labor was very high, when migrant labor was not present (unlike harvest time), and when the correct timing of agricultural tasks was most important. Consequently, this was when wage demands were made by both women and men. Transplanting is a strictly female task throughout Tamilnadu; further, in the Aruloor area (and more widely in the Kaveri Delta), it is a peculiarly female "untouchable" task. It is therefore the monopoly of the Pallar women in Aruloor; all castes believe Pallar women to be especially skilled at this difficult task. The real reason why transplanting has been delegated to Pallar women may, however, be because it is the most arduous and backbreaking of all agricultural jobs.

Dreze and Mukherjee point out that in Uttar Pradesh as well, both laborers and employers agreed that wage rises had to be extracted from employers: "They ... show a fair degree of agreement on the circumstances when the wage standard changes: it increases when a farmer cannot find labourers at the going wage and is desperate to complete an urgent task" (1989: 260). Athreya, Djurfeldt, and Lindberg do not investigate wage mechanisms in western Tiruchi District, but they make a similar observation: "The peak demand for labour is reflected in the wage rates. ... The demand for this labour reaches a peak in the beginning and end of each growth cycle" (1990: 137). Further, later in their discussion, they suggest that at least "labour gang" workers probably do have some idea of what their interests are because they collectively press for higher wages: "In order to demand higher wages and better conditions of work the labourers need some kind of a collective organization. The only such collectivity existing in the field area are labour gangs, who ... *can be regarded as a kind of proto-union*" (Athreya, Djurfeldt, and Lindberg 1990: 158, emphasis added). I have argued that with regard to the Pallar women's labor in Aruloor, this perception is, indeed, justified. But Athreya, Djurfeldt, and Lindberg immediately go on to add, "Generally these gangs get paid much above the existing minimum wage rates. In contrast, other types of daily labourers generally are paid below these rates. The latter workers also have not got the collective organization necessary to bargain for better deals" (1990: 158). This is not quite true of Aruloor. Female daily laborers in Aruloor primarily work in groups, and though these daily wage groups tend to vary in composition from day to day, the women have a sufficient awareness of collective self-interest for daily wages to be pushed up at the same time as contract (piece-rate) wages. So wage rises are demanded in *both* daily wages and contract wages when labor demand peaks.

In October 1987, Kaveri water from the Mettur Dam at last appeared in the Panguni. After a period of almost no demand for labor, there was suddenly a huge demand as all landholders immediately started transplanting paddy seedlings at the same time. Taking advantage of the very high labor demand, various groups of Pallar women from Periyar Street insisted on higher wage rates for both daily work and piece-rate contract work (e.g., transplanting) and refused to work for less. Previously, in October 1986, they had not succeeded in getting such demands met, but this time, they did. Rates for female daily work ("coolie" work) went up from Rs.4 to Rs.5, transplanting rates rose from Rs.100 to Rs.110 per acre (Rs.120 for "Japan-style" planting in rows), and ploughing rates (male piece-rate contract work) went up from Rs.15 to Rs.20 per furrow.

The wage rise that occurred in the second week of October 1987 was the result of the stubborn resistance of the Pallar women and the temporary vulnerability of their employers. In addition to the sudden plentiful supply of water in the Panguni, it started to rain heavily with the onset of the monsoon. This provided an ideal water-supply situation. Every employer was in a desperate hurry to get his paddy transplanted because the planting of the *samba* crop was already seriously delayed.

A group of Pallar women went to Pettupatti for daily wages work in the fields of Velu, a major Pallar landowner (and, ironically, the local Communist party leader), at the beginning of October. They would not normally have had access to daily wages work in another village, but one of them, Nahavalli, now a married woman in Aruloor, originally came from Pettupatti. Since Pettupatti was her natal village, she visited it regularly. Further, her elder brother was the *pannaiyal* (farm servant) of a Muthurajah who owned land around Pettupatti, so he, as the landlord's agent, regularly recruited labor and kept her informed about the availability of work there. In early October, the women workers of Pettupatti had demanded a rise in daily wage rates from Rs.4 per day to Rs.5, and they received it from Pettupatti's Pallar landholders, due to the great demand for labor. After earning the higher daily wage that day in Pettupatti, Nahavalli's group returned to Aruloor.

Back home, they told the other women about it, and from then on, the women started to demand the same wage. Soon after they heard of the Pettupatti wage rate, Sinnaponnu and Pichaiamma, who were with a group cutting the dry banana leaves off the banana trees for Annadori (a rich Muthurajah landholder), asked him to pay them Rs.5 instead of Rs.4. He refused.

Then, a couple of days later, a Muthurajah landholder called Srinivasan asked Sarusu's group to carry manure to his fields in the pouring monsoon rain so his paddy could be transplanted. They refused to work for him in this downpour unless he paid the Pettupatti rate of Rs.5. Srinivasan gave in because he was desperate: The transplanting could not be further delayed.

Sarusu's group quickly passed the word around to all the other women in the Pallar street, telling them that a higher wage of Rs.5 had been successfully won from one landholder. Immediately, all the women demanded the same rate, telling their employers that Srinivasan had already paid the higher wage. The Brahmin landlords, who had the largest holdings south of the river, were furious when they heard about the wage rise, Pallar informants claimed, and berated Srinivasan for giving in to the women's demands. So did Muthurajah landholders. They felt that agricultural costs were already high and would certainly have tried to avoid raising wages if they could have. In fact, they had succeeded in doing this in 1986, for there had been no wage increase at all that year. So the Pallar women had been demanding a higher wage for over two years. Soaring inflation had made their meager earnings even smaller (MIDS 1988), and they were very bitter about the reluctance of the landholders to grant them a raise; the small increase of one rupee for daily work was felt to be long overdue. Selvi spoke for them all when she said, with great indignation: "All the prices have gone up—so how can they refuse to pay us more? It's we who go and stand in the baking sun, transplanting, our backs bent all day—we're the ones who know how tough it is to do this difficult work— so don't we deserve to be paid for it?" But the employers view was always the same: "They're asking too much!"

The new transplanting wage rate (Rs.110, instead of Rs.100, per acre) also originated in Pettupatti. Wage rates there and in other villages near Lalgudi town tended to be higher than those in Aruloor for two reasons: because these areas still managed to produce two rice crops per year and because many landholders had gone over to lucrative banana-farming in a big way. Neither strategy would have been possible if the Tamilnadu government had not begun to provide greatly sub-sidized electricity to farmers, thus making the use of electric pump-sets a very eco-nomic means of irrigation. The fields around Aruloor had not yet been electrified in 1987, but the area's richest farmers, led by the Chettiar landlords, were vigor-ously lobbying the government and had every hope of switching from expensive diesel pump-sets to cheap electric ones at an early date. So both labor demand and wage rates were higher in the villages south of Aruloor. The rate for ploughing had been Rs.20 for over a year in Pettupatti and on "Lalgudi-side," but it had been only Rs.15 in south Aruloor. Similarly, Pallar women workers in Mela Valadi, Selvi's natal village, had been earning Rs.6 for daily wages work for over a year (though the rate was only Rs.4 in Aruloor).

However, the wage rise was not as straightforward as it seemed because em-ployers soon were demanding that the Pallar women put in an extra hour of work, and where the major landholders were concerned, the women were forced to con-cede their demand. Now, instead of working from 8 a.m. to noon, according to the usual daily routine, they had to work until 1 p.m. Thus, they actually were not getting higher wages—they were merely being paid more for more work. The fact that an extra hour of work was successfully extracted from the Pallar women even in November, which had previously been a month of peak labor demand, indicates how vulnerable they were and how much the labor situation had deteriorated, with too many workers and too few jobs.

Segmentation of the Labor Market

In October 1987, south Aruloor had just caught up with female wage rates in Pettupatti and the villages near Lalgudi, but north Aruloor had not. The central reason was the general problem: Compared to south Aruloor, north Aruloor and adjoining Nannikal village had too many female laborers in relation to the work available.

Relations between labor and capital in Aruloor differed markedly in the areas to the south and north of the Panguni River. Aruloor's landholders south of the Panguni had traditionally been served by the Pallar community of Periyar Street on "this side" (the south side) of the river. North of the river, however, landholders had had a much bigger labor market from which to choose. This was because the number of indigent, landless families was much larger, drawn from a variety of castes: Pallars, Muthurajahs, Pathmasaliyars, and Christian Paraiyars, among others (see Figure 1.2). South of the river, however, only the Pallar women of Periyar Street sought female agricultural work because the upwardly mobile Muthurajah community (of the Three Streets) had increasingly withdrawn its women from agricultural labor. North of the river, it was the impoverished Muthuraja women of Marukoil village (north of Aruloor) who were said to have the "worst" influence on wages. They were so desperately poor that they worked for even Rs.3 per day, thereby undercutting the female daily wage rate of Rs.4. This pushed down wages in north Aruloor for all women workers and was an important factor in the remarkable wage situation that arose in October 1987 when, in the very same village, employers in one part of it paid higher wages than those in the other.

In October 1987, the female daily wage rate went up from Rs.4 to Rs.5 for the Pallar women of Periyar Street, but north of the Panguni River and in adjoining Marukoil village, daily work wages stayed at Rs.4. The wages for the seasonal jobs of transplanting and ploughing went up there, however, to match rates in south Aruloor. This was largely because these seasonal activities were regarded as specialized, requiring skill and experience. Only the Pallar women of Tiruvalluvar Street (in Nannikal) had regular experience in transplanting, and hence, while the Pallar women of Periyar Street monopolized all transplanting south of the Panguni, those of Tiruvalluvar Street monopolized transplanting to the north. Ploughing was a skill shared by males of other castes, so the Pallar male control of ploughing was limited. Further, as noted earlier, widespread mechanization of ploughing was robbing Pallar men entirely of their major traditional task. Daily work wages did not go up north of the Panguni because daily labor activities (such as weeding and carrying manure) were seen as far less specialized than transplanting, allowing impoverished women of other castes to join in, too.

Arunachalam Chettiar, a charming but hardheaded man, was among the very largest landlords in Aruloor: He was reputed to hold more than a hundred acres of paddy-land. Shortly after the wage rise, the Pallar women of Periyar Street crossed the river to see if they could get daily work from him, though they usually left the river's north side to their more poorly paid fellow Pallar women of Tiruvalluvar Street. Marudambal (my favorite social commentator) was chief negotiator. This is her account of the interview: "I said to the Chettiar, 'Look, you know how high food prices are. How can we live on our present wage? You must pay us more because all other prices have gone up. That's the only reason we're asking for five rupees.' The Chettiar replied, 'You say that on your side [of the river] the landholders are paying you five rupees now. Fine—they have only a few acres, they can afford it. But I have a hundred acres—how can I afford paying five rupees?' And he told us that if we didn't accept four rupees we could look elsewhere for work. So we did." Interestingly, the Chettiar's rationale persuaded Marudambal. Though she and her group refused to work for the lower wage, they felt that he had a point; perhaps it was, indeed, "too expensive" for him to pay the higher wage because he had more land.

It was these sorts of arguments that large landholders south of the Panguni brought to bear on the Pallar women in November 1987, when they argued that an extra hour of work was their due because the new wage rate was proving "too expensive." However, the women worked for an extra hour only for those employers with larger fields, from whom they expected considerable future employment. They refused to work this extra hour for smaller landholders, to the great annoyance of the latter. This distinction makes it clear that working the extra hour, when it was rendered, was not solely a sign of the women's vulnerability but also an indication of their pragmatic common sense.

The segmented wage rates bring up an important question: Were not the Pallar women of Periyar Street afraid that the landholders of south Aruloor might employ others—for example, women from north Aruloor—who were ready to accept a lower wage? I put this question to Velayudham, who held a little land himself. He replied: "No, the landholders wouldn't call others—because then the people of this street would go and quarrel with those other women who might be called. Even more important, I wouldn't call others because then this street's women might refuse to come when I needed them. You must always be able to rely on getting labour on call. So you mustn't annoy them by calling others—instead the landholders here will agree to pay more just to be sure these women will always be ready to come when called." However, the fact that the Pallar women were being constrained by employers to work an extra hour for the same pay clearly indicates that the women had very little control of the labor market, despite Velayudham's claim; on the contrary, they were largely at the mercy of employers.

The segmented daily wage rate between south and north Aruloor changed within a month. The Pallar women of Tiruvalluvar Street demanded the Rs.5 wage when they learned it was being given in south Aruloor. A Veerakodi Vellalar woman from north Aruloor whose family held land and who herself supervised female daily labor described the process by which she had agreed to pay more: "The women [from Tiruvalluvar Street] demanded Rs.5 when they learnt that it was being given on that side [south Aruloor]. No, we didn't volunteer to give them Rs.5—they demanded it and so we had to give it. Because we learned that others in our area had paid Rs.5 too, we had to give it." Ultimately, it is the crucial fact that other employers have paid the new rate that persuades landholders to pay. The son of the Veerakodi Vellalar woman similarly described how he was persuaded to pay the new rate for ploughing: "Yes, I was surprised—I asked them who had paid them so much and they gave me the names of others [landholders]. I checked with the others, and then, as they had paid more, I paid too."

His mother also indicated that the female workforce was far more varied in north Aruloor: "The women labourers come from the Pallar and Paraiyar streets—but a few women from our own caste also go for fieldwork, just to earn another five rupees towards their family's expenses." These were only the poorest Veerakodi Vellalar women because a woman's participation in manual labor signaled the low status of her family.

Conclusion

Rudra notes that in thirty Bengali villages, the wage rise was effected by employers acting unilaterally and announcing an increase: "In most of them there was not even any collective bargaining or negotiations" (1984: 260). Pointing out that employers preempted laborers by unilaterally announcing wage rises, he observes, "This is an aspect of the patron-client relationship preventing the formation of a class out of agricultural labourers" (Rudra 1984: 261).

In contrast, in the context of Tiruchi District during the drought years of 1987–1988, the strategies that Pallar women adopted were those they perceived as being the best response to existing agricultural conditions. Even in a context of dire need where they were actually competing with each other for scarce work, they did not lose sight of their long-term collective interests. The evidence for this is their success in maintaining wage rates both for daily wages work and for piece-rate contract work. This provides striking evidence of an awareness of common interests by the Pallar women.

Rudra concludes his discussion of employer-worker relations in this way: "Even when labourers are not organized in unions they have a sense of community and an understanding of collective self-interest which is an integral part of the ethos of the village society" (1984: 265). This Dumontean formulation does not apply to Aruloor because the "collective self-interest" of Pallar women does not derive from a universal, consensual "ethos of village society" but rather *from their own distinctive socioeconomic position as "untouchable" women laborers.* No common, unifying, cross-caste "village ethos" exists in Aruloor today, nor is it likely to have ever done so, given that the ethos of each group is closely related to its socioeconomic position. On the contrary, what does exist is a clear awareness among all caste-groups of their conflicting interests, and in Aruloor, the lines of this continuing hidden battle are most sharply drawn between Pallar women laborers and their various caste-Hindu employers.

Therefore, at least as far as eastern Tiruchi District is concerned, Rudra's explanatory model does not seem very suitable. This is largely because his model assumes (1) that villages are isolated, self-contained worlds, and (2) that a "village society consensus" (Rudra 1984: 266) exists. As I have argued, Aruloor and its neighboring villages are neither isolated nor self-contained. Further, no villagewide, intercaste consensus on norms and values exists.

Pallar women *never* spoke of their employers in terms even remotely recalling the feudal loyalties of Rudra's Bengal laborers. Rudra quotes the latter as saying: "After all they have been good to us since our father's time. If we should act traitorously now, to whom shall we turn when we require any assistance?" (1984: 269). This expression of deep fealty contrasts very sharply with the bitter, critical view that Pallar women took of their employers. Their comments were astute and perceptive: They were well aware of the fact that production relations were organized to benefit their employers, not them. As Marudambal drily observed: "Those fields bear crops through *our* sweat and toil. But *they're* the ones who get all the profit!"

Rather than reciprocity between laborers and employers, what emerges in Aruloor is the strong mutuality of Pallar women within the Pallar street. This mutuality is ultimately based on caste and kinship loyalties. Further, the rigidity downward of both daily money wages and piece-rate contract wages indicates that these women workers are clearly aware of their collective interests. The absolute unity shown by the Pallar women of Periyar Street when pressing for higher wages shows that even in a context of increasingly fierce competition among them for scarce work, they are able to unite to protect their collective interests.

It is through their sense of identity as *independent providers* responsible for their impoverished families and due to their sense of self-worth that Pallar women are able to "prosecute their class interests" so vigorously. In short, the manner in which female gender is constructed among the Pallars has much to do with their difficult economic situation and with the failure of Pallar men to be providers. As Hart has said: "Women workers' capacity to contest the ideology of male responsibility in the domestic sphere—the product in part of the burden of daily provisioning in the harsh material circumstances in which they find themselves—is, I suggest, reciprocally linked with their capacity to define themselves as workers and to organise collectively in opposition to their employers. In other words, gender representations are an integral part of the politics of production and class processes" (1991: 115).

Hart is writing about Malay women in Muda, but she might just as well be writing about the Pallar women of Aruloor: In Aruloor's paddy-fields, too, gender constructs politics and politics constructs gender.

12

In God's Eyes: Gender, Caste, and Class in Aruloor

You can't observe caste rules in such a context. Caste is a man-made thing—in God's eyes there is no such thing.
    —Velayudham (Pallar)

In God's eyes there is no such thing as impurity.
    —Savitripatti (Brahmin)

I N ARULOOR POSSESSION-EVENTS, men become "female" and Brahmins become "impure." Thus, in the possession-rites, there is a change of gender (to some degree) for all men, though for Brahmin men, there is also a change of ritual status (that is parallel to a change of caste status). However, though men become "female" to some degree, they do not become women. Similarly, though Brahmin men temporarily become very impure, they do not become "untouchable."

Further, men become "female" and Brahmin men become "very impure" in order to gain power. In both cases, an apparent fall in status is incurred in order to make an actual gain. Only through being like women can men become receptive to possession. And it is only through becoming like the impure low castes that Brahmin men can shed their impermeability. Consequently, in the *Brahmin* view, the "impure" lower castes are permeable to influences: Permeability is seen as distinctively characteristic of lower-caste identity. This is contrasted unfavorably with notions of Brahmin impermeability, containedness, and self-control.

Similarly, in the view of *men* in the middle and upper castes, the "receptivity" of women is linked to their "submissiveness" and their "self-sacrifice": Forgetfulness of self and submissiveness here become the prime characteristics of women. These abilities are normally seen as inferior to men's ability to "control" and to "rule."

In these ways, the gender or caste attributes that a subject or a group regards as central or stereotypical in others depends on the positional perspective of that subject. For instance, the view that "self-forgetfulness" is quintessentially female is not a view that could arise in the lowest castes (for instance, among Pallars) because there, women's initiative, independence, and assertiveness make them appear "manlike." Thus, the upper-caste origins of such a view are betrayed.

Brahmins felt they "had to become impure" to win the grace of divine possession—but this was because, from the Brahmin perspective that saw ritual purity as central to Brahmin identity, they could not concede that they could simply reject the notion of impurity altogether. But this was the perspective adopted by the Sabarimalai pilgrims, and it is significant that it was those Muthurajahs who were successfully moving up the class ladder who were the main participants in this pilgrimage. Their participation was itself an acknowledgment that in the current socioeconomic context, they needed cross-caste allies, for the pilgrimage, quite apart from its religious dimension, also provided the possibility of more intimate social contacts with other, equally ambitious young men of different castes.

Both in the Sabarimalai pilgrimage group and at the grand Murugan festival, Muthurajah men predominated, as they did both in village numbers and in village politics. But the permutations of gender identity and caste identity that were going on in these religious contexts indicate that contrary orientations are present in these different aspects of identity.

With regard to gender, a far more conservative trend exists because Muthurajah men draw on a discourse that construct Muthurajah women as submissive and self-sacrificing. In other words, they construct Muthurajah women in the mold of ideal *upper-caste* women. This fits in with the social practices of socially aspiring Muthurajah men, for they withdraw their wives or sisters from wage-work. But these women themselves are not always happy to withdraw from agricultural wage-work, even though it is hard and backbreaking, because it is their only source of independent income.

With regard to caste, however, these Muthurajah men show a much more liberal trend: Indeed, the Sabarimalai pilgrimage has become an Aruloor institution because Muthurajah men have something to gain from it. Caste is undergoing various transformations in urban society, and society in Aruloor is strongly affected by urban mores. In the urban world, though caste identity remains important (and crucial in the sphere of marriage), class is steadily increasing in importance as a basis for limited social interaction and shared interests. Though caste remains very strong as the identity on the basis of which Non-Brahmins get reserved places in higher education and government jobs, the notion of ritual purity is becoming steadily weaker. In the urban context, cultural contestation is steadily *less* concerned with "purity" as a criterion of upward mobility—education, jobs, and salaries are beginning to count for more.

With upwardly mobile rural Muthurajahs, we therefore find *both* a liberal attitude toward caste hierarchy and a conservative attitude toward gender hierarchy. The latter is particularly manifested in the recent semiseclusion and financial dependence of Muthurajah women on their newly salaried husbands. But there is no reason why one orientation should necessarily entail the other. In middle-class, urban Non-Brahmin families in Tiruchi city, daughters are now given more education, and increasingly, they are encouraged to seek jobs.

However, in rural areas such as Aruloor, it will be many years—if ever—before the majority of young women have the options of higher education and salaried jobs. Meanwhile, the paradoxical situation of the devaluation of women in precisely those upwardly mobile groups that are "modernizing" continues. Within these groups, *the status of women falls, when that of their husbands rises.* Within these economically better-off groups, women's status relative to men's is declining. Outside these castes, in an intercaste rural world that is increasingly influenced by urban mores, the social status of these salaried men is rising, even if they belong to "low" castes, such as the Muthurajahs. Thus, both gender hierarchies and caste hierarchies are in flux because of changes in the class status of women and men. All three axes of identity are related to status: The crucial argument here is that the statuses of women and men are not necessarily identical on *any* of these three axes.

For instance, with the Muthurajahs, family groups that are upwardly mobile are ascending the class ladder because the educated male members of these families have succeeded in getting salaried jobs. But though most economists automatically assume that all members of an upwardly mobile family are of the same social class, feminist research has shown how mistaken such a view is, for it ignores the blatant economic inequality and unequal access to resources that may exist within the family (Folbre 1988; Dwyer and Bruce 1988).

Sharply unequal access to education, to jobs, and to equal pay exists for both women and men. It is Muthurajah *sons,* not daughters, who get a college education and are encouraged to seek salaried jobs. When it is a choice between spending family resources on a daughter (for instance, Lalitha, who needed a *pujai* done to remove *Naga Dosham* from her horoscope) or on a son (her younger brother Ramu who needed money for a bribe to get a job), the money is spent on the son. Significantly, this is the case even when the daughter is contributing more to family income than the son, as was the case with uneducated Lalitha. She regularly did construction wage-work and gave most of her income to her family, while Ramu, being a college student, only spent money.

Pallar households reflect the same economic inequality, for Pallar women contribute virtually all their earnings toward family subsistence, while their husbands keep a large share of their earnings to spend on themselves. In short, when household budgets are examined carefully, it emerges that there is often considerable economic inequality—and thus, class division—between close family members.

For these reasons, I argue that in salaried Muthurajah families, the male salary earner, with his far greater education, his control of economic resources, and his spending power, belongs to a different economic class from his uneducated, nonearning, financially dependent wife. He has economic power, while she is financially dependent.

My study of marriage patterns in Aruloor suggests that it is precisely this new disjunction in economic class between prospective wives and husbands that is responsible for the radical changes in marriage choice that seem to be occurring. Previously, with lower-caste Non-Brahmins, both wife and husband worked on the family land, if they had any, and both also went for agricultural wage-work. Today, because some rural men are being given an education and are acquiring salaried jobs, their social status and economic security are far higher than those of uneducated men of their own caste who continue to earn a meager agricultural income from tiny landholdings. A similar economic differentiation has not occurred among women—they have not, as a rule, received any higher education and therefore have no prospect of a salaried job themselves. Differentiation between women depends primarily upon the agricultural incomes of their fathers—this is what attracts modern grooms. So the obligation to marry Father's Sister's Daughter is disregarded when the opportunity to marry a rich stranger-bride arises, and the young man's parents justify this strategy by arguing that they need to be reimbursed for their outlay on their son's education. In this manner, the giving and taking of "dowry" has started, apparently for the first time, in rural communities that, until recently, gave "bridewealth" at marriage to their cross-kin.

Women's status relative to men's within a caste does not depend wholly on economic earnings, but it is closely related to this crucial variable. It seems likely that the high status traditionally enjoyed by Non-Brahmin women in these rice-producing areas of Tamilnadu has been closely connected within the fact that these women have shared agricultural work with men. Indeed, due to the gendered division of labor, women's work was essential for crucial "female" tasks like weeding and transplanting. Further, the remarkably close and warm relationship that Non-Brahmin women enjoy with their natal families even after marriage is also, I suggest, partly a product of women's continuing ability to contribute to the incomes of these natal families even after marriage. Non-Brahmin women of all castes regularly return home to their parents to help with harvesting and transplanting. In such a context of women's intimate involvement in the labor and agricultural earnings of both marital and natal families, it is a very fundamental socioeconomic change when married women are suddenly withdrawn from work and told by their husbands that they must henceforth depend on their husbands' earnings. Not only does this have repercussions on the gender hierarchy between wife and husband, it also has a disastrous effect on a woman's relationship with her natal family. From then on, she is no longer a direct financial asset to this natal household, and consequently, her visits may no longer be so welcome.

But there is still reason for a special relationship to continue, for the woman gives her children in marriage to her brother's children—or does she? The class differentiation that is emerging within kin has greatly weakened the traditional bonds of cross-kin marriage. Devaki, for example, did not give her beautiful daughter to her younger brother in marriage because he was only an impoverished farmer; instead, she chose to marry her daughter to a salaried bank clerk in Salem. But this strategy results in weakening a woman's relationship with her natal kin beyond repair, for she has rejected the traditional claims of her brothers in order that her children might "marry up." However, as many people said, this is the way of the world today: It is *nagarikam*, "city sophistication," to seek a high-status marriage. The ironical fact that this "modernity" is destroying the traditional high status of rural women has not been recognized, though poor parents complain bitterly of the new difficulty they have in marrying off their daughters. This fall in women's status is, arguably, the most fundamental change taking place in the current transformation of rural Tamilnadu. Yet very few researchers have turned their attention to it and to its disturbing implications (for an important exception, see Heyer 1992).

The crowning irony remains: In the developing rural economy, it is in those progressive sections of castes that are economically bettering themselves that women's status is steadily falling. And it is in those impoverished castes in which very little economic differentiation has occurred—as with the Pallars—that women's high status has, in large measure, remained intact. It is, for Aruloor's Non-Brahmin women, a bitter irony. Either, like Muthurajah women, they resign themselves to a new life of semiseclusion, a much lower status vis-à-vis their husbands, and the insecurity of complete financial dependence. Or, like Pallar women, they continue their life of unremitting struggle to feed their children, in a social context where domestic gender relations are relatively equal but where everything else is extremely unequal.

Siva and her sisters. When will they get an equal chance?

References

Alcoff, L. 1988. The identity crisis in feminist theory. *Signs* 13:3, 405–436.

Athreya, V. 1984. *Vadamalaipuram: A Resurvey.* Working Paper No. 50. Madras: Madras Institute of Development Studies.

Athreya, V., Djurfeldt, G., and Lindberg, S. 1987. Identification of agrarian classes. *Journal of Peasant Studies,* 14:2, 147–190.

———. 1990. *Barriers Broken: Production Relations and Agrarian Change in Tamil Nadu.* New Delhi and London: Sage.

Bardhan, P., and Rudra, A. 1986. Labour mobility and the boundaries of the village moral economy. *Journal of Peasant Studies* 13:3, 90–115.

Barnett, S. 1970. "The Structural Position of a South Indian Caste." Ph.D. diss., University of Chicago.

———. 1976. Coconuts and gold. *Contributions to Indian Sociology* (n.s.) 10, 133–156.

Beck, B. E. 1972. *Peasant Society in Konku.* Vancouver: University of British Columbia Press.

———. 1981. The goddess and the demon. *Purusartha* 5, 83–136.

Berreman, G. D. 1971. The Brahminical view of caste. *Contributions to Indian Sociology* (n.s.) 5, 16–23.

———. 1972. *Hindus of the Himalayas.* Berkeley: University of California Press.

Beteille, A. 1965. *Caste, Class and Power.* Berkeley: University of California Press.

———. 1969a. The future of the Backward Classes. In A. Beteille (ed.), *Castes: Old and New.* Bombay: Asia Publishing House.

———. 1969b. Caste and politics in Tamilnadu. In A. Beteille (ed.), *Castes: Old and New.* Bombay: Asia Publishing House.

———. 1974. *Studies in Agrarian Social Structure.* Delhi: Oxford University Press.

Bloch, M. 1971. The moral and tactical meaning of kinship terms. *Man* (n.s.) 6, 79–87.

Bourdieu, P. 1990. [1977]. Outline of a Theory of Practice. Cambridge: Cambridge University Press.

Bouton, M. 1985. *Agrarian Radicalism in South India.* Princeton: Princeton University Press.

Bruce, J., and Dwyer, D. 1988. Introduction. In D. Dwyer and J. Bruce (eds.), *A Home Divided: Women and Income in the Third World.* Stanford: Stanford University Press.

Buckley, T., and Gottlieb, A. 1988. *Blood Magic: The Anthropology of Menstruation.* Berkeley: University of California Press.

Burghart, R. 1978. Hierarchical models of the Hindu social system. *Man* (n.s.) 13, 519–536.

———. 1983. For a sociology of Indias. *Contributions to Indian Sociology* (n.s.) 17, 275–299.

255

Byres, T. J. 1981. The new technology, class formation and class action in the Indian countryside. *Journal of Peasant Studies* 8:4, 405–454.

Chandrasekhar, C. P. 1993. Agrarian change and occupational diversification: Non-agricultural employment and rural development in West Bengal. *Journal of Peasant Studies* 20:2, 205-270.

Chenery, H., and Srinivasan, T. N. (eds.). 1991 [1988]. *Handbook of Development Economics,* Vol. 1. Amsterdam: North Holland/Elsevier.

Clothey, F. 1978. *The Many Faces of Murukan.* The Hague: Mouton.

Daniel, E. V. 1983. Karma divined in a ritual capsule. In C. F. Keyes and E. V. Daniel (eds.), *Karma: An Anthropological Inquiry.* Berkeley: University of California Press.

———. 1984. *Fluid Signs.* Berkeley: University of California Press.

Daniel, S. B. 1980. Marriage in Tamil culture: The problem of conflicting "models." In S. S. Wadley (ed.), *The Powers of Tamil Women.* Syracuse, N.Y.: Maxwell School of Citizenship and Public Affairs.

———. 1983. The tool box approach of the Tamil to the issues of moral responsibility and human destiny. In C. F. Keyes and E. V. Daniel (eds.), *Karma: An Anthropological Inquiry.* Berkeley: University of California Press.

David, K. 1973. Until marriage do us part. *Man* (n.s.) 8, 521–535.

Deliege, R. 1988. *Les Paraiyars du Tamil Nadu.* Nettetal: Steyler Verlag.

———. 1992. Replication and consensus: Untouchability, caste and ideology in India. *Man* 27:1, 155–173.

Douglas, M. 1984. *Purity and Danger.* London: Ark.

Dreze, J., and Mukherjee, A. 1989. Labour contracts in rural India: Theories and evidence. In S. Chakravarty (ed.), *The Balance Between Industry and Agriculture in Economic Development,* Vol. 3. London: Macmillan.

Dumont, L. 1953. The Dravidian kinship terminology as an expression of marriage. *Man* 53, 34–49.

———. 1957. *Hierarchy and Marriage Alliance in South Indian Kinship.* Occasional papers of the Royal Anthropological Institute, 12. London. Also in L. Dumont, *Affinity as a Value.* (1983). Chicago: University of Chicago.

———. 1970. *Homo Hierarchicus.* Chicago: University of Chicago Press.

———. 1983. *Affinity as a Value.* Chicago: University of Chicago Press.

———. 1986. *A South Indian Subcaste.* Delhi: Oxford University Press.

Dwyer, D., and J. Bruce (eds.). 1988. *A Home Divided: Women and Income in the Third World.* Stanford: Stanford University Press.

Egnor, M. 1980. On the meaning of sakti to women in Tamil Nadu. In S. S. Wadley (ed.), *The Powers of Tamil Women.* Syracuse, N.Y.: Maxwell School of Citizenship and Public Affairs.

Eichinger Ferro-Luzzi, G. 1974. Women's pollution periods in Tamilnad. *Anthropos* 69, 113–161.

Folbre, N. 1988. The black four of hearts: Toward a new paradigm of household economics. In D. Dwyer and J. Bruce (eds), *A Home Divided: Women and Income in the Third World.* Stanford: Stanford University Press.

Foucault, M. 1977. The eye of power. Preface to Jeremy Bentham, *Le Panoptique.* Paris: Belfond.

_____. (1977). 1987. *Discipline and Punish: The Birth of the Prison*. Harmondsworth: Penguin Books.

Fuller, C. J. 1979. Gods, priests and purity. *Man* (n.s.) 14, 459–476.

_____. 1980a. The divine couple's relationship in a South Indian temple. *History of Religions* 19, 321–348.

_____. 1980b. The calendrical system in Tamilnadu. *Journal of the Royal Asiatic Society* 1, 52–63.

_____. 1988. The Hindu pantheon and the legitimation of hierarchy. *Man* (n.s.) 23, 19–39.

Good, A. 1978. "Kinship and ritual in a South Indian micro-region." Ph.D. diss., University of Durham.

_____. 1980. Elder sister's daughter marriage in South Asia. *Journal of Anthropological Research* 36, 474–500.

_____. 1981. Prescription, preference and practice. *Man* (n.s.) 16, 108-129.

_____. 1991. *The Female Bridegroom*. Oxford: Clarendon Press.

Gough, K. 1956. Brahmin kinship in a Tamil village. *American Anthropologist* 58, 826–853.

_____. 1960. Caste in a Tanjore village. In E. R. Leach (ed.), *Aspects of Caste in South India, Ceylon and North-West Pakistan*. Cambridge: Cambridge University Press.

_____. 1969. The social structure of a Tanjore village. In McKim Marriott (ed.), *Village India*. Chicago: University of Chicago Press.

_____. 1981. *Rural Society in Southeast India*. Cambridge: Cambridge University Press.

_____. 1989. *Rural Change in Southeast India*. Delhi: Oxford University Press.

Habib, I. 1983. The peasant in Indian history. *Social Scientist* 11, 21–64.

Hardgrave, R. 1969a. *The Nadars of Tamilnad*. Berkeley: University of California Press.

_____. 1969b. Religion, politics and the D.M.K. In D. Smith (ed.), *South Asian Politics and Religion*. Princeton: Princeton University Press.

Harper, E. 1964. Ritual pollution as an integrator of caste and religion. *Journal of Asian Studies* 23 (special issue), 151–197.

Harriss, J. 1982. *Capitalism and Peasant Farming: Agrarian Structure and Ideology in Northern Tamil Nadu*. Bombay: Oxford University Press.

_____. 1992. Does the depressor still work? Agrarian structure and development in India: A review of evidence and argument. *Journal of Peasant Studies* 19:2, 189–227.

Hart, G. 1986. Exclusionary labour arrangements: Interpreting evidence on employment trends in rural Java. *Journal of Development Studies* 22:4, 681–696.

_____. 1991. Engendering everyday resistance: Gender, patronage and production politics in rural Malaysia. *Journal of Peasant Studies* 19:1, 93–121.

Hawkesworth, M. 1989. Knowers, knowing, known: Feminist theory and claims of truth. *Signs* 13:3, 533–557.

Heyer, J. 1992. The role of dowries and daughters' marriages in the accumulation and distribution of capital in a South Indian community. *Journal of International Development* 4:4, 419–436.

Hiltebeitel, A. 1988. *The Cult of Draupadi*. Chicago: University of Chicago Press.

_____. 1991. *The Cult of Draupadi, 2: On Hindu Ritual and the Goddess*. Chicago: University of Chicago Press.

Irschick, E. 1969. *Politics and Social Conflict in South India*. Bombay: Oxford University Press.

Jeffery, P. 1979. *Frogs in a Well*. London: Zed Press.

Kapadia, K. 1990. "Gender, caste and class in rural South India." Ph.D. diss., University of London.

———. 1991. *Discourses of Gender and Caste in Rural South India: An Analysis of the Ideology of Impurity*. DERAP Working Paper D, 1991: 4. Bergen: Christian Michelsen Institute.

Kjaerholm, Lars. 1986. Myth, pilgrimage and fascination in the Aiyappa cult. In A. Paropa and B. S. Hansen (eds.), *South Asian Religion and Society*. London: Curzon.

Kumar, D. 1965. *Land and Caste in South India*. Cambridge: Cambridge University Press.

———. 1975. Landownership and inequality in Madras Presidency. *The Indian Economic and Social History Review*, 12, 229–261.

Lambert, H. 1992. The cultural logic of Indian medicine: Prognosis and etiology in Rajasthani popular therapeutics. *Social Science and Medicine* 34:10, 1069–1076.

Leach, E. R. 1970. *Pul Eliya*. Cambridge: Cambridge University Press.

Leach, E. R. (ed.). 1960. *Aspects of Caste in South India, Ceylon and North-West Pakistan*. Cambridge: Cambridge University Press.

Lorenzen, D. 1987. Traditions of non-caste Hinduism. *Contributions to Indian Sociology* (n.s.) 21, 263–283.

Ludden, D. 1985. *Peasant History in South India*. Princeton: Princeton University Press.

Madan, T. N. 1987. Auspiciousness and purity. In T. N. Madan, *Non-renunciation*. Delhi: Oxford University Press.

Marglin, F. A. 1977. Power, purity and pollution: Aspects of the caste system reconsidered. *Contributions to Indian Sociology* (n.s.) 11:2, 245–270.

———. 1985. Introduction. In J. B. Carman and F. A. Marglin (eds.), *Purity and Auspiciousness in Indian Society*. Leiden: E. J. Brill.

Marriott, McKim. 1976. Hindu transactions. In B. Kapferer (ed.), *Transaction and Meaning*. Philadelphia: ISHI.

McGilvray, D. B. 1982a. Mukkuvar Vannimai: Tamil caste and matriclan ideology in Batticaloa, Sri Lanka. In idem, (ed.), *Caste Ideology and Interaction*. Cambridge: Cambridge University Press.

———. 1982b. Sexual power and fertility in Sri Lanka: Batticaloa Tamils and Moors. In C. P. MacCormack (ed.), *Ethnography of Fertility and Birth*. London: Academic Press.

Mencher, J. P. 1972. Continuity and change in an ex-untouchable community of South India. In J. M. Mahar (ed.), *The Untouchables in Contemporary India*. Tucson: University of Arizona Press.

———. 1978. *Agriculture and Social Structure in Tamil Nadu*. Delhi: Allied Publishers.

———. 1980. The lessons and non-lessons of Kerala. *Economic and Political Weekly* 15:1–2, 41–43, 1781–1802.

———. 1985. Landless women agricultural laborers in India. In IRRI, *Women in rice farming*. Aldershot: Gower.

———. 1988. Women's work and poverty: Women's contribution to household maintenance in South India. In D. Dwyer and J. Bruce (eds.), *A Home Divided: Women and Income in the Third World*. Stanford: Stanford University Press.

Mencher, J. and K. Saradamoni. 1982. Muddy feet, dirty hands. *Economic and Political Weekly* 17:52, A149–A167.

Mencher, J., K. Saradamoni, and J. Panicker. 1979. Women in rice-cultivation. *Studies in Family Planning* 10:11, 408–412.

MIDS (Madras Institute of Development Studies). 1988. *Tamilnadu Economy.* Delhi: Oxford and IBH.

Mies, M. 1982. *The Lace Makers of Narsapur.* London: Zed Press.

_____. 1987. *Indian Women in Subsistence and Agricultural Labour.* New Delhi: Vistaar Publications.

Moffatt, M. 1979. *An Untouchable Community in South India.* Princeton: Princeton University Press.

Moore, H. L. 1988. *Feminism and Anthropology.* Cambridge: Polity Press.

Mukherjee, M. 1988. Peasant resistance and peasant consciousness in colonial India. *Economic and Political Weekly* 41, 2109–2120.

O'Flaherty, W. 1980. *Women, Androgynes and Other Mythical Beasts.* Chicago: University of Chicago Press.

Omvedt, G. 1988. The "New Peasant Movement" in India. *Bulletin of Concerned Asian Scholars* 20:2, 14–23.

Onions, C. T. (ed.). 1973. *Shorter Oxford English Dictionary.* Oxford: Clarendon Press.

Parry, J. P. 1974. Egalitarian values in a hierarchical society. *South Asian Review* 7, 95–124.

_____. 1979. *Caste and Kinship and Kangra.* London: Routledge & Kegan Paul.

_____. 1980. Ghosts, greed and sin. *Man* (n.s.) 15, 88–111.

_____. 1985. Death and digestion. *Man* (n.s.) 20, 612–630.

_____. 1991. The Hindu lexicographer? A note on auspiciousness and purity. *Contributions to Indian Sociology* (n.s.) 25:2, 267–285.

_____. Forthcoming. *Death in Banaras.*

Patnaik, U. 1987. *Peasant Class Differentiation: A Study in Method.* Delhi: Oxford University Press.

Pugh, J. 1983. Astrology and fate. In C. F. Keyes and E. V. Daniel (eds.), *Karma: An Anthropological Inquiry.* Berkeley: University of California Press.

Raheja, G. 1988. *The Poison in the Gift.* Chicago: University of Chicago Pres.

Ramachandran, V. K. 1990. *Wage Labour and Unfreedom in Agriculture: An Indian Case Study.* Oxford: Oxford University Press.

Randeria, S. 1989. Carrion and corpses. *Archives Europeennes de Sociologie* 30, 171–191.

Reynolds, H. 1980. The auspicious married woman. In S. S. Wadley (ed.), *The Powers of Tamil Women.* Syracuse, N.Y.: Maxwell School of Citizenship and Public Affairs.

Rudra, A. 1984. Local power and farm level decision-making. In M. Desai, Meghnad Desai, Susanne Rudolph, and Ashok Rudra (eds.), *Agrarian Power and Agricultural Productivity in South Asia.* Delhi: Oxford University Press.

Saradamoni, K. 1987. Labour, land and rice production. *Economic and Political Weekly* 22, WS2–WS6.

Scott, James C. 1976. *The Moral Economy of the Peasant.* New Haven: Yale University Press.

_____. 1985. *Weapons of the Weak.* New Haven: Yale University Press.

Scott, Joan. 1988. *Gender and the Politics of History.* New York: Columbia University Press.

Sen, G. 1985. Paddy production, processing and women workers in India. In IRRI, *Women in Rice Farming.* Aldershot: Gower.

Sharma, U. 1980. *Women, Work and Poverty in North-West India*. London: Tavistock.

———. 1984. Dowry in India: Its consequences for women. In R. Hirschon (ed.), *Women and Property, Women and Property*. London: Croom Helm.

———. 1986. *Women's Work, Class and the Urban Household*. London: Tavistock.

Shulman, D. D. 1980. *Tamil Temple Myths*. Princeton: Princeton University Press.

Singer, M. 1968. The Radha-Krishna *bhajanas* of Madras city. In M. Singer (ed.), *Krishna*. Chicago: University of Chicago Press.

Sivaswamy, K. B. 1948. *The Madras Ryotwari Tenant*. Madras: South Indian Federation of Agricultural Workers' Unions.

Srinivas, M. N. 1962a. Caste in modern India. In M. N. Srinivas, *Caste in Modern India: and Other Essays*. London: Asia Publishing House.

———. 1962b. A note on Sanskritization and Westernization. In M. N. Srinivas, *Caste in Modern India: and Other Essays*. London: Asia Publishing House.

———. 1966. *Social Change in Modern India*. Cambridge: Cambridge University Press.

Stevenson, H.N.C. 1954. Status evaluation in the Hindu caste system. *Journal of the Royal Anthropological Institute* 84, 45–65.

Tambiah, S. J. 1973a. Dowry and bridewealth and the property rights of women in South Asia. In J. Goody and S. J. Tambiah, *Bridewealth and Dowry*. Cambridge: Cambridge University Press.

———. 1973b. From varna to caste through mixed unions. In J. Goody (ed.), *The Character of Kinship*. Cambridge: Cambridge University Press.

Thompson, J. B. 1984. *Studies in the Theory of Ideology*. Cambridge: Polity Press.

Trautmann, T. R. 1981. *Dravidian Kinship*. Cambridge: Cambridge University Press.

Trawick, M. 1990. *Notes on Love in a Tamil Family*. Berkeley: University of California Press.

Wadley, S. S. 1980. Introduction. In S. S. Wadley (ed.), *The Powers of Tamil Women*. Syracuse, N.Y.: Maxwell School of Citizenship and Public Affairs.

Wadley, S. S. (ed.). 1980. *The Powers of Tamil Women*. Syracuse, N.Y.: Maxwell School of Citizenship and Public Affairs.

Weber, M. 1985. *The Protestant Ethic and the Spirit of Capitalism*. London: Unwin.

Winslow, D. 1980. Rituals of first menstruation in Sri Lanka. *Man* (N.S.) 15, 603–625.

Yalman, N. 1962. The structure of the Sinhalese kindred. *American Anthropologist* 64, 548—575.

———. 1963. On the purity of women in the castes of Ceylon and Malabar. *Journal of the Royal Anthropological Institute* 93, 25–58.

———. 1967. *Under the Bo Tree*. Berkeley: University of California Press.

Yanagisawa, H. 1984. *Socio-Cultural Change in Villages in Tiruchirappalli District, Tamilnadu, India*. Tokyo: ILCAA, Tokyo University.

Zelliot, E. 1969. Buddhism and politics in Maharashtra. In D. Smith (ed.), *South Asian Politics and Religion*. Princeton: Princeton University Press.

About the Book and Author

THIS BOOK EXAMINES two subordinated groups—"untouchables" and women—in a village in Tamilnadu, South India. The lives and work of "untouchable" women in this village provide a unique analytical focus that clarifies the ways in which three axes of identity—gender, caste, and class—are constructed in South India. Karin Kapadia argues that subordinated groups do not internalize the values of their masters but instead reject them in innumerable subtle ways.

Kapadia contends that elites who hold economic power do not dominate the symbolic means of production. Looking at the everyday practices, rituals, and cultural discourses of Tamil low castes, she shows how their cultural values repudiate the norms of Brahminical elites. She also demonstrates that caste and class processes cannot be fully addressed without considering their interrelationship with gender.

Karin Kapadia is on the faculty of the Department of Anthropology at the University of Durham, England. She has taught at the University of Sussex, the School of Oriental and African Studies (London), and at the London School of Economics and Political Science. She is currently researching gender and rural industry in South and South-East Asia.

Index